Accession no.
36186569

SATIRISTS IN DIALOGUE

D1610234

Swift and Pope were lifelong friends and fellow satirists with shared literary sensibilities. But there were significant differences – demographic, psychological, and literary – between them: an Anglican and a Roman Catholic, an Irishman and an Englishman, one deeply committed to politically engaged poetry, and the other reluctant to engage in partisanship and inclined to distinguish poetry from politics. Dustin Griffin argues that we need to pay more attention to those differences, which both authors recognized and discussed. Their letters, poems, and satires can be read as stages in an ongoing conversation or satiric dialogue: each often wrote for the other, sometimes addressing him directly, sometimes emulating or imitating. In some sense, each was constantly replying to the other. From their lifelong dialogue emerges not only the extraordinary affection and admiration they felt for each other, but also the occasional irritation and resentment that kept them both together and apart.

DUSTIN GRIFFIN is Professor Emeritus of English at New York University. He is the author of many studies and articles on eighteenth-century English literature, including *Literary Patronage in England, 1650–1800* (Cambridge, 1996) and *Patriotism and Poetry in Eighteenth-Century Britain* (Cambridge, 2002). He has edited *The Writings of Walter Burley Griffin* (Cambridge, 2008).

SWIFT AND POPE:
SATIRISTS IN DIALOGUE

DUSTIN GRIFFIN

LIS - LIBRARY

Date	Fund
15/9/15	Shr - x1

Order No.
2647813

University of Chester

CAMBRIDGE
UNIVERSITY PRESS

CAMBRIDGE
UNIVERSITY PRESS

University Printing House, Cambridge CB2 8BS, United Kingdom

Published in the United States of America by Cambridge University Press, New York

Cambridge University Press is part of the University of Cambridge.

It furthers the University's mission by disseminating knowledge in the pursuit of education, learning and research at the highest international levels of excellence.

www.cambridge.org
Information on this title: www.cambridge.org/9781107422544

© Dustin Griffin 2010

This publication is in copyright. Subject to statutory exception
and to the provisions of relevant collective licensing agreements,
no reproduction of any part may take place without the written
permission of Cambridge University Press.

First published 2010
First paperback edition 2014

A catalogue record for this publication is available from the British Library

Library of Congress Cataloguing in Publication data
Griffin, Dustin H.
Swift and pope : satirists in dialogue / Dustin Griffin.
p.   cm.
Includes bibliographical references and index.
ISBN 978-0-521-76123-9 (hardback)
1. Swift, Jonathan, 1667–1745 – Criticism and interpretation.   2. Pope, Alexander,
1688–1744 – Criticism and interpretation.   3. Swift, Jonathan, 1667–1745 – Correspondence.
4. Pope, Alexander, 1688–1744 – Correspondence.   5. Swift, Jonathan, 1667–1745 – Friends
and associates.   6. Pope, Alexander, 1688–1744 – Friends and associates.   7. Satire,
English – History and criticism.   8. Satirists, English – 18th century – Biography.   I. Title.
PR3726.G75 2010
828'.509–dc22
[B]
2010021487

ISBN 978-0-521-76123-9 Hardback
ISBN 978-1-107-42254-4 Paperback

Cambridge University Press has no responsibility for the persistence or accuracy of
URLs for external or third-party internet websites referred to in this publication,
and does not guarantee that any content on such websites is, or will remain, accurate
or appropriate.

To Matthew and Michèle

Contents

Illustrations

Acknowledgements

For their helpful comments on earlier drafts of sections of this book, I thank J. Paul Hunter and my former student Michael Schwartz-Rotenberg. For their extended and invaluable commentaries, I am indebted to Valerie Rumbold and Pat Rogers. For help with Swift's Latin, thanks to Charles Fuqua of Williams College. I regret that my long-time New York University colleague, Paul Magnuson, before his untimely death in 2006, did not know that I had begun thinking about a book partly inspired by his *Wordsworth and Coleridge: A Lyrical Dialogue* (1988).

Thanks to students in my Pope/Swift seminars at NYU in Spring 2005, Spring 2006, and Spring 2007, with whom I worked through some of the issues addressed in this book; and to the audience at the meeting of the Northeast American Society for Eighteenth Century Studies in October, 2007 in Hanover, NH, before which I presented some material from chapters 2 and 3.

Thanks also to David Vander Meulen and Julian Ferraro, who responded promptly to inquiries, and to Esmé Whittaker of the Word & Image Department at the Victoria and Albert Museum, London, for providing electronic scans of Swift's copy of the *Dunciad Variorum*.

My research was made substantially more convenient through the resources of Eighteenth Century Collections Online, as well as JSTOR and ProQuest. But every scholar wants to be able not only to see but also to touch the books. For supplying me with whatever I needed, I thank the staffs of Bobst Library, New York University, and of Sawyer Library, Williams College, especially Alison O'Grady of the Interlibrary Loan staff. Publication of this book was supported by a subsidy from the Stein Fund of New York University.

Finally, I would like to thank the editorial team at Cambridge University Press: Linda Bree, Maartje Scheltens, Elizabeth Davey, and especially my copy editor, Leigh Mueller, for her sharp eye, good sense, and gently phrased queries.

Note on texts cited

Because eighteenth-century poems and prose are now readily available from Eighteenth Century Collections Online, I cite wherever possible from eighteenth-century editions, and unless otherwise indicated texts are taken from first editions. But for the writings of Swift and Pope I wanted to take advantage of the work of authoritative modern editors who print from texts that Swift and Pope themselves might have seen. Swift's poems are cited from the edition of Harold Williams (*The Poems of Jonathan Swift*, 2nd edn., 3 vols., 1958), who prints without modernization from manuscripts, first editions, or authoritative early texts. Swift's prose is cited, with one exception, from the edition of Herbert Davis *et al.* (*The Prose Works of Jonathan Swift*, 14 vols., 1939–68), who prints from Faulkner's 1735 edition. The Davis edition will be superseded by the new Cambridge Edition of the Works of Jonathan Swift: I cite from the one volume that has appeared as this book goes to press, volume VIII, *English Political Writings, 1711–1714*, ed. Bertrand Goldgar and Ian Gadd, 2008.

Pope's poems have been cited from the The Twickenham Edition of the Poems of Alexander Pope, ed. John Butt *et al.*, 11 vols. (1939–68), except where that edition has been superseded by a volume from the Longman Annotated English Texts series, *The Dunciad in Four Books*, ed. Valerie Rumbold (1999), and the new Longman Annotated English Poets edition of *The Poems of Alexander Pope*, ed. Julian Ferraro, Valerie Rumbold, Nigel Wood, and Paul Baines, 5 vols., (1999–), of which one volume has appeared, *Volume Three: The Dunciad (1728) & The Dunciad Variorum (1729)*, ed. Valerie Rumbold (2007). Based on first editions and preserving original spelling, capitalization, and italicization, the Longman editions, which give complete texts of all three major versions of the *Dunciad*, make it almost possible to read the poems that Swift read. Pope's prose is cited from *The Prose Works of Alexander Pope: Vol. II: The Earlier Works, 1711–1720*, ed. Norman Ault (1936), *The Prose Works of Alexander Pope: Vol. II: The Major Works, 1725–1744*, ed. Rosemary Cowler (1986), and *The Memoirs of Martinus Scriblerus*, ed. Charles Kerby-Miller (1950, repr. 1988).

Rather than citing the Pope-to-Swift letters from the long-standard Sherburn edition, *The Correspondence of Alexander Pope*, ed. George Sherburn, 5 vols. (1956), and the Swift-to-Pope letters from the long-standard *The Correspondence of Jonathan Swift*, 5 vols., ed. Harold Williams, rev. David Woolley (1963–72), I have cited both series from the newly completed edition of *The Correspondence of Jonathan Swift, D. D.*, ed. David Woolley, 4 vols. (1999–2007). Woolley has updated the work of both Williams and Sherburn, following different editorial procedures, revising some dates, and printing a total of ninety-five separate letters, rather than Sherburn's ninety-two. Woolley's no. 721, the rhyming recipe for veal stew, is regarded by Sherburn as a manuscript poem rather than a letter. His no. 728, printed as a letter from Pope and Gay to Swift, is printed by Sherburn as from Gay to Swift. His no. 1198 (Pope to Swift, early October, 1735) is printed by Sherburn as part of a November 1735 letter (Woolley's no. 1230, and dated December 1735). To clarify chronology for the modern reader, I have altered Woolley's dates from old style (e.g., January 1727/28) to new (e.g., January 1728). For Pope's letters to and from other people I have cited from Sherburn, conveniently searchable through "Electronic Enlightenment."

To attempt to keep my extensive footnotes within a reasonable compass, I have where appropriate provided author and year of publication for citations of articles and books, referring the reader to the Bibliography for complete details. The *Oxford English Dictionary* is cited as *OED*, the *Oxford Dictionary of National Biography* (2004) as *ODNB*.

A Swift–Pope chronology

1667	November 30: Swift born in Dublin.
1688	May 21: Pope born in London.
1704	May 10: Swift, *A Tale of a Tub*.
1709	May 2: Pope, *Pastorals* (in Tonson's *Poetical Miscellanies: The Sixth Part*).
1710	Swift, *A Tale of A Tub*, 5th edn. (with "Apology" and notes).
1711	February 27: Swift, *Miscellanies in Prose and Verse*.
	May 15: Pope, *An Essay on Criticism*.
	November 27: Swift, *The Conduct of the Allies*.
1712	May 20: Pope, *The Rape of the Locke* (two-canto version), in Lintot's *Miscellaneous Poems and Translations*.
	August 1: Swift drafts early version of *Cadenus and Vanessa*.
1713	March 7: Pope, *Windsor-Forest*.
	April 25: Swift named Dean of St. Patrick's Cathedral, Dublin.
	September: first meeting of the "Scriblerus Club" probably takes place.
	September 9: Swift returns from Dublin.
1714	March 2: *The Rape of the Lock* (five-canto version).
	June 12: last documented meeting of Scriblerus Club.
	July 4–11: Swift, Pope, and Gay meet in Letcombe, Berkshire.
	August 16: Swift departs for Ireland.
1715	June 6: Pope's translation of the *Iliad* begins appearing.
1717	June 3: Pope, *Works*.
1720	August: South Sea Bubble bursts.
1722	August 24: Francis Atterbury, Bishop of Rochester, arrested and charged with treason.
1723	May: Atterbury trial (at which Pope testifies).
1724	March: first of Swift's *Drapier's Letters*.
	October 21: Swift, fourth *Drapier's Letter*.

1726   March 15–August 15: Swift in England.
        October 28: *Gulliver's Travels.*
1727   April 22–September 18: Swift in England (mostly with Pope in
        Twickenham).
        June 24: Pope–Swift *Miscellanies in Prose and Verse*, vols. I and II.
1728   March 8: Pope–Swift *Miscellanies*, "the Last Volume."
        May 18: Pope, *The Dunciad. An Heroic Poem.*
1729   April 10: Pope, *Dunciad Variorum*, dedicated to Swift.
1730   February 9: Swift, *Libel on Dr. Delany*, with praise of Pope.
1731   December: Swift writing *Verses on the Death of Dr. Swift.*
1732   June: Swift, *The Lady's Dressing Room.*
        October 4: Pope–Swift *Miscellanies*, vol. III.
        December 4: John Gay dies.
1733   February 15: Pope, *First Satire of the Second Book of Horace* (to
        Fortescue).
        February 20: Pope, *An Essay on Man* (Epistle I).
        March 29: Pope, *An Essay on Man* (Epistle II).
        May: Pope, *An Essay on Man* (Epistle III).
        May 1: Swift, *Life and Genuine Character of Dr. Swift.*
        December 31: Swift, *On Poetry. A Rapsody.*
1734   January 24: Pope, *An Essay on Man* (Epistle IV).
        November 27: Swift, *Works*, vols. I, III, IV.
1735   January 2: Pope, *Epistle to Dr. Arbuthnot.*
        January 6: Swift, *Works*, vol. II.
        February 8: Pope, *Epistle to a Lady.*
        February 27: John Arbuthnot dies.
        April 23: Pope, *Works*, vol. II.
        May 12: Curll's edition of Pope's *Letters.*
1737   April 28: Pope, *The Second Epistle of the Second Book of Horace
        Imitated.*
        May 19: Pope's own edition of his *Letters.*
        May 25: Pope, *First Epistle of the Second Book of Horace Imitated*
        ("Epistle to Augustus"), with praise of Swift.
1738   March 1: Pope, *An Imitation of the Sixth Satire of the Second Book
        of Horace* (completing Swift's imitation of the first part of the
        poem).
        May 16: Pope, *One Thousand Seven Hundred and Thirty-Eight.*
        July 18: Pope, *One Thousand Seven Hundred and Thirty-Eight,*
        Dialogue 2.

1739   January 19: Swift, *Verses on the Death of Dr. Swift*, edited by
        Pope and King.
        February/March: Swift's own edition of *Verses on the Death of
        Dr. Swift*.
        May 1: Pope, *Seventh Epistle of the First Book of Horace, Imitat-
        ed in the Manner of Dr. Swift*, appearing (for the first time) in
        Pope's *Works, vol. II, part II*.
1740   May 3–5: Swift's last will.
1741   April 16: Pope, *Works in Prose, vol. II*, containing *Memoirs of
        Martinus Scriblerus* and Pope–Swift letters.
        June 20: Swift, *Letters to and from Dr. J. Swift*.
1742   March 20: Pope, *The New Dunciad*.
        August: Swift declared "of unsound mind and memory."
1743   October 29: Pope, *Dunciad in Four Books*.
        December 12: Pope's last will.
1744   May 30: Pope dies.
1745   October 19: Swift dies.

Introduction. Conversing interchangeably

Any reader who picks up a book on Swift and Pope is likely to know of their long and close friendship, extending from the halcyon days of the Scriblerus Club in 1714 into the darker days of their final years in the 1740s. No such reader needs to be reminded that their friendship was memorialized – as they themselves planned – in their literary correspondence, first collected and published in 1741; that each offered famous verse tributes to the other – Pope in the dedication to the *Dunciad Variorum* and the "Epistle to Augustus," Swift in the *Libel on Dr. Delany* and *Verses on the Death of Dr. Swift;* and that they collaborated to produce four volumes of joint *Miscellanies in Prose and Verse* (1727, 1728, 1732), as well as the Scriblerian *Memoirs of Martinus Scriblerus* (1741). Students of the eighteenth century have long thought of Pope and Swift as fellow "Augustans," deploying a shared satiric language and rhetoric,[1] common satiric techniques and targets, a suspicion of the power of the unregulated imagination coinciding with a pleasure in indulging it,[2] and adopting similar and mutually supportive political stances in opposition to the government of Sir Robert Walpole. Literary historians from the time of Johnson have remarked on an affinity in their literary sensibilities, from a shared delight in the "physically impure" to a proud conviction that they were superior to all their contemporaries.[3] Pope himself suggested that the

---

[1] Pope and Swift are two of the writers used by Paul Fussell to represent "Augustan Humanism" (*The Rhetorical World of Augustan Humanism* [1965]).

[2] See W. K. Wimsatt's remark on Pope and Swift as "laughing poets of a heightened unreality" in his essay on "The Augustan Mode in English Poetry," in *Hateful Contraries: Studies in Literature & Criticism* (1965), 158.

[3] Pope and Swift, remarks Johnson, "had an unnatural delight in ideas physically impure." Swift "took delight in revolving ideas, from which almost every other mind shrinks with disgust. ... disease, deformity, and filth." From the letters of Pope and Swift one may infer that they "with Arbuthnot and Gay, had engrossed all the understanding and virtue of mankind." Part of Pope's "pretended discontent" with the world "he learned from Swift, and expresses it ... most frequently in his correspondence with him" (Lonsdale 2006: III, 212, 213; IV, 60, 75).

publication of their *Miscellanies* would show them "like friends, side by side … walking hand in hand down to posterity."[4]

Identifying similarity is often the first step toward discovering crucial difference. Beginning about a generation ago it became commonplace to distinguish between these two "Tory satirists": to observe, for example, that Swift typically speaks through adopted masks – of Bickerstaff, the Drapier, or Gulliver – while Pope typically speaks out in a voice that he encourages us to regard as his own. Or to argue that Pope typically forms an alliance with his virtuous reader, joined in opposition to fools and knaves, while Swift seizes his "gentle reader" by the nose, and thrusts him into the satire as a target. Or that Swift finds it difficult to take heroic poetry seriously, while Pope is still genuinely engaged by the idea of epic. Or that Pope seems quite comfortable in claiming to be a man of virtue and integrity, while Swift usually displays some kind of nervousness about blowing his own horn. But even those who made such distinctions still in effect regard the two poets as fundamentally aligned.

Specialists have qualified this picture of literary kinship. Those who have worked through the Sherburn and Williams (and now the Woolley) editions of Pope's and Swift's correspondence, or the full-scale modern biographies by Mack (1985) and Ehrenpreis (1962–83),[5] know that these two great friends sometimes became irritated with each other, sometimes found that their interests diverged, sometimes even misled each other as they pursued their own goals.[6] Careful readers of the correspondence will also know that the letters between Pope and Swift need to be read critically: as Johnson long ago observed, Pope "may be said to write always with his reputation in his head; Swift perhaps like a man who remembered that he was writing to Pope."[7] They are literary performances, especially on Pope's part, written with the knowledge that they will probably be passed around to admiring friends and perhaps eventually published. This does not mean that we now should view with skepticism or suspicion the affectionate words that pass between friends, but it does mean that we must not assume that the writer of a personal letter – especially one so artful and fond of tricks as Pope or Swift – is always telling the whole truth – even to a dear friend. When Pope writes to Swift that his

---

[4] Pope to Swift, February 17, 1727, in Woolley (1999–2007: III, 76).

[5] Earlier biographical treatments of the relationship include Norman Ault, "Pope and Swift," in Ault 1949.

[6] Mack (1985: 915) acknowledges that Pope was on one occasion "genuinely irritated" at Swift and that Swift must have been "equally annoyed" by Pope's "maneuverings to obtain the letters."

[7] "Life of Pope," in Lonsdale (2006: IV, 38).

"principal aim" in writing the *Dunciad* was "to perpetuate the friendship between us" (October 9, 1729, in Woolley 1999–2007: III, 257), we need not take him literally. When Swift praises (while pretending to envy) Pope for fixing more sense in one couplet "than I can do in six" (*Verses on the Death of Dr. Swift*), we should observe the layers of irony, not the least of which depends on the fact that Swift here writes not six couplets but three, and writes in tighter octosyllabic couplets that make Pope's more expansive pentameters seem almost long-winded.

More recently, other scholars have reminded their colleagues of some fundamental and underappreciated differences, both demographic and psychological, between Pope and Swift – one an Anglican and the other a Roman Catholic; one an Irishman and the other an Englishman; one by temperament a reckless extremist, the other by temperament moderate and cautious; one committed to politics, and especially Irish politics, throughout his career, and the other reluctant (until his final years) to engage in partisan politics – differences that help to produce quite different kinds of writings.[8]

It is my contention that we ought to pay more attention to these differences, if only because Pope and Swift were themselves fully aware of them, and drew our attention to those differences both in their correspondence and in their poems. The point is not just that they, like any two close friends, occasionally disagreed, or discovered that defining differences was a way of expressing affection and of articulating how the two of them are bound in a reciprocal relationship with each other. More than that, each of them seemed to find that he could more clearly discern his own path as a writer by marking the difference between his own way and that of his friend.[9] In various ways Pope and Swift each found it useful to maintain a kind of productive tension between themselves, to keep their distance, even as the other sought to draw his friend into his own orbit.

Thus, Swift invited Pope – only half-mockingly – to convert to the Church of England, but Pope politely declined. Thus Pope urged Swift to give up Irish politics – both because they were politics (rather than poetry) and because they were Irish, but Swift persisted. Thus both writers, despite repeated invitations and half-promises from 1727 until the

---

[8] See, for example, Harth 1985 and 1998 and Hammond 1998. For earlier attention to differences, see Winn 1977: 177–80. Barnett (2007: 6) recently drew attention to Swift's posthumous birth and early separation from his mother, and Pope's close relations with his parents through their lives.

[9] Harth notes "a process of self-definition, sometimes delineating their own norms and attitudes by contrasting them with those of their opposite number" (1998: 240).

end of their lives, kept finding reasons why a relatively short trip across
the Irish Sea was more than either of them could possibly conceive of
managing.[10] (Ill health may have accounted for it.)[11] Orrery, who knew
them both well, speculated that, given their prickly natures, Swift's distance from Pope in England was in fact good for their friendship: "Such
a separation prevented all personal dissensions, and fixt them in a correspondence, that constantly tended to establish their endearments; when,
perhaps, a residence near each other, might have had a very contrary
effect" (Orrery 1752: 232).[12]

Adopting this angle of vision, I want to read the works of Pope and Swift
in tandem, on the assumption that to read them in isolation is in part to
misread them, to fail to hear part of what is being said. Each often wrote for
the other, sometimes addressing him directly. Such direct address is a form
of praise, but also an invitation for a response. Each sensed that the other
was his best reader, his most important critic. And each freely imparted his
critical opinion, opinions that have usually been regarded as acutely discern-
ing: Swift readily told Pope of the risks he assumed in attacking obscure
dunces, and let Pope know that he suspected him of forming "Schemes …
of Epistolary Fame," while Pope warned Swift of being consumed by Irish
politics. Each was in some sense constantly "replying" to the other, sometimes even taking up the other's language. Failing to recognize the dialogic
nature of their writings can lead a critic astray.

An example drawn from the correspondence of the two friends can perhaps suggest the degree to which their writings must be read, as it were,
responsively – each letter, and each poem, taken as a response to an earlier
one by the other. In a well-known letter of September 29, 1725, Swift writes
to Pope that "the chief end I propose to my self in all my labors is to vex
the world rather then [*sic*] divert it" (Woolley 1999–2007: II, 606). Some

[10] Swift of course made the passage a number of times. It could prove to be an onerous journey. In
1727 it took him six days to make the roughly 200-mile trip from London to Holyhead, where
he just missed the boat, and was delayed a week by bad weather. The crossing from Holyhead
to Dublin itself normally took less than a day, but in this case the journey took two days, since
he disembarked at Carlingford, and had to ride 60 miles to Dublin. See Swift's account in his
"Holyhead Journal" (Davis 1939–68: v, 207–08). But in August, 1726, the journey from London
to Dublin only took eight days (see Swift's letter to Pope, in Woolley 1999–2007: III, 18 and n2).
[11] Pope wrote to Swift in 1737 that his doctors advised him that because of a "weakness in my
breast," any seasickness might "indanger my life" (Woolley 1999–2007: IV, 404).
[12] "It is much easier to rectify any mistake, or to cool any animosity that may have arisen, in a
letter, than to recal a passionate verbal answer, especially if uttered with all the actions, and
vehemence of anger" (1752: 150). Cf. Winn: "there were so many differences between the two in
personality and philosophy that their geographical separation may have been an important factor in their managing to remain friends" (1977: 176).

critics assume this to be a programmatic declaration that, as a satirist, he aims more at provoking and disturbing not only "the world" but also his readers, rather than amusing or delighting them with his wit. Twenty-five years ago, Philip Harth pointed out (1985: 117) that Swift's paired terms – "vex" and "divert" – are not his own: they are taken from Pope's letter of two weeks earlier, to which Swift's is a response. In that letter Pope had lightly remarked, after reflecting on the "dispersions" and "divisions" among friends, that he hoped "two or three of us" might one day gather not "to vex our own or others hearts with busy vanities ... but to divert ourselves, and the world too if it pleases" (Woolley 1999–2007: II, 597). To understand Swift's remark, you need to read it not as an incipient theory of satire, but as a *reply to Pope*. Is Swift replying in Pope's facetious vein, or is he discovering in Pope's own casual words a way to redeploy them in order to provide a serious definition of his own satiric project?

If we read the ninety-five letters in the Pope–Swift correspondence in this way we can see more clearly that the two friends are engaged in an ongoing conversation from their first acquaintance in 1713 to the final letter in 1741, often literally responding to the previous letter, each sometimes replying with a witty riposte, sometimes offering a gentle or veiled rebuke, reproach, or corrective,[13] sometimes seeking to draw the interlocutor into his orbit. (In his criticism of the obscurities in *The Dunciad*, Swift might be said to try to make Pope's poem more Swiftian, just as Pope's edited version of Swift's *Verses on the Death of Dr. Swift* seeks to make the poem more like something Pope would have written.) We should also pay as much attention to a correspondent's silences as his words, what he chooses to tell his friend and what he chooses to keep to himself. By the same token, it is useful (as widespread scholarly practice has shown) to align the flow of correspondence closely with the flow of literary projects upon which each writer is engaged. Indeed, their letters are as much literary works themselves as they are biographical documents. Arguably 'literary' from the outset, they clearly become 'literary' when they are edited and presented to the world as part of Pope's prose *Works* in 1737 and 1741.[14] Yet, especially because some manuscript letters were excluded from

---

[13] For example, Swift's June 28, 1715, letter to Pope: "I am angry at some bad Rhymes and Triplets [in his translation of the *Iliad*], and pray in your next do not let me have so many unjustifiable Rhymes to *war* and *gods*" (Woolley 1999–2007: II, 133). Johnson remarks that Pope proceeded in his translation "without regard to Swift's remonstrances."

[14] Raymond Stephanson 2007, following the lead of Howard Erskine-Hill, has recently argued that we need to pay more attention to the Pope–Swift letters in the form in which they were published in 1737 and 1741.

to add to the new volume. I have reafon to chufe the method
you mention of mixing the feveral verfes, and I hope thereby
among the bad Critics to be entitled to more merit than is my
due.

This moment I am fo happy to have a letter from my
Lord Peterborow, for which I intreat you will prefent him with
my humble refpects and thanks, tho' he all-to-be-Gullivers me
by very ftrong infinuations. Tho' you defpife Riddles, I am
ftrongly tempted to fend a parcel to be printed by themfelves,
and make a nine-penny jobb for the bookfeller. There are
fome of my own, wherein I exceed mankind, *Mira Poemata!*
the moft folemn that were ever feen ; and fome writ by others,
admirable indeed, but far inferior to mine, but I will not praife
my felf. You approve that writer who laughs and makes others
laugh; but why fhould I who hate the world, or you who do
not love it, make it fo happy ? therefore I refolve from hence-
forth to handle only ferious fubjects, *nifi quid tu docte Trebati,
Diffentis.*

Yours, &c.

LETTER XXII.

March 8, 1726-7.

MR. Stopford will be the bearer of this letter, for whofe
acquaintance I am, among many other favours, obliged
to you : and I think the acquaintance of fo valuable, ingenious,
and unaffected a man, to be none of the leaft obligations.

Our Mifcellany is now quite printed. I am prodigioufly pleas'd
with this joint-volume, in which methinks we look like friends,
fide by fide, ferious and merry by turns, converfing interchangeably, and walking down hand in hand to pofterity; not in the

O

1.1 Pope's March 8, 1727 letter to Swift, *Works of Mr. Alexander Pope, In Prose. Vol. II* (1741).

ftiff forms of learned Authors, flattering each other, and fetting
the reft of mankind at nought: but in a free, un-important,
natural, eafy manner; diverting others juft as we diverted our-
felves. The third volume confifts of Verfes, but I would chufe
to print none but fuch as have fome peculiarity, and may be di-
ftinguifh'd for ours, from other writers. There's no end of making Books, Solomon faid, and above all of making Mifcellanies,
which all men can make. For unlefs there be a character in
every piece, like the mark of the Elect, I fhould not care to be
one of the Twelve-thoufand figned.

You receiv'd, I hope, fome commendatory verfes from a Horfe
and a Lilliputian, to Gulliver; and an heroic Epiftle of Mrs.
Gulliver. The Bookfeller would fain have printed 'em before
the fecond Edition of the Book, but I would not permit it without your approbation: nor do I much like them. You fee how
much like a Poet I write, and yet if you were with us, you'd
be deep in Politicks. People are very warm, and very angry,
very little to the purpofe, but therefore the more warm and the
more angry: *Non noftrum eft, Tantas componere lites.* I ftay at
Twitnam, without fo much as reading news-papers, votes, or
any other paltry pamphlets: Mr. Stopford will carry you a whole
parcel of them, which are fent for your diverfion, but not
imitation. For my own part, methinks, I am at Glubdubdrib
with none but Ancients and Spirits about me.

I am rather better than I ufe to be at this feafon, but my
hand (tho' as you fee, it has not loft its cunning) is frequently
in very aukward fenfations, rather than pain. But to convince
you it is pretty well, it has done fome mifchief already, and
juft been ftrong enough to cut the other hand, while it was
aiming to prune a fruit-tree.

Lady Bolingbroke has writ you a long, lively, letter, which
will attend this; She has very bad health, he very good. Lord
Peterborow has writ twice to you; we fancy fome letters have
been intercepted, or loft by accident. About ten thoufand

Fig 1.1 *(Cont.)*

the printed editions in their lifetime, those originals can be examined as the raw biographical materials from which literary works were shaped.

Correspondence is not the only form of conversation. Swift and Pope of course famously collaborated on several major literary projects, from the Scriblerian *Memoirs of Martinus Scriblerus* to the several volumes of *Miscellanies in Prose and Verse* and on minor pieces such as "Bounce to Fop." In a famous letter to Swift, Pope imagined that the first two volumes of their *Miscellanies* would show them "conversing interchangeably" (Woolley 1999–2007: III, 76), suggesting that their readers would be right to see the joint project as a "conversation" between two writers, a poem by Pope "answering" one by Swift, and vice versa (See Illustration 1.1).

Even when they are not formally collaborating, I would argue that Pope and Swift are engaged in conversation as poets, and that it would be illuminating (but not sufficiently practiced by critics) to read their poems and prose as a series of "replies," advertising sometimes an affinity between two close friends, sometimes a crucial difference. Critics often note that Pope's *Dunciad Variorum* (1729) implicitly acknowledges, in part by means of an elaborate apparatus of mock-footnotes, Swift's *Tale of a Tub* (1704, 1710) as a crucial literary ancestor and a formative influence in its satire on modern writing. And it is common for critics to remark on the ways in which Swift's pictures of a lady's dressing room in effect re-write the scene of Belinda at her toilet table in *The Rape of the Lock*. Sometimes the "reply" takes the form of admiring imitation. Pope himself suggests that his own imitations of Horace "in the manner of Dr. Swift" are intended to be read as emulative tribute. (Swift, interestingly, thought them not a very good imitation.)

The principle of reply can be extended to other pairs of works. As I will suggest below, we can read *Cadenus and Vanessa* as a reply to *The Rape of the Lock*, Pope's "Epistle to a Lady" as a reply to Swift's poems to Stella (addressed, like Pope's, to a middle-aged spinster), and Swift's *On Poetry. A Rapsody* as a reply to *The Dunciad*. And for my purposes – observing and assessing the interaction of two writers who share their work with each other – it will be just as important to look at early and unpublished drafts of poems, if they have been exchanged by mail or viewed in manuscript. Thus, Pope's *Epistle to Dr. Arbuthnot* can be regarded as a reply to Swift's *Verses on the Death of Dr. Swift*, written earlier, though published later, than Pope's *Epistle*. (The Pope-revised edition of Swift's *Verses* is another reply, and Swift's quickly published edition in turn a reply to Pope's truncated one.) I will not limit my attention to pairs of major (and often-studied) poems. I will pay more attention than critics usually do to lesser-known (and less-discussed) works – Pope's pamphlets on Curll as shaped in part by Swift's earlier Bickerstaffian pieces, his Gulliverian verses as a reply to Swift's *Travels*, and *Windsor-Forest* (1713) as an oblique reply to Swift's prose pamphlet, *The Conduct of the Allies* (1711).

Before engaging further on an extended discussion of the running "conversation" between Swift and Pope, it is worth trying to determine what Pope might have meant when he imagined "conversing interchangeably."[15] It is well known that his contemporaries took great interest in face-to-face "conversation" and that they aimed to cultivate it as an art. In 1737 Swift wrote to Pope about an *Essay on Conversation* in verse he had just read.[16] Steele's ideal, in an essay on the topic in the *Tatler*, is polite conversation, as in a drawing room or coffee house, and emphasizes setting one's interlocutors at ease. Hence, even in conversation with a "Bosom Friend," it is necessary "that we should always be inclined rather to hide than rally each others Infirmities." Such politesse was thought too refined later in the century, at least by such stout conversationalists as Johnson, who famously regarded good talk (at least among male social equals) as a strenuous battle of wits.

Reports of the conversational practice of Pope and Swift are inconclusive. Swift seems to have been the better conversationalist, and to have valued it more. He loved puns and thought raillery "the finest Part of Conversation."[17] Johnson reports that he "told stories with great felicity," and took care not to dominate,[18] apparently sharing Steele's view that "Equality is the Life of Conversation."[19] Swift's early *Hints Toward an Essay on Conversation* declares that the "Ends" of conversation are to "entertain and improve those we are among, or to receive those Benefits ourselves."[20] In good conversation we learn to shed our prejudices and "correct" our judgement. At its best, an exchange between those who disagree can even

[15] Pope may have remembered the *Guardian*, No. 24 (April 8, 1713): "The Faculty of interchanging our Thoughts with another, or what we express by the word *Conversation*, has always been represented by Moral Writers as one of the noblest privileges of Reason" (*Guardian*, 2 vols., 1714, p. 140).

[16] Woolley (1999–2007): IV, 433). For earlier examples, see Laurent Bordelon, "Of Conversation," in *The Management of the Tongue* (1707); *The Art of Pleasing in Conversation* (1708), attributed to Richelieu, and translated from the French by M. de Varmonière, Sir Richard Bulstrode, "Of Company and Conversation," in *Miscellaneous Essays* (1724).

[17] *Hints Toward an Essay on Conversation*, probably written as early as 1710–12 although not published until 1763 (Davis 1939–68: IV, 91).

[18] "Life of Swift," in Lonsdale (2006: III, 212). But Johnson disapproved of Swift's "affectation of familiarity with the Great" in his conversation (2006: 212).

[19] *Tatler*, No. 225 (September 16, 1710). See also *Guardian*, No. 24 (April 8, 1713), with its several "Rules of Conversation."

[20] Davis (1939–68: IV, 92). For a discussion of Swift on conversation, see Kelly (1988: 37–56).

promote personal and political reconciliation,[21] although in practice it can just reinforce prior opinion: "That was *excellently observed*, say I. ..., where his Opinion agrees with mine. When we differ, there I pronounce him to be *mistaken*."[22] His *Polite Conversation* (1738) suggests that he savored the difference between good witty talk and bad formulaic talk, but also that he might have been as acutely aware of his own contributions to conversation as he was of those of others, and even self-conscious about them. Pope's famous story about Swift's "odd, blunt way" (obliging Pope and Gay to take money for wine they would have drunk at his table) suggests that even with close friends he could be difficult to read, and to respond to.[23] At its best, Pope's talk was thought "easy."[24] Swift himself wrote to Gay that Pope's conversation was defective because he was inattentive.[25] Remembering his two visits to England years earlier, he complained to another friend that Pope had "utterly disqualifyed [himself] for my conversation," because he "hath always some poetical Scheme in his head."[26] Johnson noted simply that Pope was not known for his wit, wisdom, or repartee: "In familiar or convivial conversation, it does not appear that he excelled. He may be said to have resembled Dryden, as being not one that was distinguished by vivacity in company."[27] Perhaps Pope thought that his ability at "conversing" might be best found in his writing. One guesses that Swift agreed with him.

One might "converse" in a face-to-face encounter or by means of letters. "You see how I like to talk to you," Pope wrote to Swift, "(for this is not writing)."[28] Both he and Swift sometimes persuaded themselves

[21] *Examiner*, 19, in Davis (1939–68: III, 35–36).

[22] *Thoughts on Various Subjects*, in Davis (1939–68: IV, 248).

[23] Osborn (1966: I, 53). Johnson repeats the story in the "Life of Swift." It seems plausible that in these conversations recorded on May 1–7, 1730, Pope was in effect retaliating for Swift's remark in his March 19, 1730, letter to Gay about Pope saying, as he left his guests with the wine all but gone,"Gentlemen I will leave you to your wine" (Woolley, III, 292).

[24] Boswell reports Marchmont telling him that Pope "was not *un homme à bons mots*. His conversation was something better – more manly. A flow of vivacity. But it was necessary he should lead the conversation. If other people talked together, he fell asleep" (Weis and Pottle 1970: 333). For reports by Chesterfield, Somerville, and Warton, see the notes in Hill's edition of Johnson's *Lives of the Poets* (III, 201). For reports by Ruffhead, Hervey, Birch, and others, see the notes in Lonsdale (2006: IV, 307).

[25] Woolley (1999–2007: III, 501).

[26] Woolley (1999–2007: III, 677). Johnson repeats the report in the "Life of Pope," in Lonsdale (2006: IV, 59). Swift does not mention that, on at least one of those visits to Pope, he himself, because of an attack of deafness, was not fit for conversation, and that Pope for that reason devoted himself to writing. For Swift's verses about that visit, see below, ch. 2, pp. III, 113.

[27] "Life of Pope," in Lonsdale (2006: IV, 56).

[28] Woolley (1999–2007: III, 759). Cf. Pope's May 28, 1712 letter to Caryll: "It is not only the disposition I always have of conversing with you that makes me so speedily answer your obliging lines" (Sherburn 1956: I, 143). The preface to a 1726 collection of Pope's letters to Henry Cromwell

that writing was even superior to conversation because "more naturall and sincere."[29] The familiar letters they exchanged with each other went beyond gracious compliment and easy wit to encompass warm expressions of admiration and affection – "I love and esteem you for reasons that most others have little to do with, and would be the same although you had never touched a pen, further than writing to me"; "You are the only Man now in the world, who cost me a Sigh every day of my Life, and the Man it troubles me most, altho' I most wish, to write to."[30] Third parties have doubted that such letters are always "naturall and sincere." In the opinion of their mutual friend Orrery, their letters were filled "with the strongest expressions of mutual esteem; but those expressions are repeated too often" (Orrery 1752: 165). They were notable, in Johnson's opinion, for being "premeditated and artificial," but Mack (a more sympathetic reader) has called them the overflow "of expressive and volatile personality."[31] The letters also include notable instances of raillery, sometimes designed as an indirect form of compliment, sometimes as a kind of reproach or reflection.[32] The problem for the reader is to try to tell the difference.

The "conversation" between writers might also be found in their mutual poems, as suggested by the "Preface" to a collection of Pope's letters to Henry Cromwell, published by Curll in 1726. Pope's letters to Cromwell are of the "Familiar" kind, and Pope is praised because he "always takes Care to suit his Style to his Subject, whether Familiar, or Sublime, or Didactic," and "has more or less varied it in every Letter." Their familiar conversation is in effect continued in their poems, including "An Epistle from Mr. Alexander Pope to Henry Cromwell, Esq.," to which a sequence of short lyrics by Cromwell is in effect an answer. (Cromwell's poems are themselves modeled on an exchange of letters – "Phaon to Sapho," "Sapho's Answer to Phaon," "Phaon's Reply"[33] – and knowingly allude to

---

[29] carefully noted that letters do not imitate conversation; only dialogue can do that. The true "End of Letter-writing is to supply [i.e., to make up for the absence of] Conversation, and not to imitate it." A letter's style "should neither come quite up to that of Conversation, nor yet keep at too great a Distance from it"(*Miscellanea. In Two Volumes* (1727) [1726]), n.p.

[29] In a 1732 letter from Swift to the Duchess of Queensberry, in Woolley (1999–2007: III, 524).

[30] Swift to Pope (August 4, 1726), in Woolley (1999–2007: II, 5); Pope to Swift (March 22, 1741)(IV, 656).

[31] Mack (1985: 186). Mack here refers to Pope's letters, but elsewhere suggests that Swift's letters were equally founded in real warmth.

[32] True raillery, as it was once understood, Swift wrote, was "to say something that at first appeared a Reproach, or Reflection; but, by some Turn of Wit unexpected and surprising, ended always in a Compliment, and to the Advantage of the Person it was addressed to" (*Hints Toward an Essay on Conversation*, reprinted in Davis 1939–68: IV, 91).

[33] Readers in the know would have assumed that the poems hinted at the relationship between Cromwell and Elizabeth Thomas, whom he sometimes called "Sapho."

Pope's own translation of Ovid's "Sapho to Phaon," first published in 1712 and reprinted in Pope's 1717 *Works*). Curll's volume also puts Pope in a kind of conversation with Tom Durfey: it prints a poem attributed to "Mr. Pope" entitled "Verses occasion'd by Mr. Durfy's adding an &c. at the end of his Name, in Imitation of Voiture's Verses on Neuf-Germain." Curll here follows common contemporary practice: the poetic miscellanies of the day often include a poem "addressed" by A to B, with a "reply" from B to A. When Pope suggested to Swift that their miscellany would show them "conversing interchangeably" he was speaking about the mutual poems – none of them, as it happens, explicitly announced as address and reply poems – in terms that their contemporaries would have understood, and that we can thus appropriately adopt.

To emphasize its literary nature, the ongoing conversation might also be called a "dialogue." Swift and Pope themselves use the term to refer to poems for two voices which present opposed points of view, as with Swift's "Dialogue Between an Eminent Lawyer and Dr. Swift" (an imitation of Horace) and "Pastoral Dialogue between Richmond Lodge and Marble Hill," or Pope's imitation of the same poem of Horace "in a Dialogue between Alexander Pope … on the one Part, and his Learned Council on the other," and the two "Dialogue[s]" between "P." and "Fr." of his *Epilogue to the Satires*.[34] My study of the "satirical dialogue" between Swift and Pope might be compared to Paul Magnuson's 1988 study of the "lyrical dialogue" between Wordsworth and Coleridge, to which it is indebted for its basic premise that poets who wrote to and for each other and commented on each other's works need to be read in tandem.[35] I also adopt Magnuson's principle of paying attention to key pairs of poems, and to the draft versions of poems, if there is evidence that the poets saw each other's work in draft. But there are some significant differences between the two pairs of writers, and between my approach and Magnuson's "methodology."

First, Wordsworth and Coleridge spent a great deal of time in each other's company, and Magnuson finds it possible to chart their responses to each other almost monthly. Pope and Swift spent relatively little time together – a series of meetings in 1713–14, Swift's visit to England in 1726, and especially the visit to England in 1727 when he stayed for some weeks with Pope in Twickenham. Their relationship, unlike that of Wordsworth and Coleridge, was conducted primarily by correspondence, and they rarely

[34] *OED* defines "dialogue" as "conversation," sometimes (2a) as "a literary work in the form of a conversation."
[35] Paul Magnuson, *Wordsworth and Coleridge: A Lyrical Dialogue* (1988).

exchanged more than half a dozen letters between them in a calendar year. Magnuson is especially interested in the succession of poems produced by Wordsworth and Coleridge, regarding "each succeeding poem [by one poet] as a commentary on a preceding one [by the other]" (1988: 139), or as parts of a single "lyric sequence" (1988: x). Pope and Swift do not "respond" to each other with such frequency, and when they do "respond," it is not just to the most recent product of the friend's pen. In the case of letters, to be sure, they often reply explicitly to what was said in the immediately preceding letter. But in the case of poems, they seem not to restrict themselves to work drafted or published in that year: in some cases there is a significantly delayed response. This is not difficult to explain: the writings of both poets were repeatedly reprinted many years later, in either authorized or pirated editions. In addition, Pope, in his capacity as editor of the four volumes of Pope–Swift *Miscellanies*, would have had before his eyes many instances of Swift's early verse and prose, to be included, excluded, corrected (at Swift's invitation), or in some way answered.

Second, Magnuson pays little attention to the traditional topic of authorial individuality. He views the poetry of Wordsworth and Coleridge as "an intricately connected whole," indeed as a "joint canon" (ix). I make no such case for the writings of Pope and Swift, even though they collaborated on several projects in which it is probably impossible to determine which parts are written by Swift and which by Pope, and even though Pope claimed that their joint *Miscellanies* would show them "walking together, hand in hand, down to posterity," and once even claimed that Swift was in fact the true "author" of *The Dunciad*. At the same time Magnuson argues that Wordsworth and Coleridge worried that their works would seem to run together, in a kind of "amalgamation" that they fought hard to resist. A special version of this anxiety, he suggests, was Coleridge's fear of being subsumed by Wordsworth's stronger literary personality. Again, I make no such claim about Swift and Pope, each of whom (so I will argue) in effect sought to make over the other in his own image, readily resisted the other's attempt, and thereby reaffirmed his own distinctiveness.[36] Although Pope was younger than Swift by some twenty years, as Swift frequently reminded him, the two writers seem to have regarded each other as equally strong personalities, and as equally powerful writers. In discussing each other's works, they tended to emphasize what distinguished them (Swift the prose writer, the political

---

[36] As Lucy Newlyn in fact argues about Wordsworth and Coleridge, in *Coleridge, Wordsworth, and the Language of Allusion* (1986).

writer, the Irish writer; Pope the poet, apolitical and English) rather than what they had in common. This authorial evasion, if that is what it is, may perhaps signal some concern on the part of Pope and Swift to preserve distinction, and deserves attention.

But to understand how Pope and Swift regarded their interrelationship, we need to strip ourselves of some modern ideas about authorship that derived from the theory and practice of the Romantic poets. In the early eighteenth century, collaboration was much more common than it was at the end of the century, when Wordsworth and Coleridge were compiling the *Lyrical Ballads*. Both Swift and Pope grew up in a literary tradition of the multi-authored text, from the miscellany to the play equipped with prologue and epilogue by another hand, from a poem introduced by commendatory poems, or by a letter from bookseller to reader, to a preface by an "editor." They also wrote at a time when much publication was anonymous (an author might have various reasons for avoiding being named) or piratical (a bookseller might well want to publish a poem under the name of a famous author, whether or not he in fact wrote it), or even scribal (in which poems – by Pope, for example – would circulate in manuscript for some time before – and even after – appearing in print).[37] In such a literary milieu the interaction between a pair of famous writers is bound to be different from that which links a pair of Romantic poets.

My method will blend a joint biographical narrative (derived from their letters to each other) with comparative analysis of some of their works, both major and minor, discovering Pope and Swift in continuous conversation with each other, and putting their writings in a kind of conversation with each other as well. The assumption underlying such comparative study is that, as Dryden put it, "great Contemporaries whet and cultivate each other."[38] (Dryden had in mind writers in the age of Augustus and painters in the age of Lorenzo de Medici; closer to our own time we might think of Picasso and Matisse.) Rather than giving equal attention to each year of the developing relationship between Swift and Pope, I will focus on five periods when their interaction seemed to be the most intense, and the most productive: the first years of their relationship, at the time of the meetings of the Scriblerus Club; the mid-1720s, when Swift was writing the *Travels* and Pope was writing the *Dunciad;* the early 1730s, when both Pope and Swift were writing and publishing at a furious rate; the late 1730s, when Swift was at the end of his writing career

[37] See Ferraro 1998.
[38] "Discourse … of Satire," *Works*, California edition (1974), IV, 12.

and Pope was adopting more openly political stances; and the early 1740s, when Pope published an edition of their joint correspondence, and the *Memoirs of Martinus Scriblerus*, the late fruit of their early Scriblerian collaboration, and when each composed both a will and an epitaph.

What might emerge from such study are better readings of some of the writings of Pope and Swift – better because more attentive to the interpersonal resonance – and a better sense of the interrelations between the writers, moved as they were sometimes to emulate and sometimes to mark out difference. It might also yield a greater understanding of the way in which authorial interaction shaped the reception of their writing. Contemporary readers in London and Dublin knew of the close friendship and collaboration between these two writers, and eagerly awaited the appearance of the latest poem by either one, that eagerness only fanned to higher heat by the regular appearance of pirated materials from Curll and other unscrupulous publishers who counted on a reader's hope for an unauthorized glimpse into the private lives of famous writers. Once established, the principle of reading a writer's work in tandem with that of a contemporary could be extended to other pairs of writers in this period, perhaps Pope and Gay, Swift and Gay, Swift and Defoe, or Fielding and Richardson.[39]

The contextual pressures of authorial interaction also shaped the production of their writing. Individual poems will inevitably look different to us if we regard them as responses to other writings, or as designed in any sense for a particular reader. To focus not on a single author but on a pair of writers whose lives and careers were intertwined is to begin to recover a fuller sense of the practical workings of authorship in an era when interaction of various kinds was common.[40] It was not only commonly *practiced*, but also commonly *represented* in contemporary texts, as a quick survey of writings by Swift and Pope will remind us. Several named critics, commenting in one way or another on the main text, are incorporated within *A Tale of a Tub* and the *Dunciad Variorum*. Both Pope and Swift address poetical epistles to friends, some of whom (e.g., Arbuthnot, Burlington, Bathurst, and Fortescue) are represented in the poem as responding. Some poems (e.g., *One Thousand Seven Hundred and Thirty-Eight*) are cast in the form of a dialogue; in others (e.g., *Verses on the Death of Dr. Swift*) a putatively independent figure is brought into the poem to provide an "impartial" view.

---

[39] Tom Jones has done a comparative reading in *Pope and Berkeley: The Language of Poetry and Philosophy* (2005). See also Brean Hammond, *Pope and Bolinbroke: A Study of Friendship and Influence* (1984). John Ross's *Swift and Defoe: A Study in Relationship* (1941) could be updated.

[40] For some preliminary speculations on Augustan collaborative authorship, see Griffin 1987.

On occasions both Swift and Pope imagined an exclusive circle to which only they – with one or two choice colleagues – might gain admission.[41] To follow their lead and focus just on two writers is of course arbitrary. A quick look at the complete *Correspondence* of Swift and Pope will show that each of them was in steady epistolary contact over a number of years with many other writers: Pope's other regular correspondents, even during the years when his exchanges with Swift were at their height, included Arbuthnot, Atterbury, Bolingbroke, Gay, and Orrery, as well as several nonliterary friends.[42] Swift was writing regularly to the same correspondents – Arbuthnot, Bolingbroke, and Gay were among his closest friends too – but also to Knightley Chetwode, Thomas Sheridan, and William King, among many others. Both Swift and Pope addressed poetical "epistles" to their contemporaries, many of them fellow writers who in one way or other responded in print: Swift addressed such poems to Gay, Young, Robert Harley, Sheridan, the Countess of Winchelsea, and Patrick Delany; Pope to Addison, Arbuthnot, Bolingbroke, Henry Cromwell, the painter Charles Jervas, and many others.[43] Eighteenth-century readers of miscellanies were furthermore invited to regard the "conversation" between a writer and the others who appeared in the same pages, often providing an "answer" to a poem written by Pope or by Swift, or a commendatory poem. In the fifth edition of Lintot's 1712 miscellany, published in 1726–27 and entitled *Miscellany Poems*, the first volume is wholly devoted to poems by Pope, but also includes commendatory poems addressed "To Mr. Pope" by Buckingham, Lady Winchelsea, Wycherly, Simon Harcourt, Parnell, Francis Knapp, Elijah Fenton, Christopher Pitt, Abel Evans, William Broome, and two anonymous poets. Granted that Swift and Pope were engaged in forms of literary conversation with several contemporaries, it is probably safe to claim that, for both of them, each was the other's most important and influential colleague.[44]

[41] Posing as the "Intelligencer," Swift proposes no other "Reward" for his ridicule of "the Follies and Corruptions of a *Court*, a *Ministry*, or a *Senate*" than "laughing with a few Friends in a Corner" (Davis 1939–68: XII, 34).

[42] They included John Caryll, Hugh Bethel, William Fortescue, and Edward Harley. In Pope's first years, before he met Swift, he exchanged many letters with Henry Cromwell and William Wycherley. In his last years, after the letters to and from Swift dropped to a trickle, he was corresponding frequently with new friends – Ralph Allen and William Warburton, for example.

[43] Other recipients of Pope's verse epistles were Bathurst, Hugh Bethel, Martha Blount, Bolingbroke, Burlington, Cobham, James Craggs, and Robert Harley. Swift also addressed poems to Carteret, Biddy Floyd, Peterborough, and Pulteney.

[44] A complete account of the relationship between Swift and Pope would have to include the letters to and conversations with third parties, in which the two principals referred to each other. In August 1723 Pope wrote to Swift that "Dr Swift lives still in England … & I find him in all the Conversations I keep" (Sherburn 1956: II, 184).

Likewise, it would be inaccurate to claim that Pope and Swift were only reacting to their contemporaries, that each was the most important single influence on the other, or even that they were persistently and primarily concerned to distinguish themselves from each other. Pope later claimed that he was "sworn to no master." In fact, as many commentators have observed, he learned from, emulated, and at the same time set himself apart from, many literary masters, including Horace, Montaigne, Cowley, Denham, Milton, and Dryden. And his poems are studded with "replies" – in the form of allusions, borrowings, echoes, and parodies – to dozens of other writers. Swift's masters, so scholars have rightly suggested, included Erasmus, Rabelais, and Sir Thomas More, Robert Burton and Samuel Butler. To understand Pope and Swift aright, we probably need to think of them as always writing with several such figures in their heads. To provide a comprehensive picture of Swift and Pope among all their masters would require a much larger canvas. In the present book I focus on part of the picture – on the ways in which each may be said to have written with the other in mind.

But in some instances, when we observe the interaction of Pope and Swift we probably need to imagine the presence of a third writer, even when that writer is not named. In many respects Pope and Swift received the same literary inheritance, and regarded themselves as descendants, or at least admirers of the same canon of classical and modern authors, from Homer and Virgil to Shakespeare and Milton. One way for them to declare an alliance or define an unbridgeable difference was to articulate their own relationship with a jointly admired master. To admire Homer and think him an inaccessible ancient is one thing; to regard oneself as his modern incarnation is quite another. Both Swift and Pope admired Cowley, but for the former it was the Pindaric odes he sought to emulate, while for the latter such odes seemed overblown, and it was the essays which revealed "the language of the heart" that Pope loved. Both Swift and Pope found that poems by Horace seemed to suit their own circumstances, and imitated them in distinctive ways. Orrery noticed a "strong resemblance" between Swift and Horace, but also a difference: Horace "is the more elegant and delicate: while he condemns, he pleases," but Swift "takes pleasure in giving pain" (Orrery 1752: 42). Pope is commonly regarded as more "delicate" than Swift – playing Horace to his Juvenal – but some have argued that Pope's "Horatian" poems of the late 1730s are perhaps designed not to imitate Horace's ingratiating manner but to mark off a difference from it. In that respect, Pope might be producing in those poems a more Swiftian Horace.

On other occasions the third writer is one about whose merits Pope and Swift disagreed. Rabelais is a little-discussed instance. As Pope knew, Swift was "a great reader and admirer of Rabelais," but he himself confessed to Spence that "I could never read him over with patience." Swift, he said, "used sometimes to scold me for not liking him enough."[45] Their disagreement about Dryden's merits is well known. As generations of critics have pointed out, Dryden was in many respects the most important of Pope's English predecessors and models.[46] But Swift harbored strong reservations about Dryden (even though he was his kinsman), if only because of the famous remark Dryden is said to have made: "Cousin Swift, you will never be a poet."[47] Swift the cleric would have been irritated by Dryden's anticlericalism and his tolerationism; Swift the Anglican would have hated Dryden's Roman Catholic apologetics; Swift the political Whig would have deplored Dryden's defense of James's royal authority. He sneered at Dryden's flatteries and mocked his dedications of multi-volume works to a multiplying set of patrons. He scorned Dryden's garrulous "Modern" manner, and his readiness, in his many prefaces, to tell the reader of "his Merits and Suffering." Dryden's fellow Roman Catholic, Pope, who knew something first-hand about the difficulties of finding patronage in a Protestant country, was more forgiving. Like Dryden, Pope did not hesitate – in the *Dunciad* and Horatian poems – to tell the reader of *his* merits and sufferings, and presumed to present himself as a sort of latter-day Horace. Particularly when Pope expresses strong admiration of Dryden, we should probably try to imagine him imagining its effect on Swift.

Steele is another writer over whom Swift and Pope disagreed: Pope remained a friend and admirer long after Swift had come to think of Steele as "nauseous Dick Steele." Addison is a fourth. Ehrenpreis remarks that "few men touched Swift as Addison and Arbuthnot did – drawing forth his liveliest conversation, setting him at ease without weakening their own dignity or Swift's – keeping his respect as well as his love. These were the ripest of all his masculine friendships' (1962–83: III. 909). Swift and Pope

---

[45] Osborn (1966: I, 55). The scolding must have been face to face, since Rabelais is not mentioned in their correspondence with each other.

[46] Dryden is an obvious model when Pope came to write *The Dunciad* (see below, ch. 2), but in his early writings (e.g. the *Essay on Criticism*) Pope conspicuously declines to suggest Dryden as a model.

[47] For recent discussion of Swift's hostility to Dryden, and of this possibly apocryphal remark, see Ian Higgins, "Dryden and Swift," in *John Dryden (1631–1700): His Politics, His Plays, and His Poets*, ed. Claude Rawson and Aaron Santesso (2004), 217–34, and Robert Philmus, "Dryden's 'Cousin Swift' Re-examined," *Swift Studies* 18 (2003), 99–103.

initially shared a high regard for Addison, but after a period of friendship, relations between Pope and Addison distinctly cooled, and Pope would later write a bitingly satirical character of his former friend.[48] And Edward Young is yet one more example: Pope includes in the *Dunciad Variorum* (1729) a note on "the sublime verses of Dr. Y" (1962–83: III, 259n), while Swift's *On Reading Dr. Young's Satires* (1733) needles Young for flattering his patrons.

Assessing the several dimensions of their literary correspondence and conversation also leads to some larger questions about their interaction as writers that I will try to address even if it proves impossible to resolve them. Looking beyond the ways in which a poem by Swift might have prompted a response from Pope, and vice versa, is it possible to sustain an argument that either one had a large-scale impact on the career of the other, pushing him in one direction or another? Did they incite each other to do their best work? Did they sometimes encourage in each other writing, thinking, or conduct – a readiness to dissimulate, or an assumption that they are superior to the second-raters who surround them – that has done them little credit in the minds of many critics?[49] Did Swift's extravagant praise of Pope's integrity encourage him to portray himself in the Horatian poems as the friend of "Virtue?" Did Pope's equally extravagant praise of Swift encourage him to portray himself proudly, in poems such as *Verses on the Death of Dr. Swift*, as the fearless friend of "Liberty?" Was it pressure from Swift that led Pope to become more personal and particular in his later satire? Did they encourage in each other what Johnson called a delight in "the physically impure?"[50] (Patrick Delany thought that the "defilement" in Swift's style and language became much more "conspicuous upon his return home from his first long visit to Mr. Pope," implying that Swift "imbibed" the "pollution" from conversing with Pope [1754: 75]). Would Pope have produced the *Dunciad* without the intervention of Swift at a crucial moment? Did Pope significantly shape any of Swift's writings, or was the latter too firmly formed, as a writer, by the time Pope met him in 1713? Would their careers have been significantly

---

[48] See further, below, pp. 20, 71–72, 154, 181, 195. Swift and Pope also disagreed about the merits of minor writers. For Pope, William Walsh was a valued literary mentor. But Swift seems to have regarded him as no better a critic than Rymer or Dennis (Woolley 1999–2007: I, 561, citing Davis 1939–68: I, 249), and may have disapproved of Walsh if only because, as Pope once wrote to Swift, he was "not only a Socinian, but (what you'll own is harder to be saved) a Whig," i.e., a Whig in religion (Woolley 1999–2007: I, 559).

[49] Johnson thought that Pope learned his "pretended discontent" with the world from Swift, whose "resentment was unreasonable, but it was sincere" ("Life of Pope," in Lonsdale 2006: IV, 60).

[50] Smedley's *Metamorphosis* (1728) sneers that both Pope and Swift delight "To *foul* and *dirt* each Place they came in, / And play some Pranks, unfit for naming" (5).

different if they had never met, or if they had managed to exchange annual visits? To the last two questions, the Earl of Orrery, who knew both Swift and Pope well, has firm answers: the "character" of Swift "as an author," he states (1752: 44), was "perfectly established" by 1709 – and in his view it always differed from Pope's.

There is probably a risk, in writing about the interactions of two writers, of taking sides, not just of discovering the writings of one to be the greater, or the character and conduct of the other to be more admirable, but of inadvertently holding or declaring a preference.[51] In this study I will make every effort to be even-handed. Having written a book quite sympathetic to Pope many years ago, in this book I make every effort to maintain critical distance. There is another risk: some readers will perhaps think I overemphasize the trivial disagreements and resentments that are an inevitable part of any close relationship, or misread as resentment or criticism what is only said tongue-in-cheek, building such moments into an argument of some deeper division between two writers aptly famed for their friendship.[52] My reply is first to argue that it is usually possible, if we read carefully, to distinguish between raillery and expressions of pique or resentment. Second, I suggest that it remains puzzling that Pope declined to gratify Swift's oft-expressed desire that he address to him one of his verse epistles – after all, he had honored many friends with such poems. Did something hold him back from honoring the man whom we regard as his greatest friend?

Finally, in emphasizing the tensions holding Swift and Pope both together and apart, I build on one of the earliest critical traditions. In 1748 Laetitia Pilkington noted in her *Memoirs* that Swift "did not think Mr. *Pope* was so candid to the Merits of other Writers, as he ought to be." Authors, he allegedly went on, "are as jealous of their Prerogative as King and can no more bear a Rival in the Empire of Wit, than a Monarch could in his Dominions."[53] In 1749 Thomas Birch wrote to Philip Yorke, Lord Hardwicke, reporting that Faulkner has told him Swift "had no Esteem for Mr. Pope on account of the

---

[51] I disagree with Brean Hammond, who suggests that students of eighteenth-century writing "nowadays have to nail their colours to the mast as either Popeans or Swiftians" ("Swift, Pope, and the Efficacy of Satire," in *Swift: The Enigmatic Dean*, ed. Rudolf Freiburg *et al.* [1998], 77).

[52] Near the end of his life Arbuthnot declared that his friendship with Pope was marked by "scarcely any of those suspicions or jealousy which affect the truest friendships." Pope was anxious enough about "scarcely" that he responded by insisting that he knew of "*not one* on my part," and edited Arbuthnot's letter so as to read in his printed edition "not been any" rather than "scarcely any" (Sherburn 1956: III, 416, 423).

[53] *Pilkington, Memoirs*, 2 vols. (1748), I, 61, 62–63. Swift (or Pilkington) seems to have had Pope's own character of Atticus in mind – "Bear, like the *Turk*, no brother near the throne" (*Epistle to Dr. Arbuthnot*, 198). Pilkington reported that Pope was "united to the Dean in the strictest

latter's jealous, peevish, avaritious & artful Temper; & that he was particularly offended with Mr. Pope's satire upon Mr. Addison, for whose Integrity, Generosity, & other amiable Qualities, the Doctor always declar'd the highest Regard."[54] By 1752, when Orrery printed his *Remarks on the Life and Writings of Dr. Swift*, reports had already circulated that "the Friendship between Pope and Swift was not so firm and perfect at the latter end as at the beginning of their lives."[55] Orrery insists on the falseness of the report, vouching for Swift's "unalterable" friendship, and avowing (on the basis of a number of private letters) that it did not "appear less fervent on the side of Mr. Pope." But he also adds that, while Swift was always forthright in his manner, Pope "could stifle resentment, and wait with patience till a more distant, and perhaps a more seasonable hour of revenge" (1752: 146). Still, he concludes his discussion by declaring that it is "my real desire of convincing you [his son, the addressee of the letters that make up his *Remarks*], that the affection of Swift and Pope subsisted as entire and uninterrupted, as their friends could wish or their enemies regret" (1752: 149).

Orrery, who regarded both Pope and Swift as his "two poetical friends" and exchanged warm letters with them both, seems to have had no motive to conceal any break between them, although his language hints more at his desire to think the Pope–Swift friendship unblemished than his conviction that it was so.[56] He was young, eager to form (and to advertise) friendships with older famous writers, and impressionable – Johnson said he "had no mind of his own."[57] And the story of some hostility on Pope's part did not die. Johnson relays the confident report that "a defamatory Life of Swift, which he had prepared as an instrument of vengeance to be used, if any provocation should be ever given" was found in Pope's papers after his death.[58]

Bonds of Friendship" (I, 50), but also declared that he was "an envious Defamer of other Men's Good Parts, and intolerably vain of his own" (II, 287).

[54] August 26, 1749, reprinted in Williams 1963: V, 275. Birch described Faulkner as "a great Confidant" of Swift. Whether he thought Swift had taken offense as early as 1722, when the character of Addison was first published, or 1735, when it was incorporated into Pope's *Epistle to Dr. Arbuthnot*, is not clear. See below, ch. 4, p. 195.

[55] The report, he says, was "very industriously spread, and not without some degree of success" (1752: 147).

[56] His reiteration of the same point in the following paragraph – "I must again repeat, that throughout the long series of letters which have been published, not the least altercations appear to have happened between Swift and Pope" (150) – suggests the urgency of his need to deny the rumor. That need seems to have led him to interpolate the words – "I love [Pope] above all the rest of mankind" into his citation of one of Swift's 1737 letters (147). As Orrery's recent editor points out, the words do not appear in the manuscript letter (*Remarks on the Life and Writings of Dr. Swift*, ed. João Fróes [2000], 250).

[57] James Boswell, *Life of Johnson* ed. G. B. Hill, rev. L. F. Powell, 6 vols. (1934–50), IV, 29.

[58] "Life of Pope," in Lonsdale (2006: IV, 61).

Johnson goes on to report that he was assured by the Earl of Marchmont, one of Pope's executors, that "no such piece was among his remains," but he plainly thought the report worth mentioning.[59] As did Thomas Tyers, who, in his *Historical Rhapsody on Mr. Pope* (1782), refers to a "satirical Life of Swift" left in manuscript.[60] Tyers's source was apparently some manuscript notes prepared by the Revd. John Lyon, reporting that "it's certain that after Pope's death, some very severe reflections on the Dean were found amongst his papers, which were destroyd." (Lyon also reported that Swift one day told a friend that "Pope's esteem for me is more through fear than Love.")[61] Johnson seemed to think that Marchmont's testimony settled the matter, and doesn't press further. But Marchmont, interviewed thirty-five years after Pope's death, may have wished to protect Pope's reputation. He was only one of several executors, and Pope's will specified that his "Manuscript and unprinted Papers" were to be delivered to Bolingbroke, "to whose sole Care and Judgment I commit them, either to be preserved or destroyed," and only to Marchmont in the event that Bolingbroke should predecease Pope, which he did not. Johnson elsewhere reported that some of Pope's manuscripts were in fact burned "by those whom he had perhaps selected from all mankind as most likely to publish them"[62] – implying that it was his executors. Bolingbroke might have had a motive: not only his anger at Pope for correcting and printing, without authorization, the manuscript of his *Idea of a Patriot King*, but also his wish to protect the reputation of his old friend Swift (if not Pope's reputation too). Mack, who is silent on the reported "defamatory life," infers that Bolingbroke destroyed some of Pope's manuscripts.[63] If Pope had prepared such a "satirical" report and held it in reserve, it would

---

[59] On the final page of Johnson's MS notes for his "Life of Pope" (BL Add. MS. 5994, fols. 159–77) appears a note reading "No writings against Swift!" (Kirkley 2002: 82). But when Boswell reported Marchmont's claim that Pope left behind no manuscripts, Johnson declared "He lies, Sir" (Weis and Pottle 1970: 338–39).

[60] 2nd edn., 1782, 95. In 1814 Nichols, a well-informed scholar who contributed to editions of Swift's *Works* in the 1760s and 1770s, printed Tyers's report without demur (*Literary Anecdotes of the Eighteenth Century*, VIII, 100).

[61] "Materials for a Life of Dr. Swift," transcribed in 1765 and interleaved into Lyon's copy of Hawkesworth's twelve-volume 1755 edition of Swift's *Works*, an early scribal transcript of which is reproduced in Elias (1998: 69). At I, 57, Hawkesworth says Swift in his 1740 will called Pope his "dearest friend" (Davis 1939–68: XIII, 154). In a 1736 letter (Sherburn 1956: IV, 42), Pope asked a friend to assure Swift that there was nothing in the world "I *admire* so much; nothing the loss of which I should *regret* so much as his genius and his virtues" (quoted by Orrery 1752: 149).

[62] *Idler* 65 (1759), in *The Idler and The Adventurer*, ed. W. J. Bate, John M. Bullitt, and L. F. Powell (1963), 202. Cf. "Life of Pope," in Lonsdale (2006: IV, 53).

[63] Mack (1982: 325 and 1985: 748). Cowler (1986: 511) reprints Elwin and Courthope's report that Bolingbroke burned Pope's secretly printed edition of his *Idea of a Patriot King*. Bolingbroke also suppressed the satirical character of Atossa in the "deathbed edition" of Pope's *Moral Essays* (Bateson 1951: 41).

not have been the first time: in 1716 he drafted and sent to Addison some severe lines, not publishing them until after Addison's death, and in 1733 he wrote and had printed (but not published) "A Letter to a Noble Lord" and sent it to Hervey as another warning.

It is curious that to my knowledge no scholar (apart from Elias) has assessed the credibility of Lyon as a witness. As a prebendary of St. Patrick's and a confidant of Swift's – "officially responsible," as Ehrenpreis notes, "for Swift during the years of incompetence"[64] – Lyon was in a good position to know of Swift's private affairs. He apparently had access to Swift's papers and understood that writers might hold back some materials as not suitable for publication: he later told Thomas Birch, for example, that he had a copy of Swift's *On Poetry. A Rapsody* that was "more complete than the printed one, but too licentious for publications" (Williams 1963: v, 275). He presumably had no access to Pope's private papers, but may have found a note reflecting some knowledge of Pope's "very severe reflections" in Swift's papers, or have received private communication from one of Pope's executors. His interest would have been to protect Swift's reputation, and he would have had no motive to invent a story about a "defamatory life" written by Pope.

The story of the "defamatory life," assuming it to be apocryphal, is still significant: for some decades after their deaths, readers who knew the work of Pope and Swift well, and had the opportunity to hear reports from eyewitnesses, *thought* there might be something in it. One does not need to invoke such reports to support an argument that Pope and Swift maintained a wary distance and independence. Among their commentators Johnson was particularly alert to the occasions when Pope and Swift resisted each other: e.g., "To Swift's edict for the exclusion of Alexandrines and Triplets [Pope] paid little regard,"[65] and "To this [resolution to retire from the world] Swift answered with great propriety, that Pope had not yet either acted or suffered enough in the world to have become weary of it" (Lonsdale 2006: IV, 60, 79). Johnson's skepticism is a good corrective to any tendency to over-identify with the objects of my study, and to any tendency to idealize any human relationship. As Ehrenpreis observed of the Pope–Swift friendship, "each … was proud to be intimate with

[64] Ehrenpreis (1962–83: III, 919). Lyon was one of the witnesses to the May 5, 1740 codicil to Swift's will.
[65] The "edict" is probably found in Swift's April 12, 1735 letter to Thomas Beach (Woolley 1999–2007: IV, 89) in which he reports that he "did prevayl" with Pope "to reject them," but that in the Homer translation (too long to require exactness in prosody) and in some recent poems he used them "out of Lazyness."

the other, and each wished to enhance his fame through the connection. Neither one could keep from making the other an instrument to serve his private ends" (III, 562). If I have emphasized those occasions where there appears to be some tension, difference, or disagreement between Swift and Pope, some fault-lines in the otherwise solid rock of friendship, or some serving of what Swift called "private ends," my objective is ultimately to correct for critical blindness, and to try to bring their relationship and their work into clearer focus.

CHAPTER I

The four last years of Queen Anne

Pope and Swift did not meet each other until the latter part of 1713, but they surely knew each other before then by reputation. Within two days of the publication of *Windsor-Forest* on March 7, 1713, Swift wrote to Stella that "Mr Pope has publishd a fine Poem calld Windsor Forrest"[1] – implying that both she and he of course knew who "Mr. Pope" was. And Pope would have had no doubt about who "Dr. Swift" was. They had mutual friends, including Addison, Steele, and Gay, as well as Lord Lansdowne (to whom *Windsor-Forest* was dedicated)[2] and had ample opportunity – in the relatively small world of literary London – to read each other's published work. From such reading, what impressions would they have formed of each other in the two or three years prior to their first meeting?

Swift was by far the more established writer. His several "Bickerstaff Papers," published in 1708, were still very much in the air, Swift's joke given new currency in April 1709 when Steele adopted Isaac Bickerstaff's name for the putative author of the *Tatler*, which continued publishing into 1710.[3] If Pope was reading the early numbers of the *Tatler*, he would have encountered Swift's "Description of the Morning," which appeared in No. 9 on April 30. Earlier that month there appeared a quite different kind of work by Swift, published anonymously, "By a Person of Quality," but probably soon known to be his: the *Project for the Advancement of Religion*. Little admired today (by readers who prefer Swift's subversive ironies), it is an essentially straightforward and non-ironic project to encourage the public practice of religion, but it was well received in

---

[1] March 9, 1713, in Williams (1948: II, 635).
[2] Ehrenpreis suggests (II, 593) that it may have been Lansdowne (before he became a peer) who introduced Pope to Swift. Lansdowne and Swift had quarreled in March 1712, but had quickly patched it up. (For details, see *Journal to Stella*, March 13 and 27, 1712.)
[3] See Pope's letter to Cromwell (May 17, 1710), alluding to Steele's adoption of Bickerstaff's name in the first number of the *Tatler* (April 1709).

its time. Pope may well not have seen it, but he probably read Steele's praise of it in the *Tatler*: "every man here has read it; and as many as have done so have approved it … it is written by one whose virtue sits easy about him, and to whom vice is thoroughly contemptible." And he probably took particular notice when Steele concluded that "The man writes much like a gentleman."[4] In the following month Swift was represented in Tonson's *Poetical Miscellanies: The Sixth Part* by two poems, "Baucis and Philemon" (an updating of an Ovidian myth of metamorphosis) and "On Mrs. Biddy Floyd" (an affecting and affectionate tribute to a woman of breeding and wit). There is every reason to think Pope read them, since his own *Pastorals* and *Episode of Sarpedon* appeared in the same volume, and since the latter of Swift's poems seems to have called forth a Popean allusion years later.[5]

In the following year (1710) Swift appeared before the public with the fifth edition of his *Tale of a Tub*, accompanied not only by the previously published *Battel of the Books* but also by a new "Apology" for the *Tale*, claiming that what had been attacked by William Wotton and others as subversive and irreligious was in fact a defense of the doctrine and discipline of the established church. Pope never left an explicit comment about the *Tale*, but, as his later allusions plainly show, he read it. If he had read it by 1710, he would had the opportunity to ponder Swift's claim (in the "Apology") that edgy wit and irony might be put to the service of religion.[6] Later that year Pope would probably have encountered Swift's "Description of a City Shower," which appeared (anonymously) in *Tatler* 238 on October 17, with a commendation by "Isaac Bickerstaff" (i.e., Steele), comparing it to the earlier "Description of the Morning" – as "another exquisite Piece of this local Poetry" – and recognizing a witty reworking of a famous storm scene in Virgil. In February 1711 Swift's poems and prose tracts (with the exception of *Tale of a Tub* and the *Battel of the Books*) that had appeared anonymously over the previous ten years or so were collected as *Miscellanies in Prose and Verse*. To them were added some pieces not published before, including the vertiginously ironic *Argument against the Abolishing of Christianity* and the sobersided but urbane *Sentiments of a Church of England Man*, where Pope could have found Swift declaring that "In order to preserve the Constitution entire in Church and State; whoever hath a true Value for both, would be sure to avoid the Extreams

---

[4] *Tatler*, No. 5 (April 21).   [5] See below, ch. 3, p. 162.

[6] Curll's *Complete Key to a Tale of a Tub*, published later that year, and also in his 1711 pirated collection of *Miscellanies by Dr. Jonathan Swift*, kept the controversial *Tub* before the reading public. Curll had also published a pirated collection of Swift's prose and verse in April 1710.

of *Whig* for the Sake of the former, and the Extreams of *Tory* on Account of the latter" (Davis 1939–68: ii, 25). This was not a bad road map for a poet like Pope, who would himself aim at a moderating middle way. And for the first time he would have had the opportunity to consider the extraordinary range of Swift's writings in a variety of genres.

By then he would also have known that Swift was a skilled political writer: his weekly *Examiner* essays, forcefully defending the policies of the Tory ministers, had begun appearing the previous summer, and would run until late July 1711. Although Pope was reluctant to commit himself to either the Tory or Whig side, he would – like many readers – probably have been attracted by Gay's welcoming praise of the *Examiner* as a paper "which all Men, who speak without Prejudice, allow to be well Writ." Although the Examiner is a Tory, Gay went on, "Men, who are concern'd in no Party, may Read him with Pleasure."[7] By late autumn of that year Swift solidified his reputation as a political writer with his best-known and most influential work to date, *The Conduct of the Allies*, a pamphlet designed to dismiss objections, particularly from Whig writers, to the peace treaty designed to end the long continental war, then being negotiated at Utrecht. Within two months it had sold 11,000 copies – an unprecedented number for a pamphlet. It, and its author (whose name soon became known), were the talk of the town. As Johnson later noted, Swift at this point had "attained the zenith of his political importance," and, "being now the declared favourite and supposed confidant of the Tory Ministry, was treated by all that depended on the Court with the respect which dependents know how to pay."[8] Pope was no dependent on the court, and in fact retained a number of connections among the Roman Catholic families of Berkshire that would have marked him as an outsider, and possibly even a Jacobite sympathizer.[9] In January 1713, however, Pope did pay court to the newly ennobled Lord Lansdowne[10] and was no doubt intrigued to meet the leading literary insider, who was to retain his power and influence – and his ability to help other writers hoping for government patronage – until shortly after Pope met him.

---

[7] *The Present State of Wit, in a Letter to a Friend in the Country* (1711), [4].

[8] Johnson, "Life of Swift," in Lonsdale (2006: iii, 196–97). It is now generally agreed that Swift had less influence on the ministers than Johnson – or Swift himself – supposed. See, for example, J. A. Downie, *Robert Harley and the Press: Propaganda and Public Opinion in the Age of Swift and Defoe* (1979).

[9] For arguments that Pope had strong Jacobite sympathies, see Erskine-Hill 1975, 1982, 1996 and Rogers 2005a.

[10] George Granville, from a family of Stuart loyalists, was made Lord Lansdowne on December 31, 1712.

Swift was of course only one of the writers Pope was reading – and trying out as a model for his own career. Others in his early years he was openly imitating include Waller, Cowley, Rochester, Chaucer, Spenser, Dorset, and Wycherley. In addition to them he was reading Dryden, the greatest poet of the previous generation, and only recently dead. (As a very young boy Pope remembered once being taken to see Dryden at Will's coffee house.) No living writer, Pope observed in his first surviving letter (December 26, 1704, to Wycherley), was Dryden's equal: "whatever lesser Wits have arisen since his Death, are but like Stars appearing when the Sun is set, that twinkle only in his absence, and with the Rays they have borrowed from him." Pope admired Dryden (for his onomatopoeic "style of sound": Sherburn, 1956: I, 23), kept his portrait in his chamber (I, 120), valued his authority (I, 44), and was already thinking about following in Dryden's path as a modernizer of Chaucer[11] and a translator of Homer. Dryden's 1697 *Virgil* had established itself as the definitive version but he had translated little more of Homer than the first book of the *Iliad*, leaving an opportunity for an ambitious writer to produce a complete Homer, as Pope (who had already published two "episodes" from the *Iliad* as a sort of trial) went on to do. But by 1710 he was reading Dryden critically – as a writer who sometimes committed faults he would try to avoid (alexandrines and triple rhymes [I, 24], hiatus [I, 57], terms of art [I, 101]) and who was less judicious than Virgil (I, 92). Dryden would always be an important model for Pope, perhaps the most important model, but not the only one.

In these years Pope was also playing with the idea that he might be a sort of reincarnation of the Restoration witty gentleman writer – Rochester, Dorset, Etherege, Roscommon, Sheffield – who constituted in effect the antithesis of the proto-professional Dryden in his own day. They were probably the models for the octosyllabic verse letter (with comic rhymes and jaunty tone) Pope wrote to Henry Cromwell in about 1707 (Ault 1954: 24ff.).[12] But the model of writer as gentleman amateur, though it continued to attract him at least as late as the 1717 Preface to his *Works*, was a pose that didn't allow for the ambition and vocational dedication he clearly felt, and though he honored the gentlemen-writers of the previous generation in his 1711 *Essay on Criticism*, he was,

---

[11] Dryden's versions of Chaucer appeared in his *Fables Ancient and Modern* (1700). Pope's "January and May; or, the Merchant's Tale" and "The Wife of Bath her Prologue" were written about 1704; the former appeared in Tonson's 1709 *Miscellanies*, the latter in Steele's *Poetical Miscellanies* at the end of 1713.

[12] See also Pope's other octosyllabics on Lintot and Durfey, probably written in 1711.

as Dennis shrewdly observed, undermining their authority, and that of the men of taste who continued to claim the right to judge the quality of writing.[13]

When he arrived in London in 1713, Pope, we can imagine, was looking about for a new literary model. By about 1712 his literary friends included Garth, Wycherley, Henry Cromwell (a very minor gentleman-poet thirty years his senior), Addison, Steele, and Gay. But Pope had outgrown Wycherley, and had surely taken Cromwell's measure. Gay was just starting out, which left Garth, along with Addison and Steele, who befriended him, and who as writers of the *Tatler* and the new *Spectator* occupied positions of influence. But oddly Steele seemed to prefer the pastorals of Ambrose Philips, and Addison provided advice about revising the *Rape of the Locke* that Pope saw fit to reject.

The most glittering writer in London, the best connected politically, and the most senior, when Pope moved into town from Binfield in February 1713, was probably Swift. They had mutual friends. By now Pope would probably have regarded Swift as a brilliant ironist and versatile (and dangerous) satirist; skilled imitator and modernizer of Ovid and Virgil; sober moralist when he chose to be; a strong defender of the Church of England; and the most powerful political writer of the day, deeply engaged with the ministry. Swift was also a model of a writer who, though strongly partisan, had friends (patrons and writers) in the other party. Not a Roman Catholic (as Dryden was), but a member of a church that shared much with his own – and repudiated the fierce antipapistry of the Dissenters (and of the Whig ministries under William and then Anne). In any case Pope not a doctrinaire Catholic but an admirer of Erasmus. Although Pope would have regarded Swift as a party-man, and he wanted to keep clear of party himself (Sherburn 1956: 1, 245), the political principles of the Church-of-England man would have seemed compatible with Pope's own professed moderation. If he heard any whispers of Swift's Jacobitism, they might not have bothered him, especially since he seems to have had the same sentimental attachments to the Stuarts. Swift was also an older man – 21 years older than the 24-year-old Pope. And Pope was comfortable with older men: in his early years he had cultivated their friendship – Betterton (b. 1635), Trumbull (b. 1639), Wycherley (b. 1640), Sheffield (b. 1648), Cromwell (b. 1659), Walsh (b. 1663), and Congreve (b. 1670). He had recently contracted friendships with Addison

---

[13] See Dennis's *Reflections Critical and Satyrical upon a late Rhapsody, call'd, An Essay upon Criticism* (1711).

(b. 1672) and John Caryll (b. 1667), and in January 1713 had found a patron in Granville (b. 1666).[14]

How would Swift, before he met Pope, have regarded this young writer? Pope too had acquired a reputation in London. His *Pastorals* had appeared in Tonson's *Poetical Miscellanies: The Sixth Part* (1709), along with the "Episode of Sarpedon" – and, as noted earlier, two of Swift's own poems. The *Essay on Criticism*, published anonymously in May 1711, was quickly identified as Pope's and, though attacked by Dennis, was praised by Addison in the *Spectator* in December. In March of the following year Pope's "Sapho to Phaon" appeared in Tonson's edition of *Ovid's Epistles*. In May his poems figured prominently in Lintot's *Miscellaneous Poems and Translations*, which included not only the first published version of *Rape of the Locke*, but also a translation of Ovid's "Vertumnus and Pomona," a translation from the *Thebaid* of Statius, and several shorter pieces. It also included praise from Gay for Pope's charming "Numbers" and "steady Judgment" that surpassed his young years. In May too "Messiah" was printed in *Spectator* 378 (where Steele saluted Pope's "wit" and "genius") – and Pope would receive further praise in the *Spectator* later that year (October 30 and November 10). In 1713 Pope joined the ranks of those welcoming the Peace of Utrecht, and Swift, as noted above, had read *Windsor-Forest* and commended the poem within two days of its appearance on March 7. Swift might not have known that Pope was also the author of pieces in Steele's *Guardian* for both March and April, but he surely knew that Pope had written a prologue for the first night (April 14) of Addison's *Cato*, which riveted the town's attention for weeks, and he probably saw Pope's *Ode for Musick*, published by Lintot in July.

From Swift's point of view – interested in befriending and promoting writers of either party – Pope was the young "rising genius" of the day, already praised by Addison in those terms, and by Steele, and Gay whose judgement Swift respected.[15] In some respects Pope appeared to be a writer with tastes and abilities like his own: he had demonstrated brilliant wit and urbanity in the *Essay on Criticism*, and a gift for Ovidian narrative. In other respects Pope appeared to be quite a different sort of writer from Swift, and not only because he had up to this point limited himself to verse. He was devoting himself (in a way that Swift was not)

[14] Pope's *Pastorals*, he later claimed, had been written as early as 1704, and "past thro' the hands" (for critical review) of a number of older writers and patrons, including Walsh, Wycherley, Granville, Trumbull, Garth (b. 1661), Halifax (b. 1661), Somers (b. 1751), and Maynwaring (b. 1668).

[15] "Rising genius" is Addison's term for Pope (and for Thomas Tickell) in *Spectator* 523.

to a career in the standard poetic genres of the day, and seemed to be aiming at literary qualities (harmony of numbers, correctness) in which Swift himself had little interest. Pope had successfully imitated the pastorals of Virgil, and demonstrated polished skill in writing odes (the genre in which Swift himself had made his initial, and on the whole unsuccessful, attempts as a poet). He seemed to be attracted to the heroic narratives of Homer and Statius (in which Swift, who had already discovered a delight in mocking the heroic, had no apparent interest). What would perhaps have been of greatest immediate interest to Swift, in his capacity as public writer, was *Windsor-Forest* – which showed that Pope, having defended the peace that Swift's *Conduct of the Allies* had promoted, might be prepared to defend other ministerial policies – and perhaps the prologue to Addison's *Cato*, which suggested how a skilled poet might make use of the political potential in a classical topic to move a contemporary audience to tears, and to virtuous action. That Pope also had friends among the Whigs probably seemed to Swift an advantage. That he was a papist didn't seem to deter this Church-of-England man, although within weeks of their meeting Swift was inviting Pope to change his religion – which, probably not coincidentally, would have made him eligible for some ministerial patronage. As it was, of course, Swift was soon to lose his power of directing the fount of governmental largesse, and to depart for Ireland and a lesser position in the church than he wanted. Pope was to look for support in another quarter – by launching a subscription to a new translation of Homer. Already equipped with a sharp sense of the changing economics that underwrote literary production, Pope seems to have understood that power was shifting from traditional patrons (the ministry and the aristocracy) to booksellers, and that the most financially successful authors would be the ones who learned how to manipulate the emerging literary marketplace while keeping the lines open to old-style patrons – such as Halifax, whose advice he prudently sought.

THE FRESHEST MODERN: *TALE OF A TUB* AND *AN ESSAY ON CRITICISM*

To judge by their (hostile) reaction, most early critics of *Tale of a Tub* focused on the religious allegory – because of its alleged profaneness and irreligion (in the eyes of Wotton and Bentley, for example). Was Pope offended at Swift's portrait of his co-religionist Peter? Probably not – an admirer of Erasmus could readily share Swift's contempt for a tyrannical papacy. Given his decision – probably in 1710 – to write a verse

essay on criticism, it would have been surprising if Pope did not know
the "Digression concerning Criticks" in the *Tub* (and the mockery of
Ancients and Moderns in the *Battel of the Books*) when he sat down to
write on what were in effect similar topics – good (and bad) critics, what
is to be learned from the precepts and practice of both the ancients and
the moderns, and (more generally) the situation of the modern writer who
aspires to join the ranks of his predecessors. If he knew of it, Swift's dedication of the *Tale* to John Lord Somers (with its mockery of the degener-
ation of the form into empty cliché) might have been of particular interest
to Pope, who two or three years later, in March 1713, was to publish an
essay "Upon Dedications" – and the hollowness of most modern ones –
in the *Guardian*.[16]

If we cannot show persuasively that Pope, when he sat down to write
the *Essay on Criticism*, had already digested Swift's *Tale of a Tub*, nor can
we make the bolder claim that he was in some sense "answering" Swift.
Pope was obviously working out of a tradition of verse essays going back
to Sheffield and Roscommon, and behind them to Horace, and if he was
"answering" anybody it was perhaps the champions of the traditional critical authority of gentlemen of breeding and taste and of the newly emerging "professional" critics such as Rymer and Dennis, the latter of whom
in 1704 had published *The Grounds of Criticism in Poetry*.[17] Nonetheless,
it is useful to read *Tale of a Tub* (5th edn., 1710) and the *Essay on Criticism*
(1711) side by side, if only to suggest that in a number of ways the young
Pope was situating himself as a modern writer in quite a different way
from the older Dr. Swift.

In *Tale of a Tub*, as Pope would have found, the narrative and the several "digressions" are placed in the mouth of one who pretends to be
the "most devoted Servant of all *Modern* Forms" (45), one of the tribe
of "*Modern Authors*" (123).[18] Indeed, since he aspires to be heard in the
crowd of modern authors all clamoring for attention, and to join the
swarm of writers already in print, he is the most recent of the Moderns: "I

---

[16] No. 4 (March 16, 1713), in Ault (1936: 76–82). When Pope wrote the closing tribute to Belinda,
promising that (despite her inevitable death) his poem would make her immortal ("'midst the
stars inscribe Belinda's name"), did he remember the closing words of Swift's *Battel*, in which,
following Virgil, he promises to a pair of dying combatants that "happy and immortal shall you
be, if all my Wit and Eloquence can make you?"

[17] Like Swift, Pope surely realized that in his survey of "criticism" he was competing with other
modern writers, not only Dennis but also Dominique Bouhours, whose *Manière de Bien Penser
dans les Oeuvres de l'Esprit* (1687) appeared in an English translation as *The Art of Criticism* in
1705.

[18] Quotations from the *Tale* are taken from Guthkelch and Smith 1958.

here think fit to lay hold on that great and honourable Privilege of being the *Last Writer*; I claim an absolute Authority in Right, as the *freshest Modern*, which gives me Despotick Power over all Authors before me" (130).[19] Like every author before him, he hopes for the "immortality" that comes from winning favor from "Prince Posterity." But the odds are long – not only are the press swarming with "Trash" and the received literary forms exhausted, the productions of all modern writers are liable to be lost in the cacophony of other modern voices, and also to fall quickly out of fashion: "nothing is so very tender as a *Modern* Piece of Wit" (43). If that were not enough, the modern writer finds lying in wait for him the murderous tribe of "Criticks," who conceive of the "True Critick" as the "Discoverer and Collector of Writers Faults" (95).

Many readers of the *Tale* have assumed that its satire, directed against the inanities and egotism of the "Moderns," is designed to direct attention to the theory and practice of the "Ancients" (and their modern defenders such as Sir William Temple), which (properly understood) might serve as true models for the aspiring writer. But as a generation of commentators have argued, Swift's satire, both in the *Tale of a Tub* and in the *Battel of the Books*, does not seem to spare the Ancients, who are often made to seem as foolish as their modern adversaries in the episode of the "battle" fought in St. James' Library. The would-be writer, so Swift's reader might conclude, must cross what amounts to a mine-field of dangers, and must cross it without much of a guide. Such a gap has opened up between Ancients and Moderns that they have quite literally come to blows. Regardless of Swift's views about the Ancients – and almost all critics conclude that Swift held conventionally admiring views of them – he could never be of their number, nor count himself their legitimate descendant, but was inevitably the "freshest" of the Moderns.[20] And Swift's own practice after his first poetic efforts at the greater Cowleyan ode (and in later years as well) suggests that in his mind the inherited literary forms – whether high epic or modest dedication, straightforward Ovidian narrative or Virgilian scene painting – have lost their currency, and that the modern writer must look, as the epigraph from Lucretius on the title page of the *Tub* suggests, for new ways of excelling ("new flowers ... from

---

[19] "Freshest" suggests not only that he is the newest, but that he is perishable, though not (yet) impaired by time, which fades every fresh flower. See *OED*, "fresh," a., 4, 7, 8, 9, 10. In the "Apology" Swift later claims that when the author wrote the *Tale* he was "then young," with "his reading fresh in his head."

[20] Cf. a phrase in Swift's July 9, 1724 letter to Carteret: "I humbly claim the privilege of an inferior, to be the last writer" (Woolley 1999–2007: II, 503).

fields whence before this the Muses have crowned the brows of none").[21]
It is perhaps for this reason that Swift is drawn to satire: as he suggests in
the "Preface" to the *Tale*, "there is very little Satyr which has not something in it untouch'd before" (Guthkelch and Smith 1958: 49).

What picture of the situation of the modern writer emerges from
Pope's *Essay on Criticism*? In some respects there is enough similarity to make difference significant. Like Swift's garrulous narrator, Pope
is self-consciously the freshest modern writer, "the last and meanest of
[the] sons" of the Ancients (196), although rather than laying claim to
a "Despotic Power over all Authors before me" he defers to the authority of the Ancients. (Or only pretends to defer: Dennis thought he acted
like "a downright Bully of *Parnassus*.")[22] Like Swift's *Tub*, Pope's *Essay*,
though technically not the author's first foray into authorship, is a sort of
debut piece in which a self-consciously young writer surveys the literary
field he is about to enter, tries out his tools, displays his wit in dazzling
virtuoso pieces, and seeks to make a bold impression. As he looks around
him, he beholds critics who regard their task as the fingering of faults,
lying in wait for him, and he launches what might be regarded as a pre-
emptive strike against them, ridiculing their bad taste, challenging their
authority. (Swift's revised *Tub* adds a set of notes ridiculing Wotton and
Bentley who attacked his first edition, and offering a mocking "Apology"
explicitly rejecting their gravest charges. Pope, perhaps realizing that he
is going to be attacked – as indeed he was within weeks – makes sure
that he discredits Dennis in advance.) And, like Swift, Pope is painfully
aware of the transience of modern writing: "Short is the Date, alas, of
Modern Rhymes." The works of the Ancients have survived 1,000 years
and more, but not the Moderns, if only because they write in a changing
language: "Our Sons their Fathers' *failing Language* see, / And such as
Chaucer is, shall *Dryden* be" (476, 482–83). That is, even the great Dryden
(who had concluded that he had to update Chaucer's English to make it
comprehensible to his contemporaries), although dead only a decade, will
himself need updating before long.[23]

Although it is broadly true, as I suggested earlier, that Pope and Swift
differed in their views of Dryden's merits, a closer look at the *Essay on*

---

[21] Swift borrows from Lucretius, *De rerum natura*, 1. 928–30. I borrow the translation from the
Rawson edition of the *Basic Writings of Jonathan Swift*, with notes (and translation) by Ian
Higgins (2002), 961.
[22] *Reflections Critical and Satyrical*, in Hooker (1943: 1, 414).
[23] Swift was likewise worried about the impermanence of the language: in *Tale of a Tub* modern
writing is impermanent because new works are "hurryed so hastily off the Scene" – displaced by
the next new ones – "that they escape our Memory" (Guthkelch and Smith 1958: 34).

Criticism suggests that Pope has subtly undermined Dryden's authority no less than Swift has. In the famous *Battel of the Books*, published with the *Tale*, Dryden (wearing an outsize helmet) is ridiculed for claiming Virgil as his father, and pretending to have inherited the mantle of classical authority. In the *Essay* Pope represents Dryden as a father whose authority has become enfeebled: just as Dryden could "see" that Chaucer's language was "failing," so one day Dryden's sons will "see" their father's failing. (Pope's unexpected verb "see" perhaps invokes one of the oldest stories about the declining authority of fathers, Noah's sons who *saw* their drunken father's nakedness.) The focus is initially on Dryden's "*failing Language*," but the next line transfers attention from the unstable language he wrote in to the obsolescent poet himself: "shall *Dryden* be." Another sign of Dryden's loss of authority in the *Essay* is that Pope conspicuously declines to name him as the model poet-critic, choosing instead to name Sheffield, Roscommon, and Walsh, although in 1710 there was no more obvious candidate than Dryden for the position.[24]

But in many ways Pope's *Essay* presents a sharply contrasting picture of the modern writer's situation, even if we adjust for the radical differences in genre (didactic verse essay and Menippean prose satire). For him the Ancients are immortal, and their old altars still green with bays (181). A modern poet may still conceive of himself as one of their inheriting "sons" – Pope makes no reference to the famous "Quarrel" of the Ancients and Moderns that had preoccupied many of his older contemporaries, including Swift. (It is telling that only two years later Pope would circulate proposals for a new translation of the *Iliad*, and that, when the first volume was published in 1715, it carried, like Swift's *Tale of a Tub*, an epigraph from Lucretius, proclaiming this time not the writer's search for "fresh flowers" but his contentment in planting his "firm feet" in the "marked footsteps" left by his predecessor, not because he is "eager to compete" but from "love.")[25]

The modern poet may find "Nature" in the works of Homer, but he can go directly to "Nature" himself, for she is still "divinely bright, / One clear, unchang'd, and universal Light" (70–71). For Pope the right-

---

[24] In being told by Walsh that "we never had any one great poet that was correct" (Osborn 1966: I, 32), the young Pope was already being encouraged to think that Dryden himself was not sufficiently "correct." Years later, his admiration for Dryden still strong, Pope could say that even Dryden "wanted, or forgot, / The last and greatest Art, the Art to Blot" (*Epistle to Augustus*, line 281).

[25] "Te sequor, O Graiae gentis Decus! inque tuis nunc / Fixa pedum pono pressis vestigia signis / Non ita certandi cupidus, quam propter Amorem, / Quod Te imitari aveo" (*De rerum natura*, III, 3–6). Pope transfers to Homer the praise that Lucretius offers to Epicurus.

thinking modern poet is not troubled by the idea that nothing is new, for he aims not at novelty but at "What oft was *Thought*, but ne'er so well *Exprest*" (298). The decorum of a didactic verse essay permits (and invites) Pope to develop quite explicit distinctions between good and bad criticism, true and false wit, the kinds of distinction sometimes found in satire but rarely in Swift's satire. Indeed, Pope's famous definition of true wit – "*Nature* to Advantage drest" – and his virtuoso demonstration of how to write wittily differ sharply from the brilliant conceited writing found in the *Tub* – for example, the famous riff on wisdom as "a Fox, … a Cheese, … a Sack-Posset, … a Hen, … a Nut" (66). Swift's wit has been described as a version of late metaphysical style, one of the sorts of wit that Pope brands as false, where "glitt'ring Thoughts" are "struck out at ev'ry Line, / … One glaring Chaos and wild Heap of Wit" (290–92). If Pope had thought to provide examples of a "wild Heap of Wit," he could not have done better than to cite the dizzying flights in Swift's *Tale*.

Swift devastatingly undermines the props of the modern writer's inheritance, but Pope finds them sturdy and more than serviceable, or shores them up. Swift laughs away (by regarding it as vacuous cliché) Horace's famous advice in the *Ars poetica* (134) that the writer aim to instruct and delight by declaring that he has served up in his "Divine Treatise" both "Diversion" and "Instruction," and has "skilfully kneaded up both together with a Layer of Utile and a Layer of Dulce" (124).[26] As if disregarding Swift's mockery, Pope reaffirms that Horace's "precepts teach but what his works inspire" (660). While Swift's satire mocks the urbane pose, detached ease, and "serenity" of the gentleman – his writing is anything but what his contemporaries would have called "easy," and systematically undermines the assumption that writing is still the preserve of the gentleman amateur with a classical education – Pope retains the old idea that good breeding ("Tho' Learn'd, well-bred; and tho' well-bred, sincere" – 635), or at least learning the ways of a gentleman ("True Ease in Writing comes from Art, not Chance, / As those move easiest who have learn'd to dance" – 361–62), is essential for good writing. Pope still finds it sound advice to remind a would-be critic that "A perfect judge will read each work of wit / With the same spirit as its author writ" (234). Swift, by

---

[26] In the "Apology" he says, in a variation of the Horatian formula, that his satire will be "useful and diverting" (Guthkelch and Smith 1958: 4), but "diverting" turns out to mean not just "entertaining" or "amusing": in the "Preface" the "Wits of the present Age" are "diverted" from their attack on "the Commonwealth" by the *Tale*, as seamen fling out a "Tub" to a whale, "to divert him from laying violent Hands upon the Ship [of state]" (40).

contrast, had ridiculed this idea by turning a spiritual into a material relationship, and then literalizing it:

Whatever Reader desires to have a thorow Comprehension of an Author's Thoughts, cannot take a better Method, than by putting himself into the Circumstances and Postures of Life, that the writer was in, upon every important Passage as it flow'd from his Pen; For this will introduce a Parity and strict Correspondence of Idea's between the Reader and the Author. (44)

In another respect too Pope's account of the position of the modern writer is quite different from Swift's. The *Essay on Criticism* conveys no sense that Pope is troubled by the sheer number of poets clamoring for attention, the difficulty of being heard in a crowd, that makes such a strong impression in Swift's *Tale*. Swift seems clearly to imagine the ways in which the literary landscape has been altered by the onset of what we now call "print culture" – the new power of booksellers, the unappeasable appetite of the printing press for new copy, the vast number of books produced each year. Pope imagines the landscape in different ways. Indeed, he makes no mention in the *Essay* of the bookseller, or of the fact that modern writing passes through the shaping hands of bookseller and printer before it reaches a reader. Although in his later poems Pope would acknowledge the inescapable presence of booksellers and the transformative power of print, in the *Essay on Criticism* he writes as if he is still in the unmediated relationship with his readers characteristic of an oral culture.

POPE'S RESPONSE TO SWIFT'S 1711 MISCELLANIES

By the time Pope's *Essay* was published – in May 1711 – he would have had little time to react to the publication of Swift's *Miscellanies in Prose and Verse*, which appeared less than three months earlier, in late February. But there is some evidence to suggest that his response took a literary form. A little more than a year after Swift's *Miscellanies* appeared, Bernard Lintot published (on May 20, 1712) a collection entitled *Miscellaneous Poems and Translations by Several Hands*. Its editor was Pope, and the collection included seven poems by Pope himself. Pope's involvement was once thought somewhat surprising, given his derisive comments about poetic miscellanies in both letters and poems. In a 1709 letter to Wycherley he had sneered at the "modern Custom" of "appearing in Miscellanies," which gave poets an opportunity to "escape by getting into a Crowd" (Sherburn 1956: 1, 60) – i.e., enabled them to present their works before the public but not to draw too much attention to their claims.

In some respects this is precisely opposite to the problem Swift playfully pointed to in *Tale of a Tub*, where anyone with "an Ambition to be heard in a crowd, must press, and squeeze, and thrust, and climb with indefatigable Pains, till he has exalted himself to a certain Degree of Altitude above them." And the Pope-edited 1712 *Miscellaneous Poems and Translations* was in this respect just the opposite – and perhaps consciously so – of Swift's 1711 *Miscellanies in Prose and Verse*. For Swift, an established author, the miscellany was a means of gathering and publishing a collection of one's own writings that made no pretense to unity of design: prose stood next to verse, satire next to straightforward "project," light verse next to Ovidian fable. For Pope, making up part of a miscellany "by Several Hands" was a way for a young poet to make a careful early appearance in print – as Pope himself did in Tonson's 1709 *Poetical Miscellanies*. Pope's disingenuousness and readiness to conceal his ambition to be heard, even to the extent of deceiving his friends, is well established. In 1712 it suited his needs to put some more poems before the public, but he was not yet ready, as he would be five years later, to publish them as a collection of *Works* under his own name. So he found a place for several pieces that he had written over the previous few years, including translations from Statius and Ovid, imitations of Rochester and Dorset (Pope's first satires), and a *jeu d'esprit* ("Verses design'd to be prefix'd to Mr. Lintott's Miscellany") laughing at the very collection of which it was a part. Of these pieces the translation from Statius – the first book of his *Thebaid* – into 864 lines of couplets was probably the most important in Pope's mind, and might have served as a kind of specimen of what a complete translation of Statius should look like. Perhaps more important for Pope, as signs of the kind of writing he was now seeking to present to the public, were the initial two-book version of *Rape of the Locke* (as the first published version of the poem was called) and what was in effect a companion piece, "To a Young Lady, with the Works of Voiture," an address to a young lady, much like Belinda, "destin'd" for marriage and advised by the poet to rely not on her currently "resistless Charms" but on "Good Humour." But all of these pieces were doubly hidden – published anonymously, and collected with the work of several other "Hands" – including the famous Samuel Butler (long dead), Thomas Betterton (recently dead), Matthew Prior, and Pope's future collaborators on Homer, Elijah Fenton and William Broome.

Pope's miscellany was in another sense a kind of response to Swift's quite different one: it contained several of his own poems that answered poems in Swift's collection. Swift's "Baucis and Philemon" aimed at comic and quasi-mock-heroic effects, transforming Ovid's lovers into simple peasants, while Pope's "Vertumnus and Pomona" presented itself as a straightforward paraphrase of Ovid, as if to suggest that one might still find a way to turn the Ancients into English without having to parody them.[27] How to make poetic use of the classics was a matter that clearly concerned Pope at this stage in his career, and he was, in this miscellany, trying out at least two strategies – one a more or less faithful following of the original, the other an updating that substituted modern circumstances for ancient. Swift's miscellany included several examples of how one might modernize the Ancients, not only "Baucis and Philemon" but also the two "Description" poems, based on Virgil's *Georgics*. The latter two poems showed how a modern poet might modernize without playing for laughs, for, while they aim at mildly satiric effects, the comedy is tempered by what feels like accurate observation, and tinged with darker hints of corruption. As Pope set about writing *Rape of the Locke* he had before him the example of Dryden's *MacFlecknoe*, to show him how heroic conventions might be parodied with sharp satiric effect. But he clearly aimed at other effects, at a more complicated combination of compliment and satire, and may have been encouraged by Swift's example.[28]

In other instances Swift's example may have inspired Pope. It was perhaps the appearance, in his 1711 *Miscellanies*, of Swift's "Apollo Outwitted," a teasing compliment addressed to Anne Finch, later Lady Winchelsea, that helped to prompt Pope in early 1714 to write an "Impromptu to Lady Winchelsea." (Pope was of course more immediately responding to Finch's own verses about a few lines in *Rape of the Locke*.) Following Swift's example, Pope addresses her as "Ardelia."[29] His "Verses design'd to be prefix'd to Mr. Lintott's Miscellany" are written in the octosyllabics that Swift deployed in several of the poems in his 1711 collection, and make use of the comic, feminine rhymes (e.g., prefer/Elzevir, besot us / Lintottus) that Swift, borrowing from Butler's *Hudibras*, had begun to make his signature tune. Pope seemed to associate this style with Swift, as suggested by a poem Pope wrote about this time but did not include in Lintot's miscellany, "The Happy Life of a Country Parson." It too is

[27] Pope later claimed to have written "Vertumnus and Pomona" as early as 1702. But he chose not to publish it until after Swift's Ovidian imitation had appeared.
[28] The jumble of objects trivial and serious on Belinda's toilet table – "Puffs, Patches, Powders, Bibles, Billet-Doux" – may have been partly inspired by the miscellany of "A new Receit for Paint," "a safe way to use Perfume," and a lover's "Billet Doux" all found in "a Lady's Ivory Table-Book" in Swift's 1711 *Miscellanies*.
[29] The poem was not published until 1741.

written in octosyllabic couplets, with feminine rhymes (band in / standing, blessing/possessing), and incorporates an inventory, introduced by
the collective "These Things ...," that Pope may have modeled on the
"Here you may read ..." that introduces the collection of "Trifles" in the
"Lady's Ivory Table-Book." The poem concludes quite literally with a nod
to Swift – "And shake his Head at Doctor S – t." When he reprinted it in
1736 Pope subtitled it "In Imitation of Dr. Swift." It is as if Pope in 1713
were trying out a prosodic measure and a comic technique, consciously
imitating the style of a contemporary, just as he had imitated the style of
his predecessors – Waller, Rochester, Dorset, Wycherley – from the preceding generation.

But the most interesting of Pope's responses to Swift's 1711 collection
may be his *Narrative of Dr. Robert Norris*, the apparently sober account,
by a reputable London doctor, of the "strange and deplorable Frenzy of
Mr. John Denn–," published in late July 1713. Pope and Dennis had been
at odds at least since 1711, when Pope in his *Essay on Criticism* laughed at
the thinly disguised "Appius," a hot-tempered critic who "reddens at each
Word you speak, / And *stares, Tremendous*! With a *threatening Eye*, / Like
some *fierce Tyrant* in *Old Tapestry*!" (585–87). Dennis, provoked by the
personal affront but also by Pope's claim to critical authority, responded
first with his *Reflections Critical and Satyrical* on the *Essay on Criticism*
and then in July 1713 with his *Remarks upon Cato, A Tragedy*, an attack on
Addison's play (for which Pope had written a prologue). Pope replied with
his *Narrative*, sharpening his portrait of the intemperate critic by having Dr. Norris now describe him as a "lunatick," elaborating on the lines
from the *Essay*: "His Aspect was furious, his Eyes were rather fiery than
lively, which he roll'd about in an uncommon manner ... I observ'd his
Room was hung with *old Tapestry*, which had several Holes in it, caus'd
... by his having cut out of it the Heads of divers *Tyrants*, the Fierceness
of whose Visages had much provoked him" (158). The lunatic's fit has been
brought on, so he tells Norris, by his spending fourteen hours a day writing his "*Remarks*" on *Cato*. The bookseller Lintot then reports to Norris
numerous previous incidents of Dennis's "Frenzy" – including a furious
reaction in his shop "on the 27th of March, 1712," to reading lines from "a
book called an *Essay on Criticism*" (166).

Pope's readers have from the first been puzzled by the *Narrative*, since
it seems so unlike his other writings, and have doubted his authorship
of it. But Ault persuasively showed that Pope was in fact the author,
which has obliged readers to reconsider the traditional claims that Pope
does not turn to satire until the later 1720s, and that, in any case, unlike

his fellow-Scriblerians Swift and Arbuthnot, his gift was for verse satire rather than for narrative prose (or Menippean) forms. The *Narrative of Dr. Norris* and the pamphlets ridiculing Curll which followed in 1715 and 1716 suggest that Pope was fully capable of writing in a style we associate with Swift. And it seems likely that Pope learned to write in that style partly by reading Swift's satirical prose, not just the Bickerstaff Papers, but also the *Tale of a Tub* and *Battel of the Books*.

The *Narrative of Dr. Norris* is a mock-authentic report, by an eyewitness, of a notably violent event in the life of a controversial contemporary. The most famous predecessor for such a report was Swift's *Accomplishment of the First of Mr. Bickerstaff's Predictions* (1709), in which Bickerstaff claimed to provide a first-hand account "of the Death of Mr. *Partrige*, the Almanac-Maker, upon the 29th Inst." – a "death" which "Bickerstaff" (i.e., Swift) had previously predicted in the first of the papers, the *Predictions for the Year 1708.*[30] By impersonating Bickerstaff the astrologer, Swift managed to conceal himself and to extend his mockery of the impostures of astrology: as is insufficiently remarked, the earnest Bickerstaff himself comes in for ridicule too. By comparison, Pope makes uses of a real person, Dr. Robert Norris (familiar to readers of newspaper advertisements), rather than an invented one, but otherwise deploys a similar strategy. Norris, who claimed to cure lunatics, comes in for incidental mockery as a "Quack," even as he reports interviewing the deranged Dennis. But his sobersided account of Dennis's "Frenzy," like Bickerstaff's circumstantial report of the death of Partridge, is designed to seem credible.

Pope then could have found a model for his mock-documentary report in Swift's Bickerstaff Papers, but he would not have found there a model for the furious language placed in the mouth of the unfortunate Dennis. In one respect Pope was simply exaggerating Dennis's outspoken and vehement critical style, or perhaps the inflated style of his failed tragedy, *Appius and Virginia*. But he could have found models for Dennis's mad raving in Swift, not only in the crazed Jack in *Tale of a Tub* and the lunatics in the "Digression on Madness," but also in the splenetic spider in the *Battel of the Books*. At least one contemporary agreed: Curll's violent address to his books at the end of *A Further Account of the Most Deplorable Condition of Mr. Edmund Curll, Bookseller* (1716) – "Now *G–d damn* all *Folio's, Quarto's, Octavo's* and *Duodecimo's!* ungrateful Varlets that you are,

---

[30] For Baines and Rogers (2007: 83) the "joke" of both Swift's Bickerstaff pamphlets and Pope's *Full and True Account* is "to give living individuals the sort of treatment they usually hand out to the dead."

who have so long taken up my House without paying for your Lodging?"
(284) – struck the memoirist William Ayre (who may have been one of
Curll's authors) as vituperative language learned from Swift's Lord Peter.[31]

By reporting the death of his victim, Swift, like the archaic satirist, in
effect "kills" him, or destroys his reputation. Pope's satire is not so murderous – he only reports that Dennis has lost his wits, or (later) that Curll
has lost the contents of his stomach. But in some respects Pope's attack has
greater force. To begin with, perhaps it would be more accurate to say that,
since Partridge's reputation had long been demolished and nobody of any
education and sense put any stock in his kind of astrology, Swift's re-kill-
ing is a kind of ritual act.[32] Our attention is shifted from the attack upon
the mortal body of Partridge to the ingenuity of the hidden satirist – for
Swift remained behind the mask of "Bickerstaff" – who proves by means
of intellectual demonstration that Partridge must indeed be dead, despite
what he might say to the contrary. But in satire, Pope seems to have sensed,
there are some punishments worse than metaphorical death. He keeps the
focus on the mind of the victim, and demonstrates that Dennis is and long
has been deranged, and that his lunacy takes the form of his furious asser-
tion of Aristotelian rules, arguably a more humiliating fate for a critic who
prided himself on his intellectual powers. When, three years later, Pope
published his *Full and True Account of a Horrid and Barbarous Revenge by
Poison, on the Body of Mr. Edmund Curll, Bookseller* (1716), another mock-
documentary account of a deplorable accident that had befallen one of
his enemies, he focused not on the mind but on "the Body" of his victim, providing a graphic description of the spectacular green vomiting that
occurred after Pope slipped an emetic into his wine, and the "plentiful
foetid Stool" with which the crisis passed. Again the account is designed
to be personally degrading. And it is plainly labeled a "Revenge," to settle
a personal score.[33] And unlike Swift, who hides behind a mask and in any

---

[31] Ayre reported that Pope "particularly mark'd" – i.e., took note of – a passage ridiculing Peter's
claims about the sacrament, including his thundering curse of his brothers – "By G-d it is true
good natural mutton, as any in Leadenhall market, and G-d confound you both eternally if you
offer to believe otherwise" (*Memoirs of Alexander Pope*, 2 vols. [1745], 1, 204). One wonders if
Curll supplied "Ayre" with the anecdote. Swiftian too is Curll's final gesture, wiping his breeches
with "the unfinish'd Sheets of the Conduct of the E of *N —m*" (285).

[32] By another reading, Partridge wasn't dead yet: he was a "passionate and radical Whig" (*ODNB*)
whose works still sold well – among uneducated readers – and continued to do so long after
Swift's ridicule.

[33] As Pope no doubt knew, the punishing of Curll would have given some satisfaction to Swift
too – in 1710–11 Curll had published several of Swift's pieces without authorization. But see
Karian (2008: 118–22), reviewing evidence that suggests Swift may have had some "involvement"
in Curll's publications.

case has no personal score to settle, Pope announces that he is the proud perpetrator, able to outdo Curll at his own game of printing scandal, lies, alleged "full and true" eyewitness accounts, and last wills.[34]

Did Pope need Swift's example to write the *Narrative of Dr. Robert Norris?* Probably not. There is a danger in assuming that Pope was essentially a delicate and cautious writer, particularly in his early career, inclined to hint dislike and to avoid open offense (rather like his later portrait of Atticus), to conceal satire under flattery (as in *Rape of the Lock*), while Swift was the more indecorous and aggressive of the two. The related danger is to assume that the flow of influence was essentially in one direction – the younger Pope in effect learning from the older Swift. Reading more of Pope's early writings reminds you that he could be indecorous and aggressive when he chose to, and that he need not be suspected of having learned such deliberate offensiveness from Swift. The two may have been attracted to each other not because Swift was looking for a protégé and Pope for a mentor, but because they had similar temperaments and tastes. This probably extends even to their common delight in what Johnson euphemistically called "physical impurity." Pope's "Verses design'd to be prefix'd to Mr. Lintott's Miscellany" concludes with praise for the usefulness of Lintot's books. The books of other booksellers – particularly those who publish the classics – are "useful but to few, / A Scholar, or a Wit or two." By contrast, "Lintot's for gen'ral Use are fit; / For some Folks read, but all Folks sh–." There wasn't much that Swift had to teach the young Pope about the literary possibilities of excrement.[35]

WINDSOR-FOREST AND CONDUCT OF THE ALLIES

Swift may have been encouraged by the publication of *Windsor-Forest* to think that Pope might be of further use to the Tory ministers.[36] But that was not to be, if only because the ministry was soon to fall. Even if it had not fallen, one wonders whether Pope would have been willing

---

[34] When Pope went on to provide "a faithful Copy of [Curll's] Last Will and Testament," in which the bookseller confesses his various publishing sins, he was perhaps borrowing from Swift's *Accomplishment*, in which Partridge also confesses on his deathbed that the predictions of astrology were nothing but "Deceits" and "Fooleries." But Pope's list of Curll's sins seems to be quite accurate, displaying what Baines and Rogers call "inside information," perhaps procured from Lintot (2007: 84).

[35] Pope himself is more likely to have learned about the poetic uses of excrement from Restoration court poets such as Rochester than from, say, Urquhart's 1708 translation of Rabelais.

[36] In 1712 he was talent-spotting for Harley and St. John, and providing encouragement to both Parnell and Diaper, each of whom was to produce a poem celebrating the Peace of Utrecht.

to be of service. Although some critics still argue that in *Windsor-Forest*
Pope steps forth onto the public stage as a political poet, celebrating (as
Virgil had done before him) his nation's military victories and the more
important arts of peace, foretelling a glorious imperial future of "Albion's
golden days" (424),[37] or (in a variant reading) even dreaming of a Jacobite
restoration,[38] it is possible (if we remember the darker side of Virgil's
Georgics)[39] to give the poem a different reading: that Pope reveals considerable misgivings about the future of England and parallel misgivings
about playing a public role as a poet.

Swift's *Conduct of the Allies* was published on November 27, 1711, about
two weeks before the Queen's speech on December 7, announcing that
negotiations to end the long continental war would soon begin. At the
time Britain was already engaged in secret negotiations – secret because
they were banned by the treaty with its allies – with the chief enemy,
France. Swift's task was to prepare the ground for the open negotiations
by discrediting those who opposed them, "the Allies" who had (so Swift
argues) not contributed sufficiently to the war effort, and the Whig
"Faction" at home, who thought that Britain should finish the job mili-
tarily, while the enemy was weak, and who (not coincidentally) benefitted
both financially and politically from continuing the war. The costs of the
war, he claimed, were being inequitably borne. While landowners were
receiving rents worth only about 3 percent of the value of the land, and
paid high land taxes (20 percent of the income they derived from rent),
the "*Monied Men*,"[40] those loaning money to the government (through
the purchase of shares in the national debt), were getting an 8–10 percent
return – and not paying punitive taxes. The sharpest part of Swift's argument was directed against what he claimed was a "Conspiracy" (86) to
prolong the war for the private benefit of the Duke of Marlborough, who
as Paymaster General had made (legal) profit by contracts to supply the
army and navy:

---

[37] See, for example, Weinbrot 1993.
[38] "Jacobite" readings of the poem were first presented by John R. Moore, "*Windsor Forest* and
William III," *MLN* 66 (1951), 451–54, and Earl Wasserman, *The Subtler Language* (1959), esp.
113–33. They were re-argued by Douglas Brooks-Davies; Erskine-Hill, who calls *Windsor Forest*
a "crypto-Jacobite poem" (1996: 71); and, most recently, by Rogers 2005a. Restoration of the
Stuarts to the throne was not beyond imagining: Oxford and Bolingbroke secretly encouraged
the Pretender to convert to Protestantism ("James Francis Edward [Stuart]," *ODNB*) – so as to
be eligible to succeed his half-sister – although there is no reason to suppose that either Swift or
Pope knew of this.
[39] Michael C. J. Putnam's *Virgil's Poem of the Earth* (1979) initiated a series of "pessimistic" readings
of the *Georgics*.
[40] *The Conduct of the Allies*, in Goldgar and Gadd (2008: 82).

We have been Fighting for the Ruin of the Publick Interest, and the Advancement of a Private. We have been fighting to raise the Wealth and Grandeur of a particular Family; to enrich Usurers and Stock-jobbers; and to cultivate the pernicious Designs of a Faction, by destroying the Landed-Interest. (100)[41]

Swift's pamphlet did its work, and negotiations began at Utrecht by the end of January 1712, while battlefield hostilities were suspended.[42] During the spring Pope was putting the finishing touches to the miscellany for Lintot. The Twickenham editors, following Ault (1949: 33), think that Pope was planning to include the original (unrevised) version of *Windsor-Forest* in the miscellany, but decided to hold the poem back for separate publication later – just as he was to hold back *The Dunciad*, originally designed for the 1727 Pope–Swift *Miscellanies*, for separate publication later.[43] They conjecture that Pope's reasons may have been "financial or political," suggesting that separate publication would be more profitable, and (without explanation) that May might be an "unpropitious" moment to publish the poem. Some development of this conjecture seems justified: perhaps Pope sensed that, as the nation prepared for a great public event, it might not be a good time to publish what was essentially a quiet "retirement poem" about the poet's delight in the shades of the Forest. Or did he sense that, once peace was assured, a poem on the peaceful pursuits of life in the Forest, adjusted to suit the new occasion, might be just the thing? (Such adaptive re-use was to prove typical practice in his later career.)[44] If this suspicion is correct, then it might have been Pope himself, rather than Granville, who initiated the transformation of *Windsor-Forest* into its published form. It would not be the only time in his career that Pope misled his readers by pretending to respond to events rather than to seize the occasion and take advantage of it.[45]

---

[41] "Family" is a hit at Marlborough, who was linked by marriage with two ministers – Godolphin and Sunderland – in the Whig Junto.

[42] The Lords, however, were not initially persuaded, voting on December 7 for a motion calling for "No peace without Spain." After the creation of twelve new peers (including Lansdowne), they reversed their positions. In the *Journal to Stella*, Swift proudly declares that in a series of resolutions on February 4, 1712 "those who spoke, drew all their arguments from my book" (Williams 1948: 480).

[43] Foxon (1991: 35), after a bibliographical analysis, suggests that the hypothesis that *Windsor-Forest* was removed for separate publication, while "wrong in detail," may be "right in essence."

[44] For example, when he found room for free-standing couplets and independent satiric characters, composed in his early years, in *The Dunciad* and the *Epistle to a Lady*, published much later.

[45] Pope told Spence several decades later that Granville "insisted on my publishing my *Windsor-Forest*" (Osborn 1966: 1, 43), but these words do not necessarily say that it was Granville who advised Pope to expand his old poem for a new occasion. Furthermore, Pope's memory was notoriously leaky: his remarks to Spence about the dates of composition are unreliable. But it would not have been uncharacteristic of Pope to mislead his interlocutor.

LIBRARY, UNIVERSITY OF CHESTER

It is also tempting to conclude that Pope's poem "responds" to the other poems on the peace, especially by Whig poets, including those by Thomas Tickell, Joseph Trapp, Nahum Tate, and the anonymous author of *Anna triumphans*.[46] But this argument cannot be sustained, since Pope had begun revising before any of them appeared, and probably concluded his revisions, in December 1712, before any except Tickell's were published.[47] It is more likely that he was "responding" to the public discussion of the ongoing treaty negotiations, which he could have followed in pamphlets, broadsides, and newspapers during the summer and autumn of 1712, and to what he anticipated other poets might well write.

At the beginning of the summer of 1712, on June 6, the Queen had addressed both houses of Parliament, presenting to them (as Swift later put it) "the Terms of a General Peace stipulated between Her and France,"[48] terms which were then to be negotiated further at The Hague, preparatory to the eventual ratification of the treaty by the several parties to it. Was it perhaps this speech that induced Pope to think about revising his poem on Windsor Forest?[49] The famous couplet – "At length great *ANNA* said – Let Discord cease! / She said, the World obey'd, and all was *Peace!*" (327–28) – which ostensibly concludes Pope's brief narrative of the "dreadful Series of Intestine Wars" in England (325) makes far more sense (since Anne did not in fact proclaim an end to the disputes that arose out of the Civil War) as a segue from domestic concerns to the international peace that she can be said to have proclaimed on June 6.[50]

However, the Queen's speech did not put an end to the paper war that continued to rage in England, as pamphleteers denounced both the nation's continental allies and its enemies and defended the government's position, or accused the ministers of betraying England's friends.[51] Arbuthnot's series of "John Bull" pamphlets, which had begun earlier in the year, ridiculing both the Dutch and the French, continued to appear. Pope, who seems to have met Arbuthnot in 1712, very probably knew of them. He

---

[46] For an extended list of poems "on the peace," see Foxon 1975.

[47] Some details in Pope's poem may have been shaped by Tickell's *Prospect of Peace*: e.g., "Sylvan Shade" (cf. Tickell, the prefatory "To the Lord Privy-Seal," line 8), "The Youth rush eager," line 148, and Tickell's "eager Youth" (p. 4).

[48] Davis (1939–68: VII, 129).

[49] The speech, printed in Swift's *Four Last Years* (Davis 1939–68: VII, 130–34), was much discussed in contemporary newspapers. Swift says it was published in Holland.

[50] Twenty-four years after it was published, Pope's couplet was associated, by his aging Jacobite friend, Mary Caesar, with the Queen's speech. See Potter (2002: 89).

[51] This pamphlet war is surveyed in Heinz Joachim Müllenbrock, *The Culture of Contention: A Rhetorical Analysis of the Public Controversy about the Ending of the War of the Spanish Succession, 1710–1713* (1997), ch. 1.

also knew writers on the other side, including Arthur Maynwaring, who had looked over Pope's "Pastorals" while still in manuscript: in June 1712. Maynwaring, coordinator of the Whig political writers on the peace, and author of a series of political pamphlets over the previous three years, published a pamphlet entitled *The French King's Promise to the Pretender.* Pope's friend Richard Steele, with whom he exchanged several letters during June and July,[52] was also working on behalf of the Whigs, reprinting in the *Spectator* (May 21, 1712) the preface to a set of sermons by the Bishop of St. Asaph, a preface which Johnson later described as so "overflowing with whiggish opinions"[53] – including the praise of William and Mary for delivering the country from "Arbitrary Power and Popery," and of the Act of Settlement, which ensured the Protestant succession – that it was ordered to be burnt by the House of Commons. In one of the letters to Steele – printed in the June 12, 1712 issue of the *Spectator* – Pope reflects on the opposing attractions of "solitude" and "publick life," indicating that he himself inclines to the former, following the path of Cowley, who sought to be only the "Companion of Obscurity." It is as if Pope is weighing the choices that present themselves to a writer in 1712: should he follow Cowley into a solitary life with the muses, or should he follow Steele, Maynwaring, and Swift, who had aligned themselves with a party and taken part in the pamphlet war, and engage more fully in "publick life?"

By the autumn of 1712 a number of poets, both Whig and Tory, began looking forward to the successful conclusion of those negotiations. The first to appear in print was Thomas Tickell, whose *On the Prospect of Peace* was published in October. Tickell shared Addison's Whig politics, and his poem received praise from Addison in *Spectator* 523 (October 30, 1712). It was addressed to the Lord Privy-Seal (John Robinson, Bishop of Bristol), one of the Queen's two chief negotiators at Utrecht, and a moderate Tory of Oxford's stripe. Tickell's poem focuses on the battles of the war just concluded; on the soldiers now returning home to peace; on Blenheim Palace, gift of a grateful nation to the Whig hero Marlborough; and on the diplomats then negotiating the treaty. Britain's Queen is praised for preserving the balance of power in Europe between "rival kings," and for extending Britain's imperial sway to the ends of the earth:

---

[52] June 1, June 18, and July 15 (Sherburn 1956: 1, 145–48). Pope contributed pieces to Steele's *Spectator* on February 4, March 3, May 14, June 13, June 18, July 8, August 8, August 14, and August 26. They dealt with topics from private life, except for those of August 8 and 14, which facetiously propose (since "the great Fountain of News, I mean the War, is very near being dried up") a new newspaper to deal with the gossipy news in the villages around London.

[53] "Life of Addison," in Lonsdale (2006: III, 7).

From *Albion's* cliffs Thy wide-extended Hand
Shall o'er the Main to far *Peru* command,
So vast a Tract whose wide Domain shall run,
It's circling Skies shall see no setting Sun…
The Line and Poles shall own thy rightful Sway,
And thy Commands the sever'd Globe obey.[54]

By the time Tickell's poem appeared Pope had probably begun revising his poem on Windsor Forest.[55] The old poem, begun as early as 1704 (and certainly by 1707) when the government was controlled by the Whigs, and the Tories (such as Sir William Trumbull) were out of office, was now being revised under a Tory ministry. But it would be too simple to suggest that Pope's poem was designed to be a "Tory" reply to the poems that "Whig" poets would inevitably produce. It is true that only a year earlier, when Swift published the *Conduct of the Allies*, the Whig and Tory views of the peace were sharply contrasted. But because the treaty was by late 1712 being welcomed on all sides, it had become difficult to distinguish the Tory view from the Whig. Writers on both sides were going to celebrate Queen Anne, the peace, British liberties,[56] and British commerce. The chief distinguishing feature was perhaps the celebration, by the Whigs, of Marlborough as a military hero whose victories paved the way for the peace.[57] Unlike Tickell, Pope makes no mention of Marlborough, and no mention of the diplomats negotiating the terms of the treaty. His version of British history emphasizes the Stuart monarchy (ignoring the Hanoverians waiting in the wings), hints that William III is just another "foreign master," and says nothing of the Revolution and Act of Settlement which (so the Whigs and moderate Tories like Harley believed and often declared) assured Britain's liberties and kept the monarchy Protestant. And as his revisions continued, his poem adopted an approach to its topic that differed from Tickell's frankly imperial triumphalism.

---

[54] *A Poem, to his Excellency the Lord Privy-Seal, upon the Prospect of Peace* ([1712], 1713 on title page), 14–15. I have borrowed the description of the poem from Griffin (2002: 51).

[55] By the end of November he was writing to Caryll that, although he admired Tickell's new poem "upon the peace," he regretted that Tickell's "description of the several parts of the world in regard to our trade" had "interfered with some lines of my own in the poem called Windsor Forest, tho' written before I saw his" (Sherburn 1956: 1, 156). See also the letter of December 5, 1712, in which he reports to Caryll that "Windsor Forest" has "undergone many alterations, and received many additions since you saw it" (1, 162).

[56] Pope's invocation of "Fair Liberty, Britannia's Goddess" (91) does not signal any specifically Whiggish sentiment: "Fair Liberty" (in contrast to "Licence") is also invoked in the *Hymn on Peace* (1713) by the Stuart loyalist, the Revd. Samuel Wesley.

[57] Several of the Whiggish poems on "the peace" – including Joseph Trapp's *Peace. A Poem* (1713), Tate's *The Triumph of Peace* (1713), and the anonymous *Anna triumphans. A Congratulatory Poem* (1713) – pour lavish praise on Marlborough.

But by the time he read Tickell's poem, Pope had apparently worked out his own scheme for expanding his old poem, his own point of view on the war and the forthcoming peace, and the way in which he wanted to characterize himself in the poem.[58] In shaping that point of view he seems to have looked back to earlier poems on the war, especially those Whig panegyrics on Marlborough's victories in war, including Addison's *Campaign* (1705),[59] and to the most famous and influential of the political polemics in favor of peace, Swift's pamphlet.

But Pope was not "responding" to Swift's *Conduct* in any simple or explicit way, and the differences between poem and pamphlet need to be acknowledged. They were published at two quite different points in the peace process, Swift's at its controversial beginnings and Pope's at its widely acclaimed conclusion. They were also written in two quite different genres, with differing rhetorical requirements. Swift was writing political polemical prose, though disguising it as a straightforward presentation of "plain Matters of Fact" (57) – which fooled Johnson, who thought the pamphlet succeeded "by the mere weight of facts." Pope drew on both the new topographical poem, as initiated in England by Denham's *Cooper's Hill*, and the much older Virgilian georgic, which linked a country's agriculture and its rural virtue with its urban culture and global empire. Swift's argument is conducted systematically, by means of a series of tightly linked points ("Thirdly..." [95], "Fourthly..." [101], "Lastly..." [103]). While it was once argued that Pope's poem is likewise carefully organized around the principle of *discordia concors*, critics now point to a series of loosely related sections that the hostile Dennis thought a mere "Rhapsody" and one modern critic regards as deliberate "discontinuities," based on a classical model.[60] Despite the generic differences, it is nonetheless possible to see that Pope adopted an approach to his topic that differed pointedly, if subtly, from Swift's.

In some respects, however, they drew water from the same rhetorical well, so much so that their modern biographers have suspected that Pope

---

[58] A December 5, 1712 letter hints that he has chosen a contemplative rather than active life, contrasting the hunter Caryll pursuing the fox and his own "Indolence & Inactivity of Body, tho my Mind be perpetually rambling, ... insensible of any Moving Power but Fancy" (Sherburn 1956: I, 163).

[59] Cf. Father Thames rising from "his Oozy Bed" (329), and Addison's "Rivers from their Oozy Beds arise" (p. 16). Addison also compares soldiers pursuing the enemy to hunters chasing deer (p. 6). The references to "blood" that flow through Pope's poem may reply to the extraordinary emphasis in *The Campaign* on the carnage of war: "Floating in Gore ... bloody Whirlpools ... bloated Corps ... Streams of Blood ... Choak'd in his Blood ... Floods of Gore ... Mountains of Slain" (pp. 12–13).

[60] Hooker (1943: II, 137); Cummings 1987.

was influenced by Swift's pamphlet.[61] Both Swift and Pope adopted rhetoric that echoed the familiar positions of both parties. Like Swift's *Conduct*, Pope's poem was broadly aligned with the landed interest (roughly speaking, the Tory view), but at the same time saw overseas trade, now recognized as central to Britain's interests (roughly speaking, the Whig view),[62] to be integrally related to the agricultural heartland, especially by means of the recurrent poetic figure that regarded the trees of Windsor Forest as destined to form the ships of Britain's merchant fleet and navy.[63] The emphasis on the navy, as opposed to the army, echoed the traditional Tory "blue water policy," with a preference for controlling the seas rather than engaging in a continental land war, especially with a standing army. Both Swift and Pope deplored any further spilling of blood and treasure, and foresaw that peace would not only promote Britain's overseas trade but also usher in a glorious future. But on some underlying matters Pope's view of the peace is pointedly different from Swift's.

The most prominent feature of Swift's pamphlet is its virulently partisan tone.[64] Pope's tone, by contrast, has rightly been called "conciliatory." He expresses sympathy with both the victors and the vanquished – each have lost "blood." He declines to mention party conflict – the words "Whig" and "Tory" are absent from the poem – except possibly to refer to "Faction" in the closing lines, without explicitly identifying "Faction" with the Whigs, as Swift had done. (Some contemporary writers deplored the "Factions" in both parties.)[65] Swift widens the gulf between the parties, while Pope tries to close it. The latter avoids any explicit reference to Marlborough, still a polarizing figure, although he may hint at his presence in lines about an apparently typical "General."[66] He treats the peace not as the political accomplishment

[61] Ehrenpreis (1962–83: II, 593n), and Mack (1985: 853).

[62] Swift argues that it is "essential to our Trade" to be able to preserve "the Balance of Power in the North" (105). Cf. his remarks on the "Disadvantage to us" of "the general Discouragement of Trade, on which we so much depend" (102).

[63] "While by our Oaks the precious Loads are born, / And Realms commanded which those Trees adorn" (31–32); "towering Oaks their growing Honours rear, / And future Navies on thy Shores appear" (221–22).

[64] Even though in principle he deplored the party-spirit, Swift adopts partisan rhetoric to accomplish a particular end – approval of the treaty. It is notable that he attacks Marlborough and his "Family" rather than the Whig party in general – as if to cordon them off as venal and self-interested.

[65] Including Simon Clement, author of *Faults on Both Sides* (1710), published on the eve of the 1710 parliamentary elections to promote the election of moderate and public-spirited men. Clement articulates the ideological position of moderate Tories such as Harley, who became Lord Treasurer in 1710.

[66] When the poem appeared in 1713, lines 107–08 read "Pleas'd in the Gen'ral's Sight, the Host lye down / Sudden, before some unsuspecting Town." For an English reader in 1713, "the Gen'ral" probably would have pointed at Marlborough, Captain-General of English forces, especially

of the Tory ministers (praised by name in several other contemporary poems "on the peace"[67]), or their diplomatic representatives at Utrecht (praised in Tickell's poem), or for that matter as the result and motive of just war, but as a magical and quasi-divine act of the Queen herself, who declares peace by fiat (327–28). Pope focuses so little on the negotiations at Utrecht that he conflates the domestic peace that brought an end to English "Intestine Wars" (325) – which Anne had no hand in bringing about – and the international peace that prevailed after the conclusion of the War of the Spanish Succession. Although the title page of his poem read *Windsor-Forest. To the Right Honourable George Lord Lansdown*, Lansdowne was complimented not as Minister but as courtier and poet.[68] Naming no one but the Queen and Lansdowne, avoiding the divisive names of Marlborough, Oxford, and St. John, Pope carefully declines to take sides.[69] His poem, like Addison's contemporary *Cato*, gives everybody something to think his own – to the Whigs the praise of liberty and trade and of England's military victories, to the country squires the praise of the land and the delights of the hunt, to the Tory Ministers the praise of peace, to the Jacobites the praise of Granville (himself a suspected Jacobite) and of the Stuart line,[70] to the loyal Protestants the praise of Anne's fifty churches.[71] By comparison to several of the partisan "Tory" poems on the peace by Parnell, Samuel Wesley, Bevil Higgons, and William Diaper, Pope's is almost ecumenical, if not apolitical.[72]

because of his policy of besieging towns in Flanders, even though (as Rogers notes – 2005a: 312) they were rarely "unsuspecting."

[67] Both Marshall Smith's *On the Peace* and Bevil Higgons's *Poem on the Peace* are inscribed to Oxford; Joseph Trapp's *Peace. A Poem* is inscribed to Bolingbroke; Parnell's *On Queen Anne's Peace* compliments both Oxford and Bolingbroke, along with half a dozen other Tory ministers; Higgons's *Poem on the Peace* compliments Oxford, Bolingbroke, and their senior ministerial colleague Simon Lord Harcourt (Keeper of the Great Seal, until he was appointed Lord Chancellor in April 1713).

[68] Lansdowne, had been a relatively junior Minister as Secretary at War from September 1710 until June 1713, when he was named Treasurer of the Household and then member of the Privy Council, while retaining his minor reputation as a courtier poet. He is recognized as a poet in Bevil Higgons's *Poem on the Peace.*

[69] Erskine-Hill 1982, 1996, and Rogers 2005a have argued that the dedication to Lansdowne signals Pope's secret Jacobite sympathies: Lansdowne's cousin was Secretary of State to the Pretender, and he himself corresponded with the Pretender after the accession of George I (*ODNB*).

[70] Some of Pope's readers may have concluded that in celebrating the fact that "a STUART reigns" (42) he was citing Anne's "hereditary title" (derived from her father) rather than her "parliamentary" one – i.e., the one granted her under the Act of Settlement. Contemporary writers such as the author of *Faults on Both Sides* recognized the distinction.

[71] Dennis complained in his *True Character of Mr. Pope, and his Writings* (1716) that Pope was "a Whig and a Tory, a virulent *Papist* and yet forsooth, a Pillar of the Church of *England*, a Writer at one and the same time, of *GUARDIANS* and *EXAMINERS*, an assertor of Liberty and of the Dispensing Power of Kings" (Hooker 1943: II, 103).

[72] Samuel Wesley's *An Hymn on Peace* (1713), which compliments Wesley's patron, Stuart loyalist and courtier John Sheffield, Duke of Buckinghamshire, is so committed to the Stuart family that it

Another prominent feature of Swift's *Conduct* is that it presents itself as having been written by a privileged insider with special access to information. Unlike other writers, he is possessed of "several Facts, which I had the Opportunity to know" (95). He knows "the real Causes" of events, even though they are "disguised under specious Pretences" (87), and assures his readers that "if the Particulars were truly related" the Queen's "Prudence, Courage, and Firmness" would be even more admired (86). (Swift suppressed whatever resentments he harbored about Queen Anne's reported refusal to make the author of *Tale of a Tub* a bishop.) By contrast, Pope claims no access to inside information, and writes as a lover of the "silent Shade" (432), drawn into political matters only because Granville, his patron, "commands" him to sing (5) – whether or not this was in fact the case. Swift presents himself as a realist about politics and war: Britain entered the war to protect what it thought were its interests – "Interest" is a recurrent term in his argument[73] – and to preserve the "Balance of *Europe*" (57). It ought always to measure the costs of its actions, and avoid the expense of taking a town "which costs us fifty times more than it is worth, either as to the Value, or the Consequences" (101). Both besieger and besieged know that the outcome is simply a matter of time and "Charge": "If you will count upon sacrificing so much Blood and Treasure, the rest is all a regular, established Method, which cannot fail" (103). Once a state calculates that prosecuting the war "brings no real solid Advantage to us" (62), then it is time to sue for peace. Pope acknowledges the ministry's argument that continuing the war is not worth the expenditure of blood and treasure – "No more my Sons shall dye with British Blood / Red Iber's Sands, or Ister's foaming Flood" (367–68) – but implicitly suggests that such calculation is an inadequate response. For him war is not politics but what an early commentator, Gilbert Wakefield, calls "horrors and devastations."[74] The taking of a town means "sudden"

---

hopes Anne's reign will be prolonged indefinitely, that she will in effect "herself Succeed" (p. 10). Bevil Higgons's *Poem on the Peace*, published in April 1713, imagines a future in which "Banquo's Race" – i.e., the Stuarts – will "possess the British Throne." William Diaper's *Dryades*, published in December 1712, compliments both Bolingbroke and his ally, the Stuart loyalist and future Jacobite Sir William Wyndham. Thomas Parnell's *On Queen Anne's Peace, Anno 1713* (designed for publication but not in fact published until 1758) praises the Tory ministers by name and denounces the "Blatant voice" of the Whig "Faction." For a contrasting view, claiming that Pope's poem, like those of Diaper, Trapp, Gay, and Philips, is "Tory-inflected," see Rogers 2005b.

[73] In his peroration Swift rhetorically asks "Is it therefore our Interest, to toil on in a ruinous War, for an impracticable End …?" and insists that, although Marlborough and the Whigs seek to serve their private interests, the "Proceedings" of the ministry "are meant to serve their Country, directly against their private Interest" (105).

[74] *Observations on Pope* (1796), 39.

painful amazement for the unsuspecting ("thoughtless") and "defence-
less" town (107–11), and triumphant exultation for the winners. While
Swift explains the international system of political and military alliances,
Pope, who never mentions the Allies, simply imagines England as the
supreme power, and all other states as "suppliant" (384), ritually bending
their knees "before a British Queen" (385). Pope ignores the political considerations that preoccupied both Swift and the negotiators at Utrecht –
the "balance of power" in Europe, whether or not France had been
sufficiently weakened, or England's interest in the "Spanish Succession."

Swift writes to persuade an audience that negotiating a peace treaty is
in the country's immediate interest; Pope, now that the treaty is about to
be signed, takes the longer view. He hails the "long-expected Days" of
peace and prosperity (355), and the displacement of military violence by
the apparently well-regulated activity of hunting. But critics have often
been struck by the bloody violence of Pope's hunting scenes (depicted as
it is with sensitivity to the victims) and the impetuousness of the "un-
wearyd's Fowler" with his "slaught'ring Guns" and hunters "rush[ing]
eager to the Sylvan War" (125, 148). The poem also foresees the displacement of bloody international conflict by international commerce. But in
the prophetic song placed in the mouth of Father Thames, Pope reveals
some concern about the long-term effects of Britain's transformation into
a trading empire:

> Thy Trees, fair Windsor! now shall leave their Woods,
> And half thy Forests rush into my Floods;
> Bear Britain's Thunder, and her Cross display,
> To the bright Regions of the rising Day. (385–88)

As British ships carry "Britain's Thunder" and display "her Cross,"[75]
it is unclear whether they are carrying on peaceful trade or projecting
British power. Is there a difference? Trees have been turning into ships
since the beginning of the poem, but now – whether as enthusiastic exaggeration or fact – "*half* thy Forests rush [as if in imitation of the rushing
hunters] into my Floods" (my emphasis). It is unclear what will remain
of the beloved Windsor Forest. Can Britain (like Rome before it) retain
the virtues associated with both retirement and agriculture as it becomes
a global empire? We may ask whether the poem confidently sees empire

---

[75] In 1736 Pope added a footnote suggesting that he had originally intended a sharper critique: in
the manuscript, so he says, he had written "bloody Cross" – linking the red cross of St. George
with the blood (of Britons and their enemies) spilled in British wars, and the "blood" spilled in
global trade.

(embodied in British ships) as the almost natural outgrowth of such virtues (embodied in its trees), or worries that the country might lose half
its soul. *Windsor-Forest*, so Pope later took pains to remind his readers,
was written at two different times, and he even marks the point – line
290 – where the earlier part (about Windsor Forest) ended. By drawing
the reader's attention to the seam, he perhaps suggest a gap between rural
and imperial England.

Swift, revealing no ambivalence in celebrating British sea power, concludes with a confident and forthright declaration of future prosperity;
Pope, more ambiguous, implicitly leaves his reader with questions. Will
the peaceful Britain of *"Albion's* Golden Days" continue to conduct a kind
of war in masquerade, "British Blood" (367) now replaced by "bleed[ing]"
balm (393)?[76] Will the seas serve to "join" or to "divide" nations (400)? Is
trade a reign of peace "for all mankind" (398), or will Britain continue to
command foreign realms? (Pope's early lines about "Realms commanded"
by British ships which bear "precious Loads" of luxury goods back to
England (31–32) have struck some readers as enthusiastic about empire,
but empire disappears in the next lines (33–36), and our attention returns
to native flocks, fruits, and flowers, suggesting that they are the gifts of
the gods.) Perhaps a universal peace will resemble the displaced "universal
monarchy" of Louis XIV. Will an "unbounded" Thames – Pope's note
indicates that he refers to the "wish that London may be made a FREE
PORT"[77] – bring prosperity "for all Mankind" (398), or just for London's
traders? When Pope calls it a "wish," he hints that it may be a fond one,
perhaps no less fond than the millenarian desire that one day "Conquest"
shall "cease, and Slav'ry be no more" (408). (Some have argued that Pope
here reveals his misgivings about, or even his opposition to, the provision
in the Treaty of Utrecht which granted to Britain the "Asiento," the lucra-
tive right to a thirty-year monopoly to sell slaves to Spain's colonies in the
New World.)[78] Although Pope and his readers in March 1713 could not

---

[76] Note that in the song of English victories that he asks Granville to sing, France will "bleed
for ever under Britain's Spear" (310), meaning that the battle of Crécy will live "for ever" in
Granville's song but perhaps hinting at desires on the part of some Whigs for more demanding
treaty terms so that French power would be reduced "for generations to come." See Bolingbroke's
Works, 4 vols. (1844), II, 315.

[77] Gibraltar, which was ceded to Britain by Spain in the Treaty of Utrecht, had been named a
free port in 1705. The note, which first appeared in 1751, may be Warburton's, and it is not clear
whether Pope approved it. But the Twickenham editors suggest that the name of Addison's Sir
Andrew Freeport embodied the hopes of many Whiggish contemporaries, and, as Rogers notes
(2004: 255n), Bolingbroke had pressed for free trade during the Utrecht negotiations.

[78] Erskine-Hill 1998 and Richardson 2001. The Asiento, cited in the Queen's June 6, 1712 speech,
was subsequently printed and discussed in the newspapers during the summer of 1712.

know that the reigning Stuart Queen, guarantor of her country's peace and plenty, would die within seventeen months, they knew well that she would be the last of the Stuarts: for Pope the problem of the "Spanish Succession" was less important than the English Act of Succession, whereby the childless Anne would inevitably be succeeded by a foreign Prince. But about that Protestant successor Pope is conspicuously silent.

Committed as he was to the Act of Settlement and a Protestant succession, Swift's *Conduct of the Allies* reveals no implicit doubts about a post-Stuart England.[79] Likewise, he displays no Popean misgivings about the justice of his country's actions and the prospects for a postwar England,[80] no misgivings about Britain's control of the slave trade,[81] and no misgivings about his own role as its champion. In his free use of "we" – "the part we have acted in the Conduct of the whole War" (57), "We have actually Conquered ... the Troops we have funished, the Armies we have paid" (80) – Swift identifies himself with his nation. By comparison Pope presents himself as a reluctant client, a "humble muse" who retreats to the shades of Windsor Forest as soon as he can. Some have regarded this as a conventional modesty trope, a decorous disguising of his secret ambition (hinted at in the opening lines) to be the "Muse" who might once again stand beside the "Monarch." When it comes time to sing "in lofty Numbers" (287), Pope several times defers to his patron, the minor poet George Granville, recently elevated to the upper house as Lord Lansdowne: "Oh wou'dst thou sing what Heroes Windsor bore, / What Kings first breath'd upon her winding Shore" (299–300):

> Here cease thy Flight, nor with unhallow'd Lays
> Touch the fair fame of *Albion*'s Golden Days.
> The Thoughts of Gods let *Granville*'s Verse recite,
> And bring the Scenes of opening Fate to light. (423–26)

---

[79] Some contemporaries were not convinced. Swift's remark that in case of some future "Tyranny and Oppression of any succeeding Princes," the Parliament might be reduced to the "fatal Necessity" of "breaking in upon the excellent and happy Settlement now in force" (27), was attacked as evidence of Jacobite leanings (Goldgar and Gadd 2008: 3–5 and 69n). Most modern scholars see no sign of Jacobitism, but Higgins (1994: 91) calls Swift's point "potentially treasonable." In a postscript Swift felt obliged to dismiss a legislative change in the succession as "a distant Case" (106).

[80] Just before the Treaty of Utrecht was signed he wrote to Stella that "now the Great Work is in effect close, and I believe it will appear a most excellent Peace for Europe, particularly for England" (*Journal to Stella*, April 3, 1713).

[81] As Richardson notes (2001: 13), the slave trade was carried on by the South Sea Company, a Harley-sponsored project in which Swift himself had invested in 1711. Both in *Conduct of the Allies* (64) and his retrospective *History of the Four Last Years* (Davis 1939–68: VII, 109), Swift regarded English trade with the Spanish West Indies, including the trade in "Negroes," as crucial to the nation's interest.

Again, this has been read as perfunctory or disingenuous, a gracious compliment to the patron that is designed to suggest not Granville's but Pope's own nascent powers.[82] But the poem hints repeatedly that Pope is uncomfortable in the role of public poet, and suggests that a writer must choose either to be a man "whom this bright Court approves, / His Sov'reign favours, and his Country loves" or one "who to these Shades retires, / Whom Nature charms, and whom the Muse inspires" (235–38). Pope is here distinguishing between the courtier poet Lansdowne and himself, but perhaps too between the path that a political writer like Swift has apparently taken – with hopes to be approved by the ministry, favored by the Queen, and honored as a patriot by the people[83] – and the path of private and poetic ambitions that Pope was considering for himself.[84] It is in this reading not a mere stage device to place the prophecy of "Albion's Golden Days" (355–422) in the mouth of Father Thames, but a sign of his reluctance to put himself forward as a public celebrant.

In this light the figure of Lodona plays a crucial part in the pattern. Not simply a piece of Ovidian decoration,[85] she serves as an emblem of poetic retirement. The poet aligns himself with her, vowing to sing her "Fate" (173–74) and perpetuate her story, gazing into the river which bears her name, as in a "Glass" which reflects not only the "headlong Mountains" but also the face of the "musing Shepherd" (211–12). Like Lodona, who longs to "repair" to her "native Shades" (201–02), the poet too retires to "these Shades" (237),[86] and longs to be borne to "sequester'd Scenes" (261).[87] Lodona's story may serve too as a cautionary tale for a poet: too "eager of the Chace" (181), she strayed "beyond the Forest's verdant Limits" (182), and met her dreaded fate. Perhaps an analogous fate awaits the poet who strays beyond the limits of Windsor Forest – that is, moves from a quiet celebration of retirement and poetry to a public forum. Perhaps for that reason Pope later advertised, by means of footnotes, that the poem was not only

---

[82] Erskine-Hill (1996: 71) reads the line as endorsement of Granville's (alleged) hopes for a "Fate" that would install James Stuart (son of the exiled "James III") as Anne's successor.

[83] Pope would probably have been aware that Swift's *Conduct* was only one of many pamphlets in the "pamphlet war" between Whig and Tory writers that raged from about 1710 to 1712.

[84] See above, p. 52.

[85] See David Hauser's "Pope's Lodona and the Uses of Mythology" (*SEL* 6 [1966], 465–82), arguing that Diana (Queen Anne) acts as protector of Arcadia (England), and Vincent Carretta's "Anne and Elizabeth: The Poet as Historian in *Windsor Forest*" (*SEL* 21 [1981], 425–37), linking Diana with Elizabeth, Lodona with an England that "strayed from its original principles after Elizabeth's reign" (433).

[86] Cf. his roaming "from Shade to Shade" (269) and his happy retreat to "the silent Shade" (432).

[87] She calls on Father Thames in vain for aid (197), but perhaps he answers her call by appearing, uncalled, to sing of the "Sacred Peace" (349–55).

written at two different times, but treats of two different topics, the Forest and the Peace, in two different "Parts." Rather than concealing the bounds between the two parts, Pope emphasizes them, as if to suggest one should pay attention to any move from Forest to a wider world. By calling the poem "Windsor-Forest" (rather than, say, "The Prophecy of Peace") Pope perhaps hints where his deepest affinities lie, and the poetic path he chooses.

Swift had chosen another path, and Pope could not have failed to observe how his fellow writer had, by contrast, placed himself squarely in the eye of the public and of the ministry. But Swift was only the most recent of a long line of writers before him who chose to align poetry with politics. Dryden was another, and Pope may well have reflected on the price Dryden paid, in his final years, for his public defenses of Anne's father, the Catholic James II. Before Dryden stood Denham, for whom the muse is like a King – "as Courts make not Kings, but Kings the Court, / So where the Muses and their train resort, / *Parnassus* stands" (lines 5–7). Denham's poem commits itself to a sustained view of English politics, both past and present, and as poet he occupies no space separate from the political sphere: Windsor for him is a political site, and for him there is no real gap between Windsor and London – the poet's eye can see both from the height of Cooper's Hill. By contrast, Pope carves out a space in Windsor Forest separate from politics, and imagines that between Windsor and London, though they are linked by the Thames, lies a significant border. In designing the original *Windsor-Forest* as a retirement poem, and in preserving the urge to retirement in the revised poem, Pope was perhaps marking his difference from Denham.

To suggest that Pope, while writing *Windsor-Forest*, had in mind both Denham and Dryden is only to acknowledge that, like any widely read poet, he is at any moment "responding" to several different predecessors or contemporaries. Swift was the leading exemplar in Pope's own day of a writer who had committed himself and his writings to the world of politics. And although he makes no reference to the choice made by Swift – a famous writer whom he had no doubt read but not yet met – we can conclude that Pope would have sensed, and that his readers would have sensed, the gap between, and the implicit dialogue between, *Windsor-Forest* and *Conduct of the Allies*.[88] This division – the choice of "poetry"

---

[88] There is no evidence to suggest that Pope knew Swift to be the author of the anonymously published *The Windsor Prophecy* (Dec. 1711), an attack on the Duchess of Somerset as an evil counselor to the Queen. (It begins with a reference to the same John Robinson to whom Tickell addressed his poem "On the Prospect of Peace.") But he must have savored the difference between the "Windsor" prophecy and his own.

vs. the choice of "politics" – was to be played out between them again in the early 1730s.

Pope's choice – a declared preference for the shades – was probably not simply a matter of his retiring temperament: in the contentious partisan atmosphere of the time it was good business for an ambitious writer. By 1713 Pope, who knew that governmental patronage of a Roman Catholic in a Protestant country was out of the question, already had his eye on where his future sources of support would come from, and already had plans for a major project, the translation of Homer. If he hoped to secure subscriptions, and the endorsement of the leading patrons of the day, including both the Whig Earl of Halifax and the Tory Duke of Buckinghamshire (each of whom in fact subscribed for ten sets), he would want to be careful to conceal any extreme political sympathies, assuming (as do Rogers and others) that he harbored them.[89]

For his part, Swift (who was not paid for his service as government propagandist)[90] continued to write pamphlets and public letters in defense of the ministry throughout the year 1712 and the first part of 1713.[91] The day before he commended *Windsor-Forest* to Stella, he told her he was at work on a draft of the "vote of Address of thanks for the Speech" that the Queen was to give when Parliament next met on April 9, announcing that the Treaty of Utrecht had been signed.[92] His draft, later edited by Oxford, congratulates the Queen "upon the General Peace you have pro-cured for all Your Allies, wherein the true Interests and just Pretensions of each are so fully provided for that the Tranquillity and Welfare of Europe will be owing (next to the Divine Providence) to Your Majesty's Wisdom and Goodness."[93] Swift's politic language, designed to assuage Whig fears that England had sold out the Allies, was too much even for Oxford: the final address refers only to "the Success of Your Endeavours for a General

---

[89] Pope's subscribers included most of the leading men of the day, including Oxford, Bolingbroke, Wyndham, James Brydges, Earl of Carnarvon (twelve sets), and even the Duke of Marlborough, along with the chief Whig writers, Addison, Steele, and Rowe. Lansdowne subscribed for ten copies (a good return on Pope's investment). The list also includes several Jacobite leaders, among them Wyndham and Lansdowne, both of whom would be arrested as a result of the 1715 Rising. See Hodgart 1978. Rogers (2005a: 118–22) brings out that there was wide support from "the community of Stuart supporters," but also from the Whig lords Somers, Sunderland, Stanhope, and Wharton.

[90] Many years later Swift told Pulteney that he never "got a farthing by anything I writ," except for *Gulliver's Travels*, for which he said Pope prudently managed the contract (Woolley 1999–2007: IV, 107).

[91] See the tracts collected in Goldgar and Gadd 2008.

[92] Williams (1948: II, 635).

[93] A facsimile of Swift's draft is reproduced in (Davis 1939–68: VI, facing p. xxviii).

Peace" (Goldgar and Gadd 2008: 215). Pope's poem had shown no concern for "the Allies" though it endorsed the "General Peace." Swift's final
address also reproduces the affirmation of the "Protestant Succession" and
"the perfect Friendship there is between Your Majesty and the House of
Hanover," a matter on which Pope had been notably silent.

Swift continued to write on behalf of the ministry, refuting Steele's
rehash of Whiggish polemic in an essay on "The Importance of the
Guardian Considered" in November 1713 and a substantial pamphlet on
The Publick Spirit of the Whigs in February 1714. But by the autumn of
1713 Swift seems to have sensed that his efforts as a Tory pamphleteer
were not going to win him the English church appointment he wanted.[94]
In October 1713 he published an imitation of Horace (part of the seventh
epistle of the first book), suggesting that a writer whose eyes are clear
will not count on the favor of statesmen. As I have argued elsewhere, the
poem is a kind of declaration of independence. (The epistle must have
struck a chord with Pope – he was later to write an imitation of the rest of
the poem "in the manner of Dr. Swift.") It begins with Swift's refusal to
accept Harley's invitation to dinner, and concludes with a symbolic resignation from the minister's patronage: "And then since you now have done
your worst, / Pray leave me where you found me first" (137–38).[95] This
was the first expression that Pope encountered of a stance that he himself
would later adopt – the writer proudly independent of patrons, the friend
and confidant of ministers but never their slave. Johnson was famously
skeptical of the reports of the "equality and independence which [Swift]
preserved in his conversation with the Ministers, of the frankness of his
remonstrances, and the familiarity of his friendship" (Lonsdale 2006: III,
197), but it appears that Pope believed in them – and modeled his own
later self-representations on them.

Swift must have sensed that Pope was not to be counted on as a political ally. But apparently he did not regard their political differences as
insuperable – perhaps because he realized that he and Pope agreed on the
main point, that the peace was good for England, perhaps too because
the reward he received for his own political service was less than he
expected.[96] Perhaps Pope's hesitation to step into the role of political poet
was prudent. Within seven months Swift had not only met the young

---

[94] In the summer of 1714 Swift worked on, but did not publish, two pamphlets on "The Present
State of Affairs" (see Goldgar and Gadd, 2008: 8, 287–311).
[95] Griffin (1996: 212).
[96] Swift was appointed Dean of St. Patrick's on April 25, 1713, and installed on June 10.

author of *Windsor-Forest* but had promised to secure subscriptions to his Homer.[97]

CADENUS AND VANESSA AND RAPE OF THE LOCK

Although both were occupied with contemporary politics in 1712–13, Swift and Pope did not limit their attention to Whigs and Tories. The first edition of *Rape of the Locke* appeared in Lintot's *Miscellaneous Poems and translations* on May 20, 1712. In the summer of that year Swift was drafting what would be published years later as "Cadenus and Vanessa." Both poems are occasional, both grounded in unique personal circumstances: Pope was invited to damp down the quarrel between two Roman Catholic families, and Swift seems to have written in order to cool down his relationship with Hester Vanhomrigh.[98] The similarities between the two poems are suggestive. Although both poems deal with private matters under code names (Belinda, Vanessa, *et al.*), they teasingly invite the reader to identify the originals. Both poems were designed to appease or "manage" an offended lady: "Belinda" because she received unwanted attentions; "Vanessa" because, after falling in love with her tutor, she had in effect been refused. Both were at first circulated privately, in part no doubt to avoid making public what was a private matter, which might have given offense; when Pope's poem was subsequently published, the lady in question in fact did take offense. Both poems parody epic conventions, particularly the celestial machinery of Homer, and both lightly satirize the nymphs and fops of the day. Both poems scramble gender roles: in *Rape of the Lock* men are diminished to lapdogs and fops, while women vent their "mighty rage"; Swift's Vanessa, with more sense and manly virtues than men, is mistaken for a boy. (In both poems a woman who speaks sense is regarded as an anomaly.) Vanessa disregards convention by avowing her passion before her lover has spoken, and assumes the "Government" of affairs (801). Women in both poems – Clarissa,

[97] Swift reportedly vowed that "the author shall not begin to print till I have a thousand guineas for him" (entry for November 2, 1713 in White Kennett's MS Diary, quoted in Johnson's "Life of Pope").

[98] Swift's original purpose remains mysterious. "Vanessa" seems not to have seen the poem until 1719 (Schakel 1994), by which time it may have served other purposes. In 1719 Swift wrote to Vanessa, complimenting her (in French) by telling her that in hiding herself as she does, "le monde ne vous connoit pas, et vous perdez l'eloge des millions des gens" (Woolley 1999–2007: II, 304). Cf. "When, after Millions slain, your self shall die" (*Rape of the Lock*, 5. 146), and the compensatory promise to render immortal "*Belinda*'s Name" (150). Was Swift half-suggesting that he publish his praise of her from "Cadenus and Vanessa?"

Thalestris, and Belinda, and Venus and Pallas – are the instigators and manipulators of events. By contrast, Cadenus seems to lack sexual power and the Baron seems to be more interested in the lock than the lady. Both poems break off at the moment of crisis: in Pope's poem the action stops when the lock disappears; in Swift's the outcome of the courtship of Cadenus and Vanessa remains secret. In each a young woman is left unmarried, with no suitor in sight. Only Swift's "conscious muse" (cf. Pope's "quick poetic eyes") knows what has happened, and he's not talking. Put this way, the similarities or parallels are remarkable. But what is their significance? Even though the two poems are basically quite different from each other, can we say that "Cadenus and Vanessa" was in any way shaped by *The Rape of the Locke*? If so, it would be the first instance in which Swift might be said to be "replying" to one of Pope's poems.

The Rape of the Locke, as noted, was published in two cantos in May 1712. "Cadenus and Vanessa," not published until 1726, may have been begun within a month or two of the appearance of Pope's poem. Swift said that "Cadenus and Vanessa" was written at Windsor in 1712 (Woolley 1999–2007: II, 639, 649). He is known to have been at Windsor in August and September of 1712, and one manuscript transcription of the poem is dated August 1, 1712 (Williams 1958: II, 684).[99] But most of Swift's editors (Williams, Ehrenpreis, and Rogers) think that it was written in the autumn of 1713, after Swift was named Dean of St. Patrick's (which would have accounted for "Cadenus," an anagram of *decanus*), and he was again at Windsor. By then Pope was apparently engaged on the revisions which would lead to the expanded version of his poem. Ault (1936: lxv–lxvii) suggests that Pope was revising as early as July 1713, when an unsigned letter from him appears in *Guardian* No. 106. As Ault shows, many details in the letter have "correspondences" in the revised *Rape of the Lock*. In late October, by which time Pope and Swift had met for the first time, Pope appears to have been "deeply ingaged" in the revisions,[100] and on December 8 he writes to Swift that the revised *Rape of the Lock* is "finished" (Woolley 1999–2007: I, 560). That Pope refers to the completion of the revisions in an informal way, in a postscript – "I have finished the Rape of the Lock, but believe I may stay here [i.e., in Binfield] till Christmas without Hindrance of Busyness" – suggests that he had probably discussed the poem with Swift earlier that autumn, perhaps before

---

[99] Fischer 2003 supports the 1712 date.
[100] See the October 23 letter to Gay: "I am deeply ingaged in Poetry, the particulars whereof shall be deferr'd till we meet" (Sherburn 1956: I, 195).

late October, when (in the same letter) Pope told Gay that Swift liked Pope's proposal to write a monthly critical account of "the Works of the Unlearned."[101] Swift and Pope had apparently met as early as August: in an August 31 letter to Caryll Pope reports his efforts at copying portraits by Charles Jervas, including three different attempts to copy his portrait of Swift, whom he refers to as one of his "friends" (Sherburn 1956: 1, 189).[102] Swift and Pope were both in London from September 20, and the first meeting of what would become the "Scriblerus Club" probably took place soon after that date. Swift, then, was writing "Cadenus and Vanessa" in the first few months of his acquaintance with Pope. This does not prove that he had the *Rape of the Lock* in mind as he wrote, but it increases the plausibility of it.

The revised five-canto version of *Rape of the Lock*, with its prefatory dedication to Arabella Fermor, was published in March 1714. By April 1716 Pope was at work on a new poem which resembled Swift's in dealing with the case of another young woman who fell in love with her tutor – "Eloisa to Abelard."[103] One year later Pope made a final addition to *Rape of the Lock*, inserting a speech by Clarissa, a parody, as his note pointed out, "of the Speech of Sarpedon to Glaucus in Homer." Meanwhile, "Cadenus and Vanessa" remained unpublished. No evidence survives to prove that Swift showed it or sent it to Pope in this form, though that remains possible. It began to circulate in manuscript form in 1723, and appeared in print for the first time in an unauthorized edition in 1726. Two years later it was included in the third volume of the Pope–Swift *Miscellanies*.[104] Pope clearly regarded it as a major poem: his role in preparing the poem – arranging for it to be the lead piece in the volume, and correcting errors in the unauthorized 1726 edition – constitutes a kind of editorial "reply."[105]

To what extent might we regard "Cadenus and Vanessa" as a reply to *The Rape of the Lock*? As Rogers notes, there are in Swift's poem "signs of

---

[101] A proposal to write "An Account of the Works of the Unlearned" – probably by Pope – had appeared anonymously in *Spectator* 457 (August 14, 1712). According to an anecdote in Goldsmith's *Life of Parnell* (1770), at some point before the revisions were completed, Parnell overheard Pope reading the poem to Swift and later translated a part of it into Latin. (Rawson and Lock, *Collected Poems of Thomas Parnell* [1989], p. 494, regard the story as "apocryphal," but they seem to refer to the reported origin of Parnell's translation.)

[102] Cf. a letter to Gay a few days earlier (August 23) in which he passes on the same report (1, 187).

[103] See the letter from Pope to Martha Blount (Sherburn 1956: 1, 338).

[104] In the 1726 edition some lines from the manuscript were omitted.

[105] Sherburn (1956: 11, 438 and n.) In the end Pope decided to include his own "Peri Bathous" in the volume, and make it the lead piece. *Cadenus and Vanessa* follows, the first item in a section headed "Miscellanies in Verse."

a pervasive debt to *The Rape of the Lock*" (1983: 658). To begin with, there are a number of verbal echoes. Near the opening of Swift's poem it is only a "brute in human shape" who can

> Engross the fancies of the fair,
> The few soft moments they can spare,
> From visits to receive and pay;
> From scandal, politics, and play,
> From fans and flounces, and brocades,
> From equipage and park-parades;
> From all the thousand female toys,
> From every trifle that employs
> The out or inside of their heads,
> Between their toilets and their beds. (41–50)

The "female toys" (47) recall the "toyshop" of the female heart at *Rape of the Lock*, 1.100, and, as Rogers suggests (1983: 659) the language of the entire passage is "sharply reminiscent" of *Rape of the Lock*. He is thinking, no doubt, of Belinda, preeminent of "the Fair" (1.40), passing from bed to toilet table; of "her new Brocade" (2.107) and the "Visits" ladies pay (3.167); of Ariel's invocation of the delights of an "Equipage" (1.45). Although Rogers doesn't make the point, of these details only the last is found in the first edition of Pope's poem, which suggests that Swift had access to a draft of Pope's revised version, perhaps in the autumn of 1713. Other apparent borrowings or allusions confirm the suggestion. Like Pope's fashionable women, Swift's air themselves in a coach ride in Hyde Park's "Ring" (l.385; cf. *Rape*, 1.44) and play at "Ombre" (l.435; cf. *Rape*, canto 3). By comparison, Vanessa "neither was coquette nor prude" (497), terms Swift need not have borrowed from *Rape of the Lock*, although he may have remembered their linkage as "graver Prude" and "light Coquettes" in *Rape*, 1.63–65. (Again, all the borrowed details are found in the 1714 *Rape* but not the 1712.)[106]

But Swift, if he was in effect replying to Pope's *Rape*, chose not just to echo but to re-write with a difference. For his celestial machinery, Swift reverts to a Homeric model – a dispute between Pallas and Venus – in place

---

[106] Other borrowed details are found in the first edition: "The murders of her eyes" (line 333), which Swift labels as mere "cant of stupid lies," recalls the "Murders of your Eye" (*Rape*, v, 145; and ii, 187 in the 1712 edition) – which Pope had deployed as at least half a compliment. When Swift finds it "Strange, that a Nymph by *Pallas* nurst, / In Love should make Advances first" (lines following 539 in three 1726 editions, and omitted in the 1727 Pope–Swift *Miscellanies*), he may allude to Pope's "strange Motive" that could "compel / A well-bred *Lord* t'assault a gentle *Belle*" (1.6–7 in the 1712 edition), or even to Belinda's aggressiveness in the game of ombre.

of Pope's diminutive Rosicrucian spirits. His heroine, Vanessa, is a woman "of wit and sense" (865), with no personal vanity or care for her toilette and clothes, quite the opposite of Belinda the coquette. Unlike Belinda, who conceals her passion for the Baron, Vanessa proclaims hers. Does Swift hint that Pope's gentle satire of "Female Errors" is too simple? If the *Rape* implies that the course of love would run smoothly to its natural end if only women would behave sensibly, Swift perhaps suggests that, in the world as it is, even a sensible woman like Vanessa will find herself without an appropriate lover. Like Belinda, she is offered unsolicited advice from those who think themselves wiser in the ways of love: each of Belinda's several advisors – Ariel, Thalestris, and even the Baron – offers unsolicited advice, and (although Pope appears to take some devious delight in speaking through them to Belinda) sets off, or sets up, the final bit of advice, offered by Pope in his own voice: "Then cease, bright Nymph! To mourn thy ravish'd Hair ..." (5.141ff.). If her first advisors are in one way or another self-interested, Pope presents himself as Belinda's disinterested but concerned admirer and rescuer: his advice is authorized by the poem. By contrast, none of Vanessa's advisors – from the "fashionable fops" who encourage her to gossip and the "glitt'ring Dames" who tell her how to dress, to her chief advisor, Cadenus himself, the stand-in for the author – is authorized by the poem: Cadenus is just as compromised by his own interests as the fops and nymphs. Some would say that Pope too hints that he has his own interests – in writing a poem ("*This Lock*") that will outlast any lock from Belinda's head and will advance his own "Name," "Fame," and career – but in effect insists that this does not compromise his advice. By undermining the advice that even Cadenus gives, Swift (to borrow a term from Ellen Pollak 1985) exposes as mere convention the "sexual myth" of male superiority and female passive beauty that Pope implicitly endorses.

Swift's poem remained unpublished until 1726, reportedly given only to Vanessa herself. But one wonders whether Swift also took his new friend Pope into his confidence, showing him, as early as the autumn of 1713 or somewhat later, a draft of "Cadenus and Vanessa." When Pope made another revision to *Rape of the Lock* – adding Clarissa's famous speech – for inclusion in his 1717 *Works* – did he have Swift's poem in mind? As noted, Pope was at work in 1716–17 on "Eloisa to Abelard," a poem that may well have put him in mind of Swift's Vanessa.[107] The evidence that

---

[107] "Eloisa to Abelard" is based primarily on John Hughes's 1713 translation of the letters of Héloise to Abelard. Ehrenpreis remarks casually that Vanessa and Cadenus were "the new Héloise and the new Abélard" (III, 313).

"Cadenus and Vanessa" helped to shape Clarissa's speech is skimpy. After all, the form of her advice to Belinda is based primarily on Sarpedon's speech to Glaucus in Homer, and the matter is an updated and somewhat worldly version of the standard wisdom of centuries of moralists. But one might regard Clarissa as a kind of Vanessa: she is an anomaly, the sole member of her sex who thinks sensibly, not surprisingly scorned by her fellow women as a prude. She also speaks in the language of Cadenus, who offers to Vanessa

> Friendship in its greatest Height,
> A constant, rational Delight,
> On Virtue's Basis fix'd to last,
> When Love's Allurements long are past. (780–83)

Clarissa's advice – urging Belinda to remember the difference between what fades and what does not fade, to build on virtue rather than love so as not to arouse passion but to win respect and esteem – is not just compatible with that of Cadenus, but, when she reminds Belinda that "good Humour can prevail" and "Merit wins the Soul" (5.31, 34), echoes that of Vanessa (herself an echo of Cadenus) when she parrots his lesson that "'Tis Merit must with her prevail" (753).

If Pope, as it was once common to argue, put "the moral of the poem" in Clarissa's mouth,[108] he may in his 1717 version have been continuing a dialogue with Swift, insisting that a poem can offer authoritative advice to women, reaffirming the difference that Swift recognized between the 1714 *Rape* and his own "Cadenus and Vanessa," in which he pointedly undermined Vanessa's advisors. But if, as has become increasingly common, it is argued that Pope invites us to regard Clarissa as just another interested party, whose advice is to be taken with a grain of salt, then we might say that, in his continuing dialogue with Swift, Pope was in 1717 conceding Swift's points that any advice in matters of love is likely to be partial and that a poem might be more effective and piquant if it preserved a degree of equivocation and ambiguity.

The dialogue may not have ended there. If, as has recently been argued, the famously inconclusive conclusion to Swift's poem (the ten lines beginning "But what Success *Vanessa* met …") were not written until 1719–20 or even as late as 1726,[109] Swift in drafting them would have had the

---

[108] Critics making this argument relied heavily on an addition to Pope's note to her speech that first appeared in Warburton's 1751 edition: "to open more clearly the MORAL of the poem." This addition may have no Popean authority.

[109] Fischer (2003: 296–301).

opportunity to react to Pope's 1717 additions to *Rape of the Lock*. And if Swift regarded Pope's ending as equivocal, perhaps he determined to match it, or even outdo it, by his ten-line addition:

> But what Success *Vanessa* met,
> Is to the World a Secret yet:
> Whether the Nymph, to please her Swain,
> Talks in a high romantick Strain;
> Or whether her at last descends
> To act with less Seraphick Ends;
> Or, to compound the Business, whether
> They temper Love and Books together;
> Must never to Mankind be told,
> Nor shall the conscious Muse unfold. (818–27)

While Pope's "Muse" (5.123) resolves speculation about the location of the missing "Lock" by declaring that it is now found in the heavens as a new star, Swift's "conscious Muse" knows but refuses to say how his story ends.[110]

SCRIBLERIAN PROJECTS

By the time Swift was at work on *Cadenus and Vanessa* and Pope was at work on the revisions to *Rape of the Locke*, the two writers had been introduced, and the famous "Scriblerus Club" may have begun to meet. The first documented meeting is not until March 20, 1714, but it appears that the group gathered earlier in the year, and probably as early as September 1713. While Swift was still in London, both he and Pope attended meetings of the Club, as shown by the verse invitations to Oxford on which they collaborated in the months of March and April 1714. By June 5, according to an invitation written in Pope's hand, Swift "had run from us in manner uncivil" – i.e., had departed for the country, and then for Ireland. Pope wrote to Swift on June 18, 1714, expressing hopes that Arbuthnot is right in thinking Swift has retired to Berkshire "to attend at full leisure to the life and adventures of Scriblerus" (Woolley 1999–2007: 1, 620). Swift remained in touch with fellow Scriblerians by letter, but seems to have contributed little thereafter to their joint projects. Pope continued to be engaged, and according to a June 26, 1714 letter from Arbuthnot to Swift "has been collecting high flights of poetry, which are very good; they are

---

[110] The dialogue continued. As Ehrenpreis suggests (1962–83: III, 607), Swift's "Journal of a Modern Lady" (1734) "may be read as a reply to *Rape*, for the Dame is a kind of Belinda-after-marriage," and Pope's "Epistle to a Lady" was in turn "influenced" by Swift's "Journal."

to be solemn nonsense."[111] Pope's collection very probably included specimens – from Blackmore, Dennis, Tickell, Ambrose Philips, and others – that eventually appeared in *Peri Bathous* (1728). Among the lines held up to mockery in *Peri Bathous* were a few written by the youthful Pope himself (though he took care to mark them as by "Anon.").[112] One wonders if the 1714 collection might have included lines from Swift's youthful Pindaric odes, perhaps the lines that prompted Dryden to remark, "Cousin Swift, you will never be a poet."

One of the earliest projects discussed was probably the "Works of the Unlearned," which has left almost no trace, though it may have indirectly contributed later to Pope's send-up of bad writing in *Peri Bathous*.[113] It seems soon to have grown into the related project of writing the "Memoirs" of one "Martinus Scriblerus," who had the misfortune of misapplying what mental and literary talents he had in everything he did. As Pope was later to tell Spence, Martinus was imagined to be "a man of capacity enough; that had dipped into every art and science, but injudiciously in each." The *Memoirs* were not to appear in print for many years, and much draft material may have been abandoned along the way.[114] It has not been possible for critics to agree about which portions may have been contributed by Pope, which by Swift, and which by the other Scriblerians, notably Arbuthnot, who is usually credited with the portions having to do with natural philosophy and medicine. Since Pope (unlike Swift) was never to produce much narrative prose satire, or to evince much taste for Cervantesque or Rabelaisian narrative, it is commonly assumed that the narrative of Martin's adventures must have been written primarily by Swift and Arbuthnot.[115] (It is striking, even a bit shocking, to read Swift's own dismissive comment to Arbuthnot in July 1714 – that Pope "who first

---

[111] Woolley (1999–2007: 1, 625–26). In his June 18, letter, Pope told Swift that the "top of my own ambition is to contribute to that great [i.e., Scriblerian] work" (1, 620–21).

[112] Ault (1954: 20–23) (with the authority of Spence, Warton, Warburton, and Ruffhead) includes in his edition of Pope's *Minor Poems* twenty-three lines in seven extracts from Pope's early verse that he published in *Peri Bathous*.

[113] When he left for Ireland Swift gave Pope a 1543 Greek and Latin New Testament, in the text established by Erasmus. Mack conjectures that there might have been an exchange of gifts, and that it was at this time that Pope gave Swift a 1543 edition of *Epistolae obscurorum virorum*, a famous humanist satire on scholastic theologians (1982: 311). Swift's gift was suitable for both an Anglican and a Catholic; Pope's (also linked to Erasmus) for fellow connoisseurs of the "Works of the Unlearned." Pope appropriates the title of Swift's book in his "Advertisement" for the *New Dunciad* (Rumbold 1999: 374).

[114] Pope left instructions that some of the Scriblerian papers were "to be burned" – apparently because they were judged unworthy to see the light (Osborn 1966: 1, 58).

[115] This is Kerby-Miller's conclusion (1950: 71).

thought of the Hint has no Genius at all to it, in my mind.")[116] However, it bears repeating that Pope had been experimenting with prose satire in his mock-journalistic reports on the misfortunes that had allegedly befallen both Dennis and Curll, and went on to write much of Martinus's commentary and notes on the *Dunciad*, and thus may have had more of a hand in the story of Martin than he is given credit for.

One Scriblerian piece to which Pope made some contribution, as suggested by surviving fragments in his hand from 1716 to 1717, is the famous "Double Mistress" episode.[117] His fellow collaborator is usually thought to have been Arbuthnot rather than Swift, who after 1714 was in Ireland and had shown less interest than the other Scriblerians in the "Memoirs." The bizarre tale of Lindamira and Indamora has led some critics to think that its authors were playing out some of the implications of contemporary notions of personal identity.[118] Pope would later go on to write verse essays about the "characters" of men and women, and to show particular interest in identifying a principle of personal identity – the "ruling passion" – and in confronting irresolvable inconsistencies.[119] Thus it does not seem implausible that he would have delighted in exploring how the Siamese twins might be two or one. It also seems apt that a tale of a composite body with two heads (and two distinct "Organs of Generation") was composed by a composite of at least two generative authors.

In the light of their nearly lifelong literary conversation, the Pope–Swift collaborations and interchanges that arose during the few months in which the Scriblerus Club met are surprisingly thin. If, as I have suggested, the colloquy between them had already begun, as each writer began to write with at least one eye on what his opposite number was writing or had written, then the verse invitations and even the first steps toward the *Memoirs of Martinus Scriblerus* are disappointing in their quantity and quality. It has become a critical commonplace to suggest that the real importance of the Scriblerus Club was not in the collaborative productions planned in its first year but in the riper fruits that appeared much later: both *Gulliver's Travels* and *The Dunciad*, it is argued, sprang from seeds planted during the few months in 1713 and 1714. Such claims can be traced to Pope, who told Joseph Spence in about

---

[116] Woolley (1999–2007: I, 630).   [117] Chapter 14, in Kerby-Miller (1950: 143–53).

[118] See Christopher Fox, *Identity and Consciousness: Locke and the Scriblerians in Early Eighteenth-Century Britain* (1989).

[119] Cf. a fragment of the Double Mistress episode in Pope's hand – referring to the "eddy of passion" by which one of the mistresses is driven – with "Quick whirls, and shifting eddies, of our minds" ("Epistle to Cobham," line 30).

1730 that Swift "took his first hints for *Gulliver*" from the "Memoirs." But it is doubtful that chapter 16 of the *Memoirs*, dealing with the "Travels" of Scriblerus, was the real seed for *Gulliver's Travels*. Pope was not a disinterested witness, and the author of *Tale of a Tub* did not need "the works of the unlearned" to write about the abuses of learning in the "Voyage to Laputa." Pope's own "Peri Bathous" (1728) might appropriately be called "Scriblerian" in origin and character, but the *Dunciad Variorum* (1729), in which Martinus Scriblerus appears as a commentator, astonishingly transcends any Scriblerian origins. When Pope edited and published the *Memoirs of Martinus Scriblerus* he in effect retrospectively established – or invented – the importance of the Club. As has recently been argued, the "Myth of Scriblerus" was in many respects a twentieth-century invention.[120] For my purposes, the most important thing to be established in the meetings of the Club was the friendship of Swift and Pope, and their readiness to correspond and collaborate, especially in the decade of the 1720s. And it is in those writings of those years that we can next trace the ongoing literary conversation.

[120] For a telling critique of overstated claims about the Club, see Ashley Marshall, "The Myth Of Scriblerus," *British Journal for Eighteenth-Century Studies* 31, 1 (2008), 77–99.

CHAPTER 2

"Drive the world before them"

"EODEM TERTIO'S"

After Swift left London in 1714 he and Pope did not see each other for nearly twelve years. And they were both preoccupied with separate matters: Swift deep in church and Irish politics, and worried about his health; Pope translating Homer, editing the poems of Parnell and Sheffield, and preparing the 1717 edition of his own *Works*. They managed to keep in touch by means of occasional letters. Although relatively few of those letters have survived – only four for the period July 1714 to July 1722 – and Swift apologizes "for seldom writing" (Woolley 1999–2007: II, 178), it seems likely that they maintained a steady if infrequent correspondence, and that some of their letters have been lost.[1] The most substantial of the surviving letters – dated by Swift January 10, 1721 – was apparently not sent. Begun, in Woolley's view, as a pamphlet of self-justification – a public review of his conduct and a defense of his political and religious principles (in a nutshell, a Whig in politics and a Tory in religion) in response to misrepresentations, it was perhaps designed as a public letter only nominally addressed to Pope, and many years later reframed as a private letter.[2] Because Pope did not see the "letter" until 1737 at the earliest, we cannot regard it as part of their "conversation" in the early 1720s. We can perhaps conclude that Swift at that time felt close enough to Pope, both personally and politically, to address the pamphlet to him. Why he did not publish the pamphlet, or send it as a private letter until much later, remains an unanswered question.

---

[1] In an August 1723 letter, for example, Pope refers to "a rebuke in a late Letter of yrs" (Woolley 1999–2007: II, 461), but the letter to which he refers is missing – unless, as Woolley thinks, Pope is referring to Swift's January 8, 1723 letter to Gay. In the same letter Pope notes that there has been "long silence" (463) on both sides.
[2] See Woolley (1999–2007: II, 354–62 and long headnote).

To some extent Swift and Pope kept in touch by means of mutual friends – "eodem tertio's," as Swift called them (Woolley 1999–2007: II, 470). Among these were old friends Arbuthnot, Congreve, Charles Ford, and Gay, to whom both Swift and Pope were writing.[3] It was probably Ford who, more than anyone, was asked to pass on remembrances.[4] Because he remained in England while Swift was exiled to Ireland, Pope, as he put it later, in effect inherited a number of Swift's titled friends: "all my friends of a later date" – and he names Oxford, Harcourt, Harley, and Bolingbroke – "were such as were Yours before … we have never met these many Years wthout mention of You" (II, 462).

Swift and Pope also kept each other in their sights through several literary projects. In the late summer or early autumn of 1716 Pope wrote a little pamphlet entitled *God's Revenge Against Punning*, with an insider allusion to Gay's recent fall from a horse.[5] Published on November 7, 1716, it quickly drew fire. Among the respondents was Swift, who immediately drafted a *Modest Defence of Punning*, dating it November 8 and capping the allusion to Gay's fall.[6] For some reason Swift withheld it from publication, perhaps, as Davis speculates (1939–68: IV, xxxiv), because he did not at first know that *God's Revenge* was Pope's, and upon discovering it chose not to "answer" his friend, or perhaps because he concluded the mini-controversy had by then played itself out. It is odd that Swift seems to have written nothing to Pope privately, though perhaps he did so in a letter that has not survived.

In the following year Swift was drawn into Pope's famous quarrel with Addison. Pope and Addison had fallen out over the merits of Pope's *Iliad* – when Addison publicly commended the rival version by Thomas Tickell – and in 1717 Pope privately sent to Addison a satiric character sketch – what proved to be the first draft of his later character of "Atticus" in the *Epistle to Dr. Arbuthnot* – but withheld it from publication. Although surviving reports conflict, what Mack calls a "suspension of hostilities" followed (1985: 282).[7] Swift, who remained on cordial terms

---

[3] Arbuthnot to Swift, December 11, 1718: "I would fain have Pope gett a patent for life for the place [of Poet Laureate]" (Woolley 1999–2007: II, 282).
[4] January 6, 1719, Swift to Ford: "Pray tell Mr. Pope that I will never be angry with him for any mark of his kindness." In other letters to Ford: "present my service to Pope": February 16, 1719, April 15, 1721, January 19, 1724.
[5] Printed in Ault (1936: 269–72).
[6] Printed in Davis (1939–68: IV, 205–10). It was one of the very few pieces of writing – apart from letters – that Swift did from 1714 until 1719.
[7] Pope later said that, after receiving the sketch, Addison "used me very civilly ever after" (Osborn 1966: I, 71–72). But William Ayre later claimed that the reconciliation failed (*Memoirs of the Life and Writings of Alexander Pope*, 2 vols. [1745], I, 100–02).

with Addison, may have played a role. Oxford saw Pope's character of Addison (Ault 1949: 112), and perhaps mentioned it to Swift. Years later Swift claimed, in a manuscript note identifying "Atticus" in the *Epistle to Dr. Arbuthnot* as Addison, that "he and Pope were at last [rec]onciled by my Advice."[8] It is not known just how Swift might at a distance have effected the reconciliation before Addison's death in 1719, whether it was by advice to Pope to withhold publication of the character or to mollify Addison some other way (Pope would later write and publish a complimentary epistle addressed to Addison) or by urging Addison to preserve his famous sang-froid.

Parnell, who died in 1718 and was a friend of both Swift and Pope, proved to be another bridging figure. In a 1717 letter to Parnell, Pope urged him to acquaint Swift "with all that esteem, affection, and remembrance, which there is no putting upon paper, and which can only be felt in the heart" (Sherburn 1956: I, 416). In 1719 Swift wrote to Ford suggesting that Pope ought to write a poem in Parnell's memory (Woolley 1999–2007: II, 288). Pope in time resolved to edit Parnell's poems, and in his edition effected an alliance with Swift by producing the poem that Swift had requested, taking the form of a dedicatory epistle to yet another mutual friend, Oxford. In that poem Pope commends Oxford in terms that reflected Swift's own view: "Above all Pain, all Passion, and all Pride, / The Rage of Pow'r, the Blast of publick Breath, / The Lust of Lucre ..." (24–26). Pope also found a way to bring Swift himself into the poem, and to link him with Parnell: it was "For *Swift* and him [i.e., Parnell]" that Oxford "despis'd the Farce of State" (9).

Pope and Swift also shared strong friendships with Francis Atterbury, Bishop of Rochester, and it was in the context of the so-called "Atterbury Plot" of 1722–23 that Pope and Swift resumed a regular correspondence. Their responses to the Atterbury case serve to affirm both what they shared and what distinguished them in these years.

Both Swift and Pope had been exchanging letters with Atterbury since 1716. Pope typically wrote on literary topics (including a second version of his character of Addison, which Atterbury admired) and the attractions of a retired life. In one letter he perhaps signaled that he had no interest in politics or in considering a conversion to Anglicanism (which Atterbury, like Swift before him, had proposed): "Contemplative life is not only my scene, but it is my habit too ... In my politicks, I think no further than

---

[8] In the presentation copy, now in the Berg Collection of the New York Public Library, of Pope's 1735 *Works* (see Illustration 4.3 below, p. 195). Swift's annotations have been very little remarked.

how to preserve the peace of my life, in any government under which I live; nor in my religion, than to preserve the peace of my conscience in any Church with which I communicate" (Sherburn 1956: 1, 454).[9] By contrast, Swift wrote to Atterbury about politics – in 1716, for example, with bitter irony about a bill to suspend habeas corpus which effected "fellowship of *slavery*" between England and Ireland. Later letters convey his worries about their mutual friend, the exiled Bolingbroke; his indignation at the appointment of unworthy men to bishoprics; and his resentment at the Whig government's treatment of Tories after 1714.

One topic which attracted the attention of all three men was the feverish speculation in South Sea Company stock in 1720, and the bursting of the Bubble in August and September of that year. Both Swift and Pope were caught up in the national frenzy and, as stockholders, suffered losses. As he reflected on the matter, Pope saw it as evidence of national folly. He wrote to Atterbury of the "universal deluge of the South Sea" (September 23, 1720). Swift, by contrast, though he first saw it as a "Mystery" and a "Frolick" (April 4, 1720, to Charles Ford), was soon (in an October 1720 letter to Esther Vanhomrigh) reporting talk of the "Ruin of the Kingdom" (Woolley 1999–2007: 11, 361). And when the bubble burst and it became clear that insiders had bid up the price of the stock and men in high places had walked away rich, Swift saw evidence of something worse than folly. In January 1721 he published a poem on "The Bubble" in which the directors of the South Sea Company emerge as the villains:

> As Fishes on each other prey
> The great ones swall'wing up the small
> So fares it in the *Southern* Sea
> But Whale *Directors* eat up all.
> When *Stock* is high they come between,
> Making by second hand their Offers,
> Then cunningly retire unseen,
> With each a Million in his Coffers. (Williams 1958: 1, 253)

And in early 1723 he wrote for Charles Ford a bitter birthday poem (not published in his lifetime) in which he pointed the finger not just at directors but at their political allies in government. If Ford were to go to London, he says, would it not arouse his "Passion"

---

[9] Mack (1985: 338) thinks this statement "the closest thing to a program of political and religious principles" that Pope ever made, but one wonders whether there was an element of rhetorical posturing and even careful political positioning (as in Swift's 1721 self-justifying pamphlet), should the letter ever be published, as it was in Pope's own edition in 1737.

To see a Scoundrel Strut and hector,
A Foot-boy to some Rogue Director?
To look on Vice triumphant round,
And Virtue trampled on the Ground. (1, 312)

It would be fifteen years before Pope (who apparently saw the lines in manuscript) wrote anything equally outspoken. Rogers calls this "one of Swift's most openly anti-Hanoverian poems to date," and compares it with the ending of the first Dialogue of Pope's *Epilogue to the Satires* (1, 137–70), which he calls "an amplification of Swift's couplet" (1983: 726–27). Ehrenpreis (1962–83: III, 372) compares it with the allegorical opening of the fourth book of the *Dunciad*.

The scandal over the bursting of the South Sea Bubble played a part in the famous "Atterbury Plot" of 1722–23. Jacobites saw an opportunity to exploit public discontent with evidence of corruption at highest levels. The Whig government tried to divert attention by ginning up evidence of a dangerous foreign-supported plot. Swift observed bitterly from a distance, but Pope was himself caught up in the affair. Twenty-two Pope–Atterbury letters from the period 1721–22 survive, fully eighteen of them from Atterbury, all on purely literary topics, enough to make Sherburn (1956: II, 93n) suspect that Atterbury – guilty, as is now clear, of treasonous correspondence with the Pretender – was generating a smoke screen, creating the impression that all of his time was taken up with innocent literary matters. After he was arrested in August 1722 and summoned to trial for treason in May 1723, Atterbury asked Pope to testify on his behalf, again apparently to confirm that in all of their dealings Pope never heard anything about Jacobite conspiracy. Pope agreed to bear "testimony of the truth in your behalf" (April 20, 1723), and nervously testified on May 7, later telling Spence that he committed several "blunders" (Osborn 1966: I, 102). Biographers have divided over Pope's knowledge of Atterbury's political activities. Mack (1945: 122) concludes that Pope at the time thought him innocent, though Cruickshanks and Erskine-Hill, in their recent study of the "Plot," suspect that Pope had "suspicions, even possibly inside knowledge" (2004: 211). Pope's letters before and after the trial convey his strong sympathy with Atterbury's suffering – Pope was worried that, as a Catholic, he himself would fall under suspicion – and in effect personalize the event, emphasizing how it affects him. In a letter to Carteret in February 1723 he deplores the loss of his friend, and affirms his own desire to be "quiet" (Sherburn 1956: II, 159–60). After Atterbury's conviction and exile, Pope wrote to Swift in August 1723 that "'Tis sure my particular ill fate, that all those I have most lov'd & with whom I have most liv'd" – he had in mind Atterbury, Bolingbroke, and Swift – "must be banish'd" (Woolley 1999–2007: ii, 462).

By contrast, Swift's reaction to the Atterbury Plot is angry. No letters between Atterbury and Swift later than 1717 have survived, but Swift followed events closely and replied to Pope's August 1723 letter by both agreeing with his sentiments about "banish'd" friends and sharpening the language to mark a difference between himself and his correspondent. He has often "made the same remark with you of my Infelicity" – a drily ironic reply to Pope's self-pitying "ill fate" – in "being strongly attached to Traytors (as they call them) and Exiles, and State Criminalls." By simultaneously citing and distancing himself from the condemnatory language of state trials, Swift confronts the political rather than the personal dimension of the affair. That is the world one must live in, and he has no faith, he tells Pope, "in you pretenders to retirement" (Woolley 1999–2007: ii, 468–69). About the same time Swift was completing work on *Gulliver's Travels*, where his response to the Atterbury trial is bitterly satiric, particularly in the famous review of the methods of detection of "Plots and Conspiracies" in the third voyage. Edward Rosenheim finds a number of open and veiled allusions to the Atterbury case through the *Travels*. In his view, Swift's response focuses not as Pope's did on Atterbury's innocence and suffering – indeed, Swift "left little indication of belief in the Bishop's actual innocence" and evinces no "profound dismay at his sufferings" (1970: 188–89) – but on tyranny and abuse of power, especially the use of informers and the manufacturing of "evidence."

LETTERS, 1723–1725

The major consequence of the Atterbury case for Swift and Pope was that it helped to bring on the resumption of a more regular correspondence between them. Pope's long letter to Swift in August 1723, just after Atterbury went into exile, was prompted by an exchange between Swift and Gay the previous winter, in which Gay reported that Pope had read over his letter before Gay sent it, and Swift grumblingly replied that Pope was apparently too "lazy" to add a few lines of his own (Woolley 1999–2007: ii, 438, 442). The subsequent exile of Atterbury must have helped Pope to think again about his other exiled friend in Ireland. In the August 1723 letter Pope professed that his greatest pleasure is one he had "learnd f[ro]m you" – "both how to gain, & how to use the Freedomes of Friendship with Men much my Superiors."[10] (Swift had claimed such freedoms, but had occasionally regarded his claims with some irony.) There are some signs that Pope thinks himself changed from the man Swift knew in London: he tells Swift in somewhat stiffly sententious language that in recent years he has led a life "infinitely more various & dissipated than when You knew me, among all Sexes, Parties & Professions," but also that the "merry vein you knew me in, is sunk into a Turn of Reflexion, that has made the world pretty indifferent to me … Aversions I have none but to Knaves, (f[or] Fools I have learn'd to bear wth) & those I cannot be commonly Civil to" (462).[11] But in other respects Pope signals to Swift that he is the same man. Perhaps remembering his own nonpartisan public stance in their time together in London, and Swift's support of the Tory ministers, Pope says that receiving "Civilities" from "Opposite Sets of People [i.e., both Whigs and Tories]" has led him to avoid "being either violent or sower to any Party." He suspects that an excess of busyness will soon "throw me again into Study & Retirement." (As noted earlier, Johnson thought that Pope was only pretending "discontent" with the world, and that he had learned "some part" of this discontent from Swift.)[12]

Swift, in reply about a month later, after rallying Pope's pretensions to retirement, goes on to tease Pope that he deserves no credit for steering clear of party rage, since he is employed as a poet, "where Faction has nothing to do … you have no more to do with the Constitution of Church and State than a Christian at Constantinople, and you are so much the wiser, and the happier because both partyes will approve your Poetry as long as you are known to be of neither" (Woolley 1999–2007: II, 469). By contrast, Swift ironically notes that because he is "sunk under the prejudices of another Education" he fears reprisals from "those in Power."

Hammond has suggested in a discussion of Swift's reading and his oppositional marginalia that "Swift read adversarially" (2003: 137). This reading practice seems to have extended to letters. What begins to emerge from their letters, through the good-natured raillery, is a determination

---

[10] Woolley (1999–2007: II, 462). In a 1721 letter Swift had boasted to Pope that he had "conversed in some freedom with more Ministers of State of all Parties than usually happens to men of my level" (II, 358). Johnson thought both Swift and Pope were fooling themselves, and were in effect paying a "servile tribute" to their aristocratic friends (Lonsdale 2006: III, 197).

[11] Pope disingenuously claims to have no "Enemies, but who were also strangers to me," and, "Whatever they writ or said I never retaliated" (Woolley 1999–2007: II, 463), concealing, even from Swift, the fact that his satirical portrait of Addison had appeared in print the previous year.

[12] Lonsdale (2006: IV, 60).

on Swift's part to define himself almost systematically as Pope's opposite. You are a poet, but I am a man of politics. You avoid party, but I
have made a choice. "I can never arrive at the Serenity of Mind you profess" (Woolley 1999–2007: II, 469) – Pope had earlier written that he had
acquired "a Quietness of Mind" (II, 462). Pope prefers fools to knaves,
but Swift "can tolerate knaves much better than Fools because their knav-
ery does me no hurt." As to friendship, "Your Notions of Friendship are
new to me." (Pope had remarked that "My Friendships are increas'd by
new ones, yet no part of the warmth I felt for the old is diminish'd,"[13]
and Swift replies that "I believe every man is born with his quantum [of
friendship], and he can not give to one without Robbing another.")[14] Still,
for all their differences, one does not doubt that Swift regards Pope as
a fellow "Man of Genius," and an ally in the ongoing battle with "the
world": "I have often endeavoured to establish a Friendship among all
Men of Genius, and would fain have it done. They are seldom above three
or four Cotemporaries and if they could be united would drive the world
before them" (II, 469). This is the earliest instance of that sense of superiority to their contemporaries that Johnson found so offensive. Swift's
language is characteristically aggressive – "drive the world before them"
(and "drive" was a more powerful verb then than it is now) – as if "the
world" were nothing more than a herd of beasts to be expelled with force
or compelled to submit to superior power.

What is also noteworthy in these two letters between fellow writers is
what is *not* said: neither Pope nor Swift gives a hint about what he is writing.
In 1723 Pope was still engaged on his ten years' labor of translating Homer,
but declines to mention it, perhaps because he knew that Swift thought he
was wasting his time.[15] By the same token Swift provides no details about
his role in Irish politics, again perhaps because he knew that Pope thought
he too was misapplying his talents. What is odd, however, is that Swift, by
then engaged for a couple of years on *Gulliver's Travels*, gives no hint that
he is writing on anything more than "the most Trifling Subjects."[16] What
made Swift – who told Ford about the project as early as 1721 – hold back
from making confidences in an intimate ally?[17] Perhaps it was his reluctance

---

[13] Woolley (1999–2007: II, 462).   [14] Woolley (1999–2007: II, 469).
[15] In a letter to Pope two years later (July 19, 1725), Swift joins Oxford in lamenting that Pope,
    obliged to translate for money, was not able to follow "your own Genius" (Woolley 1999–2007: II,
    576). Nor does Pope mention the editions of Buckinghamshire and Shakespeare.
[16] September 23, 1723 (Woolley 1999–2007: II, 470). By January 1724 Swift had completed the
    "Voyage to the Houyhnhnms" and was at work on what would become the third voyage.
[17] In April 1721 he let Charles Ford know that he was "writing a History of my Travells, which …
    gives Account of Countryes hitherto unknown" (Woolley 1999–2007: II, 372).

to speak of the *Travels* to a fellow writer until he had made more progress, perhaps a fear – expressed in later correspondence – that his letters were being opened by government spies at the post office. But did his reluctance have anything to do with his lack of full confidence in Pope?

A series of letters in 1725 suggests that Swift and Pope continued to regard each other as intimate friends and yet defined their relationship as a kind of opposition.[18] In a letter of September 14, 1725 Pope, as I have already noted, suggested that it would be a pleasure, after long absence, to meet again not "to vex our own hearts with busy vanities... but to divert ourselves, and the world too if it pleases" (Woolley 1999–2007: II, 597); and Swift (taking up Pope's language) replied two weeks later to declare that it would be his delight, contrary to Pope's, to "vex the world rather then divert it." What needs noting here is that Pope's letter had likewise taken up and replied to an idea in a previous letter from Swift. When Pope imagines that "two or three of us may yet be gather'd together; not to plot, not to contrive silly schemes of ambition, or to vex ..." (II, 597), he is remembering Swift's letter of two years earlier, imagining that "three or four Cotemporaries" (II, 469), if united, could triumph over "the world." (Pope's alteration of the number, recalling as it does "where two or three are gathered together in my name" from Matthew 18.20, pointedly insists on the innocence of his kind of gathering.) What in Swift is violent superiority turns in Pope's letter into innocent diversion. And when Pope shifts from future pleasures to present projects, he links his own work with Swift's, and yet wittily finds or constructs a difference: "Your Travels I hear much of; my own I promise you shall never more be in a strange land, but a diligent, I hope useful, investigation of my own Territories. I mean no more Translations, but something domestic, fit for my own country, and for my own time" (II, 597). This is the first mention of *Gulliver's Travels* in the surviving correspondence between Swift and Pope. (Perhaps Swift had finally mentioned it in a letter that has been lost.) But it is not unlikely that Pope knew of the *Travels* only through mutual friends, and that Swift, for whatever reason, continued to keep this work, despite its possible origins as a Scriblerian project, to himself. The turn from "Your Travels" to "my own" may simply be a piece of wit, as is the antithesis between the voyage to "a strange land" and an "investigation of my own Territories." Pope himself glosses "a strange land" as his translations of Homer, then nearing completion – he does not suggest

---

[18] Again, it is worth noting what Pope and Swift leave out of these letters: Swift says nothing about the series of *Drapier's Letters* that he had published from March to October 1724 (they were republished in Dublin as a set on October 2, 1725), Pope nothing about the published attacks on his Homer, or about the £200 he received from the government for it.

that he is yielding to Swift's advice to give up translation – and Warburton's note glosses the second (improbably) as the "Essay on Man."[19] But Pope's antithesis may also point to a difference between what would be published as *Travels into Several Remote Nations of the World* and his own *Dunciad*, a survey of the familiar and "domestic" London literary world, a tour or "progress" through his own "Territories."[20]

In his response two weeks later Swift, as noted, took the occasion to differ with Pope, preferring as he says to "vex" the world than to "divert" it. He went on, in an often-discussed passage, to declare that he had "ever hated all Nations professions and Communityes and all my love is towards individualls ... I hate and detest that animal called man, although I hartily love John, Peter, Thomas and so forth" (Woolley 1999–2007: II, 606–07). Man is rather an animal "rationis capax" than "rationale," and it is "upon this great foundation of Misanthropy ... the whole building of my Travells is erected" (II, 607). Pope is facetiously directed to "embrace" Swift's opinion immediately, and is quickly assumed to share it already ("nay I will hold a hundred pounds that you and I agree in the Point"). Two weeks later Pope declared that he in fact agreed: "I really enter as fully as you can desire, into your Principle, of Love [of] Individuals" (II, 613).

But unlike Swift he thinks of love as a widening circle, beginning with family and extending to encompass all mankind (an idea later developed in the third epistle of the *Essay on Man*), his notion of "Publick Spirit" founded on an underlying "Private one" (Woolley 1999–2007: II, 613). Developing the theme of difference within similarity, Pope at first imagines a future reunion in which they will meet "quite in peace, divested of our former passions, smiling at our own designs, and content to enjoy the Kingdome of the Just in Tranquillity": "But I find you would rather be employ'd as an Avenging Angel of wrath, to break your Vial of Indignation over the heads of the wretched pityful creatures of this World; nay would make them Eat your Book, which you have made as bitter a pill for them as possible" (II, 612 – see Illustration 2.1 below, p. 80).

Pope's purpose is difficult to decipher, and not only because of the highly metaphorical (and intertextual) language,[21] the patent exaggeration, and

---

[19] Pope does not seem to have seriously begun work on what would become the *Essay on Man* until 1729.

[20] In a letter to Swift just a month later, Pope mentions his work on "one of my Satyrs" – apparently an early draft of the *Dunciad* (Woolley 1999–2007: II, 612).

[21] Did Pope remember the language of violent force-feeding – "ram them down our throats," "cram this brass down our throats," "make us swallow his coin in fire-balls" – in Swift's fourth *Drapier's Letter* (1724)? Cf. also the "Vial" of indignation and spleen that Umbriel "breaks" over the head of Belinda (*Rape of the Lock*, IV, 85–86, 141–42).

2.1 Transcription for Earl of Oxford of October 15, 1725 Pope-to-Swift letter.

the biblical allusion. Pope playfully figures Swift as the retributive angel of Revelation (16.1), "pour[ing] out the vials of the wrath of God upon the earth" and instructing St. John to "eat" the little "book" he held in his hand, warning that "it shall make thy belly bitter" (10.9–10).[22] But while St. John *asks* the angel to *give* him the "little book," Swift "make[s]" his readers "eat." While the angel promises that, although bitter, the book will also be "sweet as honey," and will in effect prompt John's prophecy, Pope says nothing of sweetness. At one level he seems to be defining difference between himself and Swift, and deploring it, preferring that Swift, as a possible reunion approaches, get instead "into our Vortex" (Woolley 1999–2007: II, 611). But at another level Pope shows himself an acute reader of Swift, detecting or intuiting the hostile impulse within Swift to force-feed his reader with a bitter pill. In some sense Pope seems even to be encouraging Swift to continue on the path he has chosen – and that Pope helps to define – a path which would lead eventually to poems like "The Day of Judgment," in which an indignant God dismisses mankind as beneath his notice, and to Swift's own farewell to a life of *saeva indignatio* in his chilling epitaph.

In the final two letters in this extraordinary three-month epistolary sequence Swift continues to find grounds on which to distinguish himself from Pope, who pretends that they agree. Scholars have often quoted phrases from Swift's November 26 letter, but have not noted how those phrases erupt violently in the midst of routine "news," or how Swift seems to contradict himself – at one moment he wants to "Drown the World" and in the next declares that "I do not hate Mankind," at one moment adding that he is not content with "despising" the world and in the next imagining a "Hospital built for it's despisers, where one might act with safety" (Woolley 1999–2007: II, 623).[23] What may guide his shifting rhetoric is a determination to quarrel, if only playfully, with his correspondent. He mocks the language in Pope's October 15 letter as affectation ("To hear Boys like you talk of Milleniums and Tranquillity"), but then insists that his own advanced age has nothing to do with what he ironically calls his "Affection to the World": he claims his attitude has not varied since he was twenty-one years old.[24] He also quarrels with Pope's distinction between his own peaceful "content" and Swift's "wrath" and

---

[22] Cf. Ezekiel (2.8–33), who is commanded to "eat this book."

[23] The distinction between "hate" (to detest, abominate) and "despise" (to scorn, contemn, disrespect), now largely lost, was clear in Swift's day.

[24] Swift's irony was apparently missed by someone who inserted "dis" in pencil on the manuscript letter, and by Pope who in 1741 printed "Disaffection."

"indignation," declaring that "I do not hate Mankind, it is vous autr[e]s who hate them because you would have them reasonable Animals, and are Angry for being disappointed" (II, 623). Swift claims he has insulated himself from disappointment (and anger) by reducing his expectations – he seems again to be thinking of man as at best an animal "capable of reason." But he concedes taking pleasure in the contemplation of adversity and punishment: "I am no more angry with – – th[a]n I was with the Kite that last week flew away with one of my Chickins and yet I was pleas'd when one of my Servants Shot him two days after." This leads Swift to think of La Rochefoucauld, whom Pope had mentioned in his October 15 letter, reporting a plan to write a "Set of Maximes in opposition to all Rochefoucaults Principles" (II, 612). Swift gleefully pounces, serving notice that on this matter too they are "in opposition" – "Rochfoucault … is my Favorite because I found my whole character in him" (II, 623), and suggesting that what became *Verses on the Death of Dr. Swift* was already beginning to percolate in his mind. But he immediately turns to another project Popehad mentioned: "one of my Satyrs" (apparently the "Progress of Dulness," which would become *The Dunciad*) designed "to correct the Taste of the town in wit and Criticisme" (II, 612), of which Pope had quoted three lines on Ambrose Philips. Swift's reply is to warn Pope that personal satire may backfire: "Take care the bad poets do not outwit you, as they have served the good ones in every Age, whom they have provoked to transmit their Names to posterity" (II, 623–24).

   In his December 14 letter, the last in the sequence, and the last before Swift arrived in England in March 1726, Pope is full of good feeling, evidently in anticipation of Swift's visit. He professes to agree that it is best to ignore bad writers: "I am much the happier for finding (a better things than our *Witts*) our *Judgments* jump, in the notion of entirely passing all Scribblers by in silence" (Woolley 1999–2007: II, 625). And he goes on to agree with Swift on another point: "I wish as warmly as you, for the Hospital to lodge the *Despisers of the world* in," but (gently demurring) fears that the refuge would offer no safety: its inmates would already have been "dis-abled." This immediately leads Pope to contradict both himself and Swift: "I wou'd rather have those that out of such generous principles as you and I, despise it, Fly in its face, than Retire from it," and especially the "Pisspot[s]" and "*Potecaries Prentices*" of the world. He has comically argued himself into anger at "the little rogues," and pauses to remember Swift's original advice: "But I beg your pardon, I'm tame agen, at your advice" (II, 626). Like Swift's letter, Pope's gives him an opportunity, through this sustained colloquy, to explore his ambivalence about how to respond to the provokers of his contempt. It is as if the letter-writer is arguing with himself.

POPE AND *GULLIVER'S TRAVELS*

By August 1725 Swift had completed *Gulliver's Travels* and begun to tran-scribe them.[25] In March 1726 Swift was in England, where the *Travels* were to be published – anonymously, although not until late October, by which time Swift had returned to Dublin. During his four-month stay he visited a number of old friends, including Pope, whom he saw in late March in London, in early April at Twickenham, in late June and early July at Lord Burlington's in Chiswick, in London, and in Twickenham. A farewell dinner was held on August 3, but Pope was too ill to attend. Swift then spent a few days in London, including at least one meeting with Benjamin Motte to settle on publication terms, before bidding Pope goodbye in Twickenham on August 15. It has been suggested that Pope made some contribution to the August negotiations that led Motte to publish *Gulliver's Travels* on October 28,[26] but in December he told a friend that he did not see the book before its publication.[27] Why Swift never found the occasion, during their several days together, to show the manuscript to Pope has never been adequately explained.[28]

But Pope was keenly interested in the reception of the *Travels* and on November 16 wrote to Swift with a report that the book was *"publica trita manu"* – in effect being read to pieces (Woolley 1999–2007: III, 52). Oddly, Pope assured Swift that "no considerable man" was "very angry" at the book, though some "think it rather too bold, and too general a Satire, but none that I hear of accuse it of particular reflections." Did Pope not see what other readers quickly saw? Perhaps he was being discreet, lest any reference to the thinly veiled allusions in the second voyage to Walpole and the king, or to the negotiations concerning the Treaty of Utrecht (in the first voyage), be used to endanger Swift should the letter be opened at the post office.[29]

[25] His August 14 letter to Charles Ford declares ironically that the *Travels* are "admirable Things, and will wonderfully mend the World" (Woolley 1999–2007: II, 586).
[26] Ault (1949:232) assumes, on the basis of Swift's reference to Pope's "prudent management" of the contract (Woolley 1999–2007: IV, 108), that Pope was somehow involved in the negotiations with Motte. Sherburn speculates, on the basis of Pope's November 16, 1726 letter to Swift (1956: II, 412n) that it might have been Pope himself who "dropp'd" the manuscript in front of Motte's house, "in the dark, from a Hackney-Coach."
[27] In a December 1726 letter to John Caryll, who suspected that Pope must have been in on the secret, Pope insisted: "Upon my word I never saw it, till printed" (Sherburn 1956: II, 423).
[28] Swift seems to have told none of his friends in advance. Gay complained to Swift that "you have disoblig'd us, and two or three of your best friends, in not giving us the least hint of it while you were with us" (Woolley 1999–2007: III, 47).
[29] But perhaps early readers did not see "particular reflections." Gay's November 17 letter to Swift also reports that "Politicians to a man agree, that it is free from particular reflections" (Woolley 1999–2007: III, 47).

Although Gay told Swift that he was generally assumed to be the author, and that he could not be "much injur'd" by the supposition, Swift continued to withhold confirmation, in his November 17 letter to Pope, that he was indeed its author (III, 56–57). Pope, however, seems to have had little doubt, and soon resolved to reply, in his fashion, to *Gulliver's Travels*.

In February 1727 Pope wrote to Swift, expressing the hope that he had received copies of some "commendatory verses from a Horse and a Lilliputian, to Gulliver; and an heroic Epistle of Mrs. Gulliver" (Woolley 1999–2007: III, 76). These are evidently three of the set of five "Gulliverian" poems that Ault argued were written by Pope. References to the poems in two letters from Arbuthnot to Oxford in November 1726 persuaded Sherburn that Arbuthnot himself was involved in the writing (Sherburn 1956: II, 411, 417), but may only be evidence that Pope's poems were circulated for comment among his Scriblerian friends.[30] In any event, the poems were indeed published in a second edition of the *Travels*, presumably after Pope had alerted Motte to their availability. In his February 1727 letter to Swift Pope remarked, after noting Motte's desire to print the poems, that he "would not permit it without your approbation," adding disingenuously "nor do I much like them," before going on to mark a central difference between the two of them: "You see how much like a Poet I write, and yet if you were with us, you'd be deep in Politicks" (Woolley 1999–2007: III, 76). Swift presumably gave the scheme his approbation.

Pope's remark suggests a way to think about the "Gulliverian" poems that editors now assume were indeed written by Pope: they are the response, by one who regards himself as a "Poet," to a satire that is "deep in Politicks." Although designed to be published as part of the volume containing the *Travels*, and thus to signal Pope's participation alongside Swift in the larger satiric project – Pope would later claim that the *Travels* were written by "Martinus Scriblerus" – at the same time they are distinctive expressions of a Popean imagination.[31] Pope has found room, within the boundaries created by Gulliver's first-person narrative, for further invention that manages to "reply" both to Gulliver and to Swift himself.

When the second edition of *Gulliver's Travels* appeared, Lemuel Gulliver's was not the only voice to be represented. His narrative was prefaced, as was the first edition, with a note, "The Publisher to the Reader," signed by one Richard Sympson, who claimed to be a friend of

---

[30] The recipient of Arbuthnot's letters was not the Scriblerian Robert Harley, but his son Edward.

[31] The poems appeared in the second edition of *Gulliver's Travels*, published on May 4, 1727, and two days later were published separately as *Several Copies of Verses on Occasion of Captain Gulliver's Travels*. They are printed, as Pope's, in Ault (1954: 266–81).

Gulliver, and a relation "by the Mother's Side." Pope's poems, providing responses to Swift's narrative from a Lilliputian poet, Glumdalclitch
(daughter of the King of Brobdingnag), English Houyhnhnms,
Gulliver's wife, and the King of Brobdingnag, followed immediately
thereafter. (The familiar "Letter from Capt. Gulliver to his Cousin
Sympson" did not appear until 1735.) None of the poems is constructed
or presented as a "commendatory poem," with compliments to the
author for his achievement. Instead, preserving the pretense that the
reader is beholding a genuine book of travels, the poems are addressed
to Gulliver himself, not as author but as traveler. In two instances they
come from characters whose speech is represented in the *Travels*, and in
one from Gulliver's notably silent wife; the remaining two are attributed to characters invented by Pope.

The first of them is presented as a "Lilliputian Ode," and addressed "To
Quinbus Flestrin, the Man-Mountain" (the name by which Gulliver
was known in Lilliput), from "Titty Tit, Esq; Poet Laureat to his Majesty
of Lilliput. Translated into English." Both the poet's name (suggesting a
figure of little size) and his verse form (lines of only three syllables) maintain Swift's playful fiction of a land of little people. "Tit" had the additional advantage of being a nickname for a small horse (and thus a kind
of bookend to the Houyhnhnm-horse of the fifth poem). In Pope's day a
"tit" could also mean a form of retaliation or, as the *OED* puts it, "a blow
or stroke in return for another," as if Pope, himself a notably small man,
were giving Swift "tit for tat."

> In Amaze
> Lost, I gaze!
> Can our Eyes
> Reach thy Size?
> May my Lays
> Swell with Praise
> Worthy thee!
> Worthy me!
> Muse inspire,
> All thy Fire!
> Bards of old
> Of him told,
> When they said
> *Atlas* Head
> Propt the Skies:
> See! And believe your Eyes!

This "Lilliputian Ode" not only records the poet's amazement at Gulliver's great size and power, and extends the delightful play of big and small that constitutes the underlying power of Swift's fantasy, but makes its own claim to greatness ("Worthy me!"), emphasized in the final lines:

> In Mid Air
> On thy Hand
> Let me stand,
> So shall I,
> Lofty Poet! touch the Sky. (46–50)

The responsive poet (like the Lilliputian laureate) is "lofty" because his wit is sustained by a giant fiction (and fictional giant). But the claim is only partly facetious. Pope is perhaps remembering the old and ambiguous trope of "standing on the shoulders of giants," used notably by Burton and by Newton: it was a way simultaneously to pay tribute to giant predecessors, and to claim that one actually outdoes them ("sees farther"). Pope, playfully deploying the inherited conventions of the Cowleyan Pindaric ode, with its rhetorical questions and expressions of amazement, its alternating long and short lines, has ingeniously re-invented a new variant of the form,[32] in which the severely compressed lines accentuate the virtuosity of the poet, and reanimate the old idea that the admiring poet is caught up and elevated by his own sublime fancy. At the same time he perhaps reminds Swift of his own poetic beginnings with the irregular Cowleyan ode. (Swift too had designed Pindaric lines with as few as four syllables followed by others with as many as twelve.)[33] The Pindaric was designed to accommodate a lofty and rapturous response to a grand subject, and Pope deployed the form in 1713 for his *Ode for Musick. On St. Cecilia's Day* (whose lines vary in length from three syllables to eleven

---

[32] Pope's form – three-syllable lines and a concluding six-syllable line – was soon imitated in *Two Lilliputian Odes*, a pamphlet, published in May 1727 (the title page of the British Library copy is annotated "May") which dismisses the efforts of "Titty Tit, / Master Wit," who "Tries in vain, / Lofty strain, / To set forth" the "Magnitude and Worth" of "the Engine with which Captain *Gulliver* extinguish'd the Flames in the Royal Palace." Smedley's *Gulliveriana* (1728) declares that Pope's form is in fact an old one, the "ancient Fescennine" of Anacreon, often imitated by poets down to Suckling (p. 265). Smedley supplies his own feeble "Lilliputian Ode ... in imitation of Captain Gulliver." Smedley is wrong – the Fescennine is in fact a foot of three syllables – but Pope was not the inventor of the three-syllable trochaic line: Scarron used it in his epistle to Sarrazin.

[33] See, for example, the "Ode to the Athenian Society," st. VII (printed in 1691, and reprinted in 1710 and 1724), and the "Ode to Sir William Temple," st. VIII (it was not printed until 1750, but perhaps Pope saw it earlier). When Pope and Swift, in the summer of 1726, began discussing which pieces should be included in their *Miscellanies*, Swift may have supplied Pope with copies of his early verses.

syllables); his Lilliputian ode, with rigorous regularity, sustains a grammatically sound tribute, and manages quite literally to contain the grand subject within the compass of three-syllable lines.

But we should not assume that Pope's short lines are purely parodic; they may also serve as an allusion to the serious effects he produced in the *Ode for Musick*:

> Dreadful Gleams,
> Dismal screams,
> Fires that glow,
> Shrieks of Woe,
> Sullen Moans,
> Hollow Groans,
> And Cries of tortur'd Ghosts. (56–62)

Both poems demonstrate the power Swift was later to compliment when he grumbled at Pope's ability to "fix" more "sense" in two lines than he could do in six. It is noteworthy that, about the same time as he composed the Lilliputian ode, Pope composed two short verse trifles for which Swift was the chief audience – his "Lines on Swift's Ancestors" and his "Receipt to make SOUP, For the Use of Dean Swift."[34] In the former, a squib playing with Swift's plans to erect a monument to his grandfather in the church of Goodrich (also spelled Goodridge and Gotheridge), no line is longer than six syllables, and one is as short as three:

> Jonathan Swift
> had the gift,
> By fatherige, motherige,
> And by brotherige,
> To come from Gutherige.

In the latter, apparently composed after a veal dinner at Twickenham, Pope sends Swift the recipe in anapestic meter: "Take a knuckle of Veal / (You may buy it, or steal), / In a few pieces cut it, / In a Stewing pan put it." Like the Lilliputian ode, they constitute claims on Pope's part that he could match Swift's notable facility with tetrameter couplets, and go him one better by writing in trimeter.

The second of the poems responds to the second of Swift's voyages. "The Lamentation of Glumdalclitch, for the Loss of Grildrig. A Pastoral" appropriates Swift's names, and develops a plot detail that Swift supplied at the end of the "Voyage to Brobdingnag." In the final chapter Gulliver,

---

[34] They are printed in Ault (1954: 251–55), where they are associated with Swift's 1726 visit to England.

carried in his "Travelling-Box," is separated from Glumdalclitch when illness confines her to her room and Gulliver is taken for an airing. "I shall
never forget with what Unwillingness *Glumdalclitch* consented; nor the
strict Charge she gave the Page to be careful of me; bursting at the same
time into a Flood of Tears, as if she had some Foreboding of what was
to happen." And after Gulliver's traveling box is carried off by an eagle,
he laments his separation from her and empathizes with her in her distress: "in the midst of my own Misfortune, I could not forbear lamenting
my poor Nurse, the Grief she would suffer for my Loss, the Displeasure of
the Queen, and the Ruin of her Fortune" (ch. viii). Glumdalclitch drops
out of Gulliver's narrative at this point, but Pope imagines her future
without Gulliver. His poem begins just as Swift's episode ends: "Soon as
Glumdalclitch mist her pleasing Care, / She wept, she blubber'd, and she
tore her Hair." It is as if Pope had in effect converted *Gulliver's Travels*
into a collective Scriblerian project – or reminded Swift of what may have
been its Scriblerian origins – by contributing a new episode to the traveling Gulliver's adventures.

Pope's poem is cast in the form of pastoral, not his own neo-Virgilian
but Gay's mock-realistic style. Glumdalclitch's "Lamentation … for the
Loss of Grildrig" recalls the mode of Sparabella's "Wailings" for the loss
of Bumkinet, who had run off with Clumsilis in "Wednesday; or, The
Dumps," in Gay's *Shepherd's Week* (1714). But Glumdalclitch is Gulliver's
giant nursemaid rather than his sweetheart,[35] and much of the pleasure
of Pope's poem derives from her sorrowful remembrance of his adventures and mishaps at the Brobdingnagian court. Swift had supplied a
number of such episodes (Gulliver attacked by wasps, kidnapped by the
monkey, mired in cow-dung), but Pope imagines a series of new ones
(Gulliver playing with marbles the size of "rolling Rocks," leaping over
the lines on Glumdalclitch's palm, winding the key of her watch, chasing away the mite "that bore thy Cheese away"). For Swiftian adventures
that degrade Gulliver, Pope substitutes others that show him intrepid and
fearless, though comically minute. When she laments his loss, Pope borrows from his own *Rape of the Lock*. Like Belinda, who upon the loss of
her lock "in beauteous Grief appears, / Her Eyes half-languishing, half-
drown'd in Tears" (iv, 144–45), Glumdalclitch, upon the loss of Grildrig,
"lovely in her Sorrow still appears; / Her locks dishevell'd, and her Flood

---

[35] For a pastoral imagining of the attachment between creatures of discordant size, Pope perhaps
found some stimulation in Gay's masque of *Acis and Galatea* (about the comical love of the
cyclops Polyphemus for the nymph Galatea), for which he himself contributed some lines in *c.*
1716–18.

of Tears" (11–12). But the rustic details (e.g., "She gently whimpers like a lowing Cow") keep the tone light. Her cry "Was it for this ... with daily Care, / Within thy Reach I set the Vinegar?" (17–18) recalls the famous echoing cry of Thalestris: "Was it for this you took such constant Care / The *Bodkin, Comb,* and *Essence* to prepare; / For this ... /For this...?" (IV, 97–100).³⁶ And when she imagines the fate of her tiny Grildrig lost in an outsized world,

> How then thy fairy Footsteps can I find?
> Dost thou bewilder'd wander all alone,
> In the green Thicket of a mossy Stone,
> Or tumbled from the Toadstool's slipp'ry Round,
> Perhaps all maim'd, lie grov'ling on the Ground?
> Dost thou, imbosom'd in the lovely Rose,
> Or sunk within the Peach's Down, repose? (40–46)

Pope slips into the register that Ariel had used to envisage the fate of any sylph who failed to perform his duty:

> Whatever Spirit, careless of his Charge,
> His Post neglects, or leaves the Fair at large,
> Shall feel sharp Vengeance soon o'ertake his Sins,
> Be stopt in *Vials,* or transfixt with *Pins*;
> Or plung'd in Lakes of bitter *Washes* lie,
> Or wedg'd whole Ages in a *Bodkin*'s Eye:
> *Gums* and *Pomatums* shall his Flight restrain,
> While clog'd he beats his silken Wings in vain.
>
> (*Rape of the Lock,* II, 123–30)

The trick here is to scale down Olympian punishments, and to turn the mundane into the terrifying. But for Ariel's threats Pope substitutes Glumdalclitch's microscopic imagination, which envisages an ordinary patch of moss on a stone as a "green Thicket." Pope spins variations on Swift's theme, but when he goes on to imagine Gulliver "inbosom'd in the lovely Rose" and sleeping in the "fragrant Bow'r" of a "golden Cowslip's Velvet Head" he is producing effects which Swift had no interest in, and no ability to produce. Perhaps appropriating the power of Shakespeare's Puck to conjure up a fairy world, Pope displays, in response to Swift's comical adventure, a mix of pathos and delicacy that is one of the distinctive marks of one who writes "like a Poet."

---

³⁶ The "Was it for this ... ?" of Thalestris is in turn based on the "hoc erat ...?" of Aeneas in *Aeneid* II. 664.

The third of the poems is given the elaborately formal title "To Mr.
Lemuel Gulliver, The Grateful Address of the Unhappy Houyhnhnms,
now in Slavery and Bondage in England." The title may be something
of an insider's joke. Pope's "Grateful Address" borrows the language by
which Englishmen addressed their sovereign, as they did, for example, in
the address, drafted by Swift himself, thanking Queen Anne for concluding the Peace of Utrecht.[37] As with the first two poems, this "Address"
provides an opportunity for one of the creatures whom Gulliver encounters in his adventures to *speak back* to him, and by extension to *speak back*
to Swift. It was presumably prompted by Gulliver's account, in the final
two chapters of the "Voyage to the Country of the Houyhnhnms," of his
return to England, his conversations with his horses, who "understand me
tolerably well" and "live in great Amity with me" (ch. xi), and his intention to "apply those excellent Lessons of Virtue which I learned among the
Houyhnhnms," and his resolution "To lament the Brutality of *Houyhnhnms*
in my own Country, but always treat their Persons with Respect, for
the Sake of my noble Master, his Family, his Friends, and the whole
Houyhnhnm Race, whom these of ours have the Honour to resemble in
all their Lineaments, however their Intellectuals came to degenerate" (ch.
xii). But Pope shows up Gulliver's blindness. His English Houyhnhnms
turn out not to have degenerated at all: they are fully rational animals,
capable of thought and eloquence, enslaved only in body but not in mind,
and capable, furthermore, of a kind of verse unknown in the land of the
Houyhnhnms, where poems usually contain "either some exalted Notions
of Friendship and Benevolence, or the Praises of those who were Victors in
Races and other bodily Exercises." On the evidence of the printed poem,
furthermore, English Houyhnhnms, unlike their oceanic "Sires," have
acquired writing. (And, amazingly enough, they speak English!)

Pope also responds skeptically to Gulliver's resolution to apply what he
has learned. Pope's Gulliver is commended by the English Houyhnhnm
for having been "purg'd from human Crimes" by his "sweet Sojourn" in
Houyhnhnmland (5–6), and (now that he has returned home) is urged
to "spread those Morals which the *Houyhnhnms* taught," like Orpheus,
who "travell'd to reform his Kind, / Came back, and tam'd the Brutes
he left behind" (22, 19–20). But the Houyhnhnm poet tacitly abandons
hope for any general reformation. Swift's Gulliver had described to his

---

[37] The address is printed in Goldgar and Gadd (2008: 215). In Thomas Salmon's *Life of Her Late
Majesty Queen Anne* (1721), it is referred to as "this Grateful Address" (ii, 579). Swift entitled it
"The Humble Address…" See above, p. 58.

Houyhnhnm hosts the treatment of what he called "Horses" in England, where at the best they were "employed in Travelling, Racing, and drawing Chariots," and subjected to "a Bridle, a Saddle, a Spur, and a Whip" (ch. IV). The fate of "Unhappy Houyhnhnms" in England is projected to be pretty much the same:

> Compell'd to run each knavish Jockey's Heat!
> Subservient to *New-market's* annual cheat!
> With what Reluctance do we Lawyers bear,
> To fleece their Countrey Clients twice a Year?
> Or manag'd in your Schools, for Fops to ride,
> How foam, how fret beneath a Load of Pride! (25–30)

Pope's English Houyhnhnm turns out to be something of a satirist. In a bathetic conclusion, the most he hopes for is "that gentle *Gulliver* might guide my Rein!" (34). But his stoic resignation – he has "learnt to bear Misfortune, like a Horse" (32) – sets him apart from, and above, Swift's Gulliver, for whom the contemplation of human pride "breaks all the Measures of my Patience."

By assigning to the English Houyhnhnm both speech and patience Pope endows him with noble human qualities, and invites us to regard these brutes as fellow creatures, unhappily held in "Slavery and Bondage in England." Pope of course inverts the situation in Swift's Houyhnhnmland, where it is the Yahoos who are held in slavery. Critics of Swift today debate whether or not *Gulliver's Travels* is implicated in a racialist discourse, and whether or not Swift seems to endorse or attack the institution of slavery – or whether the relationship between Houyhnhnm and Yahoo, because they are defined as different species, is simply not comparable to that between white Europeans and black Africans (or Irish peasants). As noted earlier, Swift seems in his early political writings to regard the slave trade neutrally, as a valuable part of England's foreign trade. Pope, by contrast, although he discreetly conceals any reference to the fact that human slaves in his day were primarily African, seems to have shown some discomfort with the institution. Given the prominence of "Slavery" in Pope's title, and the look ahead, in *Windsor-Forest*, to a day when "Slav'ry" shall "be no more" (408), we might wonder if Pope in this Gulliverian poem quietly aims to unsettle those who congratulate themselves that slavery is not found "in England," prefer to think that human slaves are really some kind of inferior species, or, if they are indeed men, to conclude that their part is to bear their bondage with resignation. If so, then Pope is perhaps gently and quietly hinting at a blindness not only in Gulliver but also in Swift.

The fourth of the poems, "Mary Gulliver to Captain Lemuel Gulliver," imagines a sequel to Gulliver's narrative. The fourth voyage had concluded with Gulliver's return to his wife and family in Redriff. Sympson's letter, dated three years later, reports that Gulliver, having left Redriff, now lives a retired life "near Newark, in Nottinghamshire, his native Country" – without making clear whether he has taken his wife and family with him. Pope imagines that he has not, that he has left her behind in London, or that he has sought even deeper retirement with Sympson, as the "Argument" to the poem explains: "The Captain, some Time after his Return, being retired to Mr. Sympson's in the Country, Mrs. Gulliver, apprehending from his late Behaviour some Estrangement of his Affections, writes him the following expostulating, soothing, and tenderly-complaining Epistle."

In Swift's narrative Mrs. Gulliver had been only a shadowy figure, protesting at the end of Gulliver's second voyage that "I should never go to Sea any more" (her only reported speech), found to be "in good Health" at the end of the third voyage, "big with Child" at the beginning of the fourth. She greets Gulliver warmly upon his return – "my Wife took me in her Arms, and kissed me" – but Gulliver falls into a swoon, cannot tolerate her presence, and spends four hours a day conversing with "two young Stone-Horses" in his stable, his spirits revived by the smell of the groom. Pope takes up the story from there – "What, touch me not? What, shun a Wife's Embrace?" (2), imagining what Mrs. Gulliver might say, or rather write, to her estranged husband.

As Pope's "Argument" suggests, the poem is conceived as an Ovidian heroical epistle, typically sent by a woman to a man who has abandoned or been separated from her. Pope of course had produced two poems of this kind himself, the early "Sapho to Phaon" (published in a collection of translations of *Ovid's Epistles* in March 1712) and "Eloisa to Abelard" (first published in his 1717 *Works*), and his characterization of the epistle's style as "expostulating, soothing, and tenderly-complaining" reflects contemporary critical opinion. (For the affecting language of Mrs. Gulliver's letter Pope borrows, as the Twickenham editors note, from both "Sapho to Phaon" and "Eloisa to Abelard.")[38] But Pope's heroine, rather than an unmarried lover, is a wife and mother, reminding her husband of his spousal and paternal responsibilities. Yet, true to Ovidian form, she is also a passionate and jealous woman:

---

[38] They compare lines 39–45 with "Sapho to Phaon," lines 145–60, and "Eloisa to Abelard," lines 233–48; and line 73 with "Eloisa to Abelard," line 127.

Not touch me! Never Neighbour call'd me Slut!
Was *Flimnap*'s Dame more sweet in *Lilliput?*
I've no red Hair to breathe an odious Fume;
At least thy Consort's cleaner than thy *Groom.* (25–28)

Mrs. Gulliver seems to have been made most jealous by the report not of the amorous propensities of the female Yahoo who threw herself at Gulliver, but of the one he calls "the Sorrel Nag," a clearly male horse who forms an attachment to Gulliver ("I knew he had a Tenderness for me" and "always loved me"), and bids him fond farewell: "Take Care of thy self, gentle *Yahoo*" (ch. xi). Apparently Pope's Mrs. Gulliver doesn't believe her husband's story, or his report that the nags in his Redriff stable are "Stone-Horses" (horses with "stones" – i.e., uncastrated stallions) – she insists on calling one of them "the Sorrel Mare":

> Why then that dirty Stable-boy thy Care?
> What mean those Visits to the *Sorrel Mare…*
> *Where sleeps my* Gulliver? *O tell me where?*
> The Neighbours answer, *With the Sorrel Mare.* (29–30, 47–48)

Pope's joke is to provide a sexual motive for the largely sexless Gulliver, and more generally to reflect critically on his chilly indifference to his wife.

Pope's poem not only suggests how he replies to – or supplements – Swift, but also suggests another way of reading *Gulliver's Travels*. To imagine the emotional life of Mrs. Gulliver, as Pope does, is to assume that one could read the book not as a satire, in which characters are designed to facilitate ridicule, but as a psychological narrative, in which characters are endowed with an inner life with which we are invited, if only facetiously, to empathize.[39] But by parodically re-telling the story of *Gulliver's Travels* as if it were an amorous romance, Pope in fact acknowledges that as Swift designed it the narrative remains within the conventions of satire.

It also suggests that what Pope responded to in Swift's narrative is the flow of improbable incident, particularly in Lilliput and Brobdingnag.[40] But what Pope implicitly finds delightful and absurd, Mrs. Gulliver finds frightening and engaging – in the latter part of her letter she remembers her emotional response to reading Gulliver's narrative:

[39] His reading might be regarded as an early and unremarked example of what Hammond (borrowing from Bakhtin) calls the "novelization" of culture in the eighteenth century (1995: 107–12).
[40] By omitting to refer, in this or any of the five poems, to any incident in the third voyage, Pope may obliquely indicate that, like many contemporary readers, he found less pleasure in it than in the other three. It's surprising, given his apparent delight in "uncleanness," that Pope makes no reference in the Gulliverian poems to the "excremental" element in the *Travels*.

How did I tremble, when by thousands bound,
I saw thee stretch'd on *Lilliputian* Ground;
When scaling Armies climb'd up ev'ry Part,
Each Step they trod, I felt upon my Heart. (67–70)

Again, Pope in effect "replies" to Swift by re-telling Gulliver's story as
a set of romantic adventures. By doing so, he at the same time mocks
contemporary female readers who (so moralists warned) were misled into
passionate engagement by the fictions of novelists.

The last of the Gulliverian poems, "The Words of the King of
Brobdingnag, As he held Captain Gulliver between his Finger and
Thumb for the Inspection of the Sages and Learned Men of the Court,"
constitutes more of an elaboration of Swift's narrative than a "reply" to
it. Pope's Brobdingnagian King says nothing in verse that Swift's did not
say in prose. It was prompted, so its formal title indicates, by the episode in chapter III of the second voyage when the king, who has just met
Gulliver, calls in "three great Scholars" to examine him and determine
what kind of animal he is. But the king does not hold Gulliver "between
his Finger and Thumb" – that is Pope's addition – and does not on that
occasion remark on Gulliver as a man in miniature. That comes later in
the chapter, when the King turns to his first Minister and observes "how
contemptible a Thing was human Grandeur, which could be mimicked
by such diminutive Insects as I." The close to Pope's poem –

> When Pride in such contemptuous Beings lies,
> In Beetles, Britons, Bugs and Butterflies,
> Shall we, like Reptiles, glory in Conceit?
> Humility's the Virtue of the Great

– clearly echoes the words of Swift's king.

Pope also incorporates the "observations" of Swift's King (in chapter VI) in reply to Gulliver's account of "the State of Europe," leading
to the devastating condemnation that "I cannot but conclude the Bulk
of your Natives, to be the most pernicious Race of little odious Vermin
that Nature ever suffered to crawl upon the Surface of the Earth." When
Pope re-writes the King's terrible denunciation of English politics, only
the content of his charge derives from Swift:

> Yet will he boast of many Regions known,
> But still, with partial Love, extol his own.
> He talks of Senates, and of Courtly Tribes,
> Admires their Ardour, but forgets their Bribes;
> Of hireling Lawyers tells the just Decrees,
> Applauds their Eloquence, but sinks their Fees. (13–18)

The couplets have the balance and polish characteristic of Pope's later "ethic epistles."

His king speaks not to Gulliver but to "the Sages and Learned Men of the Court," and he speaks as a musing and moderate philosopher, in steady pentameter lines, rather like the urbane voice in the second epistle of the *Essay on Man* reflecting to his fellow philosopher on human pride and aiming to temper it by suggesting that, from the perspective of "Superior beings," the wisest of humans would seem no more impressive than an ape does to us. Did Pope shrink from the extremity of Swift's Brobdingnagian king, distinguishing his own temperate response to human vice from Swift's vehemence? Or was he obliquely reminding Swift that in a letter sent only a few months earlier he had insisted that it was not he who hated mankind but "vous autr[e]s" who are disappointed not to find them rational animals. In "The Words of the Brobdingnagian King" Pope may in effect be modeling for Swift the response that Swift himself claimed to be making.

MISCELLANIES IN PROSE AND VERSE (1726–1728)

It was perhaps during Swift's 1726 visit to Twickenham that he and Pope began making plans for another literary project, a joint collection of some of their works in both verse and prose. Pope's well-known description of the project, in a letter to Swift on February 17, 1727, after the latter had returned to Ireland and the first volumes of the *Miscellanies* had been printed, suggests that it can serve as a memorial to their friendship. I have already cited parts of Pope's description, but it is worth citing the whole of it here:

I am prodigiously pleas'd with this joint-volume, in which methinks we look like friends, side by side, serious and merry by turns, conversing interchangeably, and walking down hand in hand to posterity; not in the stiff forms of learned Authors, flattering each other, and setting the rest of mankind at nought: but in a free, un-important, natural, easy manner; diverting others just as we diverted ourselves. (Woolley 1999–2007: III, 76)

There is no reason to doubt that Pope genuinely invites Swift to regard the *Miscellanies*, now that they have been printed, in this way, but we should not assume that he is saying anything about the *original* design of the joint venture, or the motives that induced them to undertake it. (Nor are we bound to believe him when he claims that the book will show them in a "natural" and "un-important" manner: what their *Miscellanies* do, and what their contemporary letters do, is precisely to flatter each other, and set most of the rest of mankind at nought.) While the project may in fact have been designed as a memorial to friendship, it is just as likely that it was prompted, as was often the case with both writers, by the unwelcome action of a bookseller. The "Preface" to their *Miscellanies*, dated May 27, 1727, says as much:

> Having both of us been extreamly ill treated by some Booksellers, (especially one *Edmund Curll*,) it was our Opinion that the best Method we could take for justifying ourselves, would be to publish whatever loose Papers in Prose and Verse, we have formerly written; not only such as have already stolen into the World (very much to our Regret, and perhaps very little to our Credit,) but such as in any Probability hereafter may run the same Fate.[41]

By July 30, 1726 Curll had published a collection entitled *Miscellanea*, in two volumes, consisting of 24 "Familiar Letters written to Mr. Henry Cromwell, Esq., by Mr. Pope," a handful of "Occasional Poems by Mr. Pope, Mr. Cromwell, Dean Swift, &c," and four "Letters from Mr. Dryden to a Lady, in the year 1699."[42] The publication was without the permission of its authors, and consisted of materials that Curll had managed to acquire and put before the public as "Never before Published."[43] Curll probably calculated that readers would be eager to find out what Pope (at that moment famous as the translator of Homer) might have written when still a young and relatively unknown poet, especially in private and unguarded letters sent to a rakish gentleman and minor poet back in the days of Queen Anne. And he probably assumed that readers would be ready to buy poems by Pope, especially if they were "Never before Published," or were in any way risqué or scandalous. But if we ask why would Curll's bookbuyers would have cared to know what the obscure Henry Cromwell had written, we may be forgetting that Curll was a cunning businessman, and knew his market: a taste for the witty writings of Restoration wits survived into the 1720s – witness Pope's own editions of the poems of Buckingham (1724) and Wycherley (1728), and Cromwell was still alive. Curll seems to have designed this miscellany as a retrospective look at an earlier era, and at a world of gentlemanly authorial exchange, to which he could link two notable contemporaries, Pope and Swift.

---

[41] *Miscellanies in Prose and Verse*, 2 vols. (London, 1727), I, 3–4.
[42] For a recent discussion of Curll's *Miscellanea*, see Baines and Rogers (2007: 171–74).
[43] The lady was Elizabeth Thomas (1675–1731), a friend of Dryden – who gave her the pen name "Corinna" – and reportedly the one-time mistress of Henry Cromwell (see p. xx, above). Thomas claimed that Cromwell gave her Pope's letters, and that she sold them to Curll. It was presumably she who sold Dryden's letters to Curll as well.

The first of Curll's two volumes included a dedication to Henry Cromwell, a letter to "the editor" signed by "Corinna" (describing the contents of the volume as "a Collection of Original Letters & c. from the best Hands since the Restoration"), and a "Preface" about letters as a kind of "conversation." And it included several other short poems that the Twickenham editors conclude were written *c.* 1710–12, when Pope sent them – in manuscript form – to Cromwell. From Swift the volume included *Cadenus and Vanessa*, first published in an unauthorized edition in May 1726, and immediately seized on by Curll. The second volume promises on its title page, among other materials, "Swifteana." It includes as frontispiece a portrait of Swift, and as dedication an impudent address to Pope from "the Editor." Among the miscellaneous materials, few of them by Swift or Pope, are "A Rebus on Dean Swift. By Vanessa" and "The Dean's Answer," "A Riddle. By Dr. Delany" and "The Same Answered by Dean Swift," "A Petition to his Grace the Duke of Grafton" (by Jonathan Smedley) and "His Grace's Answer. By Dean Swift."[44] Pieces by Pope included "To Mr. Lintot. Written (as he says) by Mr. Pope," "A Version of the First Psalm. For the Use of a Young Lady," and "To the Ingenious Mr. Moore, Author of the Celebrated Worm Powder." The first had been printed in Lintot's 1712 *Miscellaneous Poems and Translations*, and by Curll is put in conversation with an imitation of it, William Pattison's "To Mr. E. Curll, Bookseller," included in the first volume. The other two had been previously attributed to Pope in print, and had drawn sharp fire from his critics.

It is usually assumed that Curll's publication offended Pope because it was unauthorized, and because the youthful letters to Cromwell were "embarrassing."[45] It also printed poems that for one reason or other – because they were immature, slight, satirical, or bawdy – both Swift and Pope did not want to put before the public over their names. (In this instance Curll did not commit the common offense of attributing to Pope or Swift poems that they in fact did not write.)[46] But they may have been most offended because Curll's *Miscellanea* put them in company with authors with whom they preferred not to appear: Henry Cromwell, Rowe, Eusden, Hill, and Broome, not to mention Jonathan Smedley (a party-writer who was later to attack both Pope and Swift in *Gulliveriana* [1728]) and William Pattison

<hr/>

44 Also included is a poem by Swift which Curll entitles "The Journal" ("Thalia, tell in sober ways …"). Swift printed it in 1735 as "The Part of a Summer."
45 See Baines and Rogers (2007: 171).
46 Indeed, for whatever reason, Curll printed two poems by Pope, the "Version of the First Psalm" and the squib on Moore, that he did not attribute to him. But in earlier volumes Curll had misattributed poems to both Pope and Swift, and the Preface to their *Miscellanies* complained of it (1, 4–5).

(one of the hack authors whom Curll reportedly maintained). Not only "in company" because they were gathered in the same pages, but because they were exposed in familiar conversation with authors they regarded as beneath them, exchanging letters, and writing familiar epistles and answer-poems. (Earlier in his career Pope had been content to appear in the mixed company of Tonson's 1709 *Poetical Miscellanies*, Lintot's 1712 *Miscellaneous Poems and Translations*, and the 1717 *Poems on Several Occasions*, the miscellany he edited for Lintot, but he now had a different conception of his own standing as a famous author, or else believed that the company among which he stood in those earlier volumes was more distinguished than the group gathered by Curll.)[47] Indeed, one can plausibly conclude that when they conspired to plan their own volumes of *Miscellanies*, Pope and Swift were concerned not merely to reaffirm their own control over their own work, but to place themselves in better company: in their own *Miscellanies* they would appear only in company with each other, and with choice friends, their old Scriblerian colleagues Arbuthnot and Gay. The authors, who knew perfectly well that they were perhaps the leading writers of their day, would appear "serious and merry by turns, conversing interchangeably." Pope's letter here preserves both the idea of conversation, central in Curll's *Miscellanea*, and the idea of mixing the "serious" and the "merry," central to the construction of the poetic miscellany for the previous quarter-century.[48] Hostile reviewers ridiculed the mix of serious and merry as a *"Chaos of old Scraps*, jumbled … designedly together, without any Order of Connexion," and recognized clearly that the two authors – "these two *Parnassian Dictators*" – had set themselves apart from, and above, all their contemporaries: "they run Riot upon, censure and abuse every other Author of any *Note*, who has wrote, of late Years, in the *Poetical* or *Polite* Way."[49]

[47] Tonson's authors included Swift, Garth, Wycherley, and Rowe. Lintot's miscellany, re-titled *Miscellany Poems*, 2 vols., reached a fifth edition in 1726–27, just as Curll's *Miscellanea* appeared. Lintot's first volume (1726) was wholly devoted to Pope's works, along with twelve commendatory poems; the second (1727) to poems "By several hands," including Dryden, Edmund Smith, the E. of D., Christopher Pitt, James Ward, Parnell, Stepney, Rowe, Samuel Butler, Mr. Hall of Hereford, and a number of anonymous authors. In the 1717 miscellany Pope appeared with a number of older writers whose manner was formed during the Restoration, including Wycherley, Mulgrave, Buckingham, Garth, Lady Winchilsea, and Sir John Birkenhead, as well as his friends Gay and Parnell, and some lesser lights such as James Ward, William Broome, and Bevil Higgons. For details, see Ault 1935.
[48] See Barbara Benedict, *Making the Modern Reader* (1996), esp. ch. 2, "Discriminating Readers in the Early Eighteenth Century." As Benedict notes, Lintot's *Miscellaneous Poems and Translations* (1712), edited by Pope, had juxtaposed the serious (Pope's translation of Statius) and the gay (his verses to Lintot), the ambitious (*Rape of the Locke*) and the slight (short pieces on love).
[49] Smedley, *Gulliveriana*, "Preface," pp. A4, xii, xxiii.

Swift seems to have delegated to Pope the lead role in compiling their *Miscellanies*. (Unlike Swift, Pope had had considerable experience in the compiling of miscellanies; furthermore, Swift seemed to have less interest than Pope in getting his work into print.)[50] After he returned to Ireland, Swift wrote to Pope, assigning him the "despotick Power" to include or omit any of his pieces.[51] And it was apparently Pope who wrote the Preface that they both signed. The implicit principles of inclusion thus probably reflect Pope's concerns more than Swift's. Apart from making it clear what company they belonged in, Pope probably acted not only to reaffirm their right to arrange and publish their poems as they saw fit, but also to prevent Curll from future piracies, by preempting him and publishing their own authorized edition of "loose Papers in Prose and Verse." As has been suggested, Pope probably did not want to waste anything worth preserving and publishing, even if it did not belong in a formal volume of "Works."[52] (This is more likely to have been of concern to Pope than to Swift, who seems to have worried less than Pope about the distinction between grave and gay.) He may have also thought he could detoxify some bawdy pieces by calling them "Sallies of Levity" composed in youth, "not our Studies, but our Follies; not our Works, but our Idlenesses" (Preface, 10).[53] Pope's Preface pretends to apologize for "the Satire interspersed in some of these Pieces," but it quickly insists that the satire was written upon "the highest Provocations" and that Pope and Swift are not "the first Aggressors" (7). Pope would make the same disingenuous claim in the *Dunciad Variorum*. Indeed, as the content of the first two volumes of the *Miscellanies* was being considered, Pope was apparently already planning to make *The Dunciad* the major and concluding piece of the third volume. This has led some to suspect that one of Pope's motives in publishing the first two volumes of the *Miscellanies* was to draw unfriendly fire – which would then provide

---

[50] As the *British Journal* observed on November 27, 1727, Pope "had often been concerned in such kind of Jobbs, and hired out his Name to stand *Centinel* before the Inventions of Booksellers; but [Swift], I had always observed, was very cautious of prefixing his Name even to such of his own Works as were published by himself" (*A Compleat Collection of all the Verses, Essays, Letters, and Advertisements, which have been occasioned by the Publication of Three Volumes of Miscellanies, by Pope and Company*, ed. Matthew Concanen and John Dennis [1728], p. 2).

[51] October 15, 1726 (Woolley 1999–2007: III, 36).

[52] As Ehrenpreis suggested, Pope seems to have concluded that even little things are "too good to be lost" (1962–83: III, 736ff.).

[53] Pope uses comparable language in his letters to Swift describing the pieces to be included: "a few loose things" or "unguarded and trifling Jeux d'Esprit" (February 16, 1733), in Woolley (1999–2007: III, 76, 594).

further justification for publishing *The Dunciad*.[54] And they did draw
fire from hostile critics, including Jonathan Smedley's *Gulliveriana: or,
a Fourth Volume of Miscellanies. Being a Sequel of the Three Volumes
Published by Pope and Swift* (1728), and so much more that Matthew
Concanen and John Dennis were able to compile and publish a 66-page
pamphlet entitled *A Compleat Collection of all the Verses, Essays, Letters,
and Advertisements, which have been occasioned by the Publication of Three
Volumes of Miscellanies, by Pope and Company* (1728), including a "List"
of every person who had been "abused in those Volumes."

What pieces then did Pope choose to include in – and exclude from –
the *Miscellanies*? Readers in Pope's day quickly noted that, although the
book was described in the Preface as a joint production, there is very little Pope in it.[55] Indeed, the first volume, except for one short piece, is
devoted entirely to Swift; almost 70 percent of the pages of the second
volume (limited like the first to prose) are devoted to two long works by
Arbuthnot (and less than one-fifth to Pope's writings, of which only *The
Key to the Lock* is more than a trifle). The third volume, published in 1728
and devoted primarily to verse, is more evenly balanced: the major work
is *The Art of Sinking in Poetry* (of which Pope was the lead author). It was
substituted for Pope's *Dunciad*, which at the last minute he decided to
publish separately.[56] Also included are thirty-six poems by Swift, twenty-
three by Pope, and seven by Gay. Although none of the pieces, in any of
the volumes, is assigned to an individual author – it is as if they are all
joint productions – contemporary readers would in fact have been able
to determine which pieces were Swift's and which were Pope's, if only
because a number of them had been previously published and attributed.

Pope's selection from Swift's work and his own also belies the implied
claim in his "Preface" that the two authors are represented in the volumes
in the same ways. Swift's major pieces of prose were excluded, *Gulliver's
Travels* (which Swift had not yet formally owned, and which in any case
had only just appeared a year earlier), the *Drapier's Letters* (which Swift
was not ready to own, and which Pope may have thought too "Irish" and

---

[54] Peter Quennell, *Alexander Pope: The Education of Genius, 1688–1728* (1968), 227–28, and Cowler
    (1986: 85).
[55] "Some OBSERVATIONS on the Preface, Advertisement, and Postscript of the Three Volumes
    Publish'd by Pope and Swift," in Smedley, *Gulliveriana* (1728), 333–35.
[56] In the initial plan, "Baucis and Philemon" and *The Dunciad* were to serve as bookends of the
    third volume, but Pope at an early point decided to begin with *Cadenus and Vanessa*. When "Peri
    Bathous" was substituted for *The Dunciad*, it was placed in first position, *Cadenus and Vanessa*
    then moving to second, and the volume ended with two "Stella" poems, including one composed
    as the book was being prepared for the press.

too occasional), the early political writings (Pope may have been seeking
to de-emphasize Swift's attention to politics), and *A Tale of a Tub*, with
the *Battel of the Books* and *The Mechanical Operation of the Spirit* (perhaps
not suitable to be associated with the Dean of St. Patrick's). But of Swift's
verse Pope included all the pieces by which Swift had built a reputation
as a poet, and which are still regarded as the major early poems: *Cadenus
and Vanessa*," "Baucis and Philemon," the two "Description" poems, seven
"Stella" poems, and the three "Progress" poems. It is as if Pope chose to
place equal emphasis on Swift's prose and verse.

His selections from his own work are different in four respects: first,
because (as noted) he devoted far fewer pages to his pieces than to
Swift's; second, because he readily reprinted pieces from Swift's own 1711
Miscellanies but included few of his own works that had already seen
print; third, because he included no significant new work of his own,
except for *The Art of Sinking*, while he printed some notable poems by
Swift that had been published recently, including *Cadenus and Vanessa*
(pirated by Curll the previous year), three "Progress" poems, and the
"Stella" poems, including one written as late as March 1727; fourth,
because he included none of the poems on which he had built a reputation – the *Essay on Criticism*, *Windsor-Forest*, *The Rape of the Lock*, *Eloisa
to Abelard*, not even the *Pastorals* or *The Temple of Fame* – and which he
had carefully collected in his 1717 *Works*. (They had also been re-printed
just the previous year in the fifth edition of Lintot's miscellany.)[57] What
he did include was a couple of dozen poems that Pope's Twickenham
editors assign to the volume entitled *Minor Poems* – juvenilia, some short
satirical portraits, a few songs and epigrams, and three of his Gulliverian
poems. The most important of the new poems was probably the 68-line
"Fragment of a Satire" (lines beginning "If meagre *Gildon* draws his
venal Quill" and ending "Who would not weep, if *A—n* were he?").
Readers today will recognize them as an early draft of lines that would
find a place eight years later in the *Epistle to Dr. Arbuthnot*. Early reviewers noticed it as an attack on Addison (even though he is not named in
the poem), and denounced Pope for attacking one who was "universally
confessd, *The greatest Genius, and best Writer of his Age*."[58] Pope's "Preface"
disingenuously apologizes for the "Raillery" at the expense of Addison,

---

[57] Pope claimed in a July 1726 letter that he was not involved in "reviewing or recommending"
Lintot's *Miscellany*, but admitted that once he heard Lintot was going to print a new edition, he
"corrected the sheets as far as they went, of my own only" (Sherburn 1956: II, 383).
[58] Smedley, *Gulliveriana*, "Preface," p. viii. Cf. also *British Journal*, November 27, 1727, in *Compleat
Collection*, p. 3.

whose name "deserves all Respect from every Lover of Learning." This
enables Pope to fire off a salvo against Addison, reminding much lesser
writers that he is a dangerous foe, and at the same time allows him to
pretend to "innocence." What Pope does not acknowledge is that the
68-line "Fragment" is not a "loose paper" that had fallen into the hands
of an unscrupulous publisher but a carefully and substantially expanded
version of a 30-line version of the same satirical portrait of "A—n," first
published (apparently from a circulating manuscript copy) in 1722 and
subsequently piratically reprinted by Curll. Curll had in fact printed the
30-line fragment in his 1726 *Miscellanea*. By publishing the 68-line version in his own *Miscellanies* Pope both reclaimed the poem and served
notice of his abilities as a satirist.

   Of his previously printed prose Pope chose to include only *The Key to
the Lock*. He omitted his contributions to the *Spectator* and the *Guardian*,
as well as his two substantial critical essays, the "Discourse on Pastoral
Poetry" and the "Preface to *The Iliad*." He was not yet ready to reprint his
early satirical pamphlets on Dennis and Curll – they were to appear in
the final volume of *Miscellanies* in 1732.

   Why Pope should have chosen to represent himself only (the "Fragment"
apart) with slight pieces of verse and prose, most of them unpublished, has
occasioned comment. Ehrenpreis guessed that Pope "did not like his best
verses to be lost in poorly paid anonymity" (1962–83: III, 742). But this collection was by no means anonymous; it paid well, and Pope might have
been able to bargain for even more by including some of his best-known
poems.[59] He had been willing for *The Rape of the Locke* to make its first
appearance in a 1712 miscellany, and had not withheld permission from
Lintot to reprint both the *Essay on Criticism* and *Windsor-Forest* in the
second edition of his *Miscellany* in 1714. Perhaps it was because Pope was
generally more careful than Swift about minimizing piracy and planning
for future editions (which might make him hold back some major poems).
Perhaps it was because, regardless of what he said about his delight in min-
gling the serious and the merry, he (unlike Swift) wished to preserve a distinction between the grave and the gay, between "Works" and *jeux d'esprit*.
As a result, the "serious" in the Pope–Swift *Miscellanies* is represented largely
by Swift, while both writers bore a hand in the "merry." (Perhaps Pope took
into account the fact that his "serious" side was currently being represented

---

[59] Motte agreed to pay £250 for three volumes. It apparently did not sell well. For a discussion of
the contract, see McLaverty (2008: 136–37).

by his translation of Homer's *Odyssey* – the final volumes of which had been published just twelve months earlier.)

When the Pope–Swift *Miscellanies* are set beside Curll's *Miscellanea*, one can see not only that the company is different: both Pope and Swift are also represented by almost completely different selections of writings. The only works that appear in both Curll's *Miscellanea* and the Pope–Swift *Miscellanies* are Swift's *Cadenus and Vanessa*, and three short pieces by Pope: the "Verses to be Prefix'd before Bernard Lintot's New Miscellany," the lines "To Mr. John Moore," and the "Verses Occasion'd by an &c. at the End of Mr. D'Urfey's Name." (Curll had in fact cast doubt on Pope's authorship of two of the pieces by entitling the first "To Mr. Lintot. Written (*as he says*) by Mr. Pope" [emphasis added], and by declining to attribute the third to anybody.) The explanation for their inclusion is perhaps that the authors, not having published these poems under their own names before, wished to establish legal claims to them.

Pope's arrangement of the pieces in each volume does not clearly reveal a single principle of organization,[60] except that the lead pieces ("A Discourse of the Contests and Dissensions" in volume I, "A History of John Bull" in volume II, and "The Art of Sinking in Poetry" in volume III) are the longest pieces in their volumes. (*Cadenus and Vanessa*, the longest of the poems, is awarded second position in volume III.) In the first volume Swift's prose pieces are not arranged chronologically by date of composition or first publication. The essays on religion are grouped together, as are the Bickerstaffian pamphlets. There are some indications that in the third volume Pope set up a kind of antiphony, six Swift poems followed by four Pope poems (the first two of which are written in Swiftian octosyllabics); another ten by Swift answered by twelve by Pope. Most (but not all) of the Gay poems are grouped together; four birthday poems for Stella are printed together – but separated from the final one (which may have been added to the volume at the last minute) – with the three other "Stella" poems. Some obvious similarities are noticed: Pope's "To Mrs. M. B. Sent on her Birth-day" is printed immediately following a set of four Stella birthday poems. A "song" is followed by a "ballad" and a short "ode." Seven epigrams, by different authors, appear together.

---

[60] Schakel (1993: 106–07) has attempted to show that in his arrangement of vol. III ("the Last Volume") Pope tried to minimize and even obscure differences between his style and that of Swift, but concedes that after the first dozen items – which include two octosyllabic poems by Pope – evidence of such an aim disappears.

"PERI BATHOUS"

In Pope's original plan for the *Miscellanies*, "Peri Bathous" (or *The Art of Sinking in Poetry*) was apparently designed to appear in a fourth and final volume, to be made up primarily of pieces in "Prose." As noted, "Peri Bathous" seems to have begun as a Scriblerian project in 1714, when Pope suggested a periodical that would discuss "the Works of the Unlearned." Nothing came of it initially, but Pope began collecting examples of bad poetry, and may have begun drafting his learned commentary on them in 1716. He picked up the project again later, and finished it up by 1727. Of the first three volumes of *Miscellanies,* the first two were to be prose, but for whatever reason Pope found no place there for "Peri Bathous." The third volume was to be mostly verse, and a long poem that had begun as "the Progress of Dulness" and was growing into *The Dunciad* was apparently designed to serve as the major work. But at the last minute Pope decided to withhold *The Dunciad* and to publish it separately. In its place he inserted *ΠΕΡΙ ΒΑΘΟΥΣ [Peri Bathous] or, Martinus Scriblerus His Treatise of The Art of Sinking in Poetry* in the third volume of *Miscellanies* (subtitled *The Last Volume*), published on March 8, 1728. (*The Dunciad* appeared anonymously just two months later.)

"Peri Bathous" was presented as a supplement to the famous treatise of Longinus, *Peri Hypsous*, translated into English by Leonard Welsted in 1712 as *The Works of Dionysius Longinus, on the Sublime: or, A Treatise Concerning the Sovereign Perfection of Writing*. While there was now "a plain and direct Road" to mark the Ancients' way to "Their hypsos, or *sublime*," no "track has yet been chalk'd out" to mark the way of modern writers to "our βαθοσ [bathos], or *profund*." As the parody suggests, modern writers are so bad that they must be trying to be dull, even following a set of rules for sinking. The rules in "Peri Bathous" are in effect an inversion of Pope's own rules for writing well, found as early as the *Essay on Criticism*.

Pope claimed that "Peri Bathous"was not written until 1727.[61] This may be another instance of his faulty memory about dates of composition, or he may have wanted to conceal the fact that he had been gathering examples of bad poetry for fifteen years.[62] Most of his examples of bad

---

[61] On the title page in editions from 1728 through 1738. The best account of the work is in Cowler 1986, incorporating notes from the 1952 Steeves edition.

[62] It was perhaps thoroughly revised in 1727. Arbuthnot was involved in the early stages of composition, but as Pope wrote to Swift in 1728, "I have entirely Methodized and in a manner written, it all, the Dr grew quite indolent in it" (Woolley 1999–2007: III, 153).

writing are in fact drawn from the poems of Blackmore, who had begun writing what Pope regarded as bad epics in the 1690s, and was still turning them out in the 1720s. That Blackmore was over seventy by 1728 – he was to die the following year – might have induced Pope not to wait any longer to publish his mock treatise in which Blackmore figured so prominently. (The fifth edition of Blackmore's *Creation* was published in 1727. That Blackmore was still being published suggests that Pope's critique was not, in the eyes of contemporaries, as "strangely old-fashioned" as has been recently claimed.[63]) Perhaps he found room for "Peri Bathous" in the third volume of *Miscellanies* because he thought that *The Dunciad* deserved its own prominence in a separate publication. But as has been suggested, Pope may have guessed rightly that publishing "Peri Bathous" would provoke his critics to denounce him – which would have provided some cover for his claim, in *The Dunciad Variorum*, that he was not the aggressor. (And, in fact, between the publication of "Peri Bathous" on March 8 and *The Dunciad* on May 18 Pope was attacked in print on at least twenty occasions.)[64] Pope may also have thought that "Peri Bathous" could serve as a prolegomenon for the forthcoming *Dunciad*. It was itself a kind of prose version of *The Dunciad*: Blackmore (who would be prominent in Book II of *The Dunciad*) appears as "Father of the Bathos"; bad writing for the stage (the focus of Book III of the poem) is ridiculed in chapter XIV, "A Project for the Advancement of the Stage"; and *"Tranquillity of Mind"* (which, in the form of sleep, is the true end of Dulness in the poem) is offered also as "the main End and principal Effect of the *Bathos*" (chapter IX). "Peri Bathous" is also a kind of guide for reading *The Dunciad*, and a guide to the art of writing about bad writing: perhaps this is what Pope meant when he told Spence that "Peri Bathous" "may well be worth reading seriously as an art of rhetoric."[65] Chapter XV, the "Receipt to make an Epic Poem," prepares the way for an epic about an unpromising subject. Chapter IX explains how "out of a

---

[63] Abigail Williams, *Poetry and the Creation of a Whig Literary Culture* (2005), p. 47. Williams is right to note that Pope's dunces – in *The Dunciad* – are basically Whig writers, and that his picture of them (particularly his emphasis on their frenzy, marginality, and poverty) draws on old stereotypes from the 1680s that were outdated by the 1720s when Whig writers had been embraced by high Hanoverian culture. But in "Peri Bathous" Pope emphasizes primarily their literary sins.

[64] The attacks are collected in the *Compleat Collection*. Pope made sure to refer to them in the Preface to the 1728 *Dunciad*, where the "Publisher" reports the *"Fact"* that "every week for these two Months past, the town has been persecuted with Pamphlets, Advertisements, Letters, and weekly Essays, not only against the Wit and Writings, but against the Character and Person of Mr. Pope" (Sutherland 1963: v, 202), and in the 1729 *Dunciad Variorum* (see below, p. 127).

[65] Osborn (1966: I, 57).

dunghill to draw gold," chapter x how to turn "lowest things" to advantage, chapter xII how to "raise what is base and low to a ridiculous visibility." (So Pope was to turn even Curll's vomit, "forever green," to his satiric advantage.) Chapter x points ironically to an egregious example of ineptness, an "ingenious artist painting the spring" who "talks of a snow of blossoms," a foretaste of the "heavy harvests" that "nod beneath the snow" in the 1728 *Dunciad* (I, 76). The poets of the bathos know well "never to magnify any object without clouding it" (chapter xI), and Pope follows the rule by presenting his Dulness in "clouded majesty" (I, 43), her "awful face" dilated by a "veil of fogs" (I, 218).

Pope learned his rules from the practice of bad writers, but he also learned them from Swift, and in particular from *A Tale of a Tub*. Pope's account of poetry as a "morbid secretion from the brain" (chapter III) derives ultimately from the theory of "vapours" in Swift's *Tub*, as does his idea that bad writers belong to their own "Society" (chapter xxx) and his adoption of the voice of a "true modern" who proposes a new "project" and "scheme" (chapter xIII). When the author of the *Bathos* congratulates himself – "Thus have I (my dear countrymen) with incredible pains and diligence, discovered the hidden sources of the Bathos" (chapter xIII) – he echoes the self-admiring phrases of Swift's Hack: "I have now with much Pains and Study, conducted the Reader ..." (Section 3) and "By forcing into the Light, with much Pains and Dexterity ..." (Section 5). The account of the "Prurient" style, its images "drawn from the two most fruitful sources or springs, the very Bathos of the human body, that is to say *** and ******** Hiatus Magnus lacrymabilis.* * * * * *," alludes to Swift's account of "that highly celebrated Talent among the Modern Wits, of deducing Similitudes, Allusions, and Applications, very Surprizing, Agreeable, and Apposite, from the Pudenda of either Sex" (Section 7), and to his mocking use of the "hiatus in MS." When an author in pursuit of "the Profound" is advised to follow the example of the "Physician," who "by the Study and Inspection of Urine and Ordure, approves himself in the Science," and to "accustom and exercise his imagination upon the dregs of nature" (chapter VII), Pope echoes the accounts of the Epicurean, in the "Digression of Madness" in *Tale of a Tub*, who "creams off Nature, leaving the Sower and the Dregs, for Philosophy and Reason to lap up." The final four chapters of "Peri Bathous," first printed as an "Appendix" and perhaps added, as Steeves suggests,[66] in 1727, put Pope's treatise in

---

[66] *The Art of Sinking in Poetry*, ed. Edna L. Steeves (1952), 181–84.

conversation with the *Tale* and several of Swift's later satiric writings. As Cowler notes, the "Rhetorical Chest of Drawers" in chapter XIII recalls the language machine in the Academy of Lagado; the instructions for making dedications, panegyrics, and satires in chapter XIV echo the "Preface" to *Tale of a Tub* (1986: 270, 271).[67] It is as if Pope were signaling that Swift was a crucial inspiration not only for "Peri Bathous" but for the forthcoming *Dunciad* as well.[68]

SWIFT AND *THE DUNCIAD* (1726–1729)

James McLaverty has recently asked whether *The Dunciad* might be given a Bakhtinian reading, as a "polyphonic" or "heteroglossic" work, in which several "voices" are heard, in colloquy or dialogical competition with each other.[69] Recognizing the features of the poem that invite such a reading (the "Prolegomena" assigned to "Martinus Scriblerus"; the several notes assigned to fictitious or real annotators (often quoting their previously printed words); the citation, on nearly every page, of passages imitated from the Ancients; the "Letter to the Publisher" signed by "William Cleland") McLaverty nonetheless concludes that the poem is "dialogic" only in a limited sense, for the several voices, in his view, do not really engage with each other as equals, but are carefully contained and controlled by Pope himself. Others have asked whether Pope is in fact clearly in control of the various voices, which sometimes threaten to overwhelm his poetic narrative. Perhaps these questions are posed too broadly, for the poem engages with various predecessor texts – by Virgil, or Dryden, or Theobald, or Giles Jacob – in various ways, although in each case Pope seeks to make the prior text in one way or another suit his purposes.[70] Among those texts are *A Tale of a Tub* and the *Battel of the Books* as well as Swift's several private letters to Pope. The poem, and in particular the *Dunciad Variorum*, might be regarded as a dialogic response to Swift, first by emulating him and joining with him in a kind of alliance against

---

[67] Cowler also notes (1986: 267) that the instructions for producing the "Pert Style" in chapter XII recall Swift's *Proposal for Correcting the English Tongue*, reprinted in the first volume of the Pope–Swift *Miscellanies* (1727).

[68] Cf. Pope's account in chapter I of the "*Lowlands* of Parnassus" (inhabited by the "Moderns") and the neighboring "*Highlanders*" (the "Ancients") who inhabit "*upper Parnassus*" with Swift's account at the beginning of *Battel of the Books* of the "two Tops of the Hill *Parnassus*," the higher inhabited by the Ancients and the lower by the Moderns.

[69] McLaverty (2001, ch. 4, "The Dunciad Variorum: The Limits of Dialogue").

[70] McLaverty (1985: 22–32) has argued that Jacob's *Poetical Register* (1719) and *Lives and Writings of our Most Considerable English Poets* (1720) prompted Pope to produce a corrective response.

a world of bad writers, but also by implicitly rejecting his advice to ignore foolish and hostile scribblers, by determining to transmit their infamy to posterity (and to turn Swift into a collaborative annotator-documentarist in the project), and by re-affirming (against Swift's skeptical rejection) the "majesty" of epic that Swift had mockingly dismissed as no longer available to modern writers.[71]

Pope seems to have begun work on a poem about bad writers (and the bad "Taste of the Town" which made them popular) as early as 1719.[72] Editors since Sutherland assume that from the start Pope focused on the idea of succession – one bad poet succeeding another, an idea most prominently developed in Dryden's *MacFlecknoe*. Pope acknowledged his indebtedness to (and his rivalry with) *his* predecessor at the opening of Book II where Tibbald's royal seat (in a phrase first appearing in the *Dunciad Variorum*) far outshines "Fleckno's Irish throne" (2), though in a footnote takes care to point out that, although his poem "bears some resemblance" to Dryden's, it is "of a character more different from it than that of the *Aeneid* from the *Iliad*." Pope evidently determined to add to Dryden's coronation scene some other elements of epic, including the celebrative games, which constitute his Book II. He appears to have seen in Swift's *Battel of the Books* a model for turning epic warriors into figures of ridicule, and in one of Swift's minor episodes may have found specific inspiration. In the midst of Swift's battle, Lucan sweeps the field until he encounters Blackmore, who, because he is protected by a god, escapes being killed. Lucan and Blackmore decide to exchange gifts – at which point Swift's narrative breaks off with a "Pauca desunt." After the hiatus the narrative apparently continues, as "Creech" (Thomas Creech, a translator of Horace) takes the field, but (in parody of Juno's formation of a shade-Aeneas to distract Turnus)

> the Goddess *Dulness* took a Cloud, formed into the Shape of *Horace*, armed and mounted, and placed it in a flying Posture before Him. Glad was the Cavalier, to begin a Combat with a flying Foe, and pursued the Image, threatning loud; till at last it led him to the peaceful Bower of his Father *Ogleby*, by whom he was disarmed, and assigned to his repose. (Guthkelch and Smith 1958: 248)

---

[71] See Rawson's acute remarks (1994: 89–94) on the "majesty of mud" in the *Dunciad Variorum*, II, 301–06.

[72] Sherburn's tentative suggestion (1929: 450) of a "possible hypothesis," seconded by Sutherland (1963: xiv) and developed by Vander Meulen (1991: 7–9), is that Pope began a poem mocking Settle, the official poet of the City of London, in late 1719. In "The Publisher to the Reader" (Rumbold 2007: 17), Pope has the publisher declare that he is informed that the poem "was the labour of full six years of [the poet's] life" – i.e., that it was begun in 1722.

Here Pope (once he had recast Swift's battle as a game) had to hand not only his goddess, but the shadowy "Poet's Form" that Dulness sets before the booksellers in the first of the epic games in Book II, the idea of Ogilby as the father of all bad poets (cf. "great fore-father, *Ogilby*," *Dunciad*, I, 248), the sleep to which they are all destined, and even the slumbrous "Bower" (cf. the "jetty bow'rs ... where bards departed doze," *Dunciad*, II, 298, 309). It is as if Pope saw an opportunity – an "opening" created by the hiatus – in Swift's narrative, and seized it. The footnote he provided in the *Dunciad Variorum* prominently acknowledges his source in Virgil, as if to distract attention from his debt to Swift.[73]

For what grew into the elaborate presentation of the poem in the *Variorum*, complete with notes, classical imitations, and commentary, editors now also conclude that Pope took inspiration from the 1716 edition of Boileau's *Oeuvres*.[74] But at some point – whether before or after he began thinking about the edition of Boileau – Pope had apparently been musing over Swift's *Tale of a Tub*, where he encountered not only mockery of bad writers but also the multiplication of prefatory texts ("Apology," "Dedication," address from "The Bookseller to the Reader, "Epistle Dedicatory," and "Preface') and satirical footnotes, with their mix of historical and fictional materials, that he was to emulate in the *Variorum* (with its elaborate "Prolegomena of Scriblerus"), and the ingenious way in which Swift skewered his adversaries by publishing a series of editions of his poem, including new material, even incorporating the protesting words of his critics.[75] But Swift's *Battel* is nowhere acknowledged in *The Dunciad* as part of Pope's inspiration. Nor is *Tale of a Tub*. The fact that no evidence survives to show that Pope ever wrote a word about either of Swift's texts is perhaps at least as well worth remarking as what Pope was able to do in reworking his models.

Swift himself was intimately involved with *The Dunciad* from an early stage, no later than 1725, when Pope sent him some lines. Swift's response,

---

[73] Sutherland (1963: 79) notes that the long-dead "Withers" (i.e., George Wither, 1588–1677), mocked at *Dunciad Variorum*, II. 126, had also been ridiculed (as "Withers") in Swift's *Battel* (pp. 226, 235), and remarks that Pope "had probably not forgotten" the episode in the *Battel* in which Dulness makes a Horace. Rumbold (2007: 46), who without comment notes that the episode in the *Battel* is "comparable" to the one in Pope, argues (10) that the controversy in the 1690s over the Epistles of Phalaris, pitting Richard Bentley against Sir William Temple, which prompted Swift's *Battel of the Books*, remained a "key reference point" for Pope, who played Temple to Theobald's Bentley.

[74] See McLaverty (1984: 99–105).

[75] Rumbold's notes (2007) point to parallels in phrasing, e.g., "Index-learning ... / Holds the eel of Science by the Tail" (*Dunciad*, I, 223–24) and "the *Index*, by which the whole Book is governed ..., like *Fishes* by the *Tail*" (*Tale of a Tub*, Section 7).

warning Pope not to waste his time ridiculing writers whose names would disappear if he would just ignore them, suggests he meant to *discourage* Pope from pursuing the project. During Swift's 1726 visit the poem came up again, and this time Swift, surprisingly enough, seems to have encouraged Pope to complete it. At least this is what Pope claimed in his nearly buried account in a footnote printed in the "Appendix" to the 1729 *Dunciad Variorum*, where he traced the poem's survival (if not birth) to a timely intervention from Swift. When Swift and Pope in the summer of 1726 were planning their *Miscellanies*, and deciding which pieces to include, Pope had apparently considered his poem, still in draft, on Settle and other bad writers, but had rejected it – and given up on it altogether. As Pope put it, they "had determin'd to own the most trifling pieces in which they had any hand, and to destroy all that remain'd in their power" – lest such abortive births should fall into the hands of Curll or another unscrupulous publisher. At that point, in Pope's melodramatic account, "the first sketch of this poem was snatch'd from the fire by Dr. *Swift*, who persuaded his friend to proceed in it"[76] – Swift having apparently believed that the nascent *Dunciad* was by no means an "abortive birth."[77] (Some critics have suggested that Swift also proposed that Theobald might be made its hero.)[78] For this reason, continues Pope's note, Swift "may be said in a sort to be the Author of the Poem, and to him it was therefore Inscrib'd." Given Swift's earlier warning, and his subsequent delegation to Pope of "despotic power" concerning the inclusion or exclusion of his own poems from the forthcoming *Miscellanies*, one wonders if the story of the manuscript snatched from the fire – which flatteringly aligns Pope with Virgil, whose *Aeneid* was fortunately snatched from the flames to which its author had allegedly consigned it – might be apocryphal. Pope often found it convenient to claim that his poems were published only at the bidding of friends or patrons.

   Pope's suggestion that Swift was in some sense "the Author of the Poem" deserves more attention than it has received. In what sense did he intend it to be taken?[79] *The Dunciad* was of course published anonymously,

[76] *The Dunciad Variorum* (1729), p. 87n, printed in Rumbold (2007: 321) and Sutherland (1963: 201n).
[77] Pope redeployed the idea of poem as abortive birth in his own account of the works laboring in Theobald's brain, where "Hints, like spawn, scarce quick in embryo lie" (*Dunciad*, I, 57).
[78] The suggestion that in 1726 Swift proposed that Pope could salvage the poem by having Settle, who had died in 1724, be replaced, or succeeded in his office as City Poet, by Theobald (who had recently given Pope offense with his 1726 *Shakespeare Restored*) was first made by Sherburn (1929: 451) where he calls it a "a safe guess."
[79] In a letter to Thomas Sheridan on October 12, 1728, about the time he was composing the note naming Swift as "Author," and the same day he wrote to Swift that the "poem is yours" since

and both Pope and Swift delighted in mystification – and sought refuge in anonymity from possible legal action. They had just published a collection of which they were regarded by contemporary critics as "Joint Authors" (see Illustration 2.2).[80] Pope perhaps wanted to claim Swift as his ally, both to gain support and to share the blame when the poem was inevitably attacked.[81] He plays with the several meanings, both literary and theological, of the word "author": even if Swift did not literally "create" or "compose" the poem he may be thought of as the one who instigated or prompted it ("author," *OED*, 1d). In the familiar religious phrase, Swift, since he rescued the poem from burning, might have been said to be the "author and preserver" of its life.[82] Pope, who had parodied the first psalm, would not have refrained from the quasi-blasphemy of addressing Swift in terms usually reserved for the divine. Indeed, the famous dedication to Swift, by addressing him with several names (as Homer addressed the Olympians), treats him facetiously as if he is indeed a god.

The idea that Swift was the "author" of the poem may derive from Swift himself. When he returned to England in 1727, and spent part of the summer with Pope at Twickenham, Swift was temporarily suffering another of his attacks of deafness, and (so he said), because he was unable to hear Pope's voice and was thus not fit for conversation, he read while Pope wrote.[83] His version of the event, "Dr. Sw– to Mr. P–e, while he was writing the Dunciad," first published in the final volume of the *Miscellanies* in 1732, was apparently written in the summer of 1727.[84]

> *Pope* has the Talent well to speak,
> But not to reach the Ear;
> His loudest Voice is low and weak,
> The *Dean* too deaf to hear.
> A while they on each other look,

"certainly without you it had never been" (Woolley 1999–2007: III, 201), Pope declared that Swift is "properly the Author of the Dunciad," for "it had never been writ but at his Request, and for his Deafness" (Sherburn 1956: II, 523). Elsewhere Pope almost always uses the word "author" to mean "writer of a book," and sometimes "authority."

[80] Smedley, *Gulliveriana*, p. x.

[81] This may explain why the title page of the first edition of the 1728 *Dunciad* misleadingly – and falsely – declared that the poem was a London reprint of a Dublin edition.

[82] Locke refers to God as "author and preserver" (*Essay on Human Understanding*, Bk. 2). The phrase derives ultimately from Acts 3.15, where God is the "author of life."

[83] Even when his hearing was good, Swift apparently did not find much conversation from Pope. In a 1733 letter, later cited in Johnson's "Life of Pope," Swift complained that Pope had "disqualifyed" himself for Swift's "conversation" because he "loves to be alone and hath always some poetical Scheme in his head" (Woolley 1999–2007: III, 677).

[84] Mack dates it near the end of Swift's visit to Pope (which concluded in August), Rogers in August.

2.2 Frontispiece to Jonathan Smedley's *Gulliveriana* (1728).

Then diff'rent Studies chuse,
The *Dean* sits plodding on a Book,
Pope walks, and courts the Muse. (1–8)

Pope jots "Hints" on "Backs of Letters," and adds line to line until –
"Behold a *Poem* rise!"

> Yet to the *Dean* his Share allot;
> He claims it by a Canon;
> *That, without which a Thing is not*
> Is, *causa sine qua non.*
> Thus, *Pope* in vain you boast your Wit;
> For, had our deaf Divine
> Been for your Conversation fit,
> You had not writ a Line. (17–24)[85]

Swift playfully regards himself as the Aristotelian efficient cause (that which prompted a thing, and "That without which a Thing is not") of Pope's poem. It is curious that Swift's witty claim to a "Share" has a slight edge to it – "*Pope* in vain you boast your Wit" – that is absent in what we might regard as Pope's reply, the allusion to Swift's intervention in the previous summer that turns Swift from philosophical cause to intervening protector.[86]

Swift's poem should not be taken literally, for he makes it sound as if the *Dunciad* were still in very rough form in August 1727, when it seems to have been finished, or nearly so, by October 1727, for Pope wrote to Swift (on the 22nd) that "My Poem ... will shew you what a distinguishing age we lived in" – i.e., an age which unfortunately could not distinguish between the pastorals of a Philips and those of a Pope, between bad poets and good. Unfortunately, Pope says, he cannot send Swift a copy, for fear (he says) that it might fall into the hands of Curll or Dennis or (worse) "our friends and Admirers" who might take their own copies.[87] Swift, he may have remembered, did not show him a copy of the *Travels* when it was published a year earlier, and his declining to send a copy of

---

[85] Pope, who presumably saw Swift's poem at the time it was written, in effect answered it by corroborating Swift's claim in the October 12, 1728 letter to Thomas Sheridan: "had he been able to converse with me, do you think I had amus'd my Time so ill?" (Sherburn 1956: II, 523).
[86] In later years Swift repeated his claim to a "Share" in the poem. In a 1732 letter he said that he had "put Mr. Pope on writing the Poem, called the *Dunciad*" (Woolley 1999–2007: III, 516). If, as commentators suggest, Pope began the poem in 1724 or earlier, Swift overstates his share.
[87] Woolley (1999–2007: III, 136). In another letter some three months later, Pope again expressed regret that he could not send Swift a copy (III, 153). Rumbold (2007: 5) notes the extreme measures Pope took "to avoid being suspected as the author."

The Dunciad might be regarded as a kind of reprisal, or perhaps only a "reply."

By January 1728 Pope reported to Swift that "my Chef d'Oeuvre, the poem of Dulness" was ready to be printed. He was apparently still undecided about the title, jokingly declaring that it would be bound and lettered on the spine *"Pope's Dulness."* Another possible title seems to have been "The Progress of Dulness" – which combined ideas of advancement, procession, removal from one place to another, and journey of state, all of which are taken up in the poem's narrative plot. Pope had already decided to include several of Swift's ironic "Progress" poems (including "The Progress of Poetry") in the third volume of the *Miscellanies*, to be published in March, and the idea of an ironic account of the "progress" of dulness might have appealed to him.[88] Somehow that name got out, and a letter in the May 11 issue of the *Daily Journal* reported that Pope was then at work on "The Progress of Dulness." But in the end Pope, by calling it *The Dunciad. An Heroic Poem,* decided to emphasize not the mock-"progress" but the poem's mock-epic frame. However, he kept alive the rumor about the "The Progress of Dulness" and disguised his own role as the author of *The Dunciad* by instructing his printer to include the announcement that there would "speedily" be printed *The Progress of Dulness. An Historical Poem,* "by an Eminent Hand." The alternative title, which poses "Historical Poem" against "Heroic Poem," allows Pope to emphasize that his poem is not only a parody of Virgil's epic but also a chronicle of recent historical events.

As early as 1727 Pope had decided to inscribe the poem to Swift, but the famous inscription was in fact not printed until the *Dunciad Variorum* of 1729, even though Pope had promised Swift as early as October 1727 that it would be addressed to him. Reasons for the delay remain unclear. The inscription was only one of several elements prepared before the publication of the 1728 *Dunciad* but withheld until the 1729 *Variorum*.[89] But perhaps Pope had not decided on the precise form that the dedication should take: it went through at least two early drafts before it was revised again for publication. In the October 22, 1727 letter, Pope sent Swift two couplets, implying that they constituted the whole of his direct address:

[88] "The Progress of Dulness" also served as an ironic riposte to the enthusiastic (and undiscriminating) account of "the Progress and Improvement of our English Poetry" (xiv) in Giles Jacob's *Lives and Writings of the English Poets* (1720). Pope, Swift, and Prior are praised, but so are Dennis, Blackmore, and Ambrose Philips.

[89] It is now clear, as Rumbold notes (2007: 3), that Pope prepared the *Variorum* well in advance of its publication, and even before the publication of the 1728 poem, "carefully staging the release of the new information and comment that would constitute much of its appeal to his readers."

Whether you chuse Cervantes' serious air,
Or laugh and shake in Rablais' easy chair,
Or in the graver Gown instruct mankind,
Or silent, let thy morals tell thy mind.[90]

These "two verses" were probably designed to appear at the beginning of Book I, where they would have needed to be supplemented by other lines that Pope may not have finished revising. Here Pope imagines that Swift can choose at will among four modes of address: deadpan, laughing, grave, and silent. The first two lines apparently focus on Swift's narrative prose satire, contrasting the mock-"serious" ironist (one of Swift's several voices) and the exuberant fantasizing of the zany narrator of *Tale of a Tub*, or the comic satirist who found mankind basically ridiculous rather than despicable. The third line turns to the "graver" religious writings (e.g., "Sentiments of a Church of England Man," which Pope had just included in the first volume of *Miscellanies*). The fourth line perhaps suggests that the "silent" example of Swift's moral conduct – since 1712 he had not written as steadily or published as often as Pope – serves to "tell" the age what lies in his mind. What unites the two couplets is the idea that Swift delights in mixing grave and gay – and as noted earlier this makes him different from Pope, who in presenting his own works prefers to keep grave and gay separate. The lines, even in their early form, mark a difference between Swift and Pope.

The line about Rabelais deserves more comment than it has received, not only because Pope and Swift, as noted earlier,[91] differed about Rabelais's merits. "Shake" perhaps suggests the helpless full-body shaking of hearty laughter, perhaps just the knowing shake of the head. "Easy chair" is oddly comfortable furniture for Swift, who rarely strikes modern readers as an "easy" writer: we prefer his "savage indignation"and Pope preferred his *bagatelles*.[92] The praise of Swift as a modern Rabelais may serve as an acknowledgement of difference between his own taste and Swift's. It may also serve as an index of Pope's view of Swift's satire. Some early critics thought Swift not as benign a laugher as Rabelais. Orrery thought Swift's satire on modern political assemblies (in chapter VIII of the third voyage of *Gulliver's Travels*) more in the manner of "the Cynic in his cell, than the free humoured *Rabelais* in his easy

---

[90] "These two verses are over and above what I've said of you in the Poem" (Woolley 1999–2007: III, 136). Swift's name also appeared elsewhere in the poem, though in less flattering contexts than Swift might have hoped (see below, pp. 124–26).
[91] See "Introduction," p. 18.
[92] Cf. Pope's imitation of Horace, Epistles, VI, I, "And Swift cry wisely, 'Vive la Bagatelle!'" (128).

chair."⁹³ Perhaps Pope's line points to a comic attitude that he wanted to encourage in Swift. The allusion to Swift's Cervantic "serious air" – that is to say, his mock-gravity – seems more apt, though it is perhaps significant that once again Pope has selected a writer in whom he showed little interest himself.⁹⁴

But something about these lines seems not to have satisfied Pope, for by January 1728 he sent Swift another draft of the "Inscriptio," in which the first couplet survives almost unchanged, but the second largely disappears:

> And Thou! whose Sence, whose Humour, and whose Rage
> At once can teach, delight, and lash the Age!
> Whether thou chuse Cervantes' serious Air,
> Or laugh and shake in Rab'lais' easy chair,
> Praise Courts and Monarchs, or extoll Mankind,
> Or thy griev'd Country's copper Chains unbind:
> Attend, whatever Title please thine ear,
> Dean, Drapier, Bickerstaff, or Gulliver.
> From thy Boeotia, lo! the Fog retires;
> Yet grieve not thou at what our Isle acquires:
> Here Dulness reigns with mighty wings outspread,
> And brings the true Saturnian Age of Lead.⁹⁵

Swift's four modes of address have now been echoed by four titles: "Dean, Drapier, Bickerstaff, or Gulliver."⁹⁶ His gravity and silence have disappeared (perhaps because they seemed out of place in a comic poem), replaced by "Sence, … Humour, … and Rage," and turned into the invocation that the first draft lacked. "And Thou" implies that Pope has previously addressed

---

⁹³ Orrery (1752: 103). Coleridge was perhaps emphasizing not similarity but difference when he described Swift as "the soul of Rabelais inhabiting a dry place." John Traugott suggests that Pope's picture of Swift as Rabelais is "less accurate than honorific," and argues that the genius of Swift and Rabelais were in fact fundamentally unlike ("*A Tale of a Tub*," in *Focus: Swift*, ed. Rawson [1971], 97–99).

⁹⁴ In a December 14, 1725 letter Pope reports to Swift that his friend Charles Jervas has "finish'd" a translation of *Don Quixote* (Woolley 1999–2007: II, 626). Woolley conjectures that Pope first heard of Swift's interest in Cervantes from Jervas. If Pope knew of Swift's plans, as early as 1728, to take part in a new translation of Cervantes (see Elias 1998), he left no record of it. Cervantes is sometimes proposed as a model for the narrative of the life of Martinus Scriblerus. When Lady Mary Wortley Montagu (a hostile witness) told Spence in 1741 that Swift "has stolen all his humour from Cervantes and Rabelais" (Osborn 1966: I, 308), she was probably thinking of Pope's lines.

⁹⁵ Woolley (1999–2007: III, 154). Sutherland (1963: 62) adopted David Nichol Smith's suggestion that Charles Ford's Latin birthday poem to Swift ("Ad Celerem"), dated November 30, 1727, "anticipates" Pope's inscription. (The poem begins by asking how best to address Swift.) But neither Sutherland nor Smith explain how Pope could have seen a poem that survives only in a rough draft found in Ford's papers. Did Swift perhaps send Pope a copy in a letter that has not surfaced?

⁹⁶ Pope may allude to the closing lines of a brief essay, "Of Plots," in Smedley's *Gulliveriana*, where "Captain Gulliver" (Swift's most recent pseudonym) is said to have several identities: "Master

somebody else, perhaps the "great Patricians" whose "selves inspire / These wond'rous works" (i, 3–4), and then turned directly to Swift, who inspired them in another sense. The four modes are now Cervantic mock-seriousness, Rabelaisian laughter, ironic praise, and political polemic.

The several titles by which Pope freely addresses Swift – "Dean, Drapier, Bickerstaff, or Gulliver" – also show his confidence: no fear lest he use the wrong one.[97] Other titles were possible: Pope might easily have chosen "Examiner" or "Cadenus." Swift is positioned, by means of his several voices and his models (Cervantes and Rabelais), as a writer of prose – and thus not an obvious model for, or a rival of, a poet. But it is odd that Pope's titles do not point to the one prose work of Swift which most shaped *The Dunciad*, and in particular the *Variorum* edition – *Tale of a Tub*. It was common knowledge that Swift was the author, but he had not yet formally acknowledged his authorship in print, and perhaps Pope tactfully sensed that Swift did not want readers to be reminded of his early scandalous book. Perhaps too Pope thought there was no simple name he could have used for Swift's "Modern" narrator.[98]

It is notable that Pope, who had previously deplored Swift's entanglement in Irish politics, now praises it. By addressing Swift as "Drapier," Pope confirms what oft was thought but never before expressed – Swift had not yet acknowledged that he was the author of the *Drapier's Letters*, so that Pope's dedication constitutes a kind of public announcement. (His lines were to appear on the title page of a 1730 reprint of the collected *Letters*.)[99] But Pope's declaration that "the Fog" has wholly "retire[d]" from Boeotian Ireland is hyperbole, and probably meant to be taken as such: Swift himself would not have agreed that Ireland in 1728 was culturally or politically superior to England.

By now the inscription was apparently complete, although there remain a few differences between this version and that in the published *Variorum*. For whatever reason, Pope was perhaps still sufficiently dissatisfied with it to omit the inscription altogether from the poem he published in May 1728. Or perhaps he hesitated to link the poem openly with Swift, since

---

Toby, alias *Gulliver*, alias *Sw–t*, alias *Examiner*, alias D–n of St. P–'s, alias *Drapier*, alias *Bickerstaff*, alias *Remarker*, alias *Journalist*, alias *Sonnetteer*, alias *Scriblerus*" (p. 237). Smedley's concluding epigraph – "Titulo res Digna Sepulchri" ("a matter worthy the title of a tombstone"), from Juvenal vi, 230 – may have suggested Pope's "whatever Title."

[97] Cf. Milton's hesitation about what name to use in addressing God ("May I express thee unblamed? … Or hear'st thou rather … ?" [*Paradise Lost*, iii, 3–7]).

[98] Ayre later referred to the "Tub Tale-teller" (*Memoirs*, i, 200).

[99] *The Hibernian Patriot* (1730), a reprint of the first collected edition, *Fraud Detected: Or, The Hibernian Patriot* (1725). Neither edition was attributed to Swift.

that might have confirmed suspicions that Pope – "Joint-Author" of the just published third volume of *Miscellanies* – was its author, and would rule out the possibility that Swift was the author.[100] Swift had to be content, for another fourteen months, with the lines in Pope's January 1728 letter, until the *Variorum* appeared in April 1729 with its formal inscription to Swift.

Swift looked forward to the publication of *The Dunciad* in May 1728, perhaps especially because he knew of Pope's plans to inscribe it to him. In late February he wrote to Gay: "Why does not Mr Pope publish his dullness, the rogues he mawles will dy of themselves in peace, and so will his friends, and So there will be neither punishment nor reward."[101] (Swift, as noted above, had been telling Pope that there is no need to attack bad writers, who will die of their own accord). A month later he wrote again to Gay, in words often quoted: "The Beggers Opera hath knockt down Gulliver, I hope to see Popes Dullness knock down the Beggers Opera" (III, 170). It is not commonly noticed that Swift is not registering his admiration of the *Dunciad* – which he has not yet seen – but his impatience to see it published and to see *The Beggar's Opera*, then in its first run in Dublin, "knockt down" just as his own *Gulliver* (published a year and a half earlier) had been "knockt down." "Knock down" is a surprisingly physical term for the way in which eagerly bought books successively supplant each other, and suggests (not wholly facetiously) an element of rough rivalry.[102] Swift had been thinking about the transience of modern fame at least since *Tale of a Tub*, where title pages, posted as advertisements, are quickly "torn down, and fresh ones in their Places," and authors are "hurryed so hastily off the Scene, that they escape our Memory, and delude our Sight" ("Dedication to Prince Posterity"). Six weeks later, on the eve of the poem's publication, Swift is still waiting, and eager to hurry Gay off the stage, as he writes to Pope: "You talk of this Dunciad, but I am impatient to have it *volare per ora* – there is now a vacancy for fame: the Beggars Opera hath done its task, *discedat uti conviva satur*" (III, 181). The classical tags from Virgil and Horace hint at the desire for the longer fame that the Ancients enjoy.[103]

[100] Vander Meulen (1991: 15) notes that the omission of the dedication to Swift left open the possibility that Swift himself was the author. (The title page of the first edition claimed that it was reprinted from an original printed in Dublin.) But since Pope's friends in their letters were openly alluding to the poem it seems unlikely that Pope was anxious to conceal his authorship.
[101] Woolley (1999–2007: III, 162).
[102] It is unclear from lexicographical evidence whether figurative uses of "knock down," meaning "overcome, vanquish, cause to succumb" (*OED*, 10a), had been previously established.
[103] *Georgics* III, 9, "fly on the lips [of men]"; *Satire* I, 1, line 119, "depart like a sated guest."

When Swift finally saw the published poem, his response to Pope was curiously muted. In a letter dated June 1 he says simply that "The Dunciad has taken wind here," and not before complaining that he has learned from a friend "your secret about the Dunciad" – apparently that the inscription would not appear until a later edition – "which does not please me, because it defers gratifying my vanity in the most tender point, and perhaps may wholly disappoint it" (Woolley 1999–2007: III, 184–85). Even though the grumbling is designed to be comic – like the confession of envy in *Verses on the Death of Dr. Swift* – it remains grumbling. Rather than being named and honored in the dedication, Swift makes only two brief appearances in the 1728 poem, both times as the victim of Curll. At II, 96, Curll prepares to seize (in order to publish piratically) the plagiarized "papers" of "M–" (rhymes with "swore," i.e., James Moore[-Smith]), but the sportive winds, restoring the "papers" to their rightful authors, "whisk 'em back to G–, to Y–, to S–" (rhymes with "up-lift," i.e., Swift). And at II, 118, Dulness assures the disappointed "C—l" that by means of her magic gift, "*C—shall be* Prior, *and C—n,* Swift."

Swift's reaction to the poem in his next letter to Pope on July 16 is still understated, businesslike, though perhaps his admiration of the poem is meant to go without saying. In his June 28 reply Pope had told Swift of plans to produce another edition, "with the inscription, which makes me proudest. It will be attended with *Proeme, Prol[e]gomena, Testimonia Scriptorum, Index Authorum*, and Notes *Variorum*." And he had asked Swift to "read over the Text" and provide any notes he thought suitable, "whether dry raillery, upon the stile and way of commenting of trivial Critics; or humorous, upon the authors in the poem; or historical, of persons, places, times; or explanatory, or collecting the parallel passages of the Ancients" (Woolley 1999–2007: III, 186).

In reply Swift provides stern advice about notes:

I have run over the Dunciad in an Irish edition (I suppose full of faults) which a gentleman sent me. The notes I could wish to be very large, in what relates to the persons concern'd; for I have long observ'd that twenty miles from London no body understands hints, initial letters, or town-facts and passages; and in a few years not even those who live in London.[104]

---

[104] Woolley suggests (1999–2007: III, 190) that Swift had read the poem in an Irish reprint in which some of the authors' names, omitted from the London edition, had been filled in. This practice was precisely what Swift was urging on Pope, and what he himself had apparently already determined to do – in the next edition.

And he finally offers full-mouthed praise: "After twenty times reading the whole, I never in my opinion saw so much good satire, or more good sense, in so many lines." (Pope must have been gratified, but evidence of any direct reply has not survived.) But Swift then returns to his suggestions for the next edition:

> I am sure it will be a great disadvantage to the poem, that the persons and facts will not be understood, till an explanation comes out, and a very full one ... Again I insist, you must have your Asterisks fill'd up with some real names of real Dunces ... I am thinking whether the Editor should not follow the old style of, This excellent author, &c. And refine in many places when you meant no refinement? And into the bargain take all the load of naming the dunces, their qualities, histories, and performances? (III, 189).

Critics usually assume that it was Swift who encouraged Pope to provide notes, but the epistolary evidence (though perhaps not conclusive) suggests that the notes were originally Pope's idea, modeled though they were on the notes in Swift's *Tub*, with its pretense that the annotator is someone other than the author, and the mixing, in the notes, of "facts" and pure invention.[105] It remains unclear exactly what kind of notes Pope had in mind. Swift takes up the idea enthusiastically, and insists that the notes serve to identify the duncees by name. Was he aware that his insistence on providing "real names of real Dunces" would ironically have the effect of transmitting their names to posterity, which he had been warning Pope against for the last several years? Whether or not Swift actually supplied notes of the sort Pope requested is not known. By October the "Variorum" was in press. On the 12th Pope wrote to Swift informing him that "The inscription to the Dunciad is now printed and inserted in the Poem," and repeating his thanks not for Swift's praise but for his role as prompter (Woolley 1999–2007: III, 201).

Does Pope's insistence in the October 12 letter that "the poem is yours" mask the point that he has turned Swift from cautionary doubter to collaborator (whether in fact or only in spirit) in his project of both ridiculing and documenting duncery? Perhaps the dedication to Swift was deferred until the *Variorum* primarily because Pope sensed that Swift's name might be better invoked there than in the 1728 "Heroic Poem." For it was in the *Variorum* that Pope most fully adopted Swift

---

[105] This point is related to the question of whether Pope, when he published the 1728 poem, already had in mind the plan to publish a "Variorum" edition. This suggestion, first advanced by Robert K. Root in 1929, has been developed by Vander Meulen (1991: 15), challenged by Shef Rogers ("Pope, Publishing, and Popular Interpretations of the 'Dunciad Variorum,'" *Philological Quarterly* 74, 3 [Summer 1995], 279–95), but reaffirmed by Rumbold (see note 89, above).

as model, and through the *Variorum* that he most fully recruited Swift as an admiring ally.

The *Dunciad Variorum* was published on April 10, 1729.[106] Now appeared in print Pope's revised dedication, in the form we recognize but which Swift was seeing for the first time (see Illustration 2.3):

> O thou! whatever Title please thine ear,
> Dean, Drapier, Bickerstaff, or Gulliver!
> Whether thou chuse Cervantes' serious Air,
> Or laugh and shake in Rab'lais' easy Chair,
> Or praise the Court, or magnify Mankind,
> Or thy griev'd Country's copper chains unbind;
> From thy Boeotia tho' Her Pow'r retires,
> Grieve not at ought our sister realm acquires:
> Here pleas'd behold her mighty wings out-spread,
> To hatch a new Saturnian age of Lead. (1, 17–26)[107]

Pope has converted what was the second part of a two-part address ("... And Thou! ...") into a free-standing invocation: "O thou!" Some lines have been rearranged, so that the parody of an appeal to a god ("Attend, whatever Title please thine ear") is given more prominence by being placed at the beginning of the paragraph. Swift, if we note the imperative verbs, is now urged not simply to "Attend" – i.e., pay attention – and "Grieve not," but rather to "Grieve not" and "behold." Here Pope underlines the idea that Swift is a kind of god: a parody of the Creator in Genesis who "saw" or beheld that his own work was good, and in Milton's account "with mighty wings outspread / Dove-like sat'st brooding on the vast abyss / And mad'st it pregnant" (*Paradise Lost*, 1, 20–22), Swift, "Here pleas'd," is urged to "behold [Dulness's] mighty wings out-spread, / To hatch a new Saturnian age of Lead." (In the January 1728 version, Dulness simply "reigns" but does not give birth.) Pope here makes Swift the unmoved mover, not the efficient cause of *The Dunciad* but its First Cause. The inscription begins with the wish to "please thine ear" and ends with the confidence that Swift is already "pleas'd" to behold the birth of a false creation, and pleased to behold Pope's account of it, or even – if we notice that the mood of the verb is still imperative – *instructed by Pope* to be pleased.

---

[106] Five days earlier Swift had responded to a letter in which Pope, perhaps thinking that he had done *his* part in commemorating their friendship, had apparently expressed his "desire" that Swift "record our friendship in verse" (Woolley 1999–2007: III, 231) – see below, pp. 138–40.

[107] In the edition Swift received, the text for line 24 in fact reads "realms acquire." Other 1729 editions give "realm acquires" – which preserves the rhyme.

Book I.   The D u n c i a d.   3

Laborious, heavy, bufy, bold, and blind,

She rul'd, in native Anarchy, the mind.

15   Still her old empire to confirm, fhe tries,

For born a Goddefs, Dulnefs never dies.

O thou ! whatever Title pleafe thine ear,

Dean, Drapier, Bickerftaff, or Gulliver !

Whether thou chufe Cervantes' ferious air,

20   Or laugh and fhake in Rab'lais eafy Chair,

Or praife the Court, or magnify Mankind,

Or thy griev'd Country's copper chains unbind ;

From thy Bæotia tho' Her Pow'r retires,

Grieve not at ought our fifter realms acquire :

25   Here pleas'd behold her mighty wings out-fpread,

To hatch a new Saturnian age of Lead.

Where wave the tatter'd enfigns of Rag-Fair,

A yawning ruin hangs and nods in air ;

R E M A R K S.

V e r s e 23. *From thy* Bæotia.] *Bæotia* of old
lay under the Raillery of the neighbouring
Wits, as *Ireland* does now ; tho' each of thofe
nations produced one of the greateft Wits, and
greateft Generals, of their age.
  V e r s e 26. *A new* Saturnian *Age of Lead.*]
The ancient Golden Age is by Poets ftiled *Sa-*
turnian ; but in the Chymical language, *Sa-*
turn is Lead.

  V e r s e 27. *Where wave the tatter'd Enfigns of*
Rag-fair.] *Rag-fair* is a place near the *Tower of*
London, where old cloaths and frippery are fold.

V e r s e 28. 31. &c. *A yawning ruin hangs and*
nods in air.———
  Here in one Bed two fhiv'ring Sifters lie,
  The Cave of Poverty *and* Poetry.
  Hear upon this place the forecited Critick on
the *Dunciad.* " Thefe lines (faith he) have no
" Conftruction, or are Nonfenfe. The two
" fhivering Sifters muft be the fifter Caves of Po-
" verty and Poetry, or the Bed and Cave of Pover-
" ty and Poetry muft be the fame, (queftionlefs)
" and the two Sifters the Lord knows who ?
O the Conftruction of Grammatical Heads ! *Vir-*
gil writeth thus : *Æn. 1.*

                                           Fronte

2.3 Pope's dedication of the *Dunciad Variorum* to Swift.

Other minor changes adjust the difference between Pope and his addressee. Swift's politics are given an English reference: in the January 1728 version Swift is said to "Praise Courts and Monarchs" (a safely generic target) and in the printed version of March 1729 to "praise the Court" (which more clearly allows a glance at the court of George II, and thus recruits Swift as an ally in a war of words against "Dunce the Second" and all he stands for). With characteristic cunning, Pope conceals the barb by claiming, in a 1729 footnote, that "Or praise the Court" is "*Ironicè*, alluding [not to the English court but] to *Gulliver's* Representations." But the tribute to Swift's "Sence," "Humour," and "Rage" – equipment for a warring satirist, and thus an apt link between the poet and his addressee – has dropped out.

Swift no doubt saw the *Dunciad Variorum* soon after publication, but, for whatever reason, Pope seems not to have sent personal copies of it to his dedicatee for some time. His letter to Swift of October 9, 1729 (six months after the poem was published), begins "It pleases me that you received my books at last." (Swift had apparently acknowledged receipt in a letter that has not survived.) Pope goes on to complain gently that "you have never once told me if you approve the whole, or disapprove not of some parts, of the Commentary, &c," and to add (disingenuously, so it now seems) that "it was my principal aim in the entire work to perpetuate the friendship between us, and to shew that the friends or the enemies of one were the friends or enemies of the other" (Woolley 1999–2007: III, 257). Did Swift not send to Pope his praise of the new edition because he suspected some slight or omission? It seems that Pope might have thought so, since his declaration about his "principal aim" follows soon after. Any innocent reader who happened upon the *Dunciad Variorum* could easily be forgiven if he failed to realize that Pope's "principal aim" was to memorialize his friendship with a writer named only four times.[108] And what the published dedication emphasizes, as the dedicatee must also have noticed, is not Swift the benevolent friend, virtuous private man (the line in the early draft about his "morals" has dropped out), or charitable neighbor but the public personae of a shape-changing writer. Swift later told Mrs. Pilkington that he thought the lines were meant as a compliment "but they are very stiff,"[109] implicitly refuting Pope's earlier claim, in the 1727 letter about the joint volume of *Miscellanies*, that he had managed to avoid the "stiff forms" of learned authors.[110] (In his own tribute

---

[108] I, 26, II, 116, II, 138, III, 331. Swift's name also appears several times in the notes. See below, pp. 124, 126, 127.

[109] *Memoirs*, 2 vols. (1748), I, 62–63. Thomas Sheridan, quoting the remark, adds a note questioning Mrs. Pilkington's veracity (*Life of the Reverend Dr. Jonathan Swift*, 2nd edn. 1787, 412).

[110] See above, p. 95.

to Pope, in the "Libel to Dr. Delany," Swift would later refer to Pope's "generous mind," virtuous "soul," "filial piety," and great "heart.") But in his reply to Pope on October 31, Swift more fully acknowledged receipt of five copies, four of which he gave to friends and the fifth he inscribed "Amicissimi au[c]toris donum" (see Illustration 2.4).[111]

He hastened to assure the wounded Pope without qualification that "I am one of every body who approve every part of it, Text and Comment," and added that he was "one abstracted from every body, in the happiness of being recorded your friend, while wit, and humour, and politeness shall have any memorial among us" (Woolley 1999–2007: III, 858). Whatever resentment Swift felt disappears in this grateful acknowledgement of the inscription.[112]

Among the materials added to the "Variorum" edition of the poem were footnotes to the four lines in which Swift had been named. The first explains that I, 24 ("Grieve not at ought our sister realm acquires") is ironical: "The Politicks of *England* and *Ireland* were at this time by some thought to be opposite, or interfering with each other: Dr. *Swift* of course was in the interest of the latter, our Author of the former."[113] The ironical "acquires" points to Swift's conviction that England had indeed been economically exploiting – or acquiring – Ireland for years. But as Rumbold notes, this is one instance in which Swift is urged not to grieve at "England's appropriation of what the Irish will be better off without" (2007: 178). Swift probably appreciated the irony, but may have thought that the note gratuitously drew attention to a sharp political difference between himself and his literary colleague.

At II, 108 Swift's name appears again ("And whisk 'em back to Evans, Young, and Swift"), authors whose writings (so Pope's note explains) had been published piratically by Curll. In the 1728 edition Swift had been in better (or at least anonymous) company: "G–" (i.e., Gay) and "Y–" (i.e., Young). It is not likely that Swift would have been happy to be classed now with the likes of Abel Evans (an admirer of Pope, but a very minor poet), or even Young (who since 1726 had been one of Walpole's pensioners, and had just published in June 1728 the fulsome *Ocean: An Ode … to*

---

[111] As noted by Woolley (1999–2007: III, 190) (though he does not comment that Swift appears to have omitted the "c" in "auctoris"). The presentation copy (which survives in the Forster Collection at the Victoria and Albert Museum) is also inscribed "Jonath. Swift. 1729." on the main title page. In a November 28, 1729 letter, Pope told Swift that he would have the second octavo edition, with some new notes, sent to him, but as of February 26, 1730 Swift had not received it (III, 271, 284).

[112] But see below (ch. 3) for some evidence that Swift was not satisfied with the dedication.

[113] The footnote first appeared here in the 1729 (octavo) editions, moved from III, 327, where it appeared in the initial quarto editions.

2.4 Title page of the *Dunciad Variorum* (inscribed by Swift "Jonath. Swift. 1729").

which is prefix's an Ode to the King): this assemblage shows the same lack of critical discrimination that Pope deplored in Giles Jacob. And II, 130 ("Cook shall be Prior, and Concanen, Swift"), with all four names now spelled out, despite the reassuring presence of Prior, does not place him in better company. How embarrassing that any reader might mistake a poem by Swift for a poem by Matthew Concanen! The footnote explains only that Concanen had slandered "Dr. Swift to whom he had obligations, and from whom he had received ... no small assistance" – which seems not to have been precisely true – and does not make clear that Concanen had in fact published several of Swift's poems without permission in a 1724 miscellany. But Swift must have felt sharper regret that, in the footnote to the following line ("And we too boast our Garth and Addison"), his own name is omitted: "Nothing is more remarkable than our author's love of praising good writers. He has celebrated Sir *Isaac Newton*, Mr. *Dryden*, Mr. *Congreve*, Mr. *Wycherley*, Dr. *Garth*, Mr. *Walsh*, Duke of *Buckingham*, Mr. *Addison*, Lord *Lansdown;* in a word, almost every man of his time that deserv'd it." How Swift must have longed to be included in this distinguished company! How could he not regret or even resent his exclusion from it? If it were to be objected that Pope had in fact not yet praised Swift in print, except in the inscription to the poem itself, Swift might well complain that it was not for lack of opportunity.[114]

There is one name in the list that Swift might not have wished there: Dryden's. And yet Pope, who had admired and modeled himself on Dryden since the beginning of his career (and before he met Swift), thought highly enough of it that he included in the *Dunciad Variorum* an extended "Parallel of the Characters of Mr. Dryden and Mr. Pope, As Drawn by certain of their Cotemporaries." Spread across two pairs of facing pages was a set of charges, illustrated by the words of hostile contemporaries, with bibliographical details in the footnotes, on "Mr. Dryden. His Politicks, Religion, Morals," followed by "Mr. Pope, His Politicks, Religion, Morals," and so on through a litany of the attacks through the years: "only a Versifyer," "understood no Greek," and "trick'd his Subscribers," concluding with "Names bestow'd on. Mr. Dryden" (ape, ass, frog, coward, knave, fool, thing) and "Names bestow'd on Mr. Pope" (ape, ass, etc.). Linking himself with the revered Dryden clearly served Pope's purposes in ways that linking himself with the controversial and partisan Swift would not. But Swift might well have imagined that Pope could surely have found room somewhere in the vast reaches of the *Variorum* for a similar catalog of attacks made jointly on Pope and Swift.

It seems possible that Pope did in fact at one point consider including in the *Variorum* such a list of joint attacks. In his October 12, 1728

<hr>

[114] Swift is named briefly, as co-author of "*Swift* and *Pope*'s Miscellanies," in an extended note to II, 46, also at II, 93, III, 146, and the "List of All our AUTHOR's Genuine Works" in the "Appendix."

letter, Pope assures Swift that "if you knew the infinite content I have receiv'd of late, at the finding yours and my name constantly united in any silly scandal, I think you would go near to sing *Io Triumphe!* and celebrate my happiness in verse; and I believe if you won't, I shall" (Woolley 1999–2007: III, 201). He could have found lists ready to hand in Curll's *Compleat Collection* and Smedley's *Gulliveriana*, both published earlier in 1728. Perhaps, however, he judged that since such catalogues of recent attacks had already been published, he would produce a list of another sort: a list of attacks on *him*, going back to 1711. And he found room in the Appendix for "A List of Books, Papers, and Verses … in which our Author was abused." Swift's name in fact appears frequently in the list: in at least eight of the entries.[115] But as the list's title suggests, Pope wanted to keep the focus on himself: at least four of the attacks listed target both Swift and Pope, although you would not know it from Pope's entry.[116]

Swift's final appearance in the 1729 poem, in lines not in the 1728 *Dunciad* – "Gay dies un-pension'd with a hundred Friends, / Hibernian Politicks, O Swift, thy doom / And Pope's, translating three whole years with Broome" (III, 326–28) – is, so Pope's note suggests, ironical, but any irony in the line about Swift is difficult to calculate, and was probably difficult for Swift to appreciate. Pope might object that he no more meant to depreciate Swift's work on behalf of Ireland than his own translation of Homer, but Swift knew well that Pope thought he was wasting his time and talent on Irish politics, regardless of the handsome compliment in the poem's inscription.[117] Pope's footnote glossing "Hibernian Politicks" gratuitously replicates most of the footnote to 1, 24, dropping only the reference to Pope's English affiliation.[118]

---

[115] See Rumbold (2007: 327–28). At a note to II, 199 Swift and Pope are listed among the victims of Oldmixon's misrepresentations, at II, 279 as joint victims of Smedley's *Gulliveriana*, and at III, 159 as jointly abused by James Ralph's *Sawney*.

[116] Pope's "List" includes Ralph's *Sawney*, Smedley's *Metamorphosis of Scriblerus*, and two other items, without indicating that in each case Swift also was attacked. (See Guerinot, *Pamphlet Attacks*, [1969], 104–06, 124–27, 133–34.)

[117] Beginning with the 1736 edition of the poem, "Hibernian Politicks" is Swift's "fate" rather than his "doom" (III, 331). The change may have been made as part of Pope's decision to remove Broome's name, at his request. But "fate" carries less sense of punishment and adverse fortune (*OED*, "doom", 2, 4), and even hints admiringly that Irish politics was Swift's "appointed lot" ("fate," 3b).

[118] Swift is named in a note in the "Appendix" to the poem as one who "may be said in a sort to be Author of the Poem" (Rumbold 2007: 321). See above, pp. 110–11. Oddly, elsewhere in the "Appendix", in the "Index of Matters Contained in this Poem and Notes," Swift's name does not appear: perhaps Pope had adopted Swift's suggestion that the "Index Authorum" (which Pope had proposed) be designed as "the names of those scriblers printed indexically at the beginning or end of the Poem" (Woolley 1999–2007: III, 189). Still, he found room in the index for Addison, Horace, Virgil, Shakespeare, and himself.

The epistolary record of the exchanges between Pope and Swift during the composition and publication of *The Dunciad* is substantial, but modern readers could wish for more – some discussion, for example, of their shared delight in uncleanness. Did Swift sense any significance in the difference between Gulliver's mortification when he is bespattered with excrement, or obliged to tend to "the necessities of nature," and Curll's happy obliviousness of the "brown dishonours of his face" (ii, 100)? A scholar who sees Pope's as an art of incorporation, flies enclosed in amber, Curll's fresh vomit woven into a "shaggy Tap'stry" (ii, 135), and scribblers imprisoned within the monument of mock-epic, and Swift's, by contrast, as an art of purgation/rejection/purifying, paring down, washing away, vomiting out, can as yet find no evidence that Pope and Swift discussed their work in these terms. Above all, perhaps, one wishes to know whether Swift reflected on the difference between his own dismissal of epic as an obsolete and exhausted form and what Rawson would much later identify as Pope's conviction that it might still serve, if only through the parodic "majesty of mud" – one of the most important and obvious ways in which *The Dunciad* "replies" to Swift's work and corrects its author.

Such matters do not – and perhaps would not – come up in the course of their correspondence. But they never saw each other face to face after Swift returned to Dublin in September 1727, before the poem was completed. Insofar as we can measure Swift's further response to *The Dunciad*, we must look at his poems of the 1730s, and in particular at "Upon Poetry. A Rapsody," not published until 1733.

CHAPTER 3

Satyrist and philosopher

In the years between the *Dunciad Variorum* (1729) and Faulkner's four-volume edition of the *Works of J. S, D. D, D. S. P. D* (1735), Pope and Swift stood together in the eyes of most of their contemporaries as a linked pair – "Swift-and-Pope," "Pope-and-Swift."[1] In their own eyes, to judge by their letters, they saw themselves allied against a world of "ignorance and barbarity."[2] The letters they exchanged during this period continue to include extraordinary – and often quite moving – professions of undying friendship, and continue as well to suggest the points on which they had not yet agreed to differ. During these years, they collaborated (with some strains) to produce the final volume in a series of joint poetic *Miscellanies* in 1732. Both appeared before the public every year, Pope (with the *Essay on Man* and a series of poetical epistles, and the beginnings of a series of imitations of Horace) remarkably prolific, and Swift much less so, although it was during these years that he wrote what are usually regarded as his most important poems – among them the *Verses on the Death of Dr. Swift*, the so-called "dressing room poems," and *On Poetry. A Rapsody*. In their poems as in their letters each seems to have borne the other constantly in mind, and we can detect the shadow of *The Dunciad* in Swift's *On Poetry. A Rapsody*, and the shadow of Swift's dressing room poems in Pope's *Epistle to a Lady*. The *Epistle from Mr. Pope to Dr. Arbuthnot* may be read as Pope's reply to the *Life and Genuine Character of Dr. Swift*. Even the *Essay on Man* seems to bear the pressure of Swift's *Travels*. In each instance the "reply" serves as a declaration of alliance, but also as a kind of counterstatement.

---

[1] In his *Author to be Lett* (1729) Richard Savage declared that in Curll's service "I wrote Obscenity and Prophaneness, under the names of *Pope* and *Swift*" (3). Lady Mary Wortley Montagu in a 1750 letter sneered that Pope and Swift were "entitle'd by their Birth and Heredity to be only a couple of Link Boys" (*Complete Letters*, ed. R. Halsband, 3 vols. [1965–67], III, 57–58).

[2] Johnson acerbically notes that to hear Pope and Swift tell it they "lived amongst ignorance and barbarity, unable to find among their contemporaries either virtue or intelligence, and persecuted by those that could not understand them" (Lonsdale 2006: IV, 60).

Perhaps underlying all of these exchanges in the early 1730s is Swift's repeated request that Pope write an "epistle to Dr. Swift," Pope's still puzzling refusal to comply, and Swift's simmering resentment.

THE LETTERS

Although the epistolary record is obviously incomplete, the thirty-three surviving letters between Swift and Pope from April 1729 through May 1735 paint the same picture of mutual admiration and affection seen in their earlier letters. Although they were not to see each other face to face after 1726, they continued to look ahead to possible meetings, perhaps in Ireland, England, or France. But the deaths of their friends Atterbury and Gay in 1732, Pope's own mother in 1733, and Arbuthnot and Peterborow in 1735 probably made them readier to reflect on the pain of their separation. "You say truly," Pope wrote to Swift in April 1733 after the death of Gay,

that death is only terrible to us as it separates us from those we love, but I really think those have the worst of it who are left by us, if we are true friends. I have felt more (I fancy) in the loss of poor Mr. Gay, than I shall suffer in the thought of going away myself into a state that can feel none of this sort of losses. (Woolley 1999–2007: III, 630)

In a May 1735 letter to Pope, the deaths of old friends Gay, Arbuthnot, and Lady Masham provoke Swift to regret his forced separation from "my best friend" (IV, 103). But the death of friends also leads Pope to imagine the ways in which separation might ultimately be overcome: I now wish, Pope goes on, that "you and I might walk into the grave together, by as slow steps as you please, but contentedly and chearfully: Whether that ever can be, or in what country, I know no more, than into what country we shall walk out of the grave" (III, 630). Pope looks back on Swift's visits to England in 1726 and 1727 as a kind of foretaste of what they might again enjoy, in another world – "The two summers we past together dwell always on my mind, like a vision which gave me a glympse of a better life and better company, than this world otherwise afforded" – but also as a reminder that, for now, Swift (though still very much in this world) is stuck in Ireland and as good as dead, "to me like a limb lost, and buried in another country" (IV, 28–29). But even if they cannot meet, perhaps they together could "leave some sort of Monument" to show "what Friends two Wits could be in spite of all the fools in the world" (IV, 405).

There is no reason to question the sincerity of these professions, or to doubt that the eternal friendship of like-minded spirits is a leading motif in the Pope–Swift letters of these years. But it is also worth noting that in the course of declaring their affinity and near-identity – Swift is "to me like a limb lost" – both friends chose repeatedly to draw attention to differences between them. Each continued to suffer from ill health, and to worry about the health of his friend, but the shared concern becomes a means of defining difference. "In one point I am apt to differ from you," Pope wrote to Swift in December 1731, "for you shun your friends when you are in those circumstances [i.e., ill], and I desire them; your way is the more generous, mine the more tender" (Woolley 1999–2007: III, 447). Or as Swift put it fifteen months later in March 1733, "You and I are valetudinarians of a direct contrary kind" (III, 616).[3] Defining difference was not only a game they played with each other. In a 1732 letter to a mutual friend, Swift remarked initially on his affinity with Pope – "Pope, Gay, and I use all our Endeavours to make Folks merry and wise, and profess to have no Enemies, except Knaves and Fools" – but immediately went on to mark an important difference: "I confess myself to be exempted from them in one Article, which was engaging with a Ministry to prevent, if possible, the Evils that have over-run the Nation; and my foolish Zeal in endeavouring to save this wretched Island" (III, 517). Pope, until the mid-1730s, preferred to avoid making his political commitments public. By contrast, Swift from the early 1720s had made clear his determination to oppose the policies of the court. In 1735 Swift explicitly urged Pope to emulate him: "I heartily wish you were what they call disaffected, as I, who detest abominate & abhor every Creature who hath a dram of Power in either Kingdom" (IV, 174). But Pope resisted, and none of his letters, Swift agreed, "have any thing to do with Party, of which you are the clearest of all men, by your Religion, and the whole Tenour of your life; while I am raging every moment against the Corruptions in both kingdoms, especially of this; such is my weakness" (IV, 432). Swift here pretends that oppositional politics is a "weakness" which Pope has avoided, but his implicit desire to get Pope to take a political stand was finally to be gratified by 1739, when Pope aligned himself with the Prince of Wales, Lyttelton, and the Boy Patriots, in open opposition to Walpole.

Walpole was one of the courtiers over whom Swift and Pope disagreed. Another was Henrietta Howard, Countess of Suffolk. Woman of the Bedchamber to the Princess of Wales (later Queen Caroline), mistress of

---

[3] Cf. Swift to Pope: "I well know how little you value life both as a Philosopher and a Christian, particularly the latter, wherein hardly one in a million of us hereticks can equal you" (Woolley 1999–2007: IV, 259).

the Prince (later George II), and a neighbor of Pope's in Twickenham, Mrs. Howard met Pope in 1717, Swift by about 1726; both became her correspondent. Swift, hoping (apparently with some encouragement from Pope) that she might use her influence with the Princess of Wales to advance his personal and political interests, sent her a gift of Irish plaid, and received some signs from her that he (as well as Gay) could expect some royal favor. Pope kept in with her (if only for the sake of their mutual friend, Martha Blount), but Swift soon decided that she was unreliable.[4] As early as November 1727, with her in mind, he wrote to Pope of his resentment at "the insincerityes of those who would be thought the best Friends" (Woolley 1999–2007: III, 141).[5] Two years later he wrote again, bidding Pope give his "humble service" to "Mrs. B" – Martha Blount – but, pointedly, "to no Lady at court" – i.e., Mrs. Howard (III, 246). Pope replied in her defense that "that Lady means to do good, and does no harm, which is a vast deal for a Courtier" (III, 258). In 1730 Swift wrote again to Pope, proposing to write a "moral letter" to her (III, 284), and in his reply Pope, perhaps fearing that Swift would give offense, asked that any such letter be sent via him, presumably so that he could censor it (III, 299). When Swift subsequently did write reproachfully to her (November 11, 1730), Pope expressed his displeasure, and Swift replied (January 15, 1731) by reaffirming his resentment of her ill treatment of him. The two friends continued to bicker over her, Swift signing off on April 20, 1731 by sending "Nothing to Mrs. Howard" – she had failed to answer the friendly letter that Pope had persuaded him to write. On July 20, Swift again complained of her "pride and negligence."

It was not only people about whom Pope and Swift pointedly expressed their disagreement to each other. They also differed about the stance to be taken as one contemplated a corrupt court and world: is it better to express resentment in bitter satire, or to rise above such feelings in philosophical detachment? Pope and Swift personalized the question, and represented each other as opponents in the implicit debate. "You like to see the inside of a court," Pope wrote to Swift in 1729, "which I do not" (Woolley 1999–2007: III, 258)[6] – meaning not that Swift delights in court

---

[4] For Mrs. Howard's relationships with Pope and Swift, see the sympathetic remarks by Mack (1985: 375–78) and Rumbold (1989: 208–31), and the more severe analysis in Ehrenpreis (1962–83: III, 587–93).

[5] For Swift's 1727 "character" of Mrs. Howard, and Pope's reply to it, see below, p. 161.

[6] Cf. Swift to Pope, April 20, 1731, where Swift refers to an earlier letter from Pope "wherein you are hard on me for saying you were a Poet in favour at Court."

news or in vicariously visiting the court, but (in a rare allusion to *Tale of a Tub*) that Swift wants to "enter into the Depth of Things" and discover "that in the inside they are good for nothing," while Pope prefers to avert his eyes from the unpleasant, or to "converse about the Surface."[7] In April 1733 Pope noted that he himself (like Swift) had satirized "false Courtiers, and Spies," and then insisted on difference: "I have not the courage however to be such a Satyrist as you, but I would be as much, or more, a Philosopher." And, as he goes on, he again sharply draws another distinction between himself and Swift: "You call your satires, Libels; I would rather call my satires, Epistles: They will consist more of morality than wit, and grow graver, which you will call duller" (III, 631). Swift had, not long before, published his *Libel on Dr. Delany* and Pope his "Epistles" to Burlington and Bathurst. Having also just published two months earlier some fairly sharp satire – the imitation of the first satire of Horace's second book ("To Fortescue"), Pope is no doubt being disingenuous, as he was at the end of the imitation itself, in which he professes to contrast *"Libels* and *Satires!* Lawless Things indeed!" with his own "grave *Epistles*, bringing Vice to light" (lines 150–51).[8] This is a reminder that we should not always take Pope at his word: the difference he claims between his own "Epistles" and Swift's "Libels" turns out, at a closer look, to blur in the smoke of irony.[9] But the distinction between "Satyrist" and "Philosopher" is preserved, reflecting Pope's turn toward a philosophical (i.e., ethical) poetry in the 1730s. Swift, he unrepentantly declares, will think such poetry "duller" than what Pope had written earlier in his career. That marks a difference between them.

And he goes on to draw another sharp contrast: "you use to love what I hate, a hurry of politicks" (Woolley 1999–2007: III, 632). What interests Pope here is the rhetoric of opposition, a means not only of staging debate but also of defining himself in relation to an imagined contrary. Perhaps Pope is habitually drawn to think in terms of antitheses – one of the principles on which his couplets are constructed. What is significant in the context of my argument is that for every instance in his letters declaring that he and Swift are the dearest of friends and completely

---

[7] Alluding to Swift's contrast between "curiosity" and "credulity" in the "Digression on Madness" (Guthkelch and Smith 1958: 173).
[8] Pope had already sent a copy of the poem to Swift (see Pope to Swift, February 16, 1733), and Swift had already reported how much he admired it (see Swift to Orrery, March 22, 1733; Swift to Pope, March 30, 1733). Swift himself had in *c.* 1729–30 written an imitation of Horace's satire (Williams 1958: II, 488–91), but there is no evidence that Pope knew of it.
[9] Harth (1998: 245) notes that Pope's distinction is not to be taken at face value.

kindred spirits, there is another instance declaring that it is a marriage of opposites.

Opposites attract, but sometimes they also seek to effect a conversion. While they persisted in their opposed stances of philosophical (and non-partisan) detachment and angry political engagement, Pope continued to press Swift to become more like him, but paradoxically drew closer to him in the process. In the same April 20, 1733 letter, Pope, catching Swift's tone, exclaims: "Drown Ireland! For having caught you, and for having kept you."[10] In his quick reply (on May 1) Swift ignored Pope's outburst, and in his next letter (on July 8) implicitly dismissed it by once again urging Pope to visit him in Ireland, where, so Swift professed, he had freely chosen to live, "a free-man among slaves, rather than a Slave among free-men, ... and absolute Lord of the greatest Cathedral in the Kingdom." But "this," as Swift concedes, is only "railery" (Woolley 1999–2007: III, 663). Two years later he takes a much darker view of Ireland: "This Kingdom is now absolutely starving; by the means of every Oppression that can be inflicted on mankind." At first he appears to agree with Pope – "You advise me right, not to trouble myself about the World" – but goes on to make clear that in the end he cannot take Pope's view, that "not troubling himself" is simply not an option: "But oppressions torture me" (IV, 175).

It is not uncommon to find that a running exchange in the correspondence spills over into a poem organized around the differences they have been exploring in their letters. One of Swift's recurrent concerns is his friend's tender digestion. As early as 1726 he worries about the frequent reports he receives about Pope's being "out of order," especially after indulging at a "great dinner" (Woolley 1999–2007: III, 4). Pope, for his part, liked to write of his native "moderation" and in 1733 offered, as a reason why he dared not visit Dublin, the "excessive eating and drink-ing of your hospitable town" (III, 689). Swift countered by grumbling to Arbuthnot that Pope is "too temperate" (IV, 16). One gets the sense that Pope's eating habits – his temperance and intemperance – were a topic on which the two friends habitually teased each other during the time they spent together. Swift was also concerned about Pope's modest income, and his failure to build up any kind of estate on which to live.[11] Pope's response, on at least one occasion, was to take a versified form. His imita-tion of the second satire of Horace's second book, published on July 4,

---

[10] Compare Swift's own "Drown the World!" (November 26, 1725, in Woolley 1999–2007: II, 623).

[11] Swift to Pope, August 11, 1729: "One reason I would have you in Ireland ... is that you may be master of two or three years revenues." Pope to Swift, October 9, 1729: "You are too careful of my worldly affairs; I am rich enough" (Woolley 1999–2007: III, 245, 258).

1734, makes use of Swift as a kind of straw man in a playful meditation about living "on little."

After putting in his friend Bethel's mouth a "sermon" about the virtues of "Temperance" and a "homely dinner," Pope describes his own life at Twickenham, where he claims to be "Content with little" and happy to offer his guests what food the neighborhood affords at his house on five acres of "rented land." At this point he imagines Swift interjecting:

> "Pray heav'n it last! (cries Swift) as you go on;
> I wish to God this house had been your own:
> Pity! To build, without a son or wife:
> Why, you'll enjoy it only all your life." (161–64)

The speech attributed to Swift works as a kind of private joke between friends. It reflects Swift's worries in the correspondence about Pope's status as a mere tenant, improving a house that stands on ground belonging to his landlord (Thomas Vernon), and that thus must itself one day belong to him. It also alludes to a sentiment expressed in the opening lines of Swift's own imitation of the sixth satire of the second book of Horace, initially published in the Pope–Swift *Miscellanies* in 1727:

> I often wish'd, that I had clear
> For Life, six hundred Pounds a Year,
> A handsome House to lodge a Friend,
> A River at my Garden's End.

Pope may have had his suspicions that this sentiment did not in fact reflect Swift's own thinking, as suggested by some lines he was later to insert into his continuation of Swift's poem.[12] Or he may simply have chosen to make use of Swift as a convenience in his own celebration of the life of the man of no property:

> What's *Property?* dear Swift! you see it alter
> From you to me, from me to Peter Walter,
> Or, in a mortgage, prove a Lawyer's share,
> Or, in a jointure, vanish from the Heir. (167–70)

Pope playfully exaggerates, imagining that those who accumulate property are literally buying it from those who give it up. Pope himself had sold his family's land,[13] while Walter was known to be buying up what

---

[12] See below ch. 4, pp. 207–09.
[13] "My lands are sold, my Father's house is gone" (*Second Satire of the Second Book of Horace*, line 155).

property he could in Dorset,[14] but Walter never bought from Pope himself. As for property "altering" from Swift to Pope, the phrase may allude to Swift's relative lack of concern for (and Pope's eager attention to) literary "property," and just possibly to a dispute about the property in their joint *Miscellanies*.[15] As a churchman, entitled to the use (but not the ownership) of rectory and deanery, Swift in fact nowhere made a plea for the virtues of owning "Property."[16] And he comically grumbled, shortly after he read the poem for the first time, about the way in which Pope had represented him: "In his last Translation out of Horace, I could willingly have excused his placing me not in that Light which I would appear; and others are of my opinion." Yet, ready to dismiss the matter, he insists that the poem "gives me not the least offence, because I am sure he had not the least ill Intention" (Swift to Oxford, August 30, 1734, in Woolley 1999–2007: III, 753). The repetition and emphasis – "not the least … not the least" – here suggests, as often with Swift, the presence of irony.

The rhetoric of opposition – "I think this, but you think that" – serves to insist on significant difference, but does not seem to put any real strain on the friendship. That is not the case, however, with a third feature of the letters of these years, the undercurrent of tension that wells to the surface when one felt that the other had implicitly violated the terms of their friendship, whether by acts of commission or omission.

Swift, as suggested, had long been concerned about his friend's material circumstances: as a Roman Catholic, Pope was barred from some positions and some forms of patronage, and without an assured source of income was obliged to translate Homer for a bookseller. Characteristically, Swift lets Pope know of his concern by drawing a distinction between them: "I am not half so moderate as you, for I declare I cannot live easily under double to what you are satisfied with" (August 11, 1729). Having been instrumental in the distribution of governmental patronage during the Harley – St. John ministry, Swift continued to think, years later, that something might yet be done for Pope, if only he (Swift) were to speak to the right person. He did speak to powerful people, highly placed in

[14] See note in Butt (1939: IV, 68).
[15] Motte bought the copyright to the *Miscellanies*, but when he failed to make a final payment Pope renegotiated the terms, and sold rights to the fourth volume to Gilliver in 1732, at which point Motte tried to get Swift to intercede. For details, see Foxon (1991: 243–44). Woolley (1999–2007: III, 535) thinks that Pope and Swift exchanged several letters – now lost – on the matter. In a 1732 letter to Motte, Swift said he had "no advantage by any one of the four volumes" (III, 563) but in fact in 1728 he had been paid at least £100 (III, 183).
[16] For Swift's investments in land, see Ehrenpreis (1962–83: III, 324–25). In a May 2, 1730 letter to Pope, Swift says he owns land which brings in £250 a year (Woolley 1999–2007: III, 308).

Walpole's government, first to John Lord Carteret, Lord Lieutenant of Ireland, and later to George Bubb Dodington, a Whig politico, suggesting to them that Pope ought to have a pension for his services to literature. Pope, however, was touchy about his independence, preferred to keep himself free of all indebtedness, and in a November 1729 letter expressed his displeasure that Swift had spoken to Dodington. Responding on February 26, 1730, Swift professed that he was "not guilty" of speaking to Dodington, and had let Carteret know Pope's "spirit" concerning a pension.

Swift proffered another unwanted favor by praising Pope in print for the very independence he insisted on and was so evidently proud of. In the *Libel on Dr. Delany*, published anonymously in February 1730, he saluted his friend as an exemplary figure in an age when poets paid court to patrons who typically distributed empty promises:

> Hail! Happy Pope, whose generous mind,
> Detesting all the statesman kind!
> Contemning courts, at courts unseen,
> Refus'd the visits of a queen;
> A soul with every virtue fraught
> By sages, priests, or poets taught:[17]
> Whose filial piety excels
> Whatever Grecian story tells:
> A genius for all stations fit,
> Whose meanest talent is his wit:
> His heart too great, though fortune little,
> To lick a rascal statesman's spittle;
> Appealing to the nation's taste,
> Above the reach of want is placed:
> By Homer dead was taught to thrive,
> Which Homer never could alive:
> And sits aloft on Pindus' head,
> Despising slaves that cringe for bread. (71–88)

In one sense this is an idealized portrait of the fiercely independent writer who refuses to lick spittle or to "cringe" – either to statesmen or booksellers, the kind of writer Swift aspired to be, and insisted he was. Refusing "the visits of a queen" – Swift alludes to a story, apparently false, that Pope had reportedly left home one day to avoid receiving a visit from Queen Caroline – serves obliquely as Swift's fantasized revenge

---

[17] Perhaps a sly re-writing of Pope's "Of all the Nurse and all the Priest have taught" (*Rape of the Lock*, 1, 30).

on Queen Anne's refusal to make him a bishop. But some details are tailored to fit Pope – his filial devotion to his mother (often cited in Swift's letters to Pope) and his Homer translation. Swift perhaps thought Pope would be pleased to have this tribute. A year earlier he had acknowledged Pope's "desire that I would record our friendship in verse, which if I can succeed in, I will never desire to write one more line in poetry while I live" (April 5, 1729, in Woolley 1999–2007: III, 231).[18] On February 6, 1730 he alerted Pope about the imminent appearance of the poem, but (perhaps sensing that Pope might not be wholly pleased) doesn't admit authorship and pretends that the poem was not meant to be published: "You will see 18 lines relating to your self, in the most whimsical paper that ever was writ, and which was never intended for the publick" (III, 279). Perhaps he suspected that Pope would object to the idea that he had been "taught" by Homer to "thrive," as if the translation had merely been a mercenary exercise rather than a bid for fame. "Thrive" may have seemed to suggest financial calculation and amoral cunning, especially since a passage less than forty lines earlier had ironically described how Congreve, having failed to find patronage, and "taught" by Prudence to adopt his would-be patron's "Party Zeal," took "proper Principles to thrive; / And so may ev'ry Dunce alive" (43–44, 47–48). And perhaps Swift suspected that Pope would not appreciate the implication that his declaration of virtuous independence was dependent on the fact that he was placed "Above the reach of want." A poet in need, like Gay, not so "happy" as Pope, could not afford to be so virtuous.[19]

Pope did indeed object, and on March 4 wrote to Swift that "We have here some verses in your name, which I am angry at. Sure you wou'd not use me so ill as to flatter me?" (Woolley 1999–2007: III, 288). It was probably not the flattery to which he objected, but the suggestion – not in a private letter but a printed poem – that he detested all statesmen and contemned all courts. For at this point in his career Pope was still trying to keep in with everybody, including Walpole.[20] Less than two weeks earlier he

---

[18] Woolley (1999–2007: III, 233) suspects that Pope had suppressed a letter (written in reply to Swift's letter of Feb. 13 and before his letter of March 6), which expressed the "desire," presumably because he didn't want to appear to have been fishing for compliments.

[19] Harth suggests (1998: 242) that Swift reminds his readers "that there is a solid economic base supporting Pope's virtue," but does not consider Pope's likely reaction.

[20] His highly placed friends at court included the Earl of Burlington, a member of the Privy Council until May 1733. A little more than a year later, in April 1731, Pope sent an early draft of his complimentary "Epistle to Burlington" to his lordship. Long regarded as a Whig, Burlington's "putative crypto-Jacobite proclivities" (suggested by recent scholars) "must remain in the realm of speculation" (*ODNB*).

had written to a friend at court, William Fortescue (a highly placed Whig MP, formerly Private Secretary to Walpole, and in 1730 named Attorney General to the Prince of Wales), in effect assuring him that he had nothing to do with Swift's lines, and that they did not reflect any disaffection on his part.[21] By April Pope apparently felt that any danger to himself had passed, and he was able to suggest, in his April 9 letter to Swift, that he was in fact pleased by the flattery of his "Virtue." But his language – "I forgive that Painter, tho there may be others who do not" (III, 299) – suggests that he knew the poem had caused offense. Three years later, by which time Pope had begun to turn away from the court, claiming that "Courts I see not, Courtiers I know not, Kings I adore not, Queens I compliment not" (III, 632),[22] he called the passage "the best panegyrick on myself, that either my own times or any other could have afforded, or will ever afford to me" (III, 594), and thanked Swift for the poem "in which I am immortal for my Morality" (III, 631). Indeed, Pope's effusive thanks – repeated again a month later when he declared that "I was more pleas'd with your Libel, than with any Verses I ever receiv'd" (III, 646) – almost suggests that he protests too much. The *Libel on Dr. Delany* may have provided not only a way for Pope to think about himself but also, as Ehrenpreis has suggested, a model of literary form: the "whole design" of the poem, he says, "the mock-dialogue form, the interweaving of literary and political themes, the opposition of apologetic and bitter tones rising to furious invective – may well have encouraged Pope ... to write his Horatian poems of the 1730s" (Ehrenpreis 1962–83: III, 650).

Here tension between friends is resolved, but that is not always the case. Elsewhere tension appears in the recurrent complaints that, although they have laid open their hearts to each other, each keeps something back. In 1733, when he first saw a copy of Pope's "Epistle to Bathurst," Swift wrote resentfully to Pope that "I never had the least hint from you about this work, any more than your former, upon Tast" (Woolley 1999–2007: III, 581). Pope then confessed (February 16, 1733) that it was he who sent the poem to Ireland, but didn't explain why he didn't send a copy to Swift.

[21] "I've had another vexation, from the sight of a paper of verses said to be Dr Swift's, which has done more by praising me than all the Libels could by abusing me, Seriously troubled me: As indeed one indiscreet Friend can at any time hurt a man more than a hundred silly Enemies" (Sherburn 1956: III, 91). Harth (1998: 242–43) thinks critics have misunderstood Pope's complaint as political embarrassment, but his argument that Pope "is distressed because Swift has innocently implicated him in his poem by the lines in which he associates Pope's attitudes with his own" seems to me a distinction without a difference.

[22] Pope's remark, earlier in the same letter, that Swift is "sensible with what decency and justice I paid homage to the Royal Family," must be a piece of conspiratorial solemn irony.

The following year it was Pope's turn to complain, after Swift had given him no alert that *On Poetry. A Rapsody* was about to be published: "You have been silent to me as to your works; whether those printed here are, or are not genuine ... I shall take it as a thing never to be forgiven from you, if you tell another what you have concealed from me" (III, 716–17). Pope did not tell Swift of his *Essay on Man* until after it was published, for fear, he says by way of apology, that his letter would be read by clerks in the post office (III, 758). Pope had other reasons to conceal his authorship: as long noted, he hoped to draw enemies into praising a new poem published anonymously. The ruse, famously, worked.

It was not only news that was withheld. Beginning in the early 1730s Pope repeatedly sought to get Swift to return copies of his letters for a projected edition of his correspondence, and Swift dragged his heels.[23] Even more important at this time, Swift, apparently unsatisfied with the tribute to him in the *Dunciad*, repeatedly sought to persuade Pope to address to him one of his poetic epistles. But Pope, who had already addressed epistles to a number of his friends, for some reason held back. "Orna me" – "adorn me" – is the theme of a number of Swift's letters in the early 1730s. The phrase comes from Cicero, who frequently asked friends to address him in their writings.[24] Swift apparently made his first use of it in a letter to Pope in January 1733, known only in the truncated version Pope later published.[25] (Did he delete the direct appeal – "Orna me" – in his edited version in 1741 because he was acutely aware that even by that date he had failed to honor Swift's request?) In his response to the original letter on February 16, Pope declares that he is "pleas'd and flatter'd by your Expression of *Orna me*," and pleased too that the "Work" he is now planning (evidently the "Moral Essays") will give him an opportunity to "insert the name and character of every friend I have, and every man that deserves to be lov'd and adorn'd" (Woolley 1999–2007: III, 595). Swift was probably looking for some greater distinction than to be mingled with the large company of "every friend I have, and every man that deserves to be lov'd and adorn'd." Six weeks later he writes again: "I heard you intended four or five Poems addressed to as many friends" (III, 616). Pope had only written vaguely of his "present Work." Swift is probably referring

[23] For a full discussion, see ch. 4, below.
[24] Rogers (1994: 194) suggests *Epistolae ad Familiares*, v, xii. 2–3. But see Isaac D'Israeli: "Orna me! was the constant cry of Cicero" (*Curiosities of Literature* [1835], 429). In a letter in April 1729 Swift acknowledged Pope's own desire that he "record our friendship in verse" (Woolley 1999–2007: III, 231).
[25] Woolley (1999–2007: III, 580–82).

primarily to rumors he has heard providing some details about Pope's plans to print what became the *Epistles to Several Persons*, four "Moral Essays" addressed to his friends Cobham, Martha Blount, Bathurst, and Burlington.[26] But he implicitly reminds Pope of his own fervent wish. Why, one wonders, did Pope not oblige the wish of a man he regarded as his dearest friend?

One explanation is that Pope thought Swift had failed to oblige *his* desire – to collect his letters for publication – and was waiting for some kind of quid pro quo. And Swift may have taken the same view. In a September 3, 1735 letter in which he reiterates his "ambition" and "desire" to have an epistle "inscribed to me" (Woolley 1999–2007: IV, 174), indeed in the immediately preceding sentences, he puts off Pope's oft-repeated requests by saying that, although he has preserved Pope's letters – implying that he has no plans to publish them himself – he has left instructions for the letters to be burned upon his death.[27] In any case, Pope eventually (in March 1736) made a tentative promise to comply with Swift's wish: "If ever I write more Epistles in Verse, one of them shall be address'd to you" (IV, 276). What he had in mind, he wrote, is a large work in four epistles (of which one was apparently to be addressed to Swift) "which naturally follow the Essay on Man." This was the second volume in the "opus magnum" that Pope was never to produce.[28] Little has been made of Pope's promise, nor has it been noticed that what Pope was offering to Swift was not the kind of poem Swift thought Pope should be writing. It was to be an exercise in Pope's philosophical rather than satirical mode. The four epistles of the poem, Pope wrote to Swift, would take up "the Extent and Limits of Human *Reason* and *Science*," the "useful and therefore attainable, and … the un-useful and therefore un-attainable," "the nature, ends, application, and use of different Capacities," and "the use of *Learning*, … the *Science* of the *World*, and … *Wit*." Was Pope consciously proposing to attach Swift's name to a "philosophical" poem of which Swift himself might disapprove, as if

---

[26] Unless he has heard something of Pope's plans for what became a series of Horatian imitations from 1733 to 1737, addressed to his friends Fortescue, Bethel, Arbuthnot, an unidentified "Colonel," Murray, and Bolingbroke.

[27] For more on this letter, see below, ch. 4. Woolley remarks (1999–2007: IV, 176) that Pope seems to have taken a small step in response to that appeal, by adding "To Dr. Jonathan Swift" to the title page of a re-issue of *The Dunciad Variorum* (published November 1735). Woolley does not notice that in 1729 Pope also changed "Grieve not at ought our sister realm acquires" (I, 24 in the quarto editions of the *Variorum*) to the more personal "Grieve not, my SWIFT, at ought our Realm acquires" (beginning with the first authorized octavo).

[28] On Pope's plans for this work, see Leranbaum 1977.

to draw Swift into his own quite different frame? Or might we see the proposed poem as a kind of delayed reply to *Gulliver's Travels*, taking up, in philosophical mode, some of the same topics – the extent and limits of human reason and science, the useful as opposed to the unuseful, the uses of learning – that Swift had taken up, in satirical mode, especially in the third and fourth voyages?[29]

It was probably not coincidental that in his response to Pope's gesture, Swift (in a letter of April 22, 1736) now told Pope that he would send copies of his letters: "my resolution is to direct my Executors to send you all your letters … and leave them entirely to your disposal" (Woolley 1999–2007: IV, 283). He goes on to say that he has "a little repined at my being hitherto slipped[30] by you in some Epistle … I expect you shall perform your promise." And his response suggests that he was in fact coming around to Pope's view that the poet ought to write as a moral philosopher: "I am amazed to see you exhaust the whole science of Morality in so masterly a manner." Seven months later Swift, in a warmly friendly letter, wrote to Pope that he continued to hope to see "more Epistles of Morality" from him, that such writings were "more usefull to the Publick, by your manner of handling them[,] than any of all your Writings" (IV, 366–67). But he also reminded Pope of the promise, expressing his continuing resentment by projecting it onto his "Acquaintance," who "resent that they have not Seen my name at the head of one [of your epistles]." Pope in fact was never to perform the promise, but he did reply to Swift's letter by sending him (in his letter of December 30) a copy of the forthcoming "Epistle to Augustus," in which Swift is handsomely praised. Perhaps Pope considered that this poem, together with the soon-to-be-published edition of his correspondence, discharged the obligation. Swift in his letter of February 9, 1737 was very pleased with the tribute, but his letter of May 31, 1737 makes clear that he is still waiting for an "Epistle to Swift." He is replying to Pope, who had insisted that Swift perform his own promise – to return his letters – and deploys the metaphor of the payment of debt: "It is true, I owe you some letters, but it has pleased God, that I have not been in a condition to pay you." Looking back over a matter that had been simmering for seven years, he notes that

[i]t was I began with the petition to you of Orna me, and now you come like an unfair merchant, to charge me with being in your debt; which by your way of

---

[29] For a discussion of the *Essay on Man* itself as a kind of reply to *Gulliver's Travels*, see below, pp. 162–67.

[30] That is, passed over, not mentioned (*OED*. IV, 2).

reckoning I must always be, for yours are always guineas, and mine farthings; and yet I have a pretence to quarrel with you, because I am not at the head of any one of your Epistles (IV, 431–32).

POPE–SWIFT MISCELLANIES (1732)

The major collaborative effort between Pope and Swift during these years was their work on the final volume of their *Miscellanies,* which appeared on October 4, 1732. Even in this project there are signs of an unresolved tension, and of what Harth has called "an increasing divergence of sympathies, interests, and goals" (1998: 240). Editors of Pope and Swift have long known of the mutual deceptions Swift and Pope practiced on each other in this episode, but the story is worth retelling in the larger context of the changing nature of their life-long relationship.[31]

The volume was projected as early as January 1729, when Pope (in an unsurviving letter) apparently asked Swift what he had been writing.[32] By January 1731 Swift had implicitly conceded to Pope the responsibilities of editor, inviting him to be "as severe a judge [of Swift's contributions to the joint collection] as becomes so good and dear a Friend" (Woolley 1999–2007: III, 356). But as work proceeded, and Pope requested copies of Swift's writings composed since the 1728 volume of *Miscellanies,* Swift's tone sometimes became frosty, as when he referred in a June 1732 letter to the papers "that you are pleased to require soon" (III, 489). Swift obliquely declined to send them, offering a series of reasons: that several things remained unfinished; that some were only meant for private amusement; that some of the published pieces could be readily found in the pages of the *Intelligencer;* that Swift would bring them with him when next he came to England; that he would be sure to leave papers to Pope in his will; that he would withhold some pieces ("Polite Conversation" and "Advice to Servants") because he was considering publishing them separately. But at the same time he provides a list of recent works that are his, implicitly suggesting that Pope include them in the forthcoming volume. Pope apparently felt no obligation to comply. Of the nine pieces named, he included five (*A Modest Proposal,* "A Vindication of Lord Carteret," "To Dr. Delany," *The Journal of a Modern Lady,* and "A Soldier and a Scholar" ["The Grand Question Debated"], and omitted four,

---

[31] See the account in Williams (1958: I, xxiv–xxviii).
[32] See Swift's letters of February 13, and March 6, 1729 (Woolley 1999–2007: III, 209, 212).

including *A Short View of the State of Ireland*, the *Libel on Dr. Delany*, *The Lady's Dressing Room*, and a squib entitled "The Place of the Damn'd." He also found room for another two pieces of prose (whose authorship Swift had not previously claimed), and seven of verse. Of his own pieces Pope included a dozen epigrams and mock-epitaphs, and five pieces in prose: the *Narrative of Dr. Norris*, three pamphlets on Curll, and *God's Revenge Against Punning*. (By adding a few footnotes identifying books no longer current, Pope may have been implicitly responding to Swift's advice about the *Dunciad*).³³ The preface to the volume, written by Pope (apparently without consulting Swift), declares that the reader "may be assured no other Edition is either Genuine or Complete, and that they are all the Things of this Kind which will ever be Printed by the same Hands." Pope perhaps thought that the calculatedly vague phrase "Things of this Kind" gave him some editorial latitude in deciding just which poems should be included in an edition of their "Miscellaneous Pieces."

Pope's omissions are noteworthy, and have drawn some comment. Of the 376 pages in the volume, Swift was responsible for nearly half (186), while Pope contributed only a little over one-sixth (69), the rest made up by their friends, including Sheridan, Gay, and Arbuthnot. Noteworthy too is the fact that as Pope arranged the volume Swift is represented by several major pieces now regarded as among his best, including *A Modest Proposal* and *The Journal of a Modern Lady* (nearly 300 lines), while Pope provided for the miscellany only some early prose and decidedly minor poems. He omitted the previously published *Epistle to Burlington* and held back a number of major poems that he was soon to publish separately, within six months of the appearance of the volume of *Miscellanies*, including the "Epistle to Bathurst," the "Epistle to Fortescue" (his imitation of Horace, *Satires* II, 1), and the first and second epistles of the *Essay on Man*.³⁴

As early as November Swift expressed some dissatisfaction with the final volume of the *Miscellanies*, in a letter to the publisher, Motte, who had his own reasons to be dissatisfied. By then Swift himself was already negotiating, through his young friend Matthew Pilkington, to deal with another London printer, William Bowyer. It suited Swift's purposes to pretend that he had little knowledge or control of the volume, and that the whole thing was Pope's idea, including the embarrassing fact that "almost

³³ For a review of Pope's changes, see Pat Rogers, "Revisions to Pope's Prose Works in the *Miscellanies* (1732)" *Review of English Studies* 57 (2006), 701–06.
³⁴ Ault (1949: 264–65) suggests that Pope was withholding poems that he planned to publish in a forthcoming edition of his works – which appeared in 1736.

six sevenths of the whole Verse part in the book" was Swift's own work (Woolley 1999–2007: III, 556) – he apparently counted pages. This implies that Swift thought Pope should have contributed more, even though including the *Libel on Dr. Delany* (which Swift told Motte he thought "the best thing I writt as I think") would have only increased the proportion of his verse in the volume. Swift may well have complained directly to Pope, but no letter from Swift to Pope between June 1732 and January 1733 has survived. (Pope's letter to Swift of December 5, 1732 is taken up with news of the unexpected death of their mutual friend Gay.) The next extant letter (probably late January 1733), surviving only in Pope's printed version and very probably edited by him, conveys no complaint about the omission of the *Libel on Dr. Delany* or the disproportion between Swift's work and Pope's, but Pope may well have deleted it, for in his reply on February 16 he takes pains to explain the editorial principles that guided his work on the *Miscellanies*. His long-winded and circuitous language seems to betray some sense that he owes Swift an explanation for a volume that perhaps seemed trivial and inconsequential in the light of Gay's recent death and of Pope's plans for a much more substantial volume, the *Essay on Man*.

Beginning with a gesture toward Swift's suggestion that Pope publish a "fair edition" of Gay's works, Pope endorses the idea "of collecting the best monuments we can of our friends, their own images in their writings," and notes that he is preparing such a monument for himself, to show that "men of Wit, or even Poets, may be the most moral of mankind." An unfortunate way, one would think, to introduce the topic of the recently published *Miscellanies*. But Pope pushes ahead with some grace:

A few loose things sometimes fall from them, by which censorious fools judge as ill of them as possibly they can, … and indeed, when such unguarded and trifling Jeux d'Esprit have once got abroad, all that prudence or repentance can do, since they cannot be deny'd, is to put 'em fairly upon that foot; and teach the publick (as we have done in the preface to the four volumes of miscellanies) to distinguish betwixt our studies and our idlenesses, our works and our weaknesses: That was the whole end of the last Vol. of Miscellanies, without which our former declaration in that preface, "That these volumes contain'd all that we had ever offended in that way", would have been discredited.[35]

---

[35] February 16, 1733 (Woolley 1999–2007: III, 594). One wonders whether the final sentence in this extract, edited by Pope, originally read "… all by which we had ever offended …" Pope is also re-writing the language of the 1725 preface, which had distinguished between "Studies" and "Follies," "Works" and "Idlenesses."

This is disingenuous in several respects. From the beginning Pope's motives included the desire to find a way decently to preserve some of his lesser pieces from oblivion, and in fact to show that the snarling satirist and soon-to-be philosophical moralist was as capable of spinning a few polished "trifling" lines as the Restoration gentleman-poets he still liked to regard as among his models. Even if the explanation might ostensibly account for Pope's epigrams, they hardly account for such powerful pieces as *A Modest Proposal* and *The Journal of a Modern Lady.*

Pope still feels the need to explain why he omitted the *Libel on Dr. Delany,* a poem which not only paid him a memorable compliment but was in Swift's own view the best of his recent writings: "It went indeed to my heart, to omit what you called the Libel on Dr. D" (Woolley 1999–2007: III, 594). Perhaps he implicitly regarded the poem as something more than an "idleness" or a "weakness," though this must mean that he dismissed the withering *Modest Proposal* as a mere idleness. Pope says nothing about why he omitted other works on Swift's list, although it is not difficult to propose plausible grounds: the *Short View of the State of Ireland* represented Swift's obsession with Irish politics that Pope continued to discourage, and the *Lady's Dressing Room* had already proved controversial enough to draw two printed attacks.[36]

Swift in his January 1733 letter had apparently also complained that the volume had been published hastily, perhaps carelessly, and without giving him adequate notice.[37] (On other occasions it suited Swift to claim he had nothing to do with publication.) Pope's response shifts the onus to Swift himself and his agent Pilkington, known to have been negotiating with Bowyer to publish a separate (and rival) collection of Swift's pieces: "The book as you observe was printed in great haste; the cause whereof was, that the booksellers here were doing the same, in collecting your pieces, the corn with the chaff." Pope allows the slur about corn and chaff to stand, and then withdraws it: "I don't mean that any thing of yours is chaff, but with other wit of Ireland which was so, and the whole in your name." And then returns to the point that he in fact did aim to separate the corn from the chaff: "I meant principally to oblige a separation of what you writ seriously from what you writ carelessly; and thought my own weeds might pass for a sort of wild flowers, when bundled up with

---

[36] *The Gentleman's Study, in Answer to the Lady's Dressing Room* (1732) and *Chloe Surpriz'd, or, The Second Part of the Lady's Dressing Room* (1732), discussed in Halsband (1970: 225–29).

[37] On December 9, 1732 Swift complained to Motte that his part of the *Miscellany* was "very incorrect" (Woolley 1999–2007: III, 563).

them" (Woolley 1999–2007: III, 594). "Separation" is disingenuous: it implies that both corn and chaff are valuable, and should simply be published separately. But the terms of the metaphor imply that Pope determined to include the corn – what Swift "writ seriously" – and reject the chaff – what he wrote "carelessly" – even though the paragraph had begun with the agreement to include only "idlenesses" and "weaknesses." Pope's shifting rhetoric suggests that he is scrambling to find a gracious way to cover himself. (His careful editing of the sentence in his printed editions of the letter – in one version "oblige a separation" becomes "oblige them to separate" – constitutes a further attempt to shift responsibility away from himself to unnamed others.)

Perhaps Pope emerges from this episode as the more offending, if only because he played the more active role. With keener interest in managing his own literary affairs to practical advantage and optimal fame than Swift, he made use of the 1732 volume of *Miscellanies* to serve his own purposes and seems to have paid little regard to Swift's. But Swift was no innocent; he was negotiating quietly for separate publication, and (as has been suggested) already beginning to make plans for what would be the major 1735 Faulkner edition of his writings, plans that he did not share with Pope. Perhaps, however, as has been recently suggested, we should regard Swift's decision to deal quietly with Faulkner not merely as subterfuge but as a "consequence" of his disappointment with Pope's role in editing the Swift–Pope *Miscellanies*,[38] or, in my terms, as a *reply* to Pope.

Swift was also quietly replying to Pope in another way – as his editor. After complaining several times to Pope in early 1733 that his latest poems were (like the *Dunciad*) obscure and needed "explanatory notes,"[39] Swift apparently took matters into his own hands. When Faulkner later in 1733 reprinted Pope's "Epistle to Bathurst" for Irish readers, the initials and blanks were filled in, and his edition was equipped with explanatory notes. Elias concludes that, without doubt, Swift "was responsible for these additions" (2000: 62), and that, during the next two years, when Faulkner reprinted other new Pope poems – the *First Satire of the Second Book of Horace* (1733), the *Epistle to Cobham* (1734), and the

---

[38] McLaverty (2008: 144). McLaverty (139–43) provides a full account of Swift's complaints, and of his dealings with Motte and Faulkner.

[39] Woolley (1999–2007: III, 580). He reported that Irish readers found "obscurity" in the "Epistle to Bathurst" "by our ignorance in facts and persons" (580). Some parts of the poem "are not so obvious to midling Readers" (616).

Epistle to Dr. Arbuthnot (1735) – names and notes were again supplied by Swift, probably with "input" from collaborators (64).[40]

Swift's critical response to *The Dunciad* is well known, and has drawn the attention of scholars. What has drawn less attention is his poetic response. Over the next few years he wrote several poems that show the *Dunciad* was very much on his mind. The most important of those poems, *On Poetry. A Rapsody* (1733), might be said to constitute Swift's most significant "reply" to the *Dunciad*.

The earliest of the *Dunciad*-related poems is "A Panegyrick on the Dean, in the Person of a Lady in the North," first printed in Faulkner's 1735 edition, where it is said to have been "written in the year 1730," or about a year after the *Dunciad Variorum* appeared. In the "Panegyrick," placed in the mouth of his friend Lady Acheson, Swift is addressed "in several views" – i.e., in the several roles in which he serves the household:

> D – n, Butler, Usher, Jester, Tutor;
> *Robert* and *Darby*'s Coadjutor:
> And as you in Commission sit,
> To rule the Dairy next to *Kit*. (39–42)

The lines are designed, of course, to parody Pope's invocation of Swift in the *Dunciad Variorum*, "O thou, whatever Title please thine ear, / Dean, Drapier, Bickerstaff, or Gulliver!" (i, 17–18). Just as Pope had addressed and praised Swift under his several "Titles" – i.e., the names under which his several works appeared in print – so Swift has Lady Acheson address him "in each capacity" in which he serves. Pope's brief invocation had in fact focused on Swift as Drapier, Bickerstaff, and Gulliver, as mock-grave Cervantean or as laughing Rabelaisian, but not on his work as "Dean." Swift's poem supplies Pope's omission, though it is the Dean viewed from the angle of the mistress of a country household, and viewed comically. She takes up his very undecanal services as "butler's mate" (notes in the Faulkner edition remark that Swift "sometimes used to direct the butler"), as "usher" ("he sometimes used to walk with the lady"), "jester" (who provides verbal and practical jokes for the family), and "tutor" ("in bad weather the author used to direct my Lady in her reading"). The Dean

---

[40] Swift may have begun editing Pope even earlier. Fischer (2000: 79) found in Samuel Fairbrother's 1732 Dublin reprint of the 1728 volume of the Pope–Swift *Miscellanies* (Teerink no. 33) authorial revisions attributable to Swift.

even acted as "coadjutor" (an ecclesiastical term for a bishop's assistant) to "Robert" and "Darby" (two of Sir Arthur Acheson's estate overseers), and co-commissioner of the dairy with the footman, Kit. To each "capacity" Lady Acheson devotes a paragraph.

What is the significance of Swift's parody? As noted earlier, Mrs. Pilkington remarked on Swift's disappointment with Pope's tribute in *The Dunciad*, particularly because his own praise of Pope in the *Libel on Dr. Delany* had been considerably warmer.[41] Perhaps too Swift regarded Pope's invocation as too concise, and focused too much on his public service – one has no sense from Pope's lines that Swift was a genial companion – and determined to see into print a more elaborated tribute to his private character, even if he had to write it himself. But the parody is also a sign of Swift's habit of self-mockery: he wants readers to find it both admirable and amusing that the Dean and Irish Patriot readily stoops to humble household tasks:

> You merit new Employments daily:
> Our Thatcher, Ditcher, Gard'ner, Baily.
> And, to a Genius so extensive,
> No Work is grievous or offensive.
> Whether, your fruitful Fancy lies
> To make for Pigs convenient Styes:
> Or, ponder long with anxious Thought,
> To banish Rats that haunt our Vault.
> Nor have you grumbled, rev'rend D – n,
> To keep our Poultry sweet and clean. (155–64)

Swift still has Pope's invocation in mind: "Whether, your fruitful Fancy lies ..." picks up Pope's "Whether thou chuse Cervantes' air ..." And the comical survey of Swift's many household "Work[s]" extends for more than 200 lines.

The last of those works is the building of a pair of outhouses, "Two Temples of magnific Size," one for "He's" and one for "She's," where the goddess Cloacina "receives all Off'rings at her Shrine" (201–07). This gives Swift an occasion for a scatalogical interlude, and he seizes it, providing a mythological account of privies in the open air in the golden age, and the deplorable invention in our "degen'rate Days," by Gluttony and Sloth, of an indoor cell or cabinet, equipped with chamber pots, so close to the bedside that "unsav'ry Vapours" now offend the "nicer Nose."

---

[41] See Ehrenpreis (1962–83: III, 671). Pilkington thought Pope's lines, compared to Swift's praise, were "cold" and "forc'd" (Elias 1997: I, 34).

Swift didn't need prompting from Pope (or from Gay's *Trivia*) to indulge his taste for scatology, but it seems likely that the account in the *Dunciad* of Cloacina ministering to Jove at his allegorical house of ease ("A place there is, betwixt earth, air, and seas ...") and attending to Curll's prayer (II, 79–94) served as a kind of poetic challenge. Swift one-ups the allegorizing Pope by installing himself as a builder of a very real cloacinal temple, and reconverting Pope's dreamily aestheticized ordure (figured in the "Mud-nymphs" Nigrina and Merdamante) to the very solid and curiously observed leavings, "With spiral Tops, and Copple-Crowns,"[42] left by "Northern Swains" beside "chrystal" country streams. Swift's turds have their own delicate architecture, the "faecal coils" (Geoffrey Hill's nice phrase)[43] exactly described, but also perhaps a twisted reminiscence of Tibbald's offering to Dulness, with its "crown" and "spire" of books (*Dunciad Variorum*, I, 139–42), and a parody of the "spires" and "crowns" of flowers that bedeck the meadows in conventional pastoral description of the day.[44]

 On Poetry. A Rapsody appeared on the last day of 1733, and constitutes Swift's boldest poetic reply to *The Dunciad*. Its subtitle has occasioned some speculation, but unnoticed is the fact that the *Dunciad* was ridiculed as a "Rhapsody" half a dozen times in Dennis's *Remarks upon the Dunciad* (1729).[45] Swift's "Rapsody" might be regarded as a defense of Pope against such attacks, and at the same time as a subtle critique both of his epic affiliations and of his political caution. Swift never alerted Pope to the poem's appearance, although Pope wrote to him a week after it was published to say that although Swift has been "silent to me as to your works; whether those printed here are, or are not genuine," he is nonetheless sure that "one ... is yours."[46] Some editors suspect that Pope refers to *On Poetry. A Rapsody*.

---

[42] Adorning the flowers as a "copple-crown" (a crest or tuft of feathers) decorates a bird's head. Cf. Swift's *Examination of Certain Abuses, Corruptions, and Enormities in the City of Dublin* (1732), on "human Excrements" in the Dublin streets, many of them "upon a strict View appearing Copple-crowned, with a Point like a Cone or Pyramid" (Davis 1939–68: XII, 220).

[43] From "Jonathan Swift: The Poetry of Reaction," in *The World of Jonathan Swift*, ed. Brian Vickers (1984), 209.

[44] "Cf. *Rape of the Lock*: "Close by those meads for ever crown'd with flowers" (III, 1), "With golden crown and wreath of heav'nly flowers" (I, 34); and cf. "Eloisa to Abelard," line 142: "Those moss-grown domes with spiry turrets crown'd."

[45] *Remarks upon Several Passages in the Preliminaries to the Dunciad* (1729), 6, 8, 12 (twice), 17, 50. James Ralph's *Sawney* (1728) called the *Dunciad* "Such a Rhapsody that one knows not where to find Head or Tail" (p. vi). Pope's own November 28, 1729 letter to Swift opens ironically with "This letter (like all mine) will be a Rhapsody" (Woolley 1999–2007: III, 271).

[46] Woolley (1999–2007: III, 716). (Pope's "genuine" probably glances at the *Life and Genuine Character*, published about eight months earlier.) No letter from Swift to Pope survives between

The full dimensions of Swift's poem as reply to Pope become clearer when we set it beside two other poems published in a pamphlet just six weeks earlier, his *Epistle to a Lady, Who Desired the Author to make Verses on Her, in the Heroick Style*, and "On Reading Dr. Young's Satires, Called the Universal Passion." Both poems, along with *On Poetry. A Rapsody*, were in the small packet that Swift sent, via Mrs. Barber, when she left Dublin for London in August 1733, to be passed to Matthew Pilkington to arrange for their publication. In the end, *Epistle to a Lady* and "On Reading Dr. Young's Satires" were published in London by John Wilford on November 15 and *On Poetry. A Rapsody* by J. Huggonson on December 31. Both publications claimed – falsely – to be a reprint of an earlier Dublin edition, presumably to defend the printers against prosecution for libel, and Huggonson took the extra precaution of removing some of the lines he thought most likely to offend the censors. The ruse and strategy failed, and shortly after the publication of *On Poetry. A Rapsody* the printer of the earlier pamphlet was arrested, suggesting that in the minds of the government the two pamphlets were linked.

Like the "Panegyrick on the Dean," much of the *Epistle to a Lady* is put in the mouth of Lady Acheson, who asks Swift to "Drop, for once, your constant Rule, / Turning all the Ridicule" (50–51), and to sing her praise "in Strain sublime" (57). The Dean then replies, declining to treat her "in Heroick Strain" (136), protesting that such a style does not befit him. But instead of rallying her on her unheroic character, he turns suddenly from her to "Wicked Ministers of State" and "the Vices of a Court" (143, 147) who call forth his "Scorn" and "Rage."

> Let me, tho' the Smell be Noisom,
> Strip their Bums; let CALEB hoyse 'em;
> Then, apply ALECTO's Whip,
> Till they wriggle, howl, and skip. (177–80)

The reference to "Caleb" – i.e., "Caleb D'Anvers," pseudonymous author of *The Craftsman*, organ of the Opposition, then sharply attacking Walpole's ministry – suggests Swift is thinking about the proper response to political corruption, and that behind Lady Acheson stands Pope, who still declined to break openly with the court, and whose recent *Dunciad* had disguised its political sympathies by focusing on bad writing rather than bad governing and by diverting his readers with a parody

his of July 8, 1733 and November 1, 1734. Was Swift's silence a sign of his preoccupation with the forthcoming Faulkner edition (as Woolley thinks: III, 718), or of some strain or coolness in his relations with Pope?

of "Heroick Style." In his epistle Swift declines "the lofty Stile" (218) that Pope had adopted, reaffirming his "paultry Burlesque Stile" (50) and even more importantly reaffirming his determination to "Sneer" (unlike the more cautious Pope) at the "Nation's Representers,"[47] the "Hirelings of St. St – s" (rhymes with "Grievance," i.e., St. Stephen's), and "Sir R – Br–s" (rhymes with "Class," i.e., "Brass").

That this is the subtext of Swift's *Epistle* seems more likely when we consider the poem with which it was originally published. "On Reading Dr. Young's Satires" has been described as a "reply to Young," a critique of his inconsistency in condemning a "corrupt social order" on the one hand, and praising the nation's "virtuous leaders" (including the King and Queen, Walpole, and the peers of the realm) on the other.[48] "If there be Truth in what you sing" of the court, says Swift, then "What *Land* was ever *half* so *blest*?" (1, 12). But if his satire on the ubiquity of vice is correct, "What *Land* was ever *half* so *curst*?" (48). Why, Swift implicitly asks, does Young not speak out, and the implicit answer (though not found in the poem) is that he is dependent on his patrons, Walpole among them. To attack Young, as Swift does here, is obliquely to attack others who, perhaps for economic reasons, pull their satiric punches. His poem in effect puts some pressure on Pope, and although Swift doesn't mention him in this poem, he would have known that, in his own *Love of Fame*, Young, in reviewing the corrupt world around him and the inadequate response from satirists, had asked "Why slumbers *Pope*?" (*Satire 1*, line 35).[49] In 1728, when Young wrote, Pope had as yet to emerge as a satirist, and Swift implicitly asks the same question again at the end of 1733.

That Young and Pope were linked in Swift's mind is clearer in *On Poetry. A Rapsody*, where they, along with Gay, are obliquely presented as the worthy poets of the day, in contrast to Cibber, who "entertains / The Court with annual Birth-day Strains" (305–06). But Swift's implicit praise has a satiric edge: Cibber attends at court,

> Whence *Gay* was banish'd in Disgrace,
> Where *Pope* will never show his Face;
> Where *Y – –* must torture his Invention,
> To flatter *Knaves*, or lose his *Pension*. (307–10)

---

[47] Cf. Swift's February 6, 1730 letter to Pope, on "the prostitute Slavery of the Representers of this wretched Country" (Woolley 1999–2007: III, 279).

[48] Ehrenpreis (1962–83: III, 770). On Young's flattery, see above, pp. 124–25.

[49] Pope quotes Young's line in the "Testimonies of Authors" included in the *Dunciad Variorum* (Rumbold 2007: 152).

While the satire on Young is apparent, Pope perhaps comes in for a share too: the *Dunciad* had famously been presented to the King, and as late as 1733 Pope was still reluctant to break with the court, and (as noted) annoyed that Swift had praised him, in the *Libel on Dr. Delany*, for "detesting all the statesman kind," for "Contemning courts, at courts unseen." By reasserting here that Pope will never show his face at court – the figure hints at a lack of courage – Swift in effect reminds him that he had unforgivably omitted the *Libel on Dr. Delany* from their 1732 *Miscellanies* volume, and urges him to live up to the praise Swift has offered him. Later in *On Poetry*, Swift (having advised the would-be poet that praising a minister of state is the way to thrive) ironically invites "ye *Popes*, and *Youngs*, and *Gays*" to "tune your Harps, and strow your Bays, / Your Panegyrics here provide" (467–69). The lines hit Young palpably, but Pope (who in the *Dunciad* had offered a mock-panegyric of the King) is perhaps half-guilty by association.

A third allusion to Pope explicitly ties Swift's poem to *The Dunciad*. After surveying the line of famously bad poets from Flecknoe to Blackmore, Swift remarks that they in effect competed with each other in their attempts to reach "the low Sublime":

> For Instance: When you rashly think,
> No Rhymer can like Welsted sink,
> His Merits ballanc'd you shall find,
> That Feilding leaves him far behind.
> Concannen, more aspiring Bard,
> Climbs downwards, deeper by a Yard. (393–98)

And Swift adds a footnote – "*Vide ... Mr. Pope's Dunciad.*"[50] Swift refers of course to the diving contest in Bk. II, in which Welsted and Concanen, among others, try to prove who "flings most filth, and wide pollutes around" (II, 267). By citing Pope, Swift acknowledges an affiliation with the *Dunciad*'s attack on the writers of Grubstreet, but also offers himself as a competitor in another kind of contest – to determine who can write better about bad writers.[51]

---

[50] Swift echoes descriptions of both Welsted – "Furious he sinks; precipitately dull" (III, 294) – and Concanen – "True to the bottom, see Concanen creep / A cold, long-winded native of the deep!" (287).

[51] Rogers (1983: 873) alleges that Swift elsewhere recalls Pope's writings: the "funeral blaze" of poems at line 220/204 (cf. *Dunciad* I, 205–12); the "ivory gate of dreams" at line 231/215 (cf. *Dunciad* III, 358). But the resemblances do not rise to the level of allusion.

Even when Pope is not cited directly, Swift may have him in his sights.
Consider, for example, Swift's presentation of "Battus," the literary dicta-
tor at Will's, who

> Reclining on his Elbow-chair,
> Gives Judgment with decisive Air.
> To whom the Tribe of circling Wits,
> As to an Oracle submits.
> He gives Directions to the Town,
> To cry it up, or run it down. (265–70)

"Battus" was a name associated with Dryden, and many editors simply
gloss "Battus" as Dryden, but, as Rogers notes (1983: 874), Swift's character
of Battus is also a generic portrait, and may recall Pope's own portrait of
Atticus in the *Epistle to Dr. Arbuthnot*. That poem was of course published
two years later than *On Poetry*, but a nearly identical version of the lines on
Atticus had in fact appeared in 1727 in the Pope–Swift *Miscellanies*:

> Like *Cato* give his *little Senate* Laws,
> And sit attentive to his own Applause;
> While Wits and Templars ev'ry Sentence raise,
> And wonder with a foolish Face of Praise.

Swift in *On Poetry* may be thus affiliating himself with Pope, but in another
sense he marks a difference. For Pope's lines were directed against Addison,
while Swift's – if only by locating Battus at Will's – were apparently aimed
at Dryden. And in the *Dunciad Variorum* Dryden had of course been
held up as Pope's ally in the extended "Parallel of the Characters of Mr.
Dryden and Mr. Pope."[52] In his later career Pope increasingly aligned himself with Dryden, his own *Dunciad* plainly modeled upon "MacFlecknoe."
Swift, who in his later career continued to find opportunities to denigrate
Dryden,[53] indirectly ridiculed him in *On Poetry* by means of a backhanded
compliment, ironically advising young poets to "Read all the *Prefaces* of
Dryden, / For these our Critics much confide in, / (Tho' meerly writ at first
for filling / To raise the Volume's price, a Shilling)" (251–54).[54] For Swift to
laugh at the expense of Pope's literary hero in a potent parenthesis – here
for padding out his poems with prefaces, as Pope might be said to have
padded out the 1728 *Dunciad* to make a fat volume of the 1729 *Variorum* –
is to put a little satiric pressure on Pope himself.

[52] Sutherland (1963: 230–35).
[53] For example, his April 12, 1735 letter to Thomas Beach (Woolley 1999–2007: IV, 88), on Dryden's
triplets, "a vicious way of Riming."
[54] The section of Swift's poem dealing with Dryden/Battus (lines 233–78) is marked – perhaps
parodically – by four sets of parentheses.

By addressing "a young Beginner" (76), directing him how to succeed in Duncenia, Swift produces a perverse and cynical parody of Pope's instructions to an aspiring poet and critic in the *Essay on Criticism*. Writing with the confidence and hopes of youth, Pope in that poem situates himself in relation to the great critics of the past, and largely disregards the world in which writers must live. Writing as an "old experienc'd sinner," Swift situates modern writers in relation to printers, their jealous contemporaries, and the political world on which they depend for support. Both Pope and Swift begin their surveys of the state of modern poetry by remarking on the sheer number of would-be poets. The occasion of the *Dunciad*, so Martinus Scriblerus explains, was the "deluge of Authors" that "cover'd the land." A bad writer, adds "William Cleland," becomes a just object of ridicule when he "sets up for a Wit." These premises provide Swift's point of departure: "All Human Race wou'd fain be Wits, / And Millions miss, for one that hits." "Judges Sovereign" in their own districts, they are organized monarchically, as the kingdom of "Duncenia." Although only one of them sits on "Parnassus' Top," Swift takes account of the notorious tendency of writers to attack each other, and addresses the latest to wear the "leaden Crown":

> how unsecure thy Throne!
> A thousand Bards thy Right disown:
> They plot to turn in factious Zeal,
> Duncenia to a Common-weal;
> And with rebellious Arms pretend
> An equal Priv'lege to *descend*. (377–82)

In *Tale of a Tub* (1704) Swift had facetiously imagined the world of modern writers as a "Commonwealth of Learning" (94) and a "Grubstreet Brotherhood" (64). Thirty years later the inhabitants of Duncenia "rail [at] and criticize" their superiors, or aim to outdo each other in sinking, as if to exemplify the standard argument against commonwealths – that they tend to degenerate into anarchy. Swift's dunces constitute a ridiculous version of the republic of letters, which by 1733 was beginning to seem less like an ideal commonwealth of merit than a highly contentious realm. (Pope had already complained – in the *Dunciad Variorum*'s prose apparatus, p. 163 – of the unlimited "Liberty of the Press" which permitted authors to publish slander of their fellows.)[55]

---

[55] Cf. *Covent Garden Journal* 23, in which Fielding notes that, as late as Pope, the realm of letters had been a monarchy, but 'After the Demise of King Alexander, the Literary State relapsed again into a Democracy, or rather indeed into a downright Anarchy" (149–54); cf. also Johnson's *Rambler* 145 (1751).

Swift's Duncenia is pointedly different from the Grub Street of the *Dunciad.* Pope's world of Dulness is an "Empire" in which happy child-like poets compete in a series of games, and a phantasmagoric interior realm of mental anarchy or lassitude, sometimes aestheticized as an oddly beautiful world of harvests nodding beneath the snow, with its own kind of muddy "Majesty."[56] Swift's is a more politicized and recognizable public place in which "ev'ry Poet in his Kind, / Is bit by him that comes behind." They all "Call Dunces, Fools, and Sons of Whores, / Lay *Grubstreet* at each others Doors." (Pope imagines a literary world in which every bad writer attacks only *him*: Swift in effect responds by reminding Pope that's "it's not only about you.") Swift himself cheerfully sneers at the inhabit- ants of Grub St., but he also hints that in a world ruled by Walpole the line between the hack and the true poet has been blurred. And everybody mouths the same clichés. Nowadays all are quick to

> Extol the Greek and Roman Masters,
> And curse our modern Poetasters.
> Complain, as many an ancient Bard did,
> How Genius is no more rewarded;
> How wrong a Taste prevails among us;
> How much our Ancestors out-sung us. (347–52)

Where does Pope figure in Swift's Duncenia? It is notable that Swift does not place him on "Parnassus' Top" as the "king" whom all the hack writers of the day "rail and criticize." He implies, of course, that Pope – along with Young and Gay – stands outside the world of Duncenia, the only three real poets in an age of scribblers. But he also hints that it is dif- ficult to sustain distinctions in the world of modern writing. Ehrenpreis argued that *On Poetry*, while pretending to advise poets to flatter the min- ister and the monarch, in fact preserves the old idea that the true poet (as opposed to a time-server like Young) displays "ideal integrity" in the face of a corrupt social world. Recognizing the tone of "bitter disillusionment" in the poem, Ehrenpreis nonetheless suggests that the poet "becomes the hero of his own work ... through his moral vision" (1962–83: III, 773, 776). But it's difficult to share Ehrenpreis's moral confidence in the face of Swift's "disillusionment," and difficult to find heroes in a poet so skep- tical and suspicious of the heroic strain, and so quick to mock any pre- tenses to loftiness. Swift may in fact be replying to the *Dunciad Variorum*, which in its survey of a world of triumphant Dulness hinted broadly, in

---

[56] See Jones (1968) on the duncer as unselfconscious children at play, and Rawson (1994: 93–94) on the "defiled grandeur" of Pope's "Majesty of Mud," which "protects his loyalties [to epic]."

the voluminous notes and even in the verse, that one heroic poet stood apart from the cultural waste land and resisted the sway of Dulness.[57] By contrast Swift considers the idea that poetry, even his own, is merely a "trade" (233), and poets merely "jobbers" (312).

What emerges most clearly from the poem (as Ehrenpreis himself recognizes) is not the poet as hero but the vile image of the "savage monsters" who sit on the thrones of Europe, "plagues and scourges of mankind," kings, whose name "denotes / Hogs, Asses, Wolves, Baboons, & Goats / To represent in figure just / Sloth, Folly, Rapine, Mischeif, Lust."[58] And in his intemperate rage Swift may again be subtly replying to Pope. Just ten months earlier, in February 1733, Pope had published his imitation of the first satire of the second book of Horace, cast in the form of a conversation between Pope and his lawyer Fortescue, in which the latter advises caution, and even suggests that Pope "write CAESAR's praise," or "Let *Carolina* smooth the tuneful Lay." (Swift in effect takes up Fortescue's advice, and dispenses it in his own poem.) Apparently dismissing his lawyer's advice, Pope insists that he will speak out, "as plain / As downright Shippen, or as old Montagne," and "expose" not only himself but also his foes and friends: "Publish the present Age, but where my Text / Is Vice too high, reserve it for the next." For Swift no vice is too high, and he models for Pope what it really means to "Publish the present Age." While Pope names only unspecified "guilty men," gamesters, and knaves (even if they wear the Garter), Swift with thinly veiled irony attacks ministers and kings.[59] While Pope still gravely pretends to steer clear of "*Libels* and *Satires*," and to write "grave *Epistles*," Swift abandons the pretense. No reader would take *On Poetry. A Rapsody* for anything but a libel. It seems likely that Pope would have regarded it as implicitly pressing him to take a bolder satiric stand.

SATIRES ON WOMEN

Swift and Pope have often been compared as satirists of women, perhaps most notably by Ellen Pollak, who some years ago disturbed the critical consensus of the day by arguing that, for all his apparent sympathy and

---

[57] For a reading of Pope as the secret hero of the *Dunciad*, see Griffin (1978, ch. 7).
[58] From a passage evidently written by Swift but removed by his own printer.
[59] Swift probably did not know that Pope had written but withheld from printing some daring lines (printed in Mack 1984: 342) that tie George II more closely to the portrait of King "Tibbald," bearing out that "Dunce the Second reigns like Dunce the First." They were never printed in Pope's lifetime.

admiration of women, Pope in fact left intact his age's "sexual myths" – its assumptions about women's inferiority to men – while Swift, despite his reputation for misogyny, exposed them to the demystifying light of reason. Swift and Pope were also remarkable for their close friendships with women, and for the persistent rumors that, though neither ever married, each had in fact contracted a secret marriage. Swift, it has been persuasively argued, probably wished to remain celibate; Pope at one time probably wanted to marry Martha Blount. Pope tended to express sympathy and even support for oppressed wives; Swift tended to assume that, regardless of the provocation, even mistreated wives needed to restrain themselves.[60] Given our evolving sense of the differences between the two writers as satirists of women and as intimate friends of women, can we argue that Swift and Pope were themselves aware of those differences, and that they in effect engaged in an ongoing conversation on the matter? Except for comments about their mutual friends Martha Blount and Henrietta Howard, their letters are largely silent on the topic of _differences_ in their views of women.[61] But the poems they wrote and published in the early 1730s suggest that they wrote with each other's poems in mind, sometimes paying tribute, and sometimes offering implicit critique. Pope's _Rape of the Lock_ still seemed to ring in Swift's ear as he wrote his "dressing room poems," and Pope's own _Epistle to a Lady_ perhaps serves as his own response to them.

The Lady's Dressing Room was the first of Swift's "dressing room poems" to be published. It may have been written as early as 1730, and was published in June 1732.[62] As Nussbaum has shown, Swift's dressing room poems take up long traditions of misogynist satire and of _remedia amoris_ reaching back to Juvenal and Ovid.[63] But among the proximate causes that prompted him to write it may have been a poem by Joseph Thurston entitled _The Toilette_, published in London in 1730. Thurston's poem, more mock-georgic than mock-heroic, emulates the arch tone of _Rape of the Lock_ and repeatedly alludes to Pope's poem.[64] Perhaps it served to remind Swift of the delighted presentation in Pope's _Rape_ of

---

[60] These are the conclusions in Rumbold (1989: 103) and Barnett (2007: 6), the best accounts of their relations with women.

[61] Swift was introduced to Martha Blount when he stayed with Pope in Twickenham in 1727. Three letters between Swift and Martha Blount (1727–28) have survived, in which they remember the "long walks" they took together (Woolley 1999–2007: III, 90–91, 163–64, 178–79).

[62] A note in Faulkner's 1735 edition claims that the poem was "written in the year 1730."

[63] Felicity Nussbaum, _The Brink of All We Hate: English Satires on Women, 1660–1750_ (1984).

[64] "Front-box" (p. 10), "Belinda's loss" (p. 11), "rich Brocade" (p. 12). With some exaggeration Ehrenpreis (1962–83: III, 689) calls the poem an "imitation of _The Rape of the Lock._"

the wondrous transformations wrought at Belinda's toilet table, and to invite him to take up the topic of the toilette himself. John Aden long ago suggested that the scene in *The Lady's Dressing Room* "reads like a burlesque of Belinda's toilet."[65] This was not the first time that Swift had taken up the materials of Pope's *Rape* and given them a darker treatment. *The Journal of a Modern Lady*, written and published in 1729, reviews the "annals of a female day," featuring a game of cards which plainly alludes to Pope's game of Ombre, and an episode of "vapours and hysteric fits" which plainly alludes to the Cave of Spleen.[66] Ehrenpreis goes so far as to say that Swift's poem "may be read as a reply to the *Rape*" (III, 607). Without claiming that Swift's poem is more than a minor piece of misogynist satire, one can argue that it was designed in part as another *corrective* reply, insisting, in Swiftian fashion, to say plainly and bluntly what Pope prefers to say with gracious obliquity and ambiguity.

A more recently published Popean text may also lie behind *The Lady's Dressing Room*. The poem's final line about "gaudy tulips" rising from "dung" has occasioned critical comment,[67] but it has not been observed that Swift is botanically accurate.[68] It might be added that the line also characterizes Swift's poem as much as it does his Celia, and that Swift may have been prompted to think about the poetic uses of dung by Pope. In the *Collection of Pieces in Verse and Prose ... on the Occasion of the Dunciad*, published at the beginning of 1732, in which Richard Savage certainly and Pope himself probably had a hand, Pope is in effect praised

---

[65] "Those Gaudy Tulips: Swift's Unprintables," in *Quick Springs of Sense*, ed. Larry S. Champion (1974), 464–67.

[66] Ehrenpreis lists a number of parallels: *The Journal of a Modern Lady*, 19 (*Rape of the Lock*, IV, 117), 48 (I, 148), 52 (III, 92), 132 (IV, 31), 174–75 (V, 41–42), 190–94 (III, 15–16), 231 (III, 49), 238 (IV, 161). He subsequently declares that "it would be absurd to compare the two pieces as poetry" (1962–83: III, 608).

[67] Rees (1973: 15–16) noted that Swift's "gaudy tulips" have a "fascinating, if minor, literary history" in Marvell ("The Mower Against Gardens") and Cowley ("Beauty"), where tulips are linked with women and "paint," and represent a flamboyant art tending toward corruption of nature. Rees does not note that Cowley has "gaudy" tulips in *Of Plants*, tr. Tate (1689), Bks. III and IV. Her history may be extended to Swift's own day – Mary Astell asks of her female readers: "How can you be content to be in the world like Tulips in a Garden, to make a fine *shew* and be good for nothing?" (*A Serious Proposal to the Ladies* [1694], 12); *Spectator* 455 mocks "fanciful People" who "spend all their Time in the Cultivation of a single Tulip" and French flowers with the "glaring, gaudy Colours." On "gaudy" cf. *Spectator* 80, where the "gaudy Colours" of girls' dresses signify "plentiful Fortunes and mean Taste."

[68] Standard advice for raising tulips called for sowing seed in "well-dunged ground" (*The Dutch Gardener: Or, The Compleat Florist* [1703], 57). Swift no doubt had his own reasons for referring to "dung." For use of pigeon dung to produce exotic colors in tulips, and for recent work on the tulip craze, see Anne Goldgar, *Tulipmania: Money, Honor, and Knowledge in the Dutch Golden Age* (2007).

for raising flowers from dung: his subject is composed of authors who are "the very Excrement of Nature … It is true that he has used Dung; but he disposes that Dung in such a Manner that it becomes rich Manure, from which he raises a Variety of fine Flowers."[69] If Swift's poem was written not in 1730, as he later claimed, but shortly before its first publication in June 1732, it may have been stimulated in part by Savage's praise of Pope: Swift may have determined to show what fine flowers a different kind of poet might raise from dung.

Did Pope decline to include *The Lady's Dressing Room* in the final volume of the Pope–Swift *Miscellanies* because he found the poem somehow unseemly? He also apparently disapproved of Swift's poems to Stella (he reportedly wished Swift "had never written them"), though he did include them in the third volume of the *Miscellanies* in 1728 – the unseemliness in this case was of quite a different kind.[70] Pope had his own ideas about the appropriate way to address or describe a woman in verse, as is suggested by his own *Epistle to a Lady*, published in 1735. Addressed to a dear friend and middle-aged spinster (who had earlier been rumored to have lived with Pope),[71] and devoted to a behind-the-scenes look at the characters of women, it may be regarded as Pope's poetic reply to both the poems to Stella (another spinster, who died at forty-seven in 1728, rumored to have been secretly married to Swift) and *The Lady's Dressing Room*.[72] This, Pope suggests, is a better way to address a sensible woman of a certain age, and the proper way to expose the naked truth about most of the rest of her sex.

Why did Pope (according to Delany) wish that Swift had never written the Stella poems? Delany thinks Pope shared Orrery's view that the poems were "of small importance," perhaps too that there was something cold about them. Orrery thought them "fuller of affection than desire, and more expressive of friendship, than of love,"[73] and that most of them

[69] From "The Publisher's Preface," n. p. Savage is probably alluding to Addison's famous praise of Virgil who in his *Georgics* "tosses the Dung about with an air of gracefulness" ("An Essay on the Georgics" [1697], in *Works of John Dryden*, vol. v, ed. William Frost and Vinton Dearing [1987], 151).

[70] Delany (1754: 103).

[71] Swift may have heard the rumor: in a 1728 letter to Martha pretending that "I continue in love with you," he wishes that she and Pope could live in Dublin, he in the Deanery and she "for reputation sake just at next door" (Woolley 1999–2007: iii, 164) – leaving unspecified whether she was more attached to Swift or to Pope.

[72] Ehrenpreis suggests, without providing details (1962–83: iii, 607n) that Pope's *Epistle to a Lady* was influenced by Swift's "Journal of a Modern Lady." Unlike Swift, as he notes, Pope provides a countervailing figure, Martha Blount, to serve as "a healthy contrast to the frivolous vices of the worldly women" (608).

[73] Orrery (1752: 44, 71, 77).

"turn upon her age: a kind of excuse perhaps for Swift's want of love."
Pope may also have shared Orrery's conviction that Swift and Stella were
secretly married. If so, then the poems might embarrass Swift as either
too warm or too cold. Pope knew from his own experience that a poem
addressed to a dear woman friend might set tongues wagging: he even
felt the need to reassure Caryll that the final line in *Epistle to a Lady* – "to
you gave Sense, Good-humour, and a Poet" – was designed as a sign that
by that stage in his life he had no intention of marrying Martha Blount.[74]
And yet (if he shared Orrery's view) he thought it impolite to mention
a lady's age – and indeed he never mentions Martha's age in the poem
addressed to her, even pretending to "forget the year" of her birth.

This is not to claim that either Pope or Swift regarded the poem as a
"reply" – there is no evidence that they did.[75] But several verbal details in
Pope's *Epistle* suggest that Swift was in the back of his mind as he wrote.
To begin with, the portrait of Chloe has persistently been associated with
Henrietta Howard, about whose character Pope and Swift had differed.
As early as 1727 Swift had in fact drafted a "character" of her, including a
dry observation on the gap between her kind words and her deeds: "She
abounds in good words and expressions of good wishes, and will concert
a hundred schemes for the service of those whom she would be thought to
favour … At the same time, she very well knows them to be without the
least probability of succeeding" (Davis 1939–68: v, 215). Pope may have
had Swift's character sketch in mind when he described Chloe's correct
conduct: "She speaks, behaves, and acts just as she ought; / But never,
never, reach'd one gen'rous Thought." It's not just that she didn't follow
through – she didn't even intend to. For Pope the gap is not between
word and deed but word and intention, perhaps a more insidious form
of hypocrisy. Swift's character focused on Mrs. Howard as a politic and
unreliable courtier; Pope's, more devastatingly perhaps, on her private
life, as an "unmov'd" friend and lover.

An element in Pope's tribute to Martha Blount at the end of the poem
might likewise have been inspired by Swift. "Shakes all together, and

---

[74] "If that line meant any such thing, it must be over. 'Tis in the preterperfect tense, *Gave a Poet*"
(February 18, 1735, in Sherburn 1956: iii, 451). Pope's remark even hints that the poem was
designed to signal to Martha herself that marriage was not in the offing.
[75] On February 16, 1733 Pope told Swift he had "written an Epistle" addressed to Martha (whom he
calls "Your Lady friend" – perhaps because, as Swift wrote in a 1732 letter, she was "the onely Girl
I coquetted in the whole half year that I lived with Mr Pope in Twitenham"), but did not offer
to send a copy. In a March 30, 1733 reply, Swift asks if the "Verses to Patty" will ever "see light"
(Woolley 1999–2007: iii, 552, 595–96, 617) – they were not published until February 1735. No
evidence of Swift's response to Pope's poem has survived.

produces ... you" recalls Swift on Biddy Floyd: "Jove mixed all up, and
his best clay employed, / Then called the Happy Composition Floyd."
But the most suggestive echo comes in Pope's early summary observation about female inconstancy: "Ladies, like variegated Tulips, show, /
'Tis to their Changes that their charms we owe" (41–42). Rawson long
ago well noted that Pope's couplet discovers both order and variety in
women, but that the comparison is ironic: it "prefaces some accounts of
strange and perverse states, but there is a pleasure, turning to gallantry,
in the image's momentary power to systematize, so that a combined ele-
gance, in the women and in Pope's ordering of their variety, survives the
sarcasm" (1973: 47). As Rawson went on to note, Pope's couplet forms
a sharp contrast with Swift's "gaudy tulips, rais'd from Dung" in *The
Lady's Dressing Room*. Pope's "variegated" (vari-colored, or marked with
spots or "stripes" – a contemporary authority speaks of the "pleasant mix-
ture of several Stripes" in a multicolored tulip)[76] of course takes the edge
off Swift's "gaudy," which implies (as did tulips to some contemporary
observers) some excess in display. And he has in effect removed the tulips
from the "confusion" (and the "dung") which produced them, converting
a cheeky insult pretending to be a compliment into a more gracious (but
equally ambiguous) bit of flattery.[77]

AN ESSAY ON MAN AND GULLIVER'S TRAVELS

The *Essay on Man* occupied Pope for much of the early 1730s. He was at
work on the poem as early as 1729, had completed the first three epistles by 1731 (they were published individually in 1733), and published the
fourth epistle in early 1734. The poem is of course addressed not to Swift
but to Henry St. John, Viscount Bolingbroke, and might be regarded as
a continuous "conversation" with his friend and mentor, explicitly named
in the first line of the first epistle and again at the close of the fourth
epistle.[78] Indeed, the poem was apparently prompted in large part by a
series of "philosophical conversations" (as Mack calls them) between Pope
and his friend as early as 1729. The question of Bolingbroke's influence on

---

76 *The Dutch Gardener*, 173. Cowley refers to the tulip's "gay and party-colour'd Coat" ("Hymn. To
    Light") and *Tatler* 218 to tulips "stained with a variety of Colours."
77 Pope elides the distinction between the "changes" in inconstant women and the "changes" of
    color from one tulip to the next, or the combination of several colors in a single flower. His praise
    of "variegated" tulips is made ambiguous by being associated with "the nice admirer": *Tatler* 218
    comments on "fantastical Tastes," e.g., those that value tulips "for their Rarity and Oddity."
78 Beginning with the collected 1734 edition, the poem was dedicated to "H. St. John L.
    Bolingbroke."

Pope's thinking, once much discussed, was settled by Mack more than fifty years ago. Bolingbroke's thought, he argued, "may be said to have transmitted to the poet the outlines of his argument and an unknown number of its subsidiary ideas. It cannot be said to have done more" (1950: xxxi). Furthermore, as Mack showed, the finished poem is significant for the differences between Pope's thought and that of Bolingbroke, who had apparently attempted (without success) to push Pope in the direction of greater heterodoxy. As in his ongoing "conversation" with Swift, Pope was concerned to mark difference from his friends and models.

Swift himself would appear to have been left out of that conversation between Pope and Bolingbroke. But a closer look at the epistolary record, and at the *Essay on Man* itself, shows that Swift was a crucial part of Pope's audience from the beginning, and suggests that behind the figure of Bolingbroke in the poem (addressed originally not as "St. John" but as "Laelius," whom Horace had praised for his philosophical retirement from public life) there hovers the presence of Swift. Normally rather reticent, even in his letters to Swift, about the poems on which is he working, and careful to conceal his authorship of the poem, even swearing his friends to silence,[79] Pope took unusual pains (as did Bolingbroke, who served in effect as his surrogate) to keep Swift informed of his progress on the *Essay on Man*.[80]

As early as November 19, 1729, in the first clear reference in Pope's correspondence to what became the *Essay on Man*, Bolingbroke in fact wrote to Swift with an extended account of an unnamed "Work" upon which Pope was already engaged. Ten days later Pope himself wrote to Swift, remarking offhandedly that the "work [Bolingbroke] speaks of with such abundant partiality, is a system of Ethics in the Horatian way."[81] (Pope typically wrote to Swift about the poem in enigmatic terms, leaving it to Bolingbroke to explain its argument in detail.)[82] Six months later he wrote to Swift again, reporting vaguely that he is "planning ... a book" to "put morality in good humour" (Woolley 1999–2007: III, 313). Pope withholds details, but wants Swift to know that he is adopting a stance strikingly different from that adopted by the author of the *Travels* and the *Modest Proposal*.

---

[79] Pope to Benjamin Motte, June 30, 1727, in Sherburn (1956: III, 438).

[80] See August 2, 1731 (Bolingbroke to Swift), reporting that Pope had finished the first three epistles, and January 6, 1734 (Pope to Swift), reporting that the fourth epistle was completed and would soon be published.

[81] November 28, 1729 (Woolley 1999–2007: III, 273). Swift replied on February 26 to say "I hope your Ethick System is towards the umbilicum" (III, 286).

[82] Swift wrote to Bolingbroke on March 21, 1730 to inquire about Pope's progress (Woolley 1999–2007: III, 295). On August 2, 1731 Bolingbroke sent Swift a detailed account of Pope's work to date (III, 421–22).

In later letters to Swift, Pope signals that his poem will reflect his resolution to turn away from politics to "higher things." On December 1, 1731
he writes to Swift and Gay that he will now "scorn" politics and aspire
to "philosophy," declaring himself glad that Swift has also resolved (in
a lost letter of recent date) to "meddle no more with the low concerns
and interests of parties, even of countries" (Woolley 1999–2007: III, 447).
Pope's language reflects his invitation to Laelius / St. John at the beginning of the first epistle to "leave all meaner things / To low ambition and
the pride of kings," and suggests that in urging a turn from politics to
philosophy Pope was addressing St. John but also at some level thinking
of Swift. Four months later Swift is explicitly invited to join the two fellow philosophers. In a joint letter from Pope and Bolingbroke to Swift,
Pope again avers that he prefers philosophy to politics, looks forward to
another visit by Swift to England, and imagines a joint project: "I fancy
if we three were together but for three years, some good might be done
even upon this Age; or at least some punishment made effectual, toward
the Example of posterity, between History, Philosophy, and Poetry" (III,
459). Although never addressed in the poem itself, Swift is brought into
the poem's conversation as a like-minded philosophical companion. It is
fitting then that, six months after the four epistles were collected and
republished, Pope wrote to Swift of his regret that Bolingbroke had in
effect deserted the team. Bolingbroke, he complains, ignores the "moni-
tory Hint given in the first line of my Essay," occupies himself too much
with "particular Men," "neglects mankind, and is still a creature of
this world, not of the Universe: This World, which is a name we give
to Europe, to England, to Ireland, to London, to Dublin, to the Court,
to the Castle, and so diminishing, till it comes to our own affairs, and
our own persons" (IV, 29). In other words, Bolingbroke concerns himself
too much with Opposition politics – his "Dissertation on Parties" papers
had been appearing in the *Craftsman* since October 1733. But it is clear
that Pope is thinking not just of English politics: "Ireland, ... Dublin, ...
[and] the Castle" refer of course to Swift's continuing engagement with
Irish politics. The letter to Swift, lamenting Bolingbroke's lapse, equally
laments Swift's own.

Swift thus figures prominently in the correspondence concerning the
Essay on Man.[83] He also figures as a factor in the poem's genesis. In one

---

[83] In his letters to Swift during the composition of the poem Pope sometimes used phrases that
appeared later in the poem, e.g. on March 23, 1728, "this world is made for Caesar" (cf. *Essay on
Man*, IV, 146), and April 1, 1733, "whatever is, is right" (cf. I. 294, IV. 394).

of Pope's earliest conversations with Spence in about 1728 he is recorded as saying that he "would engage" to counter the claims of two famous French moralists: "As L'Esprit, Rochefoucauld, and that sort of people prove that all virtues are disguised vices, I would engage to prove all vices to be disguised virtues. Neither, indeed, is true, but this would be a more agreeable subject, and would overturn their whole scheme" (Osborn 1966: I, 219). Neither Pope nor Spence says anything at this point about the *Essay on Man* (or about Swift), but editors have noticed that the idea that vices are in fact virtues was to appear in the Morgan Library manuscript of Epistle II:

> Thus spite of all the Frenchmans witty lies,
> Most Vices are but Virtues in disguise.[84]

To set himself in opposition to the Frenchman La Rochefoucauld is at the same time to set himself in opposition to Swift, who (as we have seen) told Pope that he saw his "whole character" in the French moralist. Indeed, this draft passage suggests that Pope is in effect following up his plan, first expressed in an October 1725 letter to Swift, to write "a Set of Maximes in opposition to all Rochefoucaults Principles" (Woolley 1999–2007: II, 612). The point of Pope's remark – and the reason he went out of his way to mention it – is that he knew Swift to be an admirer of La Rochefoucauld. If we follow Pope's own logic in his account of the genesis of the *Dunciad*, Swift might equally be regarded as the "author" of the *Essay on Man* – for without him "it had never been."

Some editors trace the Swiftian origin of the poem to an even earlier point. A month before mentioning La Rochefoucauld, Pope had written to Swift, in the September 1725 letter cited in chapter 2, declaring that *his* "Travels" (unlike Gulliver's) "shall never more be in a strange land [i.e., Homeric Greece], but a diligent, I hope useful, investigation of my own Territories, … something domestic, fit for my own country, and for my own time" (Woolley 1999–2007: II, 597). Warburton was the first to suggest, in his 1751 edition, that this was a reference to the already-projected *Essay on Man*.[85]

---

[84] Mack (1984: 245); Elwin and Courthope (1871–89: II, 392). These lines were not to appear in the printed poem, where Pope decided to soften the paradox, and to claim that each virtue is so near "ally'd" to a vice that it is difficult to tell "where ends the Virtue, or begins the Vice" (*Essay on Man*, II, 196, 210).

[85] See above, p. 79. Later editors have demurred, and suggested that Pope was here referring (n.b.: "something domestic, fit for … my own time") to his nascent *Dunciad*. But Pope's reference to the *Essay on Man* as his "*general Map* of Man" ("The Design") perhaps supports Warburton.

Swift makes no appearance in the printed poem, but he nonetheless haunts it as a ghostly presence. Just prior to the passage on vice and
virtue in Epistle II appear some lines on the origin of the virtues in the
passions:

> The surest Virtues thus from Passions shoot,
> Wild Nature's vigor working at the root.
> What crops of wit and honesty appear,
> From spleen, from obstinacy, hate, or fear! (II, 183–86)

Elwin and Courthope were the first editors to see a buried allusion to
Swift: "Pope probably alluded to Swift when he spoke of the 'crops of wit
and honesty' which were the product of 'spleen, obstinacy, and hate'"
(1871–89: II, 389). Mack assumes that Pope is thinking of the *Drapier's
Letters*, saluted in the *Dunciad* as a work of liberation but here surprisingly regarded as evidence of Swift's "spleen . . obstinacy, hate, or
fear."[86]

Finally, in his metaphorical "travels" across the "scene of Man" in
Essay on Man, particularly in the second epistle – where he devotes considerable attention to "The Passions, and their use" and to "the office of
Reason" – and the third – where he treats reason and instinct – Pope
takes up topics that had preoccupied Swift, particularly in the "Voyage to
the Houyhnhnms."[87] While there is no need to recapitulate the extended
commentaries on these topics in modern criticism, it is worth noting
that Pope's conclusions and Swift's are broadly similar: both apply satiric
pressure to naive notions of man as a purely "rational animal," both ridicule the pride with which human beings regard themselves as a species.
(Both implicitly agree to leave Christianity out of account in their surveys
of mankind.) The difference, of course, is that Pope finds room in his
easygoing "Horatian ethics" for instinct, passion, and even vice, while
Swift in his satiric mission points to appetites and irrationality as proof
of man's failure to measure up to his own cherished ideals. If Swift's is a
work of demolition, Pope's is one of reconstruction. In *Gulliver's Travels*,
as Orrery first suggested, Swift seems to want to "make us uneasy with

---

[86] Mack (1950: II, 185–86n). Cf. *Moral Essays*, I, 62, "While one there is who charms us with his
Spleen," taken by critics since Wakefield (*Observations on Pope* [1796], 201) to be a reference to
Swift.

[87] On March 20, 1730, Bolingbroke wrote to Swift "renouncing" his idea that "Stupidity" – i.e.,
insensibility – is a cure for "Melancholy," and noting that "Passions, says our divine Pope, as
you will see one time or other, are the Gales of life" (Woolley 1999–2007: III, 373). Bolingbroke
refers, no doubt, to famous lines from the second epistle of the *Essay*, which he has seen in draft.
Pope himself added a long paragraph to Bolingbroke's letter.

ourselves, and unhappy in our present existence."[88] But Pope's purpose, as he told Swift himself, was to "make mankind look upon this life with comfort and pleasure."

Swift's own reply to the published *Essay on Man* is measured. Despite having been briefed on the poem's progress for several years, he reported to Pope, upon its first appearance as a set of four anonymous epistles on May 1, 1733, that the *Essay* was "understood to come from Doctr Young. No body names you for it here (we are better judges, and I do not railly)" (Woolley 1999–2007: III, 637). Pope had once again not alerted Swift to the appearance of a major poem and assumed that Swift was indeed taken in. He later apologized, offering the usual reason: "I beg your pardon for not telling you, as I should have had you been in England: but no secret can cross your Irish Sea, and every clerk in the post-office had known it" (III, 758).[89] But it is in fact not clear that Swift was taken in, and he may have only been pretending ignorance – he later assured Pope that "I never doubted about your Essay on Man, & I would lay any odds, that I would never fayl to discover you in six lines, unless you had a mind to write below or beside your self on purpose" (IV, 9). In his first comment on the poem (in May 1733) Swift went on to say that "It is too Philosophical for me" (III, 636), implicitly replying impudently to Pope's ongoing campaign to turn him from "politics" to "philosophy." Eighteen months later he commended the poem's "Morals," but in language equivocal enough to raise suspicion: "I confess I did never imagine you were so deep in Morals, or that so many new & excellent Rules could be produced so advantageously & agreably in that Science from any one head." (The repeated emphasis – "*so* deep ... *so* many ... *so* advantageously" – hints at ironic mock-wonder.) And he reports he found the poem sometimes difficult to follow: "I confess in some few places I was forced to read twice" (IV, 9). Given the value Pope assigned (in his short 1734 statement on "The Design" of the poem) to "perspicuity," this is a challenging criticism. He may well have taken it to heart: Ruffhead implies that criticism of obscurity in the *Essay on Man* induced Pope to accede to the suggestion that his poem be reprinted in 1740 with Crousaz's 1739 commentary.[90]

---

[88] 1752: 326. Orrery refers here to unspecified "tracts" by Swift, apparently including *Gulliver*, of which he said elsewhere that "not only all human actions, but human nature itself, is placed in the worst light" (132).

[89] Pope added: "I fancy, tho' you lost sight of me in the first of those Essays, you saw me in the second" (Woolley 1999–2007: III, 758), as if referring to the discussion of passion in Epistle II and in Bolingbroke's March 17, 1730 letter.

[90] *Life of Alexander Pope* (1769), 222.

POPE AND *VERSES ON THE DEATH OF DR. SWIFT* (I)

Pope figures prominently in Swift's *Verses on the Death*, first as the rival poet whom Swift claims to envy –

> In Pope, I cannot read a line,
> But with a sigh, I wish it mine:
> When he can in one couplet fix
> More sense than I can do in six:
> It gives me such a jealous fit,
> I cry, "Pox take him, and his wit"

– and then as the friend who laments his death for a whole month. In the traditional reading the Pope–Swift friendship endures the most difficult of tests: Swift's jealousy reveals only the inevitability of self-love, and his confession of it reveals his honesty; given the self-concern in human nature and the transience of most grief, the fact that "Poor Pope will grieve a month" is actually a sign of how deeply he feels his loss. But Swift's irony– is "poor" a sign of pity for the grieving friend, or ironic?[91] – makes it difficult to assess his meanings, and a closer look at Pope's long involvement with *Verses on the Death* suggests that the poem in its several versions stages a kind of conversation between two friends about the very unreliability of friendship, and hints at the tensions that continued to characterize their particular friendship.

Verses on the Death was being composed in late 1731. A letter from Swift to Gay of December 1, 1731 reports that he has written "near five hundred lines on a pleasant Subject, onely to tell what my friends and enemyes will say on me after I am dead" (Woolley 1999–2007: III, 443). He had apparently written to Pope (in a letter now lost) with the same news some weeks earlier, for in his letter to Swift on the same day (December 1), Pope says that he is pleased with Swift's "design upon Rochefoucault's maxim, pray finish it." Swift was in effect taking up the thread of a conversation with Pope that had started some years earlier.[92] As I have suggested, the *Essay on Man*, of which three epistles had been completed by the time Swift began writing *Verses on the Death*, might be regarded as Pope's maxims in reply to La Rochefoucault. It is just at this time that Swift himself set out to write his own "design upon Rochefoucauld's

---

[91] "Poor" is a very common adjective in Swift's poetry, especially as a modifier for a proper name (e.g., "poor Strephon," "poor Stella") – the *Concordance to the Poems of Jonathan Swift*, ed. Michael Shinagel (1972), 625–26, lists nineteen instances. It is also common in Swift's letters.
[92] See above, p. 165.

maxim." Pope's approval of Swift's plan is perhaps surprising, unless he was even at that time contemplating the fact that the poem would serve to set off his *Essay on Man*. In his lost letter to Pope, Swift had apparently also said to him what he said to Gay, that "I have brought in you and my other friends," to which Pope replies: "I am happy whenever you join our names together" (III, 447).

Swift had probably been meditating the poem for some years, perhaps since his 1725 exchange with Pope. One critic suggests that the poem is about "the failures of friendship" and that the generative context of the poem is Swift's ongoing preoccupation in the years after 1727 with false friendship, especially as displayed by the Queen and Lady Suffolk.[93] He suggests too that the poem evinces a link in Swift's mind between friendship and death, with friends as "hedges against mutability" (Woolley 1979: 207) and as preservers (after death) of one's memory. This argument can be adapted for my purposes by noting that it is especially in his letters *to Pope* from 1727 to 1731 that Swift chooses to deal directly and prominently with these topics (see Illustration 3.1).[94]

If the two women serve as exemplars of false friends, Pope is the chief exemplar of a true friend, who will remain true unto death. On October 2, 1727 Pope writes to Swift: "I hope, as you do, that we shall meet in a more durable and more satisfactory state; but the less sure I am of that, the more I would indulge it in this" (Woolley 1999–2007: III, 130–31). To which Swift replies on October 12: "You are the best and kindest friend in the world, and I know no body alive or dead to whom I am so much obliged" (III, 131). But as Swift witnesses the death of friends, he reconsiders the idea that friendship can buffer the effects of death. After their friend Congreve died, Swift wrote to Pope on February 13, 1729 that it would have almost been better, given the pain of loss, "that I never had a friend." It would be better, he goes on, to be like an "ingenious good-humour'd Physician" of his acquaintance, who has an "abundance of friends" with whom he plays cards: "he loves them all … if one of them dies it is no more than poor Tom! he gets another, or takes up with the rest, and is no more mov'd than at the loss of his cat … is not this the true happy man?" (III, 210).[95] Swift appears to be working out, in his letter to Pope, an idea that he would

---

[93] James Woolley, "Friends and Enemies in *Verses on the Death of Dr. Swift*," in *Studies in Eighteenth-Century Culture*, ed. Roseanne Runte, vol. VIII (1979), 210.
[94] See, for example, Swift's July 20, 1731 letter to Pope (Illustration 3.1).
[95] Cf. "Tom" in the *Life and Genuine Character* (lines 15–22), who illustrates the maxim that when "We see a comrade get a fall," we "laugh our hearts out, one and all."

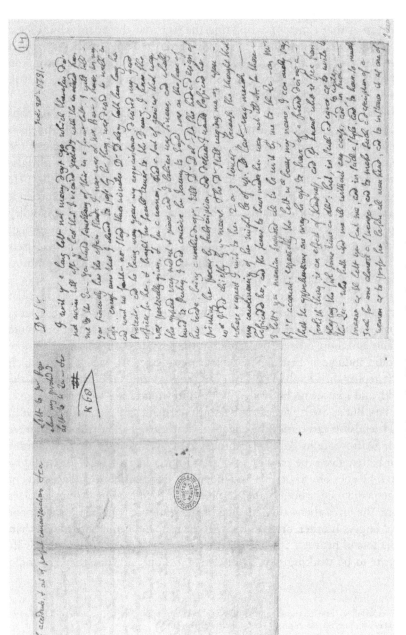

3.1 Holograph of July 20, 1731 Swift-to-Pope letter.

transform into satire in *Verses on the Death*, where Swift's "female friends" do not let news of his death interrupt their card game.[96] Swift began adding his own notes to the poem as early as May 1732 – one of the notes is dated "this present third day of May, 1732." His model was probably the *Dunciad Variorum*: one note refers to "the Character of Jemmy Moore, and ... Theobald, in the Dunciad" (200n), another to Curll's "Character in Part [which] may be found In Mr. POPE's Dunciad" (197n), a third to Lintot – "Vide Mr. Pope's Dunciad" (253n). But Pope's notes served a number of purposes, from facetious and parodic to documentary, and Swift's are highly opinionated ("three stupid Verse Writers ... notoriously infamous ... he is an absolute Dunce") but basically documentary. In this respect they are more like Pope's notes to the *Epistle to Dr. Arbuthnot*, denouncing villains (Chartres, Curll), branding political enemies (the "Whig Faction," the spineless Irish peerage and parliament), praising his friends (Pulteney, Bolingbroke), documenting slights and injuries (the Queen's failure to send the promised medals, libels written against him), and Swift's own bold acts (as the Drapier). As we saw earlier, Swift thought that the *Dunciad* needed notes, since the writers were obscure twenty miles outside of London. For the notes to his own poem Swift seems to have thought not about distance in space but distance in time. It is as if he feared that both facts known only to him and names well known to contemporary readers would one day be lost in oblivion, and wanted to make sure they would descend to posterity.

After completing a draft of *Verses on the Death*, Swift reportedly showed it to friends and visitors.[97] Although there is no evidence that it reached the eyes of Pope as early as 1732–33, that possibility should not be ruled out. But Swift did not publish it, perhaps since some of its language – especially concerning the Queen – was vulnerable to prosecution for libel.[98] About a year later there appeared a poem entitled *The Life*

---

[96] Although not named in the famous "character" of the dean at the end of the poem, Pope may be implicitly present there too, at least in Swift's mind: the closing couplet – "That Kingdom he hath left his Debtor, / I wish it soon may have a Better" – employs the same rhymes as a couplet about Pope in the "Pastoral Dialogue between Richmond-Lodge and Marble-Hill" (written in 1727): "None loves his King or Country better, / Yet none was ever less their Debtor" (83–84).

[97] Swift wrote to Pope in May 1733 that he had shown it to "all common acquaintance indifferently" but never "gave a Copy ... nor lent it out of my sight" (Woolley 1999–2007: III, 636). In an April 1733 letter he reported to Carteret that "at least fourty of both sexes" had seen it (III, 633). But Laetitia Pilkington claimed in her 1748 *Memoirs* that Swift loaned a copy of the poem to her at this time and that she memorized it and frequently recited it to friends (Elias 1997: I, 54–55).

[98] Swift wrote to Pope on May 1, 1733 that the "Verses" were "not fit to be seen until I am seen no more" (Woolley 1999–2007: III, 638).

and Genuine Character of Dr. Swift which may represent the next stage
in Swift's ongoing exchange with Pope. The authorship of the poem has
been much debated, as has its relationship with the *Verses on the Death*,
although a consensus seems now to have developed that the poem (as Pope
seemed to have thought) is indeed Swift's.[99] Scholars disagree, however,
whether it was written after *Verses on the Death*, as a distinct redaction of
it (whether as a burlesque, a self-parody, or a trial balloon), or before, as a
first draft. A case can be made, so I will argue, that it was written after-
ward and designed for print. At least one prominent critic (Herbert Davis)
has suggested that the poem is a kind of April Fool's joke – its dedication
is dated April 1, 1733 – directed against Pope. What could have changed
in the relationship between Swift and Pope that induced the former, in
the months between May 1732 and April 1733, to decide to play a joke on
his dearest friend? A review of the Pope–Swift correspondence for those
months suggests that there were several provocations.

One was the publication in October 1732 of the final volume of the
Pope–Swift *Miscellanies*, lacking Swift's *Libel on Dr. Delany*.[100] A second
was their disagreement about the posthumous publication of Gay's writings. In December 1732 Swift received news from Pope of the death of
Gay (Pope's letter of December 5): this not only made the references to
Gay in the *Verses on the Death* obsolete (for Gay is there represented as a
living rival and friend), but also raised anew the question of how writers
are remembered after their death, by an indifferent public but also by
their friends – within two months Curll was to publish an unauthorized
biography of Gay, and Pope himself, within a few weeks of Gay's death,
was deeply involved in the preparation of his papers for publication. Gay's
Achilles was performed on February 19, 1733, with a prologue probably
written by Pope, who thought the play an "original" (Woolley 1999–
2007: III, 596) and published a revised text of it on March 1. It was not
well received.[101] Swift told Pope he thought the printed play "a very poor
performance" (March 23–31, 1733: III, 615). Swift was in fact troubled by
Pope's plans, worried that he was permitting the publication of writings
that did Gay no credit.[102] (He also critiqued some lines in Pope's epitaph

---

[99] It has even been suggested that Pope himself is the author (Foxon 1975: I, 770).
[100] Rogers (1983: 845) (attributing the idea to Davis, though it is not found in his work) calls the *Life
and Genuine Character* a joke "in retaliation for the editorial methods his friend had adopted"
in preparing the volume of *Miscellanies* for the press. McLaverty (2008: 131) regards it as Swift's
"infuriated response" to Pope's work on the *Miscellanies*.
[101] *Achilles Dissected* (publ. March 2, 1733) attacked Pope for his edition of *Achilles*.
[102] "It is incumbent upon you to see that nothing more be publish'd of his that will lessen his reputation" (Swift to Pope, March 31, in Woolley 1999–2007: III, 615). See May 1, 1733, Swift to Pope,

on Gay.) In Pope's letter to Swift of February 16, 1733, these two editorial incidents – Pope's apology for his omission of the *Libel on Dr. Delany* and his preparation of Gay's papers – are linked with Pope's plan to prepare for his own "mortality" by collecting "monuments" which may serve as "images" of his mind. (This must have struck Swift as precisely what he aimed to do in *Verses on the Death*.)

Pope's letter also alludes to two other matters on which he and Swift disagreed during these months: the latter's repeated requested that Pope honor him in his writing, and that Pope visit him in Ireland. Concerning the latter, Pope once again put Swift off (he could not leave his mother in her continuing decline); concerning the former, Pope implied that he was at last prepared to comply with Swift's request, referring to "The whole scheme of my present Work" (probably the "magnum opus" of which the *Essay on Man* and the *Epistles to Several Persons* were to be parts) as providing an opportunity to address or compliment him (Woolley 1999–2007: III, 349). But Pope had by that time completed a set of epistles addressed to Cobham, Martha Blount, Bathurst, and Burlington, none of which include Swift's name. Swift must have wondered when, if ever, Pope would get around to addressing *him*.[103]

Many years ago Herbert Davis remarked (1931: 66) that a reading of their letters shows that the Pope–Swift friendship "was not wholly unblemished by moods of irritation and suspicion." As my review of the letters from the six months prior to the appearance of the *Life and Genuine Character* (October 1732 through March 1733) suggests, there were at least four grounds – not just Pope's editing of Swift, but also his editing of Gay, his deferral of Swift's requests to visit, and deferral of his requests to "Orna me" – for irritation, and grounds for reading *The Life and Genuine Character* as an oblique expression of that irritation.[104] Within days of sending the last of these letters Swift seems to have prepared and dated the dedication of *The Life and Genuine Character* to "Alexander Pope, Esq., of Twickenham in the county of Middlesex," and set in motion the process which led to the appearance of the printed poem about April 20.[105]

---

worried about publication of Gay's papers. See also Pope to Swift, April 20, 1733; Pope to Caryll, December 14, 1732.

[103] See above, pp. 140–41.

[104] The date of composition of the *Life and Genuine Character* has not been established, but the window can be defined as between May 1732 (when he was still completing *Verses on the Death*) and some point after January, but before April, 1733 (when Motte, in a July 31, 1735 letter to Swift, said he was offered the Life and Genuine Character).

[105] Ehrenpreis uncharacteristically misspeaks (1962–83: III, 757–58) in suggesting that Swift withheld *The Life and Genuine Character* from the 1732 volume as a way of "balancing accounts"

At this point the story of the poem quickly becomes complicated. Much has been written about Swift's private and public announcements (in a letter to Pope, and a subsequent notice in the *Dublin Journal*) that *The Life and Genuine Character* was in fact not "genuine," and regarding Pope's doubts about the veracity of Swift's announcements.[106] Pope's carefully phrased letter of September 15, 1733 seems to imply personal knowledge:

> The man who drew your Character and printed it here, was not much wrong in many things he said of you: yet he was a very impertinent fellow, for saying them in words quite different from those you had yourself employed before on the same subject: for surely to alter your words is to prejudice them; and I have been told, that a man himself can hardly say the same thing twice over with equal happiness: Nature is so much a better thing than artifice. (Woolley 1999–2007: III, 689)

The "words ... you had yourself employed before" implies that Pope had knowledge of the as-yet-unpublished *Verses on the Death*. The invocation of the idea that "a man himself can hardly say the same thing twice over with equal happiness" suggests that in his view the same "man" wrote both poems.

Given their history of (on the one hand) teasing or mystifying each other and (on the other) withholding information concerning authorship, it is not unlikely that the poem, and its dedication, were designed by Swift as a coded message that Pope was expected to understand. The dedication, signed by one "L. M. ... From my chambers in the Inner Temple" (said to be the "publisher"), recognizes Pope as "an intimate friend of the author" and implies (but does not explicitly state) that he has no doubt seen a copy of the poem – since it had been freely shown to "several friends" and to "any visitor," and a transcription had apparently been made and then loaned to "others." (The dedication claims only to inform Pope of how Swift came to write the poem, and how the dedicator procured a copy.) As a "superior judge and poet" Pope is expected to share the consensus with other "very good judges, and friends of the Dean" who "allow it to be genuine, ... his particular genius appearing in every line." Pope had of course just six months earlier exercised his editorial judgement, receiving

---

with Pope for omitting the *Libel on Dr Delany*. There is no evidence that Swift's poem was written before the volume appeared.

[106] For Swift's letter to Pope, see Woolley (1999–2007: III, 636). For a summary of the matter, see Williams (1958: II, 541–43), and Pope's letters to Swift of January 6, and September 15, 1734 in which he writes of Swift's "method of concealing your self" (Woolley 1999–2007: III, 716–17), and declares "I think (I say once more) that I know your hand" (III, 758).

from Swift a list of his genuine poems, and determining which of them would, and more importantly would not, appear in the final volume of *Miscellanies*. (And six years later he would publish his own revised version of Swift's *Verses on the Death*.) By publishing *The Life and Genuine Character* himself, Swift may be reaffirming control over his own work, determining the form in which it would be read – while publicly pretending not to. In an alternative theory, Pope himself has been suspected of involvement in the publication of the poem, through John Wright, who also apparently printed Epistle II of the *Essay on Man* on March 29, just three days before the date of the dedication.[107] If Pope was in fact responsible, *The Life and Genuine Character* is the first of his two attempts to edit versions of Swift's poem to make it more presentable.

Those who have compared the poems do not always agree with Swift that *Verses on the Death* is the superior version. The chief formal difference, apart from the fact that *Life and Genuine Character* is considerably shorter than *Verses on the Death*, is that the extended discussion of Swift's character appears as a dialogue between opposing speakers in the former, and as the monologue by "one indiff'rent in the cause" in the latter. Given his later editing practice, Pope would presumably have agreed with those modern critics who find the dialogical discussion of Swift's merits and defects less embarrassing than the effusive praise in the *Verses on the Death*. In tallying the differences between the two versions, critics would do well to focus on two other features: in the *Life and Genuine Character* Swift masks his attack on the Queen and Lady Suffolk (and thus renders the poem publishable), and he re-frames his presentation of Pope, whose name does not appear except in the dedication. Neither the lines about Swift's jealousy of Pope's skillful couplets nor those about Pope's month of grief appear in the *Life and Genuine Character*.[108] Although never named in the poem, Pope perhaps appears disguised as an unnamed "friend." In the *Verses on the Death* appears a passage about our inevitable envy of "our equal":

> We all behold with envious Eyes,
> Our *Equal* rais'd above our *Size;*
> Who wou'd not at a crowded Show,
> Stand high himself, keep others low?

---

[107] Williams (1958: II, 542).
[108] Did Swift perhaps want to avoid drawing embarrassing attention to Pope's apparently transitory grief over the death of Gay? Gay had of course died since the lines about his grieving "a week" had been written.

> I love my Friend as well as you,
> But would not have him stop my view;
> Then let me have the higher Post;
> I ask but for an Inch at most. (13–20)

In the *Life and Genuine Character* these lines are subtly recast, addressed to "you" – perhaps the dedicatee of the poem – and focused not on our "view" at a "crowded Show" but on the "public view" of us:

> Come tell me truly, wou'd you take well,
> Suppose your *Friend* and *You*, were *Equal*,
> To see him always *foremost* stand,
> Affect to take the *upper hand*
> And strive to pass, in *publick* view,
> For a much *better man* than *You?*
> *Envy*, I doubt, wou'd pow'rful prove,
> And get the *better* of your *Love*. (31–38)

Herbert Davis long ago suggested that the skeptical discussion of friendship in the *Life and Genuine Character* has "a special significance in a poem indirectly addressed to Pope" (1931: 65). It may especially be reflected in such lines as the following:

> I could give Instances Enough,
> That *Human Friendship* is but *Stuff.*
> Whene'er a *flatt'ring Puppy* cries
> *You* are his *Dearest Friend* – ; he lyes – . (23–26)

The letters of Pope and Swift over the previous seven years had of course repeatedly exalted "human friendship" and professed that each was the other's "dearest friend." With current reasons to be irritated with his friend (and a habit of presenting himself as Pope's opposite), Swift might well have sought to challenge Pope's effusions on friendship. Another passage seems to point even more clearly at Pope:

> Let me suppose, two special Friends,
> And, each to *Poetry* pretends:
> Wou'd either *Poet* take it well,
> To hear, the other *bore the Bell* – ?
> His *Rival*, for the *Chiefest* reckon'd,
> *Himself*, pass only for the *Second* – ? (52–57)

In 1733, when these lines were written, Pope (as Swift well knew) would have been reckoned in the minds of most readers "the Chiefest" of the English poets. Their joint appearance six months earlier in the final volume of Pope–Swift *Miscellanies* would only have confirmed the results of the comparison. In the *Verses on the Death* Swift had confessed envy of Pope, Gay, Arbuthnot, St. John, and Pulteney. In the *Life and Genuine Character* that envy is directed at one "special Friend."

If Pope thought the lines were directed at him, he left no record of it. Indeed, he was to say almost nothing about either the *Life and Genuine Character* or the *Verses on the Death of Dr. Swift* for six years, when he prepared a revised edition of the latter poem. Pope had by then published his own satirist's apology in the *Epistle from Mr. Pope to Dr. Arbuthnot* (1735), and it is worth asking whether that poem might be regarded as a deferred and oblique response to Swift's *Verses on the Death* (written 1731–32) and *Life and Genuine Character* (1733). Answering the question requires a quick review of the complicated composition history of Pope's poem, and a brief examination of the poem itself.

By the time Pope saw the *Life and Genuine Character* (and perhaps the *Verses on the Death*) in late 1732 or early 1733,[109] much of what became the *Epistle to Dr. Arbuthnot* had probably already been drafted. John Butt argued in an influential essay that Pope began work on the poem early in 1732, when he wrote some 260 lines of a poem then addressed to William Cleland, as a reply to accusations that the description of Timon's villa in the *Epistle to Burlington* (published December 1731) was a thinly disguised attack on the Duke of Chandos.[110] One of its paragraphs had been composed and even published in 1727 (the character of Atticus); what became the poem's final paragraph was drafted by December 1731.[111] Mack suggests that the various parts of the poem were probably not assembled into the form they were to take in the *Epistle to Dr. Arbuthnot* until late spring / early summer 1733. By then Pope was feeling the pressure of several new provocations, including the deaths of both Atterbury and Gay in 1732 and of his own mother in June 1733, and the publication of the *Verses address'd to the Imitator of Horace*, which appeared in March 1733. These pressures helped him to shape the developing poem, and left their plain mark on it, as Pope himself acknowledged. It was to receive further shaping by the appearance in November 1733 of Hervey's *Epistle from a Nobleman to a Doctor of Divinity*, to which Pope wrote (but did not publish) his

---

[109] Karian (2002: 98) thinks that Swift did not give a copy of *Verses on the Death* to William King until the summer of 1736.

[110] Butt (1954: 36–38), endorsed by Mack (1984: 419–54). The argument that this early draft was addressed to Cleland has been recently questioned by Julian Ferraro 2008.

[111] The former in the Pope–Swift *Miscellanies* in 1727; the latter survives in a letter Pope sent to Aaron Hill in September 1731. What became lines 406–19 was first published as an imitation of Horace in January 1732.

"Letter to a Noble Lord" in reply. (As he wrote to Swift in January 1734, Pope declined to enter "a Woman's war" with Hervey, and suppressed his letter.)[112] Final shaping came in response to the "Last Request" from the dying Arbuthnot in July 1734 that Pope continue his "noble Disdain and Abhorrence of Vice" but do so with "due regard to your own Safety." It was apparently at this time that Pope made the decision to address the poem to Arbuthnot; it was essentially complete by September 1734.[113]

During these same months – May 1733 to September 1734 – Swift was (or so he later claimed) very much on Pope's mind. They exchanged no more than a handful of letters (perhaps because both were occupied with major literary projects), but received word of each other (so Pope wrote to Swift) via the "intervening, officious, impertinence" of some mutual friends, who "repeat your slighter verses" and even printed them. This impertinence of false friends seems to have led to what Pope called "uneasiness." In September 1734, less than two weeks after reporting to Arbuthnot that the poem to him was finished, Pope wrote to Swift to apologize for his "late silence"[114] and to grumble in turn at Swift's "not answering in a very long time." But he said nothing about the forthcoming *Epistle*. Was it because he remembered Swift's repeated request that he inscribe an epistle to him? Although any misunderstanding seems to have been patched up in Swift's letter of November 1, 1734 – "I did never imagine you to be either inconstant or to want right notions of Friendship" (Woolley 1999–2007: IV, 8) – the friendship may have begun to enter its cooler phase. On December 19 – two weeks before its publication – Pope first mentioned to his old friend the *Epistle to Dr. Arbuthnot*, in a throwaway remark about what he had been writing: "I redeem now and then a paper that hath been abandon'd several years; and of this sort you'll soon see one, which I inscribe to our old friend Arbuthnot" (IV, 28).

In what in effect constituted Pope's public defense of his satiric practice, and of his readiness to speak out boldly, it is perhaps surprising that Swift (who had been urging Pope to be bold) is nearly invisible. He makes only two brief appearances in the published *Epistle*, as one of the circle of the young Pope's admiring friends at line 138 – "And *Congreve* lov'd, and *Swift* endur'd my Lays" – and at lines 275–76: "'I found him close with

[112] Woolley (1999–2007: III, 717).
[113] See the letters exchanged by Pope and Arbuthnot in the summer of 1734 (Sherburn 1956: III, 416–17, 423–24, 428–29, 430–31).
[114] Woolley (1999–2007: III, 757). Swift had written to Oxford on August 30, 1734 to complain that Pope "hath quite forsaken me, for I have not heard from him many Months" (III, 753).

Swift' – 'Indeed? no doubt' / (Cries prating *Balbus*) 'something will come out'." "[E]ndur'd" in the former may be affectionate irony, but one early reader, Wakefield, thought it "admirably expresses Swift's supercilious-ness of judgement" (232). It also has its own Swiftian resonance: "endure" is common in Swift's poems.[115] As for the latter, no one could have observed Pope literally "close with *Swift*" for nearly eight years – since Swift had last visited Twickenham in 1727. As it happens, both references to Swift are products of late revision. In the manuscript versions, the list of Pope's early friends did not include Swift; his name must have been inserted about 1733. About that time too Pope revised "I saw him walk with Swift" into the more suggestive "I found him close with *Swift*," hint-ing at intimate exchange and conspiracy. Pope may have designed the phrase to allude flatteringly to Swift's own imitation of Horace's *Satire* II. 6, in which Swift and Harley are said to be "Always together, *tête à tête*" (86), and Swift is regarded as "The closest mortal ever known" (104).[116] Pope substitutes himself for Harley, and substitutes poetry for politics. In Swift's imitation the "close" man declares that in fact he has nothing to say, and keeps his own counsel. In Pope's epistle the two friends are observed to be "close"[117] – shut up together, as if engaged in some secret matter – and from their conference "something" – perhaps a new poem – will surely come out.

But rather than emphasize his closeness to Swift, Pope's poem in sev-eral respects seems to suggest that his practice is in fact different. His *Epistle* and Swift's two related poems are only superficially similar – satiric apologies, drawn up "piecemeal" over a long period, medleys of disparate formal elements, including snatches of colloquial dialogue. All three are very much poems about friends and enemies. But the differ-ences between the poems are telling. Swift's poems concern false friends as much as true ones, and declare that even true friends have their own "private ends." By contrast, Pope's friends are bulwarks, and arouse not the slightest suspicion. Swift's strategy is to imagine what others will say after he dies; in the *Epistle to Dr. Arbuthnot* it is Pope who survives while his dear friend Gay dies. In *Verses on the Death* Swift imagines himself as a legator, leaving behind an inheritance of writings, a record of public

---

[115] Cf. especially "To all my Foes, dear Fortune, send / Thy gifts, but never to my Friend: / I tamely can endure the first, / but, this with Envy makes me burst" (*Verses on the Death of Dr. Swift*, 67–70).

[116] In Swift's poem Harley in his *tête à tête* with Swift asks if he has "nothing new to day / From *Pope*, from *Parnel*, or from *Gay*?" (73–74).

[117] *OED*, "close," a. II. 17, "intimate, confidential."

service, and funds to found a hospital for the insane. Pope by contrast presents himself as a kind of legatee, heir of a circle of admired older writers. The most significant difference lies in the management of self-praise. As is clear from his later editing of Swift's *Verses on the Death*, Pope found the eulogistic monologue at the end of the poem (from one allegedly "indifferent") an embarrassing sign of vanity in his friend. His own poem contains at least as much self-commendation as Swift's *Verses on the Death*, and makes the poet his own defender. But Pope's strategy, as has often been noted, is to arrange the various parts of the poem – an arrangement probably accomplished during the revision in 1733 – so as to make the repeated declarations that he is only a Friend of Virtue appear as the understandable responses to provoking attacks and malicious misrepresentations of an essentially peace-loving man. It is noteworthy that, unlike Swift, Pope does not imagine scenes – the card table, the customer at Curll's shop, the gathering at the Rose – at which he is not present. He is careful not to let his interlocutors speak more than a line or two: the effect is not to dramatize a scene but to report it (and thus more effectively contain it in his dismissive summaries). And by determining at some point in his revisions to frame the poem as an *epistle* to a named friend, Pope makes clear that his imagined interlocutors are not full participants in a *dialogue*.[118] In focusing on the element in his satiric character that he wants most to define him, Pope also seems to have determined to set himself apart from Swift, reaffirming (once more), against his friend's urging to the contrary, that he would rather enlist under the banner of poetry and ethical philosophy than of politics. At the climax in the closing lines of *Verses on the Death*, Swift's eulogist declares that "FAIR LIBERTY was all his cry." In a passage unobtrusively tucked some fifty lines from the end, Pope declares, as if in response, "Welcome for thee, fair Virtue! All the past: / For thee, fair Virtue! welcome ev'n the *last*!" (358–59).

In another important way too, Pope's *Epistle to Dr. Arbuthnot* serves to mark his difference from Swift: he, unlike his friend the Dean, affirms his identity as an author in the emerging "print culture." As Stephen Karian has argued (2002: 79), Swift's rhetorical strategy in *Verses on the*

---

[118] Pope's insertion of "incipit. / Epistle to Arbuthnot / (1)" at the top of the penultimate leaf of the ur-poem, reproduced in Mack (1984: 432), marks the point at which the poem was converted from an address to "the Man of Friendship" (identified by Butt and Mack as Cleland), or perhaps an address to an anonymous "Friend," to an epistle addressed to Arbuthnot. As Butt notes, it is "open to doubt" that Pope authorized Warburton's conversion of the poem from epistle to dialogue (1939: 93).

Death is to try to locate his posthumous identity outside the book trade.[119] Booksellers are presented as Swift's adversaries, Curll and Lintot serving as exemplars of "inaccurate attribution, unauthorized publication, and the corrupt marketplace" (Karian 2002: 79). The former cobbles together "Three genuine [i.e., apocryphal] Tomes of *Swift's* Remains" (198), and a year later the latter struggles to remember Swift's name: "His way of Writing now is past" (265). The eulogy delivered at the Rose – which says almost nothing about his writings (the eulogist regards himself as "no judge" of "his works in verse and prose") – represents Swift's attempt to appeal over the heads of the booksellers directly to the public. But the naming of several of Swift's published works in the poem's notes, so Karian suggests (2002: 79), indicates Swift's regretful acknowledgement of "the difficulty, perhaps impossibility, of authors reaching the public except through the book trade."

By contrast, Pope in his *Epistle* not only reaffirms himself as published author but embraces that identity. Like Swift, Pope seeks to correct what he regards as a false image of himself, but for Pope that false image is found *in print* – in the "Advertisement" to the poem he names the published texts that attack him – and must be countered by his *publishing* a corrected version. He not only devotes his life to the muse, but resolves to "publish" (135), and accepts with equanimity the fact that his writings are advertised for sale ("What tho' my Name stood rubric on the walls? / Or plaister'd posts, with Claps in capitals? / Or smoaking forth, a hundred Hawkers load, / On Wings of Winds came flying all abroad," 215–18). Where Swift's enemies are his false friends in private and public life, Pope's are the cowardly critic Atticus, the corrupt court poet Sporus, and the proud patron Bufo. Lintot emerges not as a mercenary man of business but as an established figure in the literary world: he is introduced (61–62) as Pope's bookseller, a man with sense enough to refuse a dull poem. Swift had imagined Curll's readiness to exploit his death for gain:

> He'll treat me as he does my Betters,
> Publish my Will, my Life, my Letters,
> Revive the Libels born to dye;
> Which Pope must bear as well as I. (201–04)

---

[119] Cf. "The poem's organization suggests that Swift's reputation is ultimately based not on his published works, nor on the opinions of those enemies or friends who knew him. Rather it depends on some general public memory" (2002: 79). Elsewhere Karian notes (2008: 100) that Swift may have recognized that it was Curll "who allows [him] to live beyond his death."

Pope seems to have remembered this triad: *will, life, letters*. Apparently answering this passage in Swift's poem, he concedes that he faces the same fate but implicitly shrugs it off: he merely notes that Curll "prints my Letters" (113) – as if this is simply one of the occupational hazards of being an author in print.[120] Even though an unnamed writer "aspers'd his life" [376], Pope lets it go. (He will let Budgell write "whate'er he pleased, except his *Will*" (379) – Budgell having notoriously forged the will of Matthew Tindal.) He will "laugh" at "The Tale reviv'd, the Lye so oft o'erthrown" (350). Swift imagines a future in which his works are out of date and out of print, but hopes his name will survive in popular memory. Pope assumes that the "Information" he provides – bolstered as it is by his documentary notes – will clear his name in the minds of his own contemporaries, and he appears to share none of Swift's anxiety about posterity: his *Epistle* seems of a piece with expressions of confidence in his letters that his writings will survive "to Posterity."[121]

Pope would make not make a further reply to *Verses on the Death of Dr. Swift* until 1739, when he helped to produce an edition of the poem. By that time relations between the two poets had become more complicated and more strained, and it is to the writings of the later 1730s that I now turn.

---

[120] Pope is extraordinarily disingenuous here: Curll had without authorization printed some of Pope's letters in 1726, but by the time he published the *Epistle to Dr. Arbuthnot* Pope had already initiated the famous scheme that would trap Curll into publishing the *Letters of Mr. Pope* in May 1735.

[121] Cf. the 1727 letter to Swift on their *Miscellanies*, showing them "walking down hand in hand to posterity" (Woolley 1999–2007: III, 76), and a 1742 letter to Warburton: Warburton's editorial work will cause both "Me & my Writings" to "make a better figure to Posterity" (Sherburn 1956: IV, 428).

CHAPTER 4

In the manner of Dr. Swift

The year 1735 was Pope's busiest as a publishing writer: in that year alone, as his bibliographer notes, there appeared not only the *Epistle to Dr. Arbuthnot* and the *Epistle to a Lady*, but also a major collected edition – his *Works*, vol. II – as well as Curll's edition of his *Letters* (which Pope insisted was unauthorized, but which he in fact orchestrated). In addition to these highlights, there were, according to Griffith's *Bibliography*, numerous re-issues and revisions: sixty-eight publications in all in what might be thought Pope's *annus mirabilis*. For the remainder of the 1730s Pope continued to be prolific: his own authorized edition of his *Letters* appeared in 1737, and he extended his sequence of Horatian imitations with two new poems in 1737 and three more in 1738. These were followed in the same year by two original "Horatian" poems, the two dialogues of *One Thousand Seven Hundred and Thirty-Eight* (later published as the *Epilogue to the Satires*). As the decade closed he was developing relationships with several key new friends – the Revd. William Warburton, Ralph Allen, and the young George Lord Lyttelton – and allying himself more openly with the political Opposition to Walpole.

Swift meanwhile, at the age of sixty-eight, was already suffering regularly from fits of "Giddyness" and "deafness" and complained that his "Memory is going fast."[1] He in effect set out to put his literary affairs in order, completing the publication of a four-volume edition of his works in January 1735, organized along quite different principles from Pope's *Works*. Only two new poems – *The Legion Club* (1736) and *Verses on the Death of Dr. Swift* (written much earlier, but not published until 1739) – and one new piece of prose – *A Compleat Collection of Genteel and Ingenious Conversation* (1738) – would appear in print for the ten-year remainder of his lifetime. Some things he planned to withhold until he was safely dead and beyond prosecution: in 1736 he let the English

---

[1] See, for example, his May 12, 1735 letter to Pope (Woolley 1999–2007: IV, 103).

printer Motte know that he had "some Things which I shall leave my Executors to publish after my Decease [perhaps the *Verses on the Death of Dr. Swift*, at that date still unpublished], and have directed that they shall be printed in London."[2] (He had apparently not given up his long preference that his works be published in London – the literary capital – rather than Dublin.) Faulkner's four-volume edition of the *Works* was reprinted and expanded to six volumes in 1738,[3] with the addition of *The Conduct of the Allies, and the Examiners* (vol. v) and *The Publick Spirit of the Whigs, & c. and Polite Conversation* (vol. vi). A volume containing *Letters To And From Dr. J. Swift, D. S. P. D.* appeared in 1741, and in 1746 was reissued as vol. vii, along with vol. viii, *Directions to Servants*.[4]

Pope and Swift continued to correspond – seventeen letters between them have survived, written between 1735 and 1741. Most of their correspondence concerns Pope's wish to include his letters to Swift in his authorized editions, and Swift's apparent unwillingness to comply. It is perhaps the tension that emerges in the correspondence which gave rise to the report that reached Orrery's ears that "the Friendship between Pope and Swift was not so perfect at the latter end as at the beginning of their lives."[5] But the two old friends found time to collaborate in 1736 on an amusing trifle, *Bounce to Fop. An Heroick Epistle from a Dog at Twickenham to a Dog at Court*. It was during these years too that Pope's poems, by becoming more politically confrontational, were to become more "Swiftian." (Indeed, he published one Horatian poem "Imitated in the Manner of Dr. Swift" and another in which he completed a poem Swift had earlier imitated.) This convergence throws into relief the charged episode in 1739 when Pope played a major role in editing (and in effect re-writing) Swift's *Verses on the Death of Dr. Swift* for a London edition, and Swift responded by publishing his own edition – restored from Pope's editorial surgery – in Dublin. In a sense this incident – separate publication by Pope and Swift of a key Swift poem in London and Dublin in 1739 – replicates the separate publication of their collected *Works* in 1734–35. If in the years after 1727 Pope and Swift imagined themselves "walking down hand in hand to posterity," in the half-decade after 1735 they increasingly marked out their own paths.

[2] Woolley (1999–2007: iv, 305).   [3] Teerink no. 42.
[4] Teerink no. 44.   [5] See above, "Introduction."

COLLECTED WORKS: SWIFT'S (1734–1735)
AND POPE'S (1735)

It is perhaps no coincidence that major editions of the writings of both Swift and Pope appeared within months of each other in 1734–35. The stories of the preparation of the two editions are well known to specialists, but are worth reviewing from the points of view of the two principals. When Swift's edition is regarded from Pope's perspective, and Pope's from Swift's, what emerges is a record of dissimulation, equivocation, and surprising silence. When the editions themselves are set side by side and examined bibliographically, what emerges is a set of clear differences in the ways the two writers present themselves to their readers.

The seeds of the four-volume edition of Swift's *Works*, finally published in 1734–35, can perhaps be found, so Ehrenpreis suggests, as early as 1732.[6] That might explain why Swift wrote to Pope on June 12, apparently putting off a request that he send more material for a final miscellany volume, dismissing much of his recent writing as "little accidental things," at best "tolerable or bad," and promising that he has already provided in his will "that all my Papers of any kind shall be delivered you to dispose of as you please."[7] Pope, for his part, so Ehrenpreis conjectures, hastened the publication of the final 1732 volume of *Miscellanies* because he had got wind of a plan, hatched by the London printers Motte and Bowyer, to gain copyright to some of Swift's recent work so as to publish their own edition. Swift's own plans may have come into sharper focus by December 1732, when, dissatisfied with Pope's editing of the final volume of their joint *Miscellanies* (which appeared in October), and in particular with Pope's decision not to include the *Libel on Dr. Delany*, he wrote to Motte that he had "cause to believe that some of our printers will collect all they think to be mine, and print them by subscription."[8] This seems to be a clue that Swift had himself closed with the Irish printer, George Faulkner.

On February 9, 1733 Faulkner printed proposals for a subscription edition of Swift's works.[9] Pope perhaps first heard of the project when he read the proposal, reprinted on the final leaves of the Dublin edition of his own

---

[6] See Ehrenpreis (1962–83: III, 744). I draw on Ehrenpreis's account (744–51), largely based on an analysis of Swift's letters, of the genesis of his *Works*. Woolley concurs that for four months from June through September 1732 Swift "engaged covertly in a scheme to publish his own recent prose and verse independently in London" (1999–2007: III, 491).
[7] June 12, 1732 (Woolley 1999–2007: III, 489).
[8] December 9, 1732 (Woolley 1999–2007: III, 564). See also his November 4, 1732 letter to Motte.
[9] They are reproduced in Davis (1939–68: XIV, 42–43).

imitation of *The First Satire of the Second Book of Horace*, published by
Faulkner on March 2. In his proposal Faulkner took notice of the "three
volumes" of miscellanies "published six years ago" in which Swift's work
had been "mingled" – thus pointedly ignoring the final volume which
Pope had published only five months earlier – and announced that he was
responding to the wish that a "new compleat Edition of [Swift's] Works,
should be printed by it self." He promised to include two Drapier letters
"never printed before" and "many original Poems, that have hitherto only
gone about in Manuscript." Pope would have concluded that Faulkner
had Swift's cooperation, and would have been confirmed in his earlier
fears that the new edition was in several respects designed to rival his 1732
Pope–Swift *Miscellanies*.

On April 20 Pope wrote to Swift, asking when "your collection [will]
come out" (Woolley: III, 631) – initially a spring 1733 date had been projected. Swift replied on May 1, pretending that the idea for the edition was
Faulkner's, and claiming that he himself had discouraged the project and
resolved to take no part in it: "I am grown perfectly indifferent in every
thing of that kind. This is the very truth of the story" (III, 638).[10] As his
emphatic language suggests (recalling the famous truth-claim by Virgil's
Sinon cited at the end of the *Travels*), Swift was again delighting in mis-
direction, even with his closest friends (though possibly expecting Pope
to see through his disingenuous claim). But Swift, scholars now agree,
was quietly involved in the editing, and was to remain involved after the
volumes began to be printed.[11] He was also cooperating with Faulkner
in securing subscriptions: in a letter to Oxford on February 16, delivered
by Faulkner himself, Swift, although pretending that the edition "very
much discontents me," nonetheless recommends the bearer.[12] Oxford was
to subscribe, but Pope (for whatever reason) did not: did he expect that
Swift would send him a complimentary copy? On September 1 Pope wrote
to Oxford asking him, as a subscriber, to send one copy of "Dr Swift's
Miscellanies" to Lord Peterborough. To refer to the forthcoming *Works*
as Swift's "Miscellanies" is perhaps to confirm that Pope continued to see
them as a rival to the Pope–Swift *Miscellanies*. In a sense they were, since

[10] Swift told the same story to other correspondents: Charles Ford on October 9, 1733 (Woolley
1999–2007: III, 693), Oxford on February 16, 1734 (III, 722), William Pulteney on March 8, 1735
(IV, 67).
[11] See the August 30, 1734 letter to Oxford (Woolley 1999–2007: III, 753), in which he reports that
he has given Faulkner "some Difficultyes by ordering certain Things to be struck out [of the
forthcoming *Works*] after they were printed."
[12] Woolley (1999–2007: III, 722). Oxford subscribed for five sets, as did Bolingbroke, to whom
Swift also sent a letter commending Faulkner (cf. III, 721–22).

Swift was to reprint several of his pieces that had appeared earlier in the joint *Miscellanies*, as well as the *Libel on Dr. Delany* that Pope had omitted from the 1732 volume, and Faulkner's advertisement had noted that one volume would contain "the Prose Part of the Author's Miscellanies." But Pope, sensitive as he was to the significance of titles, and still smarting at the prospect that Swift would publish a volume of "Works" before he himself could do so, perhaps deliberately chose a depreciating term to dismiss the importance of the edition.

The *Works of J. S., D. D., D. S. P. D.,*[13] its projected publication date much delayed, began appearing in November 1734, the first three volumes (including "The Author's Miscellanies in Prose," "His Poetical Works," and "The Travels of Captain *Lemuel Gulliver*") on November 27, the fourth ("His Papers Relating to *Ireland*") on January 6, 1735. The works are distributed into the various volumes by several conflicting principles, crudely generic (prose vs. poetry) as well as topical (Ireland). The very title of the first volume – "Miscellanies in Prose" – suggests the variety or miscellaneity of Swift's work. The first 90 of 115 "Poetical Works" are arranged in roughly chronological order, 1701 to 1731, each poem identified as "Written in the Year – ." But thereafter chronology largely breaks down. A major poem such as *On Poetry. A Rapsody* (494 lines) is squeezed between "A Love Song in the Modern Taste" (32 lines) and "The Dog and Thief" (20 lines). Each of the volumes contained a frontispiece portrait: volume I a formal but plain half-length of the author, in full wig and clerical garb, with a title "The Reverend Dr. J. SWIFT, D. S. P. D"; volume II an elaborate sculptural group containing the same portrait within a small medallion, backed by the sun, and surrounded by two female figures (one of whom reaches up to place a laurel wreath on the head in the medallion, the other helmeted, perhaps representing "Britannia") and several *putti*, a scroll bearing the words "The Poetical Works of J. S. D. S. P. D.," and at the bottom a line from Horace ("Quivis speret idem" – "anyone may hope for the same"). The frontispiece to volume III is a portrait of "Captain Lemuel Gulliver" (in his own hair, and looking rather more like Swift himself than the "Gulliver" whose portrait – by Hyde – appeared in the 1726 *Travels*), and the impudent Horatian tag "Splendide mendax" ("egregious or glorious liars"). In volume IV Swift is seated in an upright armchair (but not Rabelais's "easy chair"), beside a table on which sits pen and ink and a couple of sheets near his right hand representing his writings, apparently receiving with his left hand a petition (or

---

[13] Doctor of Divinity, Dean of St. Patrick's Dublin.

4.1   Frontispiece to vol. IV of *The Works of J. S., D. D., D. S. P. D.* (1735).

perhaps an address of thanks) from a female figure (representing Ireland?), his right foot trampling a helmeted male figure (representing England?), with a nursing mother in the foreground, and two winged *putti* hovering above, in order to place a wreath on his head (see Illustration 4.1). Below the cut is the famous Horatian phrase, "Exegi Monumentum Aere perennius" (the first line of Ode III, 30).[14]

The four frontispieces, giving four faces of Swift, the Dean, the Poet, Capt. Gulliver, and the Irish Patriot, perhaps echo the four "titles" in Pope's inscription to *The Dunciad*. Each is suited to the volume which it introduces. Dr. Swift in plain clerical garb is the author of plain-spoken prose. The same figure glorified by rays of the sun is the author of "poetical works," who aspires to eternal fame and the laurel wreath: the context of the legend from Horace's "Ars Poetica" (Epistle to the Pisos), "Quivis speret idem," suggests that, although the language of his poetry is deceptively ordinary, any reader who tries to reproduce it will find it more difficult than he thinks.[15] The portrait of Gulliver suggests that Swift both is and is not to be confused with his sea captain, and the much-discussed Horatian tag – "Splendide mendax" (from Ode III, 11 – like the daughter of Danaus who lied to her perjured father in order to save her husband) – suggests that he is a teller of plausible tales and a liar in a good cause, that he both is and is not to be trusted.[16] The final portrait of the seated cleric, about to receive a wreath from above, together with the soaring line from Horace – "I have built a monument more lasting than brass" – suggests that it is for his "Papers relating to Ireland" that Swift looks for his real fame, yet wittily reminding his readers that it was his Drapier's Letters that helped to defeat Wood's *brass* half-pence.

Read as a kind of response to Pope's famous inscription to "Dean, Drapier, Bickerstaff, or Gulliver," the portraits confirm Pope's sense of Swift's delight in adopting poses, and of the importance of Swift's Drapier-project. But they may also act as a corrective, reminding us as they do that Swift was also a "Poet" (an identity that Pope's inscription did not recognize), that he aligned himself not only with satire but also with the epistolary and lyric Horace,[17] and that he was not only a jester and ironist but also a defender of liberty and an aspirant for literary fame.

---

[14] Faulkner's advertisement had promised that "The Author's Effigies curiously engraven by Mr. Vertue, shall be prefixed to each Volume."

[15] "Ex noto fictum carmen sequar, ut sibi quivis / speret idem, sudet multum frustraque laboret / ausus idem" (240–42), rendered in the Loeb edition: "My aim shall be poetry, so moulded from the familiar that anybody may hope for the same success, may sweat much and yet toil in vain when attempting the same."

[16] Swift would have found the Horatian tag associated with travelers in *Tatler* No. 254, where it appears at the head of an essay about the "Invention" and "unbounded Imagination" of travelers.

[17] Among the poems in vol. II was Swift's version of Horace's Ode I, 14.

The first volume of Swift's *Works* contains no front matter except for a long list of subscribers (Pope not included) and an unsigned "Publisher's Preface" declaring cautiously (or coyly) that the volumes contain

works supposed to be written by the Rev. Dr. S ... We do not find that the supposed Author did ever put his Name to above two Compositions ... we are assured he never owned to his nearest Friends any Writings which generally passed for his ... the supposed Author was prevailed upon to suffer some Friends to review and correct the Sheets after they were printed; and sometimes he condescended, as we have heard, to give them his own Opinion.

Faulkner's language (if it is his), perhaps supervised by the author, distances Swift from the edition in several ways: not only is he only the "supposed Author" (who preferred to publish anonymously), but he took no active steps to ensure that the copy was correct (merely yielding to the entreaties of unnamed persons to permit "some Friends" to review the sheets, and reportedly giving his own opinion not to the printer but to the said "Friends").

The charade was presumably seen through by readers, who could find in the four volumes writings that had already appeared under Swift's name in his 1711 volume and in the Pope–Swift *Miscellanies*. They could also find a variety of trivial and ephemeral pieces that Swift chose to include, as well as the substantial *Libel on Dr. Delany* (198 lines), which had appeared (sometimes attributed to "Dr. Sw–t" or "D–n S–t") in a number of unauthorized editions between 1730 and 1734. The effect of reprinting pieces that had recently appeared in the Pope–Swift *Miscellanies* (where they were designed to emphasize what the two writers had in common) was to *separate* his work from that of his friend.

Virtually no comment from Pope on Swift's four-volume edition has survived. In his letter of September 15, 1734 he complies with Swift's pretense that he was himself not directly involved in it: he is "glad you suffer'd your writings to be collected more compleatly than hitherto, in the volumes I daily expect from Ireland; I wish'd it had been in more pomp, but that will be done by others: yours are beauties, that can never be too finely drest, for they will ever be young" (Woolley: III, 758). Pope pretends that Faulkner's edition (perhaps because it is Irish) will be a modest one. His language describing what a proper edition would look like ("more pomp," "never too finely drest," "ever ... young") might even hint that he expects that Swift's executors will prepare a sumptuous posthumous edition of Swift's "Remains." His conversations with Spence yield only the comment in August 1735 that "Swift's edition [was] under his own eye" (Osborn 1966: I, 55). Pope's letter to Swift of December 19–26,

1734 (written a month after the edition began appearing) says nothing of it, and his next surviving letter to Swift is dated November 1735. The eleven-month gap between letters is not unique in their correspondence, but it is clear that some letters were lost, and plausible to think that, especially since Pope was already collecting his correspondence for the heavily edited 1737 edition, some were suppressed.[18]

Even before he could have seen Swift's *Works*, Pope was making plans for his own collection, and reporting them to Swift: "I shall collect all the past in one fair quarto this winter, and send it you, where you will find frequent mention of your self" (September 15, 1734, in Woolley 1999–2007: III, 758).[19] Pope implicitly makes the point that, unlike Swift, he himself ("I shall collect …") is the originator of the collection. (In fact, it appears likely that his friend Jonathan Richardson the Younger was the editorial supervisor.)[20] And he implicitly invites Swift to think of it as in a sense directed to him as prime reader. Was he also conscious that Swift had asked to have an epistle addressed to him, and was he here offering a kind of substitute? He anticipates that Swift will laugh at him for playing the philosopher in the *Essay on Man* (a poem which figures prominently in Pope's 1735 volume): "I have only one piece of mercy to beg of you; do not laugh at my gravity, but permit me to wear the beard of a philosopher, till I pull it off, and make a jest of it myself" (III, 758–59). In fact, Swift had apparently already told Bolingbroke and Oxford – but not Pope himself – that he approved of his "moral essays."[21] Pope's edition, as advertised by Gilliver in February 1735, was to be "beautifully printed in quarto and folio." (Faulkner's advertisement had promised that Swift's writings would be "beautifully printed on a fine Paper in *Octavo*, neatly bound in *Calves* Leather.")

---

[18] Swift's May 12, 1735 letter to Pope apparently answers a lost letter from Pope. In another letter that does not survive, Pope wrote to Swift around the beginning of July 1735; Swift's answer of September 3 (Woolley 1999–2007: IV, 173) refers to the letter but says nothing about either volume of *Works*. Woolley suspects that Pope suppressed both his April 1735 and his July 1735 letters to Swift (IV, 175–76n).

[19] Swift is in fact mentioned eight times: *Dunciad* I, 17–26 (the inscription), III, 321 ("Hibernian politics, O Swift …)", and two other places in *The Dunciad* (II, 116, 138), the "Epistle to Oxford," 9 ("For Swift and him …"), the *Epistle to Dr. Arbuthnot* ("Swift endur'd my lays … I found him close with *Swift*"), the Imitation of Hor. *Sat.* II, 2 ("cries Swift … dear Swift"), and the imitation of Donne's fourth satire ("Swift, for closer style").

[20] See Griffith (1922–27: 282).

[21] In a June 27 letter to Swift, Bolingbroke says: "I am glad you approve his moral essays. they will do more good than the sermons and writings of some who had a mind to find great fault with them" (Woolley 1999–2007: III, 745). On August 30, 1734 Swift wrote to Oxford about their friend Pope: "His Time hath indeed been better employd [than in writing to me] in his Moral Poems, which excell in their kind, and may be very usefull" (III, 753).

When Pope's edition appeared in April 1735, several of its features signal some marked differences from the edition of Swift that had been published only months before. It is published in London of course, rather
than Dublin, and as promised in quarto and folio rather than the smaller
octavo. The author is announced on the title page not by initials but by
his full name – *The Works of Mr. Alexander Pope* – confirming the established difference between a writer who liked to speak through masks and
one who increasingly identified the speaker of his poems to be none other
than the historical Alexander Pope of Twickenham. The title page also
carries as an epigraph some famous lines from Cicero – "Haec studia
adolescentiam alunt, senectutem oblectant; secundas res ornant, adversis
perfigium & solatium praebent; delectant domi, non impediunt foris; per-
noctant nobiscum, peregrinantur, rusticantur" (identified as from "Cicero
pro Arch.") – and a vignette described by Griffith as "a shield bearing a
bust portrait of Pope, etc." (1922–37: II, 280). Together, the Latin lines
and the shield (held upright by two *putti*, one of whom has a lyre) and
portrait (a profile in the Roman manner) suggest that the author is one
of the ancients. The lines are taken from Cicero's "Pro Archia Poeta," his
oration in defense of the Greek-born poet Aulus Licinus Archias, accused
of being neither a Roman citizen nor a resident of Rome: "These studies
[literary works] nourish youth and amuse old age; they adorn prosperity
and offer refuge and solace to adversity. At home they delight, and out
in the world they don't hinder us. They see us through the night, travel
abroad with us, and retire with us to the country" (my translation).

Applied to Pope's own case, the lines suggest that he too has unjustly
come under suspicion from the political authorities, and that his poems
contain nothing offensive – on the contrary, that they provide both solace
and innocent pleasure.[22]

Instead of a prefatory "Publisher to the Reader," Pope's edition prints
an address from "The Author to the Reader" (signed by "A. Pope"), in
which the author plainly speaks in his own voice: "All I had to say of my
Writings is contained in the Preface to the first of these Volumes [i.e., the
1717 preface] ... And all I have to say of Myself will be found in my last
Epistle [i.e., the *Epistle to Dr. Arbuthnot*]." Later in the volume, at the
head of the section containing the imitations of Horace and Donne, there
also appears an "Advertisement" in which the author himself refers to the
"Clamour raised on some of my Epistles," i.e., the accusations that in
the "Epistle to Burlington" (1731) Pope had ridiculed his patron Chandos

---

[22] Pope had previously printed the lines from Cicero as the epigraph to his 1717 *Works*.

under the character of Timon, and that in the "Epistle to Bathurst" (1732) he had recklessly satirized a number of public figures.

Collected in this volume – announced as volume II of the author's works – were the major poems published since the appearance of volume I in 1717: the "Ethic Epistles" (i.e., *An Essay on Man*, 1731–35); a set of "Epistles," including what we know as the four "Epistles to Several Persons" or "Moral Essays" (first published 1731–35), and epistles to Addison (1720), Oxford (1722), and Arbuthnot (1735); a set of "Satires," including two imitations of Horace and two of Donne; a set of ten "Epitaphs"; and the *Dunciad Variorum* (1729). Of these, only three poems were new (the second satire of Donne, and epitaphs on Dorset and on Elijah Fenton). The principle of organization is generic, Pope displayed as the master of five different established genres: the verse essay, the verse epistle, the verse satire, the epitaph, and the mock-epic.[23]

Omitted were any works published in 1717 or earlier (unlike Swift's *Works*, which included pieces first published in his 1711 collection). Omitted also were a number of poems Pope apparently judged to be too minor to be part of an edition of his *Works*, among them "To Mrs. M. B. on her Birthday" (first published in 1724), and several epitaphs and epigrams. (Swift had chosen to include several such minor or ephemeral poems.) Left out too were several pieces that linked Pope to Swift: his "Lines on Swift's Ancestors" (written in 1726 but left unpublished), his "Receipt to Make Soup. For the use of Dean Swift" (published only in an unauthorized broadside), his published Gulliverian poems, and other pieces that he had previously printed in the volumes of the Pope–Swift *Miscellanies*. In "The Author to the Reader" he acknowledges that there were a few pieces he had "written, or joined in writing with *Dr.* Swift, *Dr.* Arbuthnot, or *Mr.* Gay," declaring that he regards them as "too inconsiderable to be separated and reprinted here."[24] (He nonetheless takes the trouble to specify precisely which pieces in the Pope–Swift *Miscellanies* were his.) The effect, despite what he says, is to *separate* his poems from those of Swift. What is more, Pope's edition is clearly constructed along different editorial principles from those of Swift,

[23] In 1736, when he produced a four-volume edition in small octavo of his *Works*, he departed slightly from generic organization: the first volume reprinted the original poems from the *Works* of 1717, the second included the "Epistles" and "Satires" from the 1735 edition, the third the "Fables, Translations, and Imitations" from the 1717 *Works*, and the fourth the *Dunciad Variorum*.

[24] Benjamin Motte, printer of the *Miscellanies*, in his July 31, 1735 letter to Swift expressed surprise and perhaps displeasure to find that Pope in his 1735 *Works* "owns so little in the four volumes [of *Miscellanies*]; and speaks of these *few* things as *inconsiderable*" (Woolley 1999–2007: IV, 153).

THE

W O R K S

O F

Mr. *ALEXANDER POPE.*

VOL. II.

To the Revd Dr Swift, from the Author.

A 2

4.2 Title page of *The Works of Mr. Alexander Pope. Vol. II* (1735). Presentation copy, inscribed by Pope "To the Revd. Dr. Swift, from the Author."

designed as a kind of monument to his major work, the achievement on which he thought his reputation would rest, Swift's designed more – as Pope sensed – as a miscellany.

Pope sent a copy of his edition as a present to Swift, inscribing it "To the Revd. Dr. Swift, from the Author" (see Illustration 4.2). Apart from his acknowledgment of its imminent receipt,[25] Swift made no other response

[25] In a May 12, 1735 letter to Pope (Woolley 1999–2007: IV, 104), who had apparently written to Swift that the book had been sent.

68   *E P I S T L E S.*

While Wits and Templers ev'ry fentence raife,
And wonder with a foolifh face of praife.   205
Who but muft laugh, if fuch a man there be?
Who would not weep, if Atticus were he!
    What tho' my Name ftood rubric on the walls?
Or plaifter'd pofts, with claps in capitals?
Or fmoaking forth, a hundred hawkers load,   210
On wings of winds came flying all abroad?
I fought no homage from the race that write;
I kept, like Afian Monarchs, from their fight;
Poems I heeded (now be-rym'd fo long)
No more than thou, great GEORGE! a Birth-day Song.
I ne'r with Wits or Witlings paft my days,   216
To fpread about the itch of Verfe and Praife;
Nor like a puppy dagled through the town,
To fetch and carry Sing-fong up and down;
Nor at Rehearfals fweat, and mouth'd, and cry'd, 220
With handkerchief and orange at my fide;
But fick of Fops, and Poetry, and Prate,
To Bufo left the whole Caftalian State.

4.3 Swift's marginal annotations on "Atticus" in his copy of *The Works of
Mr. Alexander Pope. Vol. II* (1735).

to Pope – at least none that has survived. But he did respond silently –
by making a number of annotations on the pages of the volume. Some
merely identify the historical figures behind Pope's Clodio, Bufo, Sporus,
and others – as if Swift were supplying the footnotes that he once told
Pope his poems needed. Beside the severe character of "Atticus," Swift
wrote "Addison is the Person meant, and [dese]rved it in some measure,"
adding (as I have noted earlier) that "he and Pope were at last [rec]onciled
by my Advice" (see Illustration 4.3).

Some of the marks – x's in the margin – seem to indicate that Swift took note of each time his name was mentioned in Pope's text. Most interesting are the occasions where he marks his sharp dissent from Pope's favorable judgement about the character of two public figures whose names appear in the first "Moral Essay." Beside the final line praising Cobham, Swift wrote: "The Partiality of a Friend to one who little deserves it to my knowledge." Beside Pope's line, in the same poem, that "The gracious Chandos is belov'd at sight," Swift wrote: "Not by me, who know him to be a Lyar."[26] Although Swift was ready to write to Pope about some of their differences of opinion, there were some disagreements that he did not care to discuss.

While Pope was preparing the 1735 edition of his *Works* he was also engaged in another major literary project: the publication of his letters. The story of how he made use of Curll to publish an unauthorized edition – thus enabling Pope to say that he was now *required* to publish an accurate record – is once again well known to specialists, but is worth reviewing from Swift's point of view.[27] For Pope's tireless efforts to gather the originals of his correspondence were largely focused on Swift – any letters addressed to Swift would adorn Pope's volume and help to ensure sales and readers. Displeased with Pope's efforts as editor since the 1732 volume of *Miscellanies*, Swift was not eager to cooperate, and Pope deployed various stratagems and deceptions to persuade him. In the end Swift complied, and Pope was able to publish not only the *Letters of Mr. Alexander Pope, and Several of his Friends* (1737) but also the *Works of Mr. Alexander Pope, in Prose. Vol. II* (1741), containing the Pope–Swift letters. Pope's Victorian editors, who first reported the two interrelated stories (of Pope's dealings with Curll, and his subsequent dealings with Swift), were highly censorious. In 1956 the editor of Pope's letters regarded the intrigue and the deception with equanimity, but since then the literary biographers and historians who have examined the matter have, even as they acknowledged Pope's dishonesty, treated it so sympathetically as virtually to pardon it, or diverted judgement by

---

[26] Swift's copy, a made-up volume whose pagination is not consecutive, survives in the Berg Collection in the New York Public Library. Because the pages were trimmed after the annotations were made, some letters were cut and must be inferred.

[27] The account in Baines and Rogers (2007: 246–73) largely reaffirms the accounts of Ralph Straus, *The Unspeakable Curll* (1927) and Sherburn 1956.

inviting us to delight in how Pope had outsmarted the "unspeakable" Curll.[28] Historicist scholars have argued that Pope was simply following widespread eighteenth-century practice. Perhaps it is now time for the pendulum to swing back the other way a little, and to make room in the story for a clear-eyed look at what the episode says about the strains in the relationship between Swift and Pope in their later years. Such evidence as there is must be found in the Pope–Swift letters, not only in the surviving letters but (with the help of Woolley, who regards both Pope and Swift with unsparing eyes) in the inferences to be drawn from the letters apparently suppressed.

Pope seems to have hatched his plan to publish his own letters no later than 1733, perhaps as early as 1729, when he published *The Posthumous Works of William Wycherley*, which contained a number of letters exchanged between Wycherley and the young Pope.[29] Later that year, in a letter to Swift, Pope seemed obliquely to float the idea of publishing their own letters. After reporting that he had recently had returned to him "several of my own letters" from fifteen or twenty years earlier, he compared those affectedly witty letters with the ones – written more "negligently" and "openly" – that he wrote to Swift: "I smile to think how Curl would be bit, were our Epistles to fall into his hands" (Woolley, III, 271). Swift saw through Pope's obliqueness, writing slyly in reply two months later that Pope has in effect confessed to "Schemes … of Epistolary fame" (III, 283). In his own reply on April 9, 1730, Pope insists that he has no such "schemes," but at the same time implicitly confirms that he has been thinking of collecting a "Volume" of letters:

I've kept some of your Letters and some of those of my other friends. These if I put together in a Volume, (for my own secret satisfaction, in reviewing a Life, past in Innocent amusements & Studies …) do not therefore say, I aim at Epistolary Fame: … the Fame I most covet, indeed, is that, which must be deriv'd to me from my Friendships. (III, 299)

There the project lay until, in late 1733, when Curll announced plans for a forthcoming life of Pope and asked for materials, Pope saw an opportunity to advance it.[30] He then began the clandestine dealings with Curll

---

[28] See Winn 1977 and Mack 1985. Baines and Rogers 2007 take a more even-handed view.
[29] This is the consensus view of Sherburn (1956: I, xiv), Mack (1985: 653), and Winn (1977: 184). Pope had tried to get his letters returned from correspondents as early as 1712, but seems not to have thought about preparing an edition of his own correspondence until 1729.
[30] In December 1732, after the death of John Gay, Swift's letters to Gay were transcribed for Oxford's Harleian Library, no doubt with Pope's knowledge, and returned to Swift.

which ended when octavo printed sheets of Pope's edited letters were delivered by unidentified agents to Curll's door. Curll had by then caught on to Pope's manipulations, and by exposing them tried without success to secure Pope's cooperation, but he went on in any case to publish in May 1735 the first volume of the *Letters of Mr. Pope, And Several Eminent Persons*, soon re-issued as *Mr. Pope's Literary Correspondence*. Two more volumes followed later in the year. These volumes provided Pope the cover he wanted for publishing his own authorized edition.

He immediately (probably in July) began to press Swift to return his letters. (Curll's volumes had not printed any letters to or from Swift, only because he had not laid his hands on them.) Pope's own letter has not survived, probably suppressed (along with many subsequent such requests – no such requests appear in Pope's 1741 volume) by its author, who did not wish to leave evidence that he was actively engaged in the edition. In his letter Pope apparently insisted to Swift that their letters were safer with him than in Ireland. On September 3 Swift replied by declaring that Pope "need not fear any Consequence in the Commerce that hath so long passed between us," and that he had left "strict orders" with his literary executors "to burn every Letter left behind me." In any case, Swift added, their letters had nothing in them but "innocent friendship" (Woolley 1999–2007: IV, 174).

Why Swift should have put off his dear friend's request has been much discussed. Sherburn conjectured, based on a report from Faulkner, that Swift had his own plans to publish his letters (1956: I, xvii). Swift's letter provides another reason: immediately after his comments on their letters Swift without transition declared that "I have the ambition, & it is very earnest as well as in hast to have one Epistle inscribed to me while I am alive …. I must once more repeat Cicero's desire to a friend, *Orna me*" (Woolley 1999–2007: IV, 174). It seems likely that Swift assumed Pope thought their *Miscellanies* and a volume of their letters would serve as a monument to their friendship, and was countering with his own oft-stated preference.

In his next letter to Pope on October 21, Swift again drags his feet: his letters have only "Nature and Friendship" (Woolley 1999–2007: IV, 203). Over the winter of 1735–36 Pope continued his campaign, writing at least three times – the letters have not survived and were perhaps suppressed.[31] He also began to recruit their mutual friend Orrery to serve as

---

[31] See Sherburn (1956: IV, 11), and Woolley, who cites "undoubted suppressions" (1999–2007: IV, 278n).

an intermediary. In what survives of Pope's March 25 letter to Swift, he promises that "If ever I write more Epistles in Verse, one of them shall be address'd to you" (IV, 276). This may have been the promise Swift was waiting for, for on April 22 he replied that it was his "resolution" to "direct my Executors to send you all your letters" (IV, 283), implying perhaps that Pope must first perform his promise of addressing an epistle to him. Still the letters were not delivered. The heavily edited version of Pope's letter to Swift of August 17 says nothing of the letters – except obliquely to note that he will "preserve all the memorials I can, that I was of your intimacy" – but deals rather bluntly with Swift's censure of Bolingbroke. Woolley observes that the "severe and uncompromising tone" of Pope's rebuke hints that the portion edited out "was a firmer demand for the return of the letters" (IV, 343). Another exchange of letters, now lost, apparently followed in September and October.[32]

It appears that Pope's next move was to increase the pressure on Swift by leaking to Curll two letters written to Swift by Bolingbroke and himself; they appeared in Curll's *New Letters of Mr. Pope* (November 1736).[33] Swift's December 2 letter to Pope makes no reference to Curll's pamphlet, but again expresses his hope to see more "Epistles of Morality" from Pope: "and I assure you, my Acquaintance resent that they have not seen my name at the head of one" (Woolley 1999–2007: IV, 366). In his December 30 answer Pope makes sure that Swift feels Curll's pressure: he warns Swift that the letters he is "too partially" keeping in his own hands "will get out in some very disagreeable shape," reporting disingenuously (in case Swift has not heard) that "this last month Curl has obtain'd from Ireland two letters ... which we wrote in the year 1723." Pope goes on to comment on his new friends, the "Boy Patriots," and reflects on Time's power to alter all things: "not our friends only, but so much of our selves is gone by the mere flux and course of years, that were the same Friends to be restored to us, we could not be restored to our selves, to enjoy them."[34] Is he obliquely indicating that both he and Swift have changed, and that their friendship is not the same as it was? It is almost as if, for practical

---

[32] On the basis of other letters, Woolley infers an unrecovered exchange between Swift and Pope (1999–2007: IV, 367n). Winn (1977: 189) agrees.

[33] Sherburn (1956: IV, 50) thinks Pope arranged for the letters to reach Curll. Winn concludes that "it is hard to believe that [Pope] was not behind Curll's pamphlet" (1977: 188). Curll later claimed that the letters were "given" to him by "a Person of the *first rank*," and Woolley guesses that the letters were given surreptitiously to Curll by Pope's close friend Bathurst (1999–2007: IV, 381n).

[34] Pope encloses in this letter (or in a subsequent letter which does not survive) his translation of Horace's Epistle II. 2.72–78, on loss of friends: "Years foll'wing Years, steal something ev'ry Day, / At last they steal us from our selves away."

purposes, Swift has died: "those friends who have been dead these twenty years, are more present to me now, than these I see daily. You, dear Sir, are one of the former sort to me, in all respects, but that we can, yet, correspond together."

By this time Pope must have given up any hopes that he could include his letters to Swift in the forthcoming volume, already announced. When the *Letters of Mr. Alexander Pope, and Several of his Friends* was published in May 1737 it contained only three Pope–Swift letters (among them the letters leaked to Curll).[35] But having apparently formed plans for another volume, to contain the letters exchanged with the most famous of his "Several ... Friends," Pope continued his efforts to recover the Swift letters. On March 23, 1737 Pope, picking up a theme from earlier letters, wrote to Swift that he would like to "leave some sort of Monument, what Friends two Wits could be in spite of all the fools of the world" (Woolley 1999–2007: IV, 405). He also continued to work through Orrery, and by late May his campaign had succeeded. Although there is no explicit statement from Swift that he will send the letters to Pope, or that Pope may print them (and Sherburn [1956: IV, 71] thought that Swift was still displaying "unwillingness" to return the letters), we can probably infer as much, for on May 31, 1737 Swift wrote to Pope that he had gathered some sixty letters from Pope "in a folio cover" and that "I found nothing in any one of them to be left out" (Woolley 1999–2007: IV, 432).

What caused Swift to yield? Possibly the tribute to him in Pope's *First Epistle of the Second Book of Horace Imitated* (the "Epistle to Augustus"), published on May 25, just six days before the date of Swift's letter.

> Let Ireland tell, how Wit upheld her cause,
> Her Trade supported, and supply'd her Laws;
> And leave on SWIFT this grateful verse ingrav'd,
> The Rights a Court attack'd, a Poet sav'd.
> Behold the hand that wrought a Nation's cure,
> Stretch'd to relieve the Idiot and the Poor,
> Proud Vice to brand, or injur'd Worth adorn,
> And stretch the Ray to Ages yet unborn. (221–28)

Pope's lines suggest that he had seen and remembered the as-yet-unpublished *Verses on the Death of Dr. Swift*, which revealed Swift's concern at how he will be remembered after his death, and which closed with an allusion to Swift's legacy "To build a House for Fools and Mad.: / And

---

[35] Pope sent a presentation copy to Swift (see Sherburn 1956: IV, 71).

shew'd by one satyric Touch, / No Nation wanted it so much." Pope's lines in fact serve – particularly when one considers the striking clause "leave on SWIFT this grateful verse ingrav'd" – as a kind of epitaph engraved on a tombstone.

Pope had in fact sent him a copy of the passage in his letter of December 30, 1736, and Swift had replied on February 9, 1737 that the lines, when published, "are to do me the greatest honour I shall ever receive from posterity" (Woolley 1999–2007: IV, 386). In the May 31 letter Swift notes that he has just read the "Epistle to Augustus" in published form: "it was sent me in the English Edition, as soon as it could come" (IV, 432).

The lines would have gratified Swift not only because they paid tribute to his political tracts – presumably the *Universal Use of Irish Manufacture* and the *Drapier's Letters* – but also because Pope recognized him with his own highest term of praise, "a Poet." That Pope could write such lines at a time when he was probably irritated with Swift's unreadiness to comply with his repeated requests to return his letters is perhaps a sign that the disagreement between them did not reduce Pope's high admiration of his friend. But when we recall the importance Pope assigned to the project of publishing his letters, and the energy he devoted to retrieving them, we have to ask whether the tribute to Swift in the "Epistle to Augustus" needs to be regarded in another light: was Pope's praise calculated, at least in part, to prompt Swift to return the letters?

And did Swift suspect any calculation? It is noteworthy that, after reporting he has just read Pope's printed "Epistle to Augustus," he remarks that some "curious" readers in Ireland "are looking out, some for flattery, some for ironies in it; the sour folks think they have found out some." Swift may be referring to the famous ironies undermining the ostensible praise of "Augustus" (i.e., George II), but, in language carefully chosen, he turns his attention back to the praise accorded to *him*: "But your admirers here, I mean every man of taste, affect to be certain, that the Profession of Friendship to Me in the same poem, will not suffer you to be thought a Flatterer." Well, is it or isn't it flattery? "[A]ffect to be certain" and "Profession of Friendship" leave it unclear what the men of taste, regardless of what they say, actually believe. And Swift, writing as a master of equivocation to a reader equally adept, momentarily allows for the possibility that he shares their concealed suspicions. What immediately follows – "my happiness is that … in spight of you the ages to come will celebrate me, and know you were a friend who loved and esteemed me, although I dyed the object of Court and Party-hatred" – sounds like full-hearted gratitude, except for the curious "in spight of you," which may mean "regardless of your slippery and equivocal ironies."

At any rate, something is still bothering Swift, and it had in fact emerged earlier in the letter: "It was I began with the petition to you of *Orna me*, and now you come like an unfair merchant, to charge me with being in your debt [i.e., presumably complaining that Swift would not comply with his repeated requests] ... and yet I have a pretence to quarrel with you, because I am not at the head of any one of your Epistles" (Woolley 1999–2007: IV, 432). Perhaps Sherburn was right – and Swift was by this letter not yet complying with Pope's request.

But Pope was continuing to work on Swift through Orrery, who was often at the deanery in the following month. On June 14 Orrery reported to Pope that "He has not yet put the Letters into my Hands," but on June 23 Swift wrote to Pope that when Orrery returned to England in about ten days, "he will take with him all the letters I preserved of yours" (Woolley 1999–2007: IV, 445). And, as if to suggest that the long dispute is over, he closes the letter warmly: "Farewel my dearest and almost only constant friend." On July 23 Orrery wrote to Swift that Pope has "his letters" (IV, 464).

All the more surprising that this is the last extant letter between Pope and Swift for fourteen months. But we should not assume that once Pope achieved his objective he stopped writing letters to Swift. Or jump to the conclusion that Swift sulked in resentful silence. They seem to have exchanged letters, but it is perhaps significant that they have not survived.[36] Pope apparently wrote a letter, since lost or suppressed, between late July and November 1737, and another on July 25, 1738 (also lost), in which, so Woolley thinks, he must have re-opened the matter of the manuscript letters. Swift's reply on August 24 indicates that he is confused about whether or not he has already sent letters to Pope, or is holding them until after his death. (Swift himself complained in the letter about his failing memory.) The subsequent epistolary record is disappointingly thin.[37] Pope wrote on October 12, primarily to pass on a recommendation for one of Lyttelton's dependants, and then to talk – in language that might be thought warm, or formulaic – about their friendship, bearing evil, and being remembered: "Nothing of you can die, nothing of you can suffer, nothing of you can be obscured, or locked up from esteem

---

[36] Was the alleged "defamatory life" of Swift perhaps composed during this period?
[37] The last letter printed in 1741 is the one dated August 8–24, 1738, Pope choosing to omit the final half-dozen.

and admiration, except what is at the Deanery" – i.e., his mortal body (Woolley 1999–2007: IV, 546). Swift wrote back six months later, with a recommendation for his cousin Deane Swift (IV, 575), and again two weeks later (on May 10, 1739) with another recommendation. As Woolley notes, it is the last surviving letter from Swift to Pope. A week later Pope replied with a long and chatty letter full of personal and poetical news, including some ten lines to be inserted in "the next New Edition of the Dunciad."[38]

The closing chapter in the story of the publication of the Pope–Swift letters in 1741 is (as Mack suggests) a "painful" one, even in the accounts most sympathetic to Pope. Because the details have been as well established as they are likely to be, it is sufficient here to summarize a tale told by others of (on Pope's side) vanity, manipulation, equivocation, dissimulation, and outright lies, and (on Swift's side) acquiescence and perhaps some confusion. In May of 1740, Pope, wishing to make it appear that the Pope–Swift letters were first printed by others in Ireland, had them privately printed in London and sent to Swift with an anonymous letter, signed only by Swift's "Obliged *Country-Men*," asking him to look over the volume (identified by scholars as the "clandestine volume") and, if he approved, to "bestow it on the Publick" (Woolley 1999–2007: IV, 617). Swift apparently reviewed the letters, added some notes,[39] and (implicitly consenting to publication) passed the volume on to his printer, Faulkner.[40] When Faulkner notified Pope of his plans to print, Pope sent a stern demand that he cease and desist. Pope recovered the "clandestine volume" along with Faulkner's printed sheets. The latter (containing materials Swift added) he used to complete his own edition, published on April 16, 1741 as the *Works of Mr. Alexander Pope, in Prose. Vol. II*.[41] The volume contained eighty-nine letters, of which sixty-two constituted the Pope–Swift correspondence (about two-thirds of the number Sherburn

[38] They would actually not appear until 1743, as II, 305–14 in the *Dunciad in Four Books*. No letters survive for the next year, though Pope apparently wrote to Swift at least twice. Woolley infers a letter about February 15, 1740, and another after April 18, 1740.
[39] But not the long letter of 1720–21 which laid out his political principles. Scholars once thought Swift had inserted this letter, but now, following Elias ("The Pope–Swift Letters (1740–41): Notes on the First State of the First Impression," *Publications of the Bibliographical Society of America* 69 (1975), 323–43), agree that it was inserted by Pope in London before the volume was sent to Dublin. Pope insisted (in a December 27, 1740 letter to Orrery) that Swift never actually sent the letter but that he had seen the text in its form as a "Pamphlet" (Sherburn 1956: IV, 310). Woolley (1999–2007: IV, 362) conjectures that Swift did not send it to Pope until June 1737.
[40] Sherburn (1956: I, xviii) concludes that Swift knew what was going on, and was cooperating, Winn (1977: 194) that Swift "probably … wanted the letters published."
[41] The volume also included the *Memoirs of Martinus Scriblerus*, the *Art of Sinking*, and several miscellaneous prose pieces

and Woolley have printed), along with twenty-seven others, mostly letters between Swift and Gay, or Swift and Bolingbroke. A note from "The Booksellers to the Reader" stated – which was technically true, as far as it went – that Swift's letters had been "copied from an Impression sent from *Dublin*, and said to be printed by the Dean's Direction" (i, xli). This gave Pope what he wanted: the appearance that the Irish edition was published first, and grounds on which he might state to readers that the whole idea was Swift's, not his.[42]

Less than a month before his edition appeared, Pope wrote to Swift on March 22 what would be his final letter to him. Warm expressions of undying friendship – "nothing shall make me forget you, and I am persuaded you will as little forget me" – are followed by a complaint, astonishingly disingenuous, but carefully delivered, about the volume that he had so skillfully, and deviously, guided into print: that in fact the edition "was not of my erecting, but yours."

I must confess a late Incident has given me some pain; but I am satisfyed you were persuaded it would not have given me any... As far as it was Your Will, I cannot be angry, at what in all other respects I am quite uneasy under. Had you ask'd me, before you gave them away, I think I could have proposed some *better Monument* of our Friend[sh]ip or at least of *better Materials*: And you must allow me to say, This was not of my erecting, but yours. (Woolley, IV, 656)

To pretend to the world is one thing; but to pretend to his dearest friend – and to do so in words that simply cannot be regarded as witty or playful equivocation that both correspondents can enjoy – is another. As Mack concludes: "Certainly, Pope's conduct in this episode was discreditable by any standard ... [He] lied and lied again to maintain his cover ... When all extenuating considerations have been balanced in, Pope's willingness throughout the affair to lay his own scheming on the backs of others is painful to behold" (1985: 671).

Interestingly enough, Swift scholars have in recent years been more reluctant to judge Pope harshly. Ehrenpreis (1962–83: III, 883–98) took a detached view of the matter, focusing on Pope's motives, strategy, and skill, on Swift's failing memory and his connivance, and on the role played by several willing tools. Woolley finds that in Pope's final letter, despite the "genteel equivocation" involved in assigning responsibility for publishing the volume to Swift, the warm sentiments of friendship

---

[42] Faulkner's edition in fact appeared in June 1741.

"so beautifully and touchingly expressed ... ring true" (Woolley 1999–2007: IV, 657n). "Ring true" seems just and Swift would probably have found them gratifying. Whether Pope in fact felt them is impossible to say, even if we suspect that by this time Pope was more interested in being able to show to the world that he and Swift had been friends and allies than he was in pursuing the friendship itself. But, after all he and Pope had been through together, how (we might ask) can Swift have found Pope's words about their letters to be anything but a deep disappointment? (Perhaps it is our disappointment rather than Swift's.) Pope could not of course be expected to tell the whole truth – for his letter might fall into the wrong hands, or even be used by Swift against him. But one so skilled in equivocation might have come up with language that Swift would have known how to interpret.

Pope's holograph letter survives. It was endorsed by Swift's cousin, Deane Swift, "Curious/Pope." The letter was not added to the Faulkner edition in June 1741 – it did not reach print until Scott's 1824 edition.[43] Unless "Curious" reflects Swift's own view of the letter, he left no response to it. There are several ways in which to interpret his silence. First, that letters exchanged after April 1741 were lost or suppressed. Second, that because Swift's health was declining rapidly – he was to be declared mentally incompetent a little over a year later – he wrote no further letters to Pope. (Only one letter from Swift to any correspondent after that date survives – a very brief note of recommendation on June 6, 1741.) Third, that he understood the terms on which the letters had been published and, having cooperated, implicitly agreed with them. And that he knew Pope well enough by now for the language of the March 22 letter not to surprise him.

POPE'S SWIFTIAN SATIRES

While trying to get Swift to return his letters, so as to be able to present them to the world as evidence of a long friendship, in 1737–39 Pope was simultaneously engaged in another set of projects that would also present the two of them as collaborators – two imitations of Horace begun by Swift and completed, by Pope, in Swift's manner. Swift had, decades earlier, imitated parts of two poems by Horace – the sixth satire of the second book, and the seventh epistle of the first book. Pope revisits the Horatian originals, completing the parts that Swift did not imitate. As with the

---

[43] For these bibliographical details, see Woolley (1999–2007: IV, 656–57n).

edition of the letters, there is a subtext. Just as the attempt to collect letters of friendship served to expose some strains in their relationship, the
imitations of Horace are presented so as to make clear that their ways of
imitating Horace are in fact distinct.

These poems were not the first instances in which Pope picked up
Swiftian material and revised it. About the time of his visits to Pope at
Twickenham in 1726 and 1727 Swift apparently conceived a satiric trifle
designed as an epistle from Pope's dog Bounce (an honest country dog) to
a fawning lapdog who lives at court. The poem parodies the conventional
contrast between country integrity and courtly compliance, and (in the
light of their ongoing conversation about whether one should attempt
to keep in with the court) might even be Swift's coded advice to Pope
that he ought to imitate his own dog and be prepared as an independent
poet to utter a "manly Roar." Swift drafted the poem as early as 1726–27,
or possibly as late as 1731–32. A copy passed into Pope's hands, and he
revised it probably by 1735, and published it in 1736 as "Bounce to Fop. An
Heroick Epistle from a Dog at *Twickenham* to a Dog at Court." The poem
was published separately in both London and Dublin and attributed on
its title page (in the London edition) to "Dr. S – t." On his copy of the
London edition, just after these words, Oxford wrote "much altered by
Mr Pope."[44] It is not known which parts of the poem are Pope's, but they
preserve Swift's typical manner (octosyllabic couplets, comic rhymes).
The final lines, in compliment to "Master *Pope*," were presumably written by Swift, but by printing them – and in particular the final line in
which Pope is said to have resolved to "roar in Numbers worthy *Bounce*"
(94) – Pope may possibly be signaling that he is preparing to take up the
challenge Swift had thrown down most recently in his lines in praise of
Pope's refusal to "lick a *Rascal Statesman's* Spittle" or "*cringe* for Bread" in
the *Libel on Dr. Delany*.

Pope's own further reply to the poem is perhaps his famous epigram,
"Engraved on the Collar of a Dog which I gave to his Royal Highness"[45]
(a dog mentioned in "Bounce to Fop"), written about 1737: "I am his
Highness' Dog at *Kew; /* Pray tell me Sir, whose Dog are you?" The poem
distills to a single tetrameter couplet – proof of Swift's rueful complaint
that Pope "can in one Couplet fix / More Sense than I can do in six" – the

[44] I draw these details from Rogers's definitive account ("The Authorship of 'Bounce to Fop': A
Re-examination," *Bulletin of Research in the Humanities* 85, 3 [1982], 241–68.) of the poem's composition and publication.
[45] The Prince of Wales.

epistle's leisurely and conventional satire on courtiers as leashed pets. It may also hint that even in keeping in with the Prince of Wales, Pope is determined to preserve a clear-sighted awareness of the dangers of dependence that both he and Swift liked to think they had avoided in complimenting each other on their independence.[46]

It was about a year later that Pope turned again to a Swiftian poem and refashioned it. By then he had nearly completed his own series of Horatian imitations, the first of them published in 1732 when he accepted Bolingbroke's suggestion that Horace's own literary situation aptly "hit his case." Swift's imitation of the sixth satire of Horace's second book ("I often wish'd that I had clear") was written about 1714 but not published until it appeared in the Pope–Swift *Miscellanies* in 1727 and then in Faulkner's 1735 edition. It adapts Horace's account of his attendance on Maecenas, finding a modern analogy in his own attendance on Robert Harley. At one point in Swift's imitation Harley asks if he has "nothing new to-day / From *Pope*, from *Parnel*, or from *Gay*?" (73–74). It is as if Pope resolved to supply what had been requested.

In late 1737 he arranged to have their mutual friend Bathurst send Swift what purported to be a transcript of the poem, with twenty lines quietly interpolated after the first eight lines of Swift's printed version, which report that Swift's fondest hope, to have "clear / For Life, six hundred Pounds a Year" with a "handsome House," garden, and terrace walk, has now been realized.[47] Bathurst disingenuously remarks that the transcript he sends Swift "has some very good lines in it wch are not in the Printed Copy" (implying that Swift himself wrote them and had perhaps forgotten them, when in fact they are Pope's imitation of Swift's manner). He notes that Swift had "left off without going thro' the Epistle, the fable of the Country & City Mouse is as prettily told as any thing of that kind ever was," and invites Swift to look through his papers to see if he had in fact finished the whole poem, and if not to complete his imitation now.[48] Swift apparently declined to complete the poem, which cleared the way

---

[46] Pope continued to be susceptible to the attentions of royalty. See his May 17, 1739 letter to Swift, reporting a visit to his house from the Prince. Frederick, he wrote, had been showing "a distinction beyond any Merit or Pretence on my part" and had made some gifts (Woolley 1999–2007: IV, 580).

[47] Some (e.g., Williams) have thought these twenty lines were written by Swift himself, but Ehrenpreis (1962–83: II, 742, n3), Rogers (1983: 673), and Woolley (1999–2007: IV, 47–71n) think them Pope's. Some scholars once attributed the final eight lines of Swift's imitation (printed in 1727) to Pope, though the consensus now is that Swift himself added them for the 1727 *Miscellany*. He printed them in the Faulkner edition.

[48] Bathurst to Swift, October 5, 1737, in Woolley (1999–2007: IV, 470).

for Pope to complete it himself, or, rather, to publish what he himself had probably already composed.

Pope's interpolation, especially its opening lines – "All this is mine but till I die; / I can't but think 'twould sound more clever, / To me and to my Heirs for ever" – serve to continue teasing Swift about his alleged concern for "property" (cf. "What's Property? dear Swift!" from Pope's imitation of the second satire of Horace's second book), and contrast Pope the life-tenant with Swift the would-be owner and legator. Pope also picked up the imitation where Swift left off, producing in eighty-eight lines a version of Horace's story of the town and country mouse. He later told Spence that he "thought I had hit [Swift's] style exactly," by which he meant that his imitation was "familiar, lively, and with odd rhymes."[49] Pope's poem can be regarded both as a reply to Swift and as a work of emulation, but also as a kind of challenge: I can write in your manner as well as you can. He even concludes the poem with a cry, not found in Horace, from the country mouse that seems calculated to appeal to Swift: "Give me again my hollow Tree! / A Crust of Bread, and Liberty." It is as if Pope reminds the champion of Irish political liberties that for him the most important sense of the term is the personal freedom of private life. In 1742 he told Spence that he sent a copy to Swift (perhaps only lines 9–28, and probably misremembering that he had Bathurst send it for him), who replied (so Pope reported) that he "did not think it at all a right imitation of his style" (Osborn 1966: 1, 59).

Pope's imitation was published in March 1738, its title page reading *An Imitation of the Sixth Satire of The Second Book of Horace. Hoc Erat in Votis, &c.* "The first Part done in the Year 1714, By Dr. Swift. The latter Part now first added, And never before Printed." Pope's name was not on the title page. Thus, authorship of the "latter part" remains unspecified. Nor does the title page claim that the "latter Part" is meant to be in the style of Swift. A publisher's "Advertisement," perhaps supplied by Pope after he discovered that Swift thought it a poor imitation of his style, distinguished Pope's style from Swift's:

The World may be assured, this Publication is no way meant to interfere with the *Imitations* of *Horace* by Mr. *Pope*: His Manner, and that of Dr. *Swift* are so entirely different, that they can admit of no Invidious Comparison. The Design of the one [i.e., Swift, or is it Pope?] being to sharpen the Satire, and open the

[49] Schakel (1993: 110–12) suggests that several of Pope's later poems exhibit elements of Swift's manner, including abrupt openings, parenthetical insertions, piling up of details, and Hudibrastic rhymes.

Sense of the Poet; of the other [i.e., Pope?] to rend his native *Ease* and *Familiarity* yet more easy and familiar.

A year later (May 1739) Pope claimed part-authorship of the poem by including it in his own *Works, vol. II, Part II*, where in the table of contents it is said to be "By Dr. *Swift*, and Mr. *Pope*," as if the poem were a collaboration, all of it jointly written: the publisher's "Advertisement" is dropped, and Pope makes no indication of which parts of the poem are his.[50] Pope's manner of proceeding is characteristically oblique and mystifying, even in his approach to his old friend, as well as the reading public.

The Sixth Satire of the Second Book of Horace appeared in Pope's 1739 *Works* immediately before another joint production, *The Seventh Epistle of the First Book of* Horace. *Imitated in the Manner of Dr.* Swift." Said to be "By Mr. *Pope* and Dr. *Swift*," it is another poem which confirms the link between the two poets, but also distinguishes between them. Swift had written and published in 1713 *Part of the Seventh Epistle of the First Book of Horace Imitated*. It imitated lines 46–98 of Horace's original, the passage beginning "Strenuus et fortis causisque Phillipus agendis / clarus..." ("Phillipus, the famous pleader, a man of vigour and courage ...'), adapting Horace's address to Maecenas to fit his own relationship with "*HARLEY*, the Nation's great Support." The Twickenham editor thinks Pope's part of the poem – he imitates only what Swift left undone, the first forty-five lines of Horace – may have been written in the autumn of 1737 (at precisely the same time Pope had written part of the *Sixth Satire of the Second Book*). Once again Pope picks up a poem left unfinished by Swift, and completes it "in the Manner of Dr. *Swift*." Here too that "Manner" means tetrameter couplets, feminine rhymes, and colloquial diction and tone. Although in his imitation of Horace's *first* epistle to Maecenas (the 1738 poem beginning "St. John, whose love indulg'd my labours past"), Pope had found a way to apply the poem to his own relationship to Bolingbroke, his imitation of *this* epistle to Maecenas, as Butt suggests (1939: IV, 268), does not seem to have a real-life addressee: it is as if Pope is addressing Swift. Some lines do indeed seem to apply to the quiet life Pope was (publicly) leading at Twickenham, ready, he says, if necessary, to give up luxuries.

---

[50] *The Second Satire of the First Book of Horace* ("Sober Advice from Horace") was first published in 1734 as "In the Manner of Mr. Pope" with a mock-dedication to Pope signed by "Bentley." The poem was included in Pope's 1739 *Works, vol. II* with the same subtitle but no dedication.

> South-sea Subscriptions take who please,
> Leave me but Liberty and Ease...
> Give me, I cry'd, (enough for me)
> My Bread, and Independency! (65–66, 69–70)

Again Pope pointedly chooses a word, "Liberty" (based on Horace's *otia liberrima*), that for Swift typically carried a political meaning, to define a private life characterized by "Ease" (classical *otium*), free from care and obligation.

Pope concludes his imitation of the Horatian original by referring the reader to Swift's imitation, which began where Pope left off:

> To set this matter full before you,
> Our old friend Swift will tell his Story.
> "Harley, the Nation's great Support," –
> But you may read it, I stop short.

Pope thus implicitly invites comparison with Swift's style but – despite the implication in the table of contents – chooses not to reprint Swift's lines. Why he chose to say the poem was "By Mr. *Pope*, and Dr. *Swift*" remains a mystery.[51]

Also printed in the 1739 *Works* were two other poems that suggest Pope was experimenting with Swift's manner and implicitly aligning himself with his old friend and fellow satirist: the two dialogues of *One Thousand Seven Hundred and Thirty-Eight*, first published separately in 1738. Critics have long remarked that they are perhaps Pope's most "Swiftian" satires – more outspoken than his earlier manner, more "Juvenalian," readier to name names and hit hard, more like Swift's *Upon Poetry. A Rapsody* and the *Libel on Dr. Delany* from early in the decade of the 1730s. In retrospect, we can perhaps see in Pope's lines in praise of Swift as political poet and savior of his country's rights in the "Epistle to Augustus" (May 1737) a sign that he is himself ready to speak out.[52]

By 1738 Pope had for several years been moving closer to the political Opposition to Walpole, cultivating friendships with Lyttelton (Secretary to Frederick, Prince of Wales) since the end of 1736, and through him with the "Boy Patriots," who were looking to the disaffected Prince as a potential leader. And he knew Swift would be pleased with his nascent political awakening: in March 1736 he wrote to Swift of "a race sprung up

---

[51] In the 1740 *Works* Pope omitted the attribution from the table of contents.
[52] John Barber wrote to Swift from London on June 23, 1737 that Pope's lines had given such "great offence" to the government that the Privy Council debated whether Pope "should not be taken up for it" (Woolley 1999–2007: IV, 448).

of young Patriots, who would animate you" (Woolley 1999–2007: IV, 277), and in December of his forming an acquaintance with some "young men, who look rather to the past age than the present, and therefore the future may have some hope of them ... Two or three of them have distinguish'd themselves in Parliament, and you will own in a very uncommon manner, when I tell you it is by their asserting of Independency and contempt of Corruption" (IV, 380). (It was enclosed in this letter that Pope sent the lines on Swift that were soon to appear in the "Epistle to Augustus.") Two years later he named Lyttelton to Swift as "one of the worthiest of the rising generation," and commended to Swift one of Lyttelton's dependants (IV, 545); Swift and Lyttelton subsequently exchanged several letters of mutual compliments.

Pope's *One Thousand Seven Hundred and Thirty-Eight* (later re-titled the *Epilogue to the Satires*), it is sometimes said, stages a dialogue about the merits of "delicate" and "insinuating" "Horatian" vs. lashing "Juvenalian" satire, or between general satire and particular satire, but it also replays in much sharper terms and with different dialogists, a "Poet" and his "Friend," the old disagreement between Swift and Pope about keeping in with the court or denouncing it from outside. It is in these two "Dialogues" that Pope, to whatever degree he hedged his bets in his dealings with individual courtiers,[53] most emphatically chooses a "Juvenalian" satire, and implicitly adopts a Swiftian perspective on a corrupted government. In retrospect one can see that Pope has been moving toward this perspective at least since 1736. Swift approved: in an August 24, 1738 letter to Pope and Bolingbroke, he commended the just-published poem: "I take your second Dialogue that you lately sent me, to equal almost any thing you ever writ" (Woolley 1999–2007: IV, 535). What in particular he admired he does not say, but based on follow-up reference to "facts and persons" specified in the poem it seems safe to assume that Swift was pleased to have Pope name names.

It seems likely that Pope knew Swift would be pleased. (Such a reaction would of course have increased the likelihood that Swift would return his letters, and indeed it was in one and the same letter that Swift complimented Pope's "second Dialogue" and reported that his letters were "sealed up in bundles" and sent to his cousin, Mrs. Whiteway, with instructions to deliver them to Pope upon his decease.) Pope had in the

---

[53] See his May 17, 1739 letter to Swift: "I am very well with all the Courtiers, I ever was or wd be acquainted with; at least they are Civil to me, wch is all I ask from Courtiers, & all a wise man will expect from them" (Woolley 1999–2007: IV, 580).

"Dialogues" come closer to Swift's outspoken political poems of the early 1730s. Swift himself, after the *Libel on Dr. Delany*, published no significant political poems, except for *The Legion Club* (1736), written in denunciation of the Irish House of Commons which in March 1736 voted 110–50 in support of a resolution to refuse tithes to the clergy. The poem was published in London in 1736, in a pamphlet entitled *S – t contra omnes. An Irish Miscellany*, and it seems likely that Pope saw it.[54] It is plausible to consider Pope's "Dialogues" as an emulative reply, not an imitation but a separate and distinct way of lodging a public "protest"[55] by one isolated man against a world gone bad – one just man *contra omnes*. Swift's poem is bitter invective, delivered in tetrameter couplets that approach the Hudibrastic in their feminine rhymes, sarcastic tone, and general sense of human brutality. It is organized as a guided tour of the new Irish Houses of Parliament, led first by Clio (muse of history) and then, when she flees, the "Keeper" – a title suggesting that the building housing the "Legion Club" is in effect a "Mad-House" (99). Within are the inmates:

> There sit *C – s, D –*, and *H –*,
> How they swagger from their Garrison.
> Such a Triplet could you tell
> Where to find on this Side Hell?
> *H –*, and *D –*, and *C –*,
> Souse them in their own Ex-crements …
> Bless us, *Morgan*! Are thou there Man?
> Bless mine Eyes! Art thou the Chairman? (181–86, 189–90)

Pope's "dialogues" are quite different, both in their formal structure and in their presentation of the figures of the muse and the poet. Swift's muse, Clio, initially "obedient" (75), "unbars the Gate" to the madhouse but then creeps away in fright (131–32). Pope's Muse hands him his "sacred Weapon" (212), "forbids the Good to dye, / And ope's the Temple of Eternity" (234–35). Swift's poet is consumed with anger and loathing, roundly concluding the poem with a curse: "May their God, the Devil confound 'em." (In two manuscript versions there follows a couplet exempting a virtuous minority of legislators: "except the righteous 52 / To whom immortal Honour's due.") In the first "Dialogue" Pope's poet regards the world not

[54] Several manuscript copies also circulated. The title perhaps retained a biblical resonance for Swift's contemporaries. In the Vulgate an angry God is said to execute judgement "contra omnes" (Numbers 16.22, Jude 1.15 – cf. Genesis 16.12, where the outcast Ishmael's hand is raised "contra omnes").

[55] In his May 17, 1739 letter to Swift Pope calls *One Thousand Seven Hundred and Thirty-Eight* "my *Protest*" (Woolley 1999–2007: IV, 580).

with wrath but with cool detachment – "Yet there was one who held it in disdain." In the second, a proud warrior in "Truth's defence" retains a high-minded faith in virtue and in virtuous men – and he names a few Opposition Whigs, including Pulteney, Chesterfield, and Marchmont. In return, Truth "guards the Poet … / And makes Immortal, Verse as mean as mine" (246–47). Swift's poem (without the manuscript addition) thus ends with the poet denouncing everybody – "contra omnes" – and Pope's with the virtuous poet in splendid isolation, and the promise of immortal fame for a few virtuous men. One wonders if Pope had perhaps seen the manuscript ending of Swift's poem.

Pope's "Dialogues" constitute a bold step toward a more "Swiftian" kind of political satire and toward a public embrace of the political Opposition to Walpole. But herein lie two ironies. At the very moment he is aligning himself with Swift Pope is also battling with him over the recovery of the letters; and just as he implicitly announces that he has joined the political Opposition to Walpole, that Opposition had begun to display its weakness and ineffectiveness. Even as he was praising Lyttelton and the Prince of Wales in *One Thousand Seven Hundred and Thirty Eight*,[56] Pope was already hinting that some of the "Patriots" had pulled in their horns ("*Patriots* there are, who wish you'd jest no more," says the "Friend" to the "Poet" at I. 24), and were now simply like everybody else: "In Soldier, Churchman, Patriot, Man in Pow'r, / 'Tis Av'rice all, Ambition is no more!" (I, 161–62).[57]

Pope's suspicions about the "Patriots" emerge more distinctly in the fragmentary "One Thousand Seven Hundred and Forty," a poem drafted in 1740 but left unfinished at his death. Here the "Patriot Race" (4) are no more likely to save Britain than the "wicked men in place" (3–4). Although Pope spares them with a dash, he makes plain that even the leading Opposition Whigs "C[arteret]" and "P[ulteney]" are frauds. (These are two names that would have especially drawn Swift's attention – he had known the former since his years – 1724–30 – as Lord Lieutenant of Ireland and was still corresponding with him as late as 1737, and he complimented Pulteney in a footnote to *Verses on the Death* in 1739,[58] and

[56] Dialogue I, 45–48; see also the implicit allusion to the Prince at Dialogue II, 92–93.
[57] In notes added to the poem in 1751 Warburton perhaps reflects the disillusionment that Pope was already feeling in 1738. "Patriots," he says, was an "appellation … generally given to those in opposition to the Court. Though some of them (which our author hints at) had views too mean and interested to deserve that name."
[58] "Mr. William Pulteney, from being Mr. W – 's intimate Friend, detesting his Administration, opposed his Measures, and joyned with my Lord Bolingbroke, to represent his Conduct in an excellent Paper, called the Craftsman, which is still continued." See further, below, p. 231.

exchanged letters with him in 1740.) The most damning words are reserved for Pulteney, who (so went the sneers), like everyone else, surely had his price – in this case a peerage: "Thro' Clouds of Passion P – 's views are clear, / He foams a Patriot to subside a Peer" (9–10). By ridiculing Pulteney, Pope in effect parts company with Swift. Pope's brilliant and prophetic lines reduce Pulteney's political oratory to the airy foam on a tankard of beer in the hand of a tavern statesman – the unspoken rhyme on "beer"/"peer" completes the haughty put-down.[59]

In its anger and its disillusion Pope's "One Thousand Seven Hundred and Forty" is yet more akin to Swift's "Legion Club" than his 1738 "Dialogues" were. His fragment – and Swift's poem was also once thought unfinished – is pockmarked with names of corrupted politicians, most of them (as in Swift's "Legion Club") indicated only with first initial and a dash. Like the "Legion Club," it is organized as little more than a catalog of names, a string of satiric epigrams:

> Grave, righteous S – joggs on till, past belief,
> He finds himself companion with a thief.
> To purge and let thee blood, with fire and sword,
> Is all the help stern S – wou'd afford.
> That those who bind and rob thee, would not kill,
> Good C – hopes, and candidly sits still.
> Of Ch – s W – who speaks at all,
> No more than of Sir Har – y or Sir P – .

Pope's poem remained unpublished in his lifetime, nor is there any record that Swift ever saw a draft of it. One can only speculate about his grim satisfaction in its bleakness if he had.

POPE AND *VERSES ON THE DEATH OF DR. SWIFT* (II)

Pope's several imitations of "the manner of Dr. Swift" in the late 1730s, like his edition of their letters finally published in 1741, suggest the increasing complexity of their relationship: affinity and difference, admiration and wary distance. A third joint project from those years – the publication by Pope and William King of the first printed edition of Swift's *Verses on the Death of Dr. Swift* in London in January 1739, and the quick publication of a very different version of the poem by Swift in Dublin in February 1739 – displays the same complexity. Pope, so I have argued, had already

---

[59] For the suspicions about Patriots in Pope's late poems, I borrow several sentences from Griffin (2002: 58–59).

taken an opportunity to "reply" to Swift's *Verses on the Death* in his own *Epistle to Dr. Arbuthnot* (which Swift probably knew in manuscript). His part in the 1739 publication of Swift's poem can be seen as a further reply, but also needs to be set in the context of Pope's other ongoing efforts to present himself to the public as Swift's friend and ally.

Swift had told Pope in 1733 that the poem would not be published until after his death.[60] But he later apparently changed his mind. Probably because he did not want to associate himself openly with its publication, and because he still thought of London as the literary center and the place where his writings should appear, he began making arrangements by 1735 to have it published, by others, in England. His initial approach was apparently to William King, Principal of St. Mary's Hall in Oxford, a Jacobite, a neo-Latin poet of some distinction, and an admirer of the author of *Gulliver* and the *Drapier's Letters*. Swift did not meet King until 1734–35, when the latter had business in Dublin.[61] What brought them together was probably King's satiric poem, *The Toast* (1732), in which Swift was praised as a "great Bard" who "repell'd the Brass Thunder, by darting his own," and his enemies ridiculed. Swift, who had read the poem upon its publication,[62] no doubt enjoyed the praise, but may have been particularly interested in the Dunciadic "Notes and Observations" (in both English and Latin) to King's poem, one of which salutes Swift as a "Patriot" and a "Genius" for his *Drapier's Letters*.[63] It was the kind of documentary note appended to a satiric poem that Swift himself had composed for *Verses on the Death*,[64] and perhaps encouraged Swift to think that King could be entrusted with an important part of his literary legacy.

When King determined to expand *The Toast* to four books, he reported to Swift on his progress, and apparently sent him the manuscript before it

---

[60] Woolley (1999–2007: III, 638).

[61] See Ehrenpreis (1962–83: III, 803–04).

[62] See his October 15, 1732 letter to Charles Ford (Woolley 1999–2007: III, 547).

[63] "The Poet here insinuates the Attempt, which was made about the year 1723 by *Wood* and his Patrons to carry off all the Gold and Silver, the current Coin of this Country, in exchange for Brass Half-pence, and which was defeated by some Excellent Pieces written on that occasion by Dr. S – t, the present Dean of St. P – 's, than whom no Country can boast a greater Patriot, and no Age has produced a greater Genius" (p. 84). The language of the note was sharpened in the 1736 revision of the poem (e.g., "*Wood* and his Accomplices," "an unlimited Coinage of base Half-pence," "this iniquitous Project").

[64] Probyn (1986: 62) has suggested that King's notes, inspired as they were by the *Dunciad*, "may have provided Swift with a textual model." This assumes that at least some of Swift's notes were written after October 15, 1732 – but at least one of them was written, so Swift claimed, on "the third Day of May, 1732."

went to the printer.[65] When it appeared in 1736 it was inscribed to Swift, and came equipped with a prefatory "Epistola ad Cadeni," itself adorned with notes, of which the first (glossing "Cadenus") provided the kind of glowing tribute that Swift must have wanted from Pope. It came clothed in the dignity of Latin:

J. SWIFT, D. D. D. S. P. D. sui saeculi deliciae, nec tam patriae, quam humani generis decus. Si virtutes illius contemplemur, nemini secundus; si divinum mentis ingenium, omnibus major. Cujus humanitatem, eloquentiam & eruditionem merito colebat SCHEFFERUS[66] noster ... Hanc coloniam semel iterumque in libertatem vindicavit, in aeternam vindicaturus, bona si sua norint coloni. (pp. xii–xiii)[67]

("... The delight of his age, the ornament not only of his country but of the human race. If his virtues are contemplated, second to no one; if the divine genius of his mind, greater than all. His humanity, eloquence, and learning our Scheffer deservedly honors ... And for the first time he has set free this colony, destined to set it free forever, if the colonists know their own good.")

The Latin was part of King's mock-epic apparatus, but it also cloaks in semi-obscurity a potentially revolutionary idea, and might have struck Swift as the traditional means of ensuring that it would survive to posterity. One remembers that Swift wrote his own epitaph in Latin, and that its closing words – "Libertatis Vindicatorem" – echo King's final compliment.

Perhaps in return for this fulsome praise Swift had apparently promised to give a manuscript of *Verses on the Death* to King in the summer of 1735 (Woolley 1999–2007: IV, 187),[68] but apparently had second thoughts, because King did not actually acquire "the little MS" until almost two years later.[69] Yet another went by before King wrote to Orrery, on July 8, 1738, that "Roch [i.e., the poem on the maxim of La Rochefoucauld] is in the press and shall certainly be published in September or the beginning of the next Term. I believe I mentioned to you the accidents which had

---

[65] King later said that Swift read "the greatest part of it in the manuscript" and was "chiefly pleased with the notes" (*Political and Literary Anecdotes of his Own Times*, 2nd edn. [1819], 97–98, qtd. in Probyn (1986: 62).

[66] King pretended that the poem had originally been written in Latin by "Frederick Scheffer."

[67] King echoes a letter from Cicero to Curio, *Epistolae ad Familiares*, II, 5 ("in veteram dignitatem et libertatem vindicaturus") and Virgil's *Georgics*, II, 458 ("sua si bona norint").

[68] See King's letter of September 20, 1735 (Woolley 1999–2007: IV, 187–88), apparently alluding both to Swift's poem (a "paper") and to his own ("my defence").

[69] King told Mrs. Whiteway (November 9, 1736) that he intended to take the poem to London and have it published. It was possibly carried over from Ireland by Orrery (who later delivered the manuscript of the "History of the Four Last Years" – see Orrery to Swift, July 23, 1737).

retarded the publication of this work so long, when I had the honour of seeing you last" (qtd., IV, 554). Woolley thinks King delayed publishing it for fear of prosecution, and that by the summer of 1738 Swift turned to Pope (via Orrery) to move things along.

In late September 1738 Pope wrote to Orrery, returning the manuscript of the poem, and reporting that, in his opinion, "the latter part ... is inferior to the beginning, the Character too dry, as well as too Vain in some respects, & in one or two particulars, not true" (Woolley 1999–2007: IV, 542). Although Pope wrote to Swift on October 12, 1738, he did not mention *Verses on the Death* (or the letters he was still trying to recover). It was presumably either Pope (or Orrery) who advised King, perhaps while the latter visited Twickenham in late December, to alter the "Character."[70] King later implied that Pope was the most influential voice; others who were present – or passed on their advice – apparently included Bolingbroke, Orrery, and Erasmus Lewis.

King seems to have accepted what he described as a consensus in which he joined. In early January he wrote to Swift somewhat nervously: "At length I have put *Rochefaucault* to the press, and about ten or twelve days hence it will be published. But I am in great fear lest you should dislike the liberties I have taken" – with the "advice and approbation" of Swift's friends in England. If after seeing the printed version Swift wants to publish the poem "as intire as you put it into my hands," he would try to arrange for it (Woolley 1999–2007: IV, 553–54). When the poem was published two weeks later, it had been substantially edited: the "character" from the "indiff'rent" speaker at the Rose was recast as dialogue between two speakers, one of them favorable and one not; only about 40 lines from the 175-line "character" with which the poem ends were retained, and in their place were substituted 62 lines drawn from the *Life and Genuine Character*. Some of the most striking lines in the poem we know are omitted, including the declamatory "Fair LIBERTY was all his Cry" (347); the bitter description of exile in Ireland: "Pursu'd by base envenom'd Pens, / Far to the Land of Slaves and Fens; / A servile Race in Folly nurs'd, / Who truckle most, when treated worst" (395–98); and the proud lines about the *Drapier's Letters*: "The DEAN did by his Pen defeat / An infamous destructive Cheat. / ... Nor Witness hir'd, nor Jury pick'd, / Prevail to bring him in convict" (407–08, 429–30). Cut too were the accounts of Swift's efforts in 1714 to "reconcile his Friends in Power"

[70] King told Swift he was at Twickenham during Christmas week (Woolley 1999–2007: IV, 554). It may have been then that final editorial decisions were made.

(366) and the restoration of the "dangerous Faction" (379) – the Whigs at Queen Anne's death. The poem was published without Swift's notes, though it is not absolutely certain that the manuscript given to King included the notes.

Shortly after publication King wrote again to Swift, still worried that the author would disapprove, and explaining that some cuts (e.g., "the story of the medals," and "that part of the poem which mentions the death of Queen Anne, and so well describes the designs of the ministry, which succeeded upon the accession of the late King") were made out of political caution, and with the "advice and opinion" of "all the rest of your friends on this side of the water" (Woolley 1999–2007: IV, 557). King was assuming that the London edition had not yet arrived in Dublin, and was evidently trying to prepare his most important reader. A week later, on January 30, 1739, when he wrote to Mrs. Whiteway, he was still worried: "I doubt much whether he will be satisfied with the manner in which he finds it published." Again King explained that he "consented in deference to Mr. Pope's judgment, and the opinion of others of the Dean's friends in this country" (IV, 559). By mentioning Pope's name he perhaps meant to shift the blame, but also to invoke the literary authority of a man well known to be Swift's great friend.

No letter from Swift to Pope or to King during these weeks has survived. But his rage and resentment can be inferred, for sometime in February Faulkner published an edition of the poem in Dublin, pretending on its title page to be a reprint of the London edition but restoring the material that King, at Pope's advice, had cut, and printing the extensive notes. Still, Faulkner left numerous blanks, especially for the name of the Queen, Lady Suffolk, and Walpole (e.g., "Sir R – 's Levee" (189), "Cries B*" (192), "Mr. **'s intimate Friend" (194n). Whether this is a sign of Faulkner's caution, or Swift's, is not clear. With the poem appeared a "Publisher's Advertisement" – "We are informed by the supposed Author's Friends, that many Lines and Notes are omitted in the *English* Edition" – inviting any persons who have seen "the Original Manuscript" to "help us to procure those Omissions." Faulkner also left space at the bottom of the printed pages for readers to write in notes.

Faulkner wrote to announce his intentions to the London bookseller, Bathurst, who on March 5 (several weeks after the Dublin edition was published) carried Faulkner's edition and the cover letter (now lost) to King. If the Dublin edition, published without any warning, was designed to embarrass both King and Pope, it worked: King wrote the next day to Mrs. Whiteway that he was "not a little mortified" to discover that "the Dean is much dissatisfied with our manner of publication, and that so many lines have been omitted." King now felt obliged to provide further explanations, and to do so borrowed the language of Pope's letter to Orrery: (1) "the latter part of the poem might be thought by the public a little vain, if so much were said by himself of himself"; (2) "He lash'd the vice, but spared the name" was "strictly speaking" not true; (3) he had cut the final two lines of the poem – "That Kingdom he hath left his Debtor, / I wish it soon may have a better" – because "I did not well understand them; a *better* what?"

The central fact in this stage of the poem's publication history is that Swift and Pope apparently never wrote directly to each other about plans for publication of the poem, or reactions to it. All the correspondence that has survived was through intermediaries – Orrery, King, Mrs. Whitelaw, and Faulkner. This is not surprising: it's very likely that neither one wanted to be obliged to embarrass the other, or to lodge a complaint, or even to explain himself. Each had an established record of erecting smokescreens to conceal his publication plans. Even if they had written to each other, we cannot assume that the letters would have been candid. So we largely have to infer their motives.

Pope's motives for editing *Verses on the Death* might seem clear enough from his September 1738 letter to Orrery: the "Character," in his opinion, was "too dry," "too Vain," and contained some statements that were "not true" (Sherburn 1956: IV, 130). "Dry" reminds us that Pope in his Horatian satires prefers the interchange of conversation to the continuous flow of a single voice. It is easy enough to see why he might have thought the speaker "at the Rose" who delivered an allegedly "impartial" character was a device too easily seen through, and that the praise would be read as self-praise. But it is not obvious why Pope should have found this objectionable. For in his own poems he was not shy about presenting transparently self-flattering portraits. In his *One Thousand Seven Hundred and Thirty-Eight*, he had acknowledged his pride: "Yes, I am proud; I must be proud to see / Men not afraid of God, afraid of me" (II, 208–09). And it is easy to agree that several of the statements made in the "character impartial" are "not true." It was obvious enough that, despite the claim, Swift had not in fact "spared the name" of his satiric victims. But Pope had not been meticulously truthful in his own statements about his life, not in his poems and not in his letters to Swift.

The explanation for Pope's disapproval might lie elsewhere. As we have seen, advising on the publication of Swift's poem was only one of Pope's Swift-related literary projects in 1738–39. He had by then recovered copies of his letters to Swift, and was in the process of editing them. He may have thought he had an interest in keeping Swift out of political trouble and in keeping his moral reputation intact, so that linking himself to Swift – as he planned to do in the publication of their letters – would not reflect badly on him. Since King himself had in *The Toast* praised Swift's efforts on behalf of liberty and his "defeat" of Wood's half-pence, we can probably safely infer that it was Pope who advised him to remove language that might be construed as politically inflammatory. This is perhaps surprising, since Pope had just that year published the politic-ally outspoken *One Thousand Seven Hundred and Thirty-Eight*. But if it was Pope who suggested that the "character impartial" be recast as dia-logue, it would have been consistent with his own recent satiric prac-tice: the interchange between two speakers in the two "Dialogues" of *One Thousand Seven Hundred and Thirty-Eight* is more animated than in any of his previous poems, and would have had the effect of making Swift's satiric apologia more like his own. Pope probably also had disinterested motives: he may simply have been concerned to preserve his friend's repu-tation from criticism of any kind. But he in effect wanted to play a role in shaping that reputation, and usually chose to emphasize the laughing rather than the angry and indignant side of Swift, which King described, when he reported on the poem's successful reception in England, as "that inimitable turn of wit and humour so peculiar to himself" (Woolley 1999–2007: IV, 559), which for him (and for Pope) constitutes "a just and a beautiful satire" (IV, 562).

Swift's motives are more difficult to infer, since no letter or comment from him on the matter survives. By 1738, it seems clear, he hoped to have the poem published in London, with as much of his satire as the bookseller would dare to print. Given King's praise of him as a fearless defender of liberty, he probably did not consider that King might be per-suaded by Swift's friends to make cuts. Once he saw King's edited text, he determined to publish his own version, restoring the cuts and making sure the notes were included. How closely he worked with Faulkner it is not possible to say. Faulkner's title page pretended that he was reprinting the London edition, when he had in fact apparently received a copy of the original manuscript from Swift himself, and thus did not need the help. His "Publisher's Advertisement," inviting readers to supply lines and names missing from the English edition may or may not have been written with Swift's advice or consent. Two hypotheses seem plausible. The first is Probyn's – that Faulkner, working with limited authority from Swift, but still working independently, was genuinely seeking information from those with access to manuscripts so as to be able to print a more complete edition after Swift's death. Faulkner, so Probyn suggests, "knew more than he could say and possessed more than he could print" (1986: 61).[71] An alternate hypothesis is that Faulkner and Swift were working together, agreed that prudence required a text with asterisks and blanks, but sought to stimulate readers to seek out annotations from the several manuscript copies of the poem and to pass them on. In effect, Swift sought to have a poem too daring for print circulate by the private routes of the old scribal culture. Faulkner, for his part, was free to try to acquire material he could use for a later printed edition. This second hypothesis is consistent with Karian's idea that Swift fundamentally distrusted printers and booksellers and attempted to appeal over their heads to a broader public opinion, shaped as it was by both printed and scribal documents.[72] The poem as Swift wrote it apparently did descend to posterity, but it took some time. The version in Faulkner's first posthumous edition of Swift's *Works* (1746) provides very little new material. It was not until Williams's reconstruction of the poem and the notes in 1937 that a reasonably accurate version of Swift's original text was printed. And even today it is unclear which of the notes, derived from eight different contemporary manuscripts, were authorized. Swift may still not have succeeded in controlling the way he is remembered by posterity.

[71] Probyn (1986: 57) thinks Faulkner did not have a manuscript of the notes, or had them in "provisional form" and did not have Swift's express authority to publish them.
[72] See above, pp. 180–81. Many contemporary readers implicitly responded to Swift's appeal, annotating printed copies of the poem, adding notes not found in Faulkner's edition. Whether or not such manuscript notes have authorial sanction has been debated. See Probyn 1986 and Stephen Karian, "Reading the Material Text of Swift's *Verses on the Death*," *Studies in English Literature* 41 (2001), 515–44.

CHAPTER 5

Last things

The publication of the rival editions of *Verses on the Death of Dr. Swift* by Bathurst and Faulkner in January–February 1739 and the rival editions of the Pope–Swift letters by the same two printers in April–June 1741 bring to a kind of conclusion what had been an ongoing literary conversation between the two old friends since their initial meeting in 1713. Sadly, it is as if they had nothing more to say to each other. For Swift, the conclusion coincided with the close of his literary life. His health declined rapidly after February 1740. He had written virtually nothing new since *The Legion Club* (1736) and had played a close supervisory role in nothing but the *Compleat Collection of Genteel and Ingenious Conversation*, published in 1738 but written much earlier. His correspondence declined, especially to friends in England: after January 1739 we have only twenty-three of his letters. His last surviving letter of any kind is dated June 1741, and in August 1742 he was declared legally incompetent, and his affairs placed in the hands of guardians. Pope, however, his health as fragile as ever but more than twenty years younger, continued writing with some vigor. By the time *Verses on the Death* appeared he was taking up a new set of friends, the "Boy Patriots," Ralph Allen, and the man who would be in effect his literary executor, William Warburton.

At first glance, it comes as a disappointment to realize that although Pope continued to correspond with at least two men who had long been friends and correspondents of Swift – Bolingbroke and Orrery – his letters to and from them are with one exception silent about Swift and his condition. From Bolingbroke, however, Pope could have had little news of Swift: no letters between Swift and Bolingbroke after 1738 have survived. Orrery is a similar case: he and Pope wrote often to each other during the years 1742–44[1] but Orrery was no longer in direct touch with

---

[1] These warm and friendly letters made Orrery think that he would be remembered at Pope's death. But he was bitterly disappointed that "notwithstanding all the many and high assurances

Swift either. In a letter to Swift dated July 7, 1741, he reports facetiously that "Mr. Pope .... obeys your commands, and flings away much time upon me" (Woolley 1999–2007: IV, 658), but no subsequent letter from him to Swift has survived. Pope continued to exchange letters about Swift's deteriorating condition with Mrs. Whiteway (November 22, 1742) and Deane Swift (December 4 and 19, 1742; April 4, 1744), who, in at least one letter (since lost), seems to have passed on news of Swift. Pope's only response, on November 17, 1743 (Sherburn 1956: IV, 483), is to say "I am sorry to hear of the Dean." (Swift had been declared incompetent more than eighteen months earlier, so this is probably not news of the legal event.) It is plausible to suspect that Pope shared the sentiment Orrery expressed to Deane Swift on December 4, 1742: "the man I wished to live the longest, I wish the soonest dead. It is the only blessing that can now befal him" (Woolley 1999–2007: IV 665).

But even if Swift and Pope exchanged no letters after 1741, they might still be said to have continued their conversation. A review of their writings in their closing years suggests that they had each other in mind as they wrote. It also suggests that they understood, as we can understand now, the common ground that both linked and distinguished them. Pope still had several major literary projects underway. His "opus magnum," first announced in a letter to Swift in 1734, was still engaging him on his deathbed. Also occupying him during the years 1740–43 were revisions to two Swift-related works, the *Dunciad* (last given a thorough revision in 1729) and the Pope–Swift *Miscellanies*, last revised in 1732. Swift wrote virtually nothing, but what he did write – his last will and testament, and his epitaph – tell a great deal about the way he chose to define himself and the way he wanted to be remembered. Pope too wrote a will, and not only one but several epitaphs for himself. By examining them closely and comparing them to Swift's epitaph, we get a final look at the differences that they made clear, as it were, in stone.

MISCELLANIES (1741) AND THE DUNCIAD (1742–1743)

By the summer of 1740, as he was preparing his *Works in Prose, vol. II*, Pope was corresponding with the printer Charles Bathurst concerning a new edition of the Pope–Swift *Miscellanies*, apparently offering to act as informal editor (correcting mistakes, and deleting, inserting,

of friendship, gratitude, and affection in these Letters, *he forgot me in his will. Mens curva in corpore curvo*" (Orrery's own manuscript note, quoted in Sherburn 1956: IV, 521n).

and rearranging material). In the first letter of an ongoing correspondence with Bathurst, who had acquired copyright to the volume from
Motte, Pope suggested that a new edition would be "for his [i.e., Swift's]
Honour" (August 29, 1740, in Sherburn 1956: IV, 259). But it is clear, as
Sherburn notes, that Pope was also serving himself, for he wanted to
print as his own some pieces that had appeared anonymously in the
1732 *Miscellanies*. Thus on February 3, 1741 he wrote to Bathurst: "I sent
you a Catalogue of some additional pieces yet unprinted which might
be inserted in the two or three Vols. of Miscellanies" and a list of other
pieces that might be "removed into my volume" (IV, 333–34). The pieces
"yet unprinted" included two slight poems by Pope – an "Impromptu to
Lady Winchelsea" and a recently written epigram on Bishop Hough –
that he was not prepared to acknowledge as his own but did not want
to lose altogether.[2] Items to be "removed into my volume" were several
unattributed prose pieces from the *Miscellanies*.[3] "Removed" is mislead-
ing: Pope did not ask Bathurst to transfer them from the new edition of
the *Miscellanies* to Pope's own volume, but to print them first in his *Works
in Prose, vol. II* (published in April 1741) and subsequently to confirm, in
the new arrangement in the forthcoming volume of *Miscellanies* (published in July 1742), that they were "By Mr. Pope" or "By Dr. Arbuthnot
and Mr. Pope." The purpose of the new arrangement, made clear on the
title page, is to separate pieces written "By Dr. Swift" from those written
"By Mr. Pope." Thus, although it has been suggested that the effect of
Pope's 1741 *Works in Prose* (which also included the *Memoirs of Martinus
Scriblerus*) was to advertise Pope's links to his old Scriblerian friends,[4] it
is more accurate to say that he manages simultaneously to link himself to
Swift and to distinguish himself from him.

Pope was also working on what was to become *The New Dunciad*.
If Swift was in a sense "the author" of the 1728 *Dunciad* and the 1729
Dunciad Variorum, Warburton might be said to be "the author" of the
1742 *New Dunciad* and the 1743 *Dunciad in Four Books*. In a September
20, 1741 letter to Warburton, Pope refers to his plans "to complete the
Dunciad," a phrase to which Warburton in his 1751 edition added the

2 "[Y]et unprinted" is not quite accurate. The former was written in 1714 and not printed until
1741, when it appeared in Bayle's *General Dictionary*, probably taken from a circulating manuscript. The latter was marked with an asterisk, indicating that it was not written by Swift. Neither
poem was included in Pope's *Works* in his lifetime, or in Warburton's 1751 edition.
3 "Thoughts on Various Subjects," "The Art of Sinking in Poetry," "Virgilius Restauratus," "An
Essay … Concerning the Origine of Sciences," "The Memoirs of P. P., Clerk of this Parish," several essays from the *Guardian*, and "A Key to the Lock."
4 Kerby-Miller (1950: 64).

footnote: "He had then communicated his intention to the Editor, of adding a fourth book to it." He also acknowledges that he has asked Warburton to provide a "Commentary" not only on the *Dunciad* but on all his poems. (Pope, it will be recalled, had earlier invited Swift to contribute notes for the *Variorum*.) What is more, he describes the projected "General Edition" of the poems in terms that suggest Warburton was not only commentator but also companion: "I hope Your Friendship to me will be then as well known, as my being an Author, & go down together to Posterity" (Sherburn 1956: IV, 362). This is of course the same language Pope had used in a 1727 letter to Swift about their forthcoming *Miscellanies*: "methinks we look like friends walking down hand in hand to posterity" (Woolley 1999–2007: III, 76).[5] In 1727 Pope had imagined two friends and fellow writers "in a free, un-important, natural, easy manner." In 1741 the "weak Poet" needs the "Commentator" to lend a "crutch" to "help him to limp a little further than he could on his own Feet." Perhaps Pope could not imagine that the solemn Warburton could conduct himself in a "free, un-important, natural, easy manner," but in other respects the future Bishop of Gloucester seems to have supplanted the Dean of St. Patrick's.[6]

In the following months Pope reported to friends – both Hugh Bethel and Ralph Allen – his progress on the new poem, but by then he was no longer writing to Swift.[7] *The New Dunciad* was published on March 20, 1742. Pope sent presentation copies to several friends, but there is no record that he sent a copy to Swift. Soon, prompted in part by the publication of the notorious *Letter from Mr Cibber, to Mr Pope* on July 24, 1742, Pope was working on a complete revision of the *Dunciad Variorum*, substituting Cibber for Theobald, who was no longer in the news, and adding as pompous commentator "Richardus Aristarchus," a satirically reinvented Richard Bentley. (Pope made no changes to the lines or notes in which Swift is named.)[8] Pope had republished the *Variorum* several times (in 1735, 1736, and 1741) since its first appearance, making small

---

[5] See above, ch. 2.
[6] By providing an often-solemn "Commentary," Warburton adopts a role that makes him less like a Swiftian learned wit than like the pedantic Martinus Scriblerus. Rumbold (1999: 11) notes that Warburton's "aggressive pertinacity" in his defense of the orthodoxy of Pope's *Essay on Man* made him act "not entirely unlike the attitude that Pope deplored in Theobald and Bentley."
[7] See his January 1, 1742 letter to Bethel and his February 8, 1742 letter to Allen (Sherburn 1956: IV, 377, 387).
[8] Except to add to the "List" of attacks on himself (in the Appendix) two items which linked him to Swift: *Gulliveriana Secunda*, advertised in November 1729 but never published, and *Dean Jonathan's Paraphrase on the 4th Chapter of Genesis*.

revisions or additions each time. In a May 1739 letter to Swift, Pope had enclosed a draft of ten new lines on the obscure writers of the pro-min-istry *Daily Gazeteer* to be added to Book II in the "next New Edition of the Dunciad" (Woolley 1999–2007: IV, 580–81). These lines were in fact not published until the revised four-book version of the poem appeared in October 1743, and they were probably the only part of the *Dunciad in Four Books* that Swift ever saw.[9] Slightly revised when they finally appeared in print, the lines ironically memorialize the pro-Walpole daily journalists as "Sons of a Day" – since the papers for which they wrote "lasted but a day" (II, 314n). Who were they – "Ask ye their names?" (II, 309). Pope declines to name them, and remembers them only as "the Gazetteers" (314). Perhaps Pope sent the lines to Swift because they implicitly answer Swift's advice, more than twenty years earlier, that he "take care the bad poets do not outwit you."[10] In these lines Pope largely accepts Swift's counsel about being careful not to transmit names, here naming only "Mother Osborne" and "ruful Paxton,"[11] but also resists it, for when the lines were published he printed two footnotes explaining that "Osborne" was in fact a pseudonym (312n) and providing a detailed account of the funding of the "Gazetteers" with public money (314n).

It is tempting to speculate what Swift, had he seen it, would have thought of the expanded poem. He would presumably have been pleased that Pope added to the "Testimonies of Authors" Swift's six-line tribute from the *Libel on Dr. Delany*, in the climactic final position. Pope now confirms what he wrote to Swift in 1733, that he regards the lines as "the best panegyrick on myself, that either my own times or any other could have afforded,[12] but Swift would probably have been happier if Pope had not seen fit to omit the apparently still offensive reference to his detest-ing "all the statesman kind" and his contemning "courts." This might be considered the final occasion in their joint careers on which Pope edited Swift's work. (Not included in the "Testimonies" until this edition, des-pite several opportunities to insert them in re-issues of the *Variorum* in 1735, 1736, and 1741, the lines, which he must have known Swift would never see, may represent Pope's final acknowledgement that Swift was his

---

9 The Twickenham Edition of the poem, which prints the 1729 and 1743 versions, obscures the fact that in two cases lines about Swift were first revised in the 1735 and 1736 editions. See chs. 2 and 3, above.

10 See above, ch. 2.

11 "Ruful Paxton" disappeared by the time the poem was published, replaced by the punning "Monumental Brass" (II, 313).

12 See above, p. 139.

most credentialed and influential admirer, and a final tribute to his old friend.)

It is plausible to assume that Swift would have liked the defiant Miltonic spirit in which Pope described (in a 1742 letter to Bethel) his anticipation of the furious response he thought the poem would stir up: "But a Good Conscience a bold Spirit, & Zeal for Truth, at whatsoever Expence, of whatever Pretenders to Science, or of all Imposition either Literary, Moral, or Political; these animated me, & these will Support me" (Sherburn 1956: IV, 377).[13] And he would have been pleased to see Pope renew the ridicule of Bentley as editor and commentator (in large part because of his notorious 1732 edition of *Paradise Lost*) that Swift himself (in response to Bentley's 1697 *Dissertation* on the epistles of Phalaris) had initiated almost forty years earlier.

LAST WILLS

By 1740 both Swift and Pope knew that they were nearing the ends of their writing careers, and their lives. Both left detailed wills, providing for legacies, appointing literary executors, leaving instructions about both the disposal of their papers and the words they wanted carved on their monuments. We might think of the wills of Swift and Pope as their final literary works – both were published shortly after their authors' deaths, Pope's in 1744 and Swift's in 1746.[14] Among the intended – or at least imagined – readers were the two old friends themselves. Swift had on several occasions in the past written to Pope about the literary provisions in previous drafts of his will. On February 26, 1730 he told Pope that he had "ordered in my will that my body shall be buried at Holy-head."[15] (This perhaps began as an insider joke: Pope would have known that Swift thought Holyhead a bleak place, but at least it was not Ireland, and it was the first stopover on the way to England.)[16] On June 12, 1732, he wrote that he had "ordered in

---

[13] For a recent discussion of the role of *Paradise Lost* in the four-book *Dunciad*, see Valerie Rumbold, "Milton's Epic and Pope's Satyr Play: *Paradise Lost* in *The Dunciad in Four Books*," *Milton Quarterly* 38 (2004), 138–62.

[14] *The Last Will and Testament of Alexander Pope* (1744); *The Last Will and Testament of Jonathan Swift, D. D.* (1746). Pope's is printed in Mack (*The Garden and the City: Retirement and Politics in the Later Poetry of Pope*, 1731–1743 [1969], 263–65) and in Cowler (1986: 506–08), where it is well annotated (509–13); Swift's in Davis (1939–68: XIII, 145–58).

[15] Woolley (1999–2007: III, 285). Cf. a 1735 letter to Pope: "I will not lie in a Country of slaves" (IV, 203).

[16] See Swift's "Holyhead, September 25, 1727," a poem inscribed in his "Holyhead Journal" but not printed until 1882, where in the final lines he imagines it would be better freely to go to his grave even in Holyhead "Than rule yon isle [Ireland] and be a slave." But by 1737 Swift was serious: a

my Will" – presumably a new will – "that all my Papers of any kind shall be delivered to you to dispose of as you please" (Woolley 1999–2007: III, 489). In another letter four years later he wrote that he had resolved "to direct my Executors [in a new will] to send you all your letters, well sealed and pacqueted, along with some legacies mentioned in my will, and leave them entirely to your disposal" (IV, 283–84). In 1740 he probably assumed that Pope would in time read a printed text of his last will. Pope was less communicative about his testamentary intentions, and his last will was not drawn until twenty months after his final letter to Swift, but we can perhaps still think of the last wills of Swift and Pope as the final exchange in a lifelong conversation.

Swift's last will is dated May 3, 1740 (with a codicil on May 5), while he was still "of sound Mind, although weak in Body." Much of it is devoted to his detailed instructions for establishing a "Hospital" for "Idiots and Lunaticks" and for the disposal of his leases and real property. A few sums of money and his personal effects are bequeathed to a series of relations and friends, although only one is named as a "friend": to Pope, "my dearest Friend," is left "my Picture in Miniature, drawn by *Zinck*, of *Robert* late Earl of *Oxford*." (As a close friend of both Swift and Pope, Oxford was an appropriate link between them, just as he had been when Pope named Swift in his "Epistle to Oxford"; Bolingbroke, another close friend of both, was – perhaps surprisingly – not named in the will.) What Swift emphasizes is the warmth of his affection – "dearest Friend" – but not his admiration or esteem. Those tributes surprisingly go to Queen Anne – "of ever Glorious, Immortal, and truly Pious Memory, the real Nursing Mother of all her Kingdoms" – and to Alexander Macaulay, a Dublin lawyer, for his "truly honourable Zeal in Defence of the legal Rights of the Clergy, in Opposition to all their unprovoked Oppressors." (Perhaps less surprising when we remember that in his own epitaph Swift paid tribute to himself as a zealous defender in the face of oppression.) Having earlier told Pope that he would leave him "some legacies," he now only left a miniature. A few books were left to the Revd. Francis Wilson, but almost all of Swift's library (more than 650 volumes), including presentation copies from Pope,[17] was sold at auction in February 1746.

draft will and codicil dated April 1737 (reprinted in Davis 1939–68: XIII, 198–99) leaves instructions for his body to be transported to Holyhead and buried there, and his April 1737 letter to Mrs. Whiteway (Woolley 1999–2007: IV, 425) confirms that his body is to be transported to Holyhead "for my Burial in the Church of that Town, as directed in my Will."

[17] Williams (*Dean Swift's Library* [1932], 55) thinks it "probable" that most of Swift's volumes of Pope – the six-volume *Iliad*, the five-volume *Odyssey*, the *Works* of 1717, the *Dunciad Variorum*, the *Works* of 1735, the *Letters* (1737), the *Works … Containing Epistles and Satires* of 1737, and the

Not specified in the will is what is to happen to Swift's unpublished papers, earlier promised to Pope. Swift had given away much manuscript material in the late 1730s – Pope's letters were returned to him; some letters to "Stella" were given to Mrs. Whiteway, who later passed them to Deane Swift. She later reported to Pope that Swift carefully "burnt most of his writings unprinted [including a number of sermons], except for a few loose papers."[18] But Swift in fact took care to leave in trusted hands the manuscript material that he wanted printed, including *The Four Last Years* and *Directions to Servants*.[19] Some manuscripts were found in Swift's study after his death by the Revd. John Lyon, who claimed Swift had made a present of them to him. (Some of these were given to Thomas Wilkes, and by him to Hawkesworth, who published them.)[20]

By contrast to Pope (as we shall see), Swift seems to have cared little what happened to his books and most of his papers (including, for example, the unpublished "Satirical Elegy on the Death of a Late General"[21]), despite his early assurances to Pope that they would be left to him. Since Pope's letters had already been returned to him, Swift may have considered that he had performed his promise. If Swift in fact changed his mind, it is reasonable to suspect that he had several reasons for not leaving unpublished papers to his "dearest Friend": after repeated requests Pope had still not addressed one of his epistles to him, and this may have continued to cause resentment; he had been pressed hard and repeatedly to return Pope's letters, which may have actually deterred him from sending Pope any further material; and, most important, he disapproved of Pope's editing of the *Verses on the Death* and may have suspected that his editorial judgement was unsound.

Pope's last will was drawn up on December 12, 1743 – before he could have seen Swift's. He specifies legacies, keepsakes, and books for family and friends (the largest bequest going to Martha Blount) – nineteen persons in all. If by dealing early and at greatest length with his wish to set up a lunatic hospital Swift was signaling his chief concern as

Works in Prose, vol. II of 1741 – were presentation copies. But according to Passman and Vienken (2003: II, 1490–97), only three (the 1729 *Dunciad Variorum*, the 1735 *Works*, the 1737 *Letters*) contain inscriptions, and only the *Dunciad Variorum*, the 1735 *Works*, and the 1741 *Works* contain Swift's hand-annotations.

[18] Woolley (1999–2007: IV, 622).

[19] *Directions to Servants*, published less than a month after Swift's death, seems to have been in Faulkner's hands before Swift died. The manuscript of the *History of the Four Last Years* – not published until 1758 – was delivered by Orrery to King in 1737.

[20] I take the details about Swift's manuscripts from Williams, *Dean Swift's Library*.

[21] Williams suspects that it passed into the hands of Deane Swift, who may have been the one to give it to the editors of the *Gentleman's Magazine*, where it was published in 1764.

legator, Pope for his part signaled his priorities by disposing first of his
"Manuscript and unprinted Papers,"[22] which he left to Bolingbroke (or
if deceased to Marchmont), and the "Property of all such of my Works
already printed" to Warburton, including those "as he hath written, or
shall write Commentaries or Notes upon" – thus providing an induce-
ment to Warburton to write such commentaries. Orrery is not named
in the will.[23] Nor is Swift. By December 1743 Pope knew that Swift had
already been judged legally incompetent, and was thus not fit to bear any
responsibility. But why was he not at least left a keepsake of some kind?
Although legally incompetent – with the legal status of a child – Swift
could legally have inherited, just as a child could. Perhaps Pope thought
him no longer able to remember his friends, dead in all but name.

EPITAPHS

Before providing for the disposal of their earthly goods, Swift and Pope
in their wills made provision, as was customary in their day, for the burial
of the body, the erection of a monument, and the words to be carved on
it. This act in itself makes their deaths into literary occasions, offering to
each a final opportunity to define the way he will be remembered, and
offering to readers a last means of assessing the differences between them.
Among the readers we can place Swift and Pope themselves: although
neither ever saw the other's monument, each had an opportunity – well
before death – to know what words would be inscribed on it. And each
seems to have *wanted* the other to know.

The inscription on Swift's monument is well known to anybody who
has read or even heard about him; the words on Pope's are perhaps known
only to specialists. But not enough has been noted about the fact that the
words of their epitaphs (Swift's in Latin and Pope's in English), which we
like to think spring from something deep within their authors, in fact
had a significant pre-history in both Latin and English writers, and may
have been re-deployed with some irony. And not enough has been said
about the fact that the epitaphs that Swift and Pope composed were in
some sense the ripe fruits of an intermittent discussion in their letters
about epitaphs, conducted over many years, and that each epitaph was
designed with the other in mind as primary reader.

---

[22] Pope's will leaves no trace of his efforts, beginning about September 1743, to leave to Martha
Blount a house in London he intended to purchase. For details, see Rumbold (1989: 287–89).
[23] He was angry about it. See note 1, above.

Swift began thinking about his own epitaph as early as 1730: in the February 26, 1730 letter to Pope, after mentioning his orders to be buried at Holyhead, Swift notes that he has also ordered "an Epitaph, of which this is a part."[24] In the original letter (since lost) an epitaph presumably followed, but in the surviving transcription of the letter, done for the Earl of Oxford, a blank line follows these words. Pope did not print the letter in his edition, but we may assume that he read the original, and knew of the epitaph, and thus knew that Swift wanted him to read it.[25] Between 1730 and 1740 Swift changed his mind about where he wanted to be buried. It is impossible to say whether he also changed the words of his epitaph, or whether Pope in the 1730 letter had had an early opportunity to preview what Yeats called "the greatest epitaph in history."[26]

During the 1730s Swift was not only thinking about his *own* epitaph (and more generally about what he would like said of him after his death). On April 20, 1731 he wrote to Pope about the Latin inscription he had arranged to have placed on a monument for the Duke of Schomberg, a Huguenot hero who died at the Battle of the Boyne and whose grave, forty years later, was still left without what he regarded as a proper memorial (Woolley 1999–2007: III, 383): linked in Swift's mind already were the ideas of indignation and epitaphic inscription.[27] And in the 1730s he was also linking such inscription with the idea of liberty. In 1735 he wrote admiringly to Pulteney that he was bequeathing him an epitaph, "Ultimus Britannorum," because "you preserved your spirit of liberty, when your former colleagues had utterly sacrificed theirs; and if it shall ever begin to breathe in these days, it must intirely be owing to yourself and one or two friends."[28] For his part, Pope had been composing epitaphs

---

[24] Woolley (1999–2007: III, 285). And perhaps as early as April 1729, when he wrote to Pope, citing Fulke Greville's epitaph – "here lies, & c. who was friend to Sir Philip Sidney" – and noting that "To be remembred for ever on the account of our friendship, is what would exceedingly please me" (III, 231).

[25] In some verses published in the *Gentleman's Magazine* in 1733 and later in Faulkner's 1735 edition, Swift playfully responded to two birthday gifts by ordering that the gifts be placed "around my Tomb … As Trophies" and the birthday poems that accompanied them "be grav'd on either Side in Columns" (Williams 1958: 611).

[26] From his introduction to *The Words upon the Window-Pane*, in *Wheels and Butterflies* (1934), p. 15.

[27] Johnson (1953: 822) makes the point that in one draft of the inscription (published in the *Gentleman's Magazine*) Schomburg was said to have been treated with indignity – *indignabundi*, in Swift's Latin – by heirs who would not trouble themselves to erect even a plain monument. What is more significant is Swift's own indignation.

[28] Woolley (1999–2007: IV, 65–66). Cf. Bolingbroke's *Idea of a Patriot King*: "the utmost that private men can do … is to keep the spirit of liberty alive in a few breasts" (in *Letters, on the Spirit of Patriotism* [1749], 113).

since, while recovering from a dangerous illness in 1710 and "forc'd, like many learned Authors, to write my own Epitaph," he proposed (in a letter to Cromwell) a brief inscription in Latin.[29] In February 1732 he sent a draft of his epitaph on Gay to Swift, who replied with a critique two months later. Several of Pope's epitaphs were published in the 1732 volume of Pope–Swift *Miscellanies*.[30] Swift knew of the epitaphs Pope had published in his 1735 *Works*, including one to Sir Henry Withers, honored as "the last true Briton" (a phrase Swift might have remembered when he wrote to Pulteney),[31] and another to Trumbull, who "At length enjoys that Liberty he lov'd."[32] In 1736 Pope wrote to Swift, suggesting that he leave Ireland and come "live and die with me," even proposing fancifully that they share an epitaph: "And let *Tales Animae Concordes* ["Such Harmonious Souls"] be our Motto and our Epitaph."[33] By the time he wrote his will, Swift also knew that Pope had been thinking further about his own epitaph, since he had published in his 1738 *Works* an "Epitaph. For One who wou'd not be buried in *Westminster-Abby*."[34] In his 1741 *Works* Pope included another epitaph on himself.

The first of Pope's three late epitaphs for himself was in fact the inscription designed for the family monument in Twickenham Church, placed there after the death of his mother in 1733. Although nominally designed for his parents – "PARENTIBUS BENEMERENTIS FILIUS FECIT" ("To his well-deserving Parents the Son erected this") – Pope already had it in mind that the inscription would also be his own. Its opening words, "D. O. M. /

---

[29] "Nothing wou'd be properer," he wrote to Cromwell on May 17, 1710 (Sherburn 1956: 1, 87), "than Obliviscusque meorum, obliviscendus et illis" ("forgetting my friends, and by them forgotten", from Horace, *Epistle* 1, 11, line 9). In the same letter Pope suggests that La Fontaine's epitaph (published in 1671 and quoted in Sherburn 1956: 1, 87n) on himself might suit him. Six years later he composed another epitaph on himself, modeled on an epitaph by Tibullus, and enclosed it in a letter to Lady Mary Wortley: "Here stopt by hasty Death, Alexis lies, / Who crost half Europe, led by Wortley's eyes!" (I, 369).
[30] The volume included Pope's translation of a two-line Latin epitaph "apply'd to F. C. [i.e., Francis Charteris]," an "Epitaph [of By-Words]," and a mock-"Epitaph" ("Well then, poor G – lies under ground"). The first volume of Pope–Swift *Miscellanies* in 1726 included Pope's mock-epitaph on "P. P." The 1732 volume also included a satiric epitaph ("Here continueth to rot …") on Francis Charteris (a kind of emulative response to Swift's "Satirical Elegy" on Marlborough) which Pope later incorporated into the notes to his *Epistle to Bathurst*, where he attributed it to Arbuthnot.
[31] Swift wrote to Pulteney before he received a copy of Pope's 1735 *Works*, but he could have read the epitaph on Withers in the *Grub-Street Journal*, no. 50 (December 17, 1730).
[32] Pope later adapted the line for a 1743 epitaph on Rowe: "Thy Soul enjoys that Liberty it lov'd" (Ault 1954: 400). The Trumbull epitaph was first published in 1717.
[33] March 25, 1736 (Woolley 1999–2007: IV, 278). Pope may have remembered Swift's invocation, seven years earlier, of Fulke Greville's epitaph (see above, p. 231).
[34] The *Works* were not published until May 1739, although the title page read "1738." See below, pp. 233–35.

ALEXANDRO POPE …,[35] are designed so as to fit both his father (also named Alexander) and himself, and in 1735 when he included in his *Works, Vol. II* the text of the inscription in a long footnote to his *Epistle to Dr. Arbuthnot* he added to the final line "ET SIBI" ("and to himself"), two simple words that had the effect of anticipating his own death and quietly and economically transforming the inscription into an epitaph for the son as well as the parents. ("ET SIBI" was not actually carved on the monument until after his death in 1744.)[36] By omitting to provide even the name of the son, and by remembering him only as a "filius," the inscription suggests, without saying so, that his chief virtue was Virgilian filial piety.[37] But the word between "FILIUS" and "ET SIBI" – "FECIT" (lit. "made," or "erected") – serves to emphasize that the son was a "maker" of verbal texts. And by publishing the inscription as a footnote to a verse epistle from a self-consciously famous poet, Pope makes sure his reader will know of both his moral and poetic, his private and public virtues. Those who soon after his death arranged for the publication of *The Last Will and Testament of Alexander Pope* saw to it that the private virtues would be made known to a wider public: they included an English translation of the text of Pope's Latin inscription.

Three years later Pope published in his *Works … Vol. II. Part II* (1738) an "Epitaph. For One who wou'd not be buried in *Westminster-Abby*."[38] Again he designs an inscription for himself without saying so: his name never appears in the text. The poem is perhaps by its title "carefully distanced from autobiography" (Rumbold 1989: 14), but Pope's habitually careful attention to self-presentation suggests that he may have been giving this epitaph a public trial before claiming it as his own:

> Heroes, and Kings! your distance keep,
> In peace let one poor Poet sleep,
> Who never flatter'd Folks like you,
> Let Horace blush, and Virgil too.

[35] "D. O. M." was a common abbreviation for "Deo Optimo Maximo" ("To God the Best and Greatest"), and in the period typically found in Roman Catholic (and usually continental) epitaphic inscriptions.

[36] When he incorporated the inscription into his 1743 last will and testament, he directed that in addition to "ET SIBI," his executors should add nothing more than "Qui obiit anno 17– aetatis –."

[37] Scodel (1988: 618) rightly notes Pope's "highly self-conscious, indeed ostentatious gesture of modesty."

[38] To distinguish it pointedly from the immediately preceding epitaph in the 1738 volume: "On *James Craggs*, Esq in *Westminster-Abby*." The poem was reprinted in Pope's editions of his *Works* in 1739, 1740, and 1743.

Although putatively designed for one who would not be buried there, the inscription paradoxically assumes that the reader is standing in Westminster Abbey: "Heroes, and Kings" are more likely to wander past the tombs in the Abbey than to find themselves before the obscure site of a retired poet, and where else than in the Abbey might one more readily find "Heroes, and Kings," either dead or alive? Both those who visit this scene of majesty and spectacle and those whose bodies lie nearby are admonished to keep their distance. Here Pope wittily reverses the conventional epitaphic directive to the passer-by to "pause" or "stay" or "draw near."[39] He also reverses the usual custom whereby a subject must wait to be summoned before approaching a king: here it is the King who must hold back. But Pope's ostensible purpose is not to suggest that the poet is mightier than a king or hero: the poet is still but a "poor Poet" who just wants a little sleep. This pretended modesty, of course, serves to mask self-conscious dignity and pride.[40] As Mack has suggested (1985: 733), Pope's epitaph was perhaps inspired by the erection of Gay's monument in the Abbey in 1738. Five years before that, in 1733, Pope himself had written and published an epitaph for Gay, dismissing as insignificant the fact "that here thy Bust / Is mix'd with Heroes, or with Kings thy dust." Now Pope goes one step further and, imagining an epitaph appropriate for himself, banishes those same heroes and kings. As Scodel observes (1988: 625), Pope's stance "recalls the proudly solitary figure" at the end of the first dialogue of the *Epilogue to the Satires* (also published in 1738) who beholds the spectacle of lawlessness and corruption in high places and "held it in disdain."

It is not only "Heroes, and Kings" who are rebuked: "Horace..., and Virgil too" are called to account because in their time they flattered Augustus, even when they pretended to be unable to do so.[41] Pope perhaps thinks of Horace's "Epistle to Augustus," and his care, in his own imitation of it, published just a year earlier, to put ironic distance not only between himself and his king, but also between himself and his poetic

---

[39] He may also have seen and remembered the opening vocative in Prior's manuscript "Epitaph": "Nobles, and Heralds by your leave, / Here lyes what once was MATTHEW PRIOR" (printed in H. Bunker Wright and Monroe K. Spears, eds., *The Literary Works of Matthew Prior*, 2nd edn., 2 vols. [1971], I, 195).

[40] "Poor" as an adjective is less common in Pope's poetry than in Swift's. But cf. "Yet like the Papists is the Poets State / Poor and disarm'd, and hardly worth your hate" (*Second Satire of John Donne*, line 12) and "Poor guiltless I" (*Epistle to Dr. Arbuthnot*, line 281).

[41] Scodel notes that Horace and Virgil pretend to decline to praise the great, but in the course of professing their inadequacy manage to "praise the great in the very process of refusing" (1988: 628). Pope here insists that he really does not flatter.

model, Horace; and of his turn away from Horace in the outspoken and un-Horatian *One Thousand Seven Hundred and Thirty-Eight*. Virgil's Aeneas was a model for Pope's *pietas* in the inscription for the family monument, but in this epitaph Virgil the poet is judged to be too complicit with his imperial master.

Scodel (1988: 615) argued that Pope's epitaphs serve to "distinguish him from his literary precedessors" – among whom he names Cowley and Prior, along with Horace and Virgil. But it is also true that Pope's epitaph serves to distinguish him from his greatest literary contemporary. In one respect, the calculated and leveling familiarity of "Folks like you" (reducing "Heroes, and Kings" to the status of mere "Folks"), the poem sounds Swiftian.[42] And both poets reject the Horatian way, either implicitly or explicitly. But by insisting he is but a "poor Poet," Pope implicitly reaffirms the distinction between poet and political writer that had informed his correspondence with Swift for ten years. By distinguishing between poet and hero, he distinguishes himself from one who in his epitaph adopts the heroic stance of Vindicator of Liberty. And by adopting a partly facetious tone – the Twickenham editors think Pope did not mean the epitaph "to be taken too seriously"[43] – Pope's poem differs from Swift's undeniably solemn inscription. Pope was to publish a third epitaph on himself, but not before Swift composed the famous lines he wanted carved on his own tombstone. When Swift devised his will in May 1740, he specified that he wished to have a black marble monument set up in the "great Isle" of St. Patrick's Cathedral, "with the following Inscription in large Letters, deeply cut, and strongly gilded": "Hic depositum est Corpus Ionathan Swift S. T. P. [Sanctae Theologiae Professoris][44] Hujus Ecclesiae Cathedralis Decani, Ubi saeva Indignatio Ulterius Cor lacerare

[42] Johnson's *Dictionary* notes that "folk" and "folks" are "now used only in familiar or burlesque language," and gives two citations from Swift. See also "Kings, like private Folks, are bought and sold" ("To Mr. Gay"), "Lye down obscure like other Folks" (*Libel on Dr. Delaney*), "like other Folks" (*Cadenus and Vanessa*). Pope uses "folks" only four other times in all his poems. The word is much more common in Swift's poems, where it appears thirty-five times. But "folks" is common in Pope's letters.
[43] Ault (1954: 376). But Warburton disagreed, and had it incised on a monument in Twickenham Church.
[44] The title Swift claimed for himself only here has not been discussed. In the *Verses on the Death* (composed 1731, printed 1739) he identified himself as "D. S. D" – "Dean, St. [Patrick's], Dublin." In his fragmentary prose autobiography (probably composed c. 1714) he is "D. D., and D of St. P" (Davis 1939–68: v, 191). On the title page of the 1735 Faulkner edition he is "D. D. D. S. P. D." – "Doctor of Divinity, Dean, St. Patrick's Dublin." In the opening sentence of his will he is "Doctor in Divinity, and Dean of the Cathedral Church of St. Patrick, Dublin." Swift's instructions were not exactly followed: carved on the monument are the initials "S. T. D." (i.e., "Sanctae Theologiae Doctor" – "Doctor of Sacred Theology").

nequit. Abi Viator Et imitare, si poteris, Strenuum pro virili Libertatis Vindicatorem. Obiit Anno ___ Mensis ___ Die Aetatis Anno ___." Although modern readers have found the words thrilling, Orrery thought Swift's Latin inelegant, harsh, and "scarcely intelligible."[45] Because of the differences between Latin and English syntax, it is more difficult than is usually acknowledged to translate literally. The Latin can be rendered into English as: "Here is laid the body of Jonathan Swift, Professor of Sacred Theology, Dean of this Cathedral Church, where savage indignation can lacerate his heart no longer. Go, Traveler, and imitate, if you can, one who strenuously championed liberty to the utmost of his ability ...".[46]

In an essay published more than fifty years ago, Maurice Johnson (1953: 818–19) observed that the epitaph consists of three parts: identification of the deceased; observations on his condition; and an exhortation to the reader. (Johnson does not remark that the three parts are initiated by *hic, ubi,* and *abi,* the last two terms echoing each other in the ear, and the first two perhaps playing grimly with the common phrase *hic et ubique.*) Johnson defended Swift from charges, then current, that his epitaph displayed excessive bitterness, gloom, and "disappointed egotism," by demonstrating the conventionality of Swift's language – that in his day it was not uncommon to write one's own epitaph; to offer oneself high praise; to declare that the deceased has escaped from a worse to a better place; or to exhort the passer-by with a chill reminder of what awaits him too.[47]

In some respects Johnson is correct: even monumental inscriptions for Anglican bishops up to Swift's day were almost all in Latin, and commonly deployed vestigial elements from Roman gravestones (e.g., "Abi Viator"), urging the *lector* to *imitare* or *aemulare* the virtues of the deceased. The academic degree of Doctor of Divinity is commonly rendered "Sanctae Theologiae Professoris" (sometimes abbreviated to "S. T. P.") or "Sanctae Theologiae Doctor" (sometimes abbreviated to "S. Th. D.") rather than "Divinitas Doctor."[48] And it was not uncommon in the

---

[45] "An harsher epitaph has seldom been composed. It is scarce intelligible, and if intelligible is a proof how difficult a task it is, even for the greatest genius, to draw his own character, or to represent himself and his actions in a proper manner to posterity" (Orrery 1752: 263).

[46] A literal translation would have to recognize that *strenuum vindicatorem* is not an adverb–verb phrase "strenuously championed," but an adjective–noun phrase, "strenuous champion." "Pro virili" is short for "pro virili parte" (a phrase Swift could have found in Cicero).

[47] Johnson seems to have been particularly responding to F. R. Leavis, who in his well-known 1952 essay on "The Irony of Swift" remarked acerbically that "Saeva indignatio is an indulgence that solicits us all, and the use of literature by readers and critics for the projection of nobly suffering selves is familiar" (*The Common Pursuit* [1952, repr. 1962], p. 86).

[48] See John Le Neve, *Lives and Characters, Death, Burials, and Epitaphs of all the Protestant Bishops* (1720).

period to celebrate the deceased, whether Whig or Tory, as a defender of English liberty.[49] But in other respects Swift's epitaph is unconventional, especially in its silences. He was a student of epitaphs in an age that paid attention to them and took them seriously,[50] had himself composed both mock-inscriptions and serious epitaphs, and was alert to the significance of details. It is common in an epitaph of the period to acknowledge God's will or the merits or mercy of the Redeemer, but Swift's epitaph is silent on these points. (Contrast the inscription on Pope's family monument, with its conventional beginning: "D. O. M.") He focuses on the body and says nothing of the soul.[51] Unlike those epitaphs for Anglican clergymen who looked forward to resurrection (e.g., "Hic in spe resurgendi depositum jacet ..." or "Hic in spem resurrectionis reponuntur ..."),[52] Swift's leaves the body in the grave. The *pax* it attains is not the beginning of serenity but the end of torture. Unlike most epitaphs, which offer for imitation virtues and actions within the reach of the reader, Swift's offers the vigorous defense of liberty, and his "imitare, *si poteris*" (unusual in epitaphs) implies that imitation of such heroic action may in fact be well beyond the capacity of the typical *viator*.[53]

The searing phrase "Ulterius Cor lacerare nequit" strikes many as quintessentially Swiftian in its violence and materiality. Johnson (1953: 822) compared an anecdote reported by Delany (1754: 148–49): Swift once asked "a friend" (probably Delany himself) whether the "corruptions and villainies of men in power" did not "eat his flesh, and exhaust his spirits."

[49] The epitaph of the regicide Edmund Ludlow calls him "Patriae Libertatis Defensor" in a volume Swift owned (Ludlow, *Memoirs*, 3 vols. [1698–99], I, xii); William III "Preserved the Liberty and Religion / Of *Great-Britain*" (*Select Epitaphs* [1755], II, 93). In a nine-page epitaph the Duke of Marlborough was said to be, like William, "Assertor of our Liberty" (Thomas Lediard, *Life of John Duke of Marlborough* [1743], Appendix, xxiii). John Toland's epitaph for himself included the phrase "Libertatis assertor" (*Collection of Several Pieces by Mr. John Toland*, 2 vols. [1726], I, lxxxviii). Bolingbroke (who died in 1751) was praised in an epitaph as devoted "By Zeal to maintain the Liberty / ... of Great Britain" (II, 220). Delany suggests that Swift honored both William III and the Duke of Schomberg (see above, p. 231) because they "struggled for the liberties of these kingdoms against the repeated attempts of arbitrary power" (1754: 186n).

[50] In addition to the collection of *Select Epitaphs* (1755), cited above (which included twelve epitaphs by Pope), a two-volume collection of *Select and Remarkable Epitaphs*, edited by John Hackett (in which Pope features prominently – and his "Heroes, and Kings ..." is printed) appeared in 1757. Johnson's critical essay on Pope's poetic epitaphs was published in 1756.

[51] Contrast his will, in which Swift begins by bequeathing his "Soul to God, (in humble Hopes of his Mercy through JESUS CHRIST) and my Body to the Earth" (Davis 1939–68: XIII, 149).

[52] Inscriptions for Archbishop Thomas Lamplugh (Le Neve, *Lives and Characters*, 275) and William Lloyd (d. 1674), Rector of St. Petrox, in Devonshire (http:members.lycos.co.uk/john_richards/petrox).

[53] Did Swift remember King's "bona si sua norint," in which the "si" also hints that in fact Swift's countrymen will not come to recognize what is good for them? Yeats's free version of Swift's Latin ("Swift's Epitaph") – "Imitate him if you dare ..." – perhaps catches Swift's implication.

But it seems more likely that in the epitaph Swift was mordantly reworking an elegiac convention. That the tears of the bereaved "pierced the
heart" or "rent the heart" was already a cliché by the time Swift wrote his
"Satirical Elegy on the Death of a Late Famous General" (1722):

> Behold his funeral appears,
> Nor widow's sighs, nor orphan's tears,
> Wont at such times each heart to pierce,
> Attend the progress of his hearse.[54]

Instead of the wounded heart of the bereaved, Swift focuses in his epitaph
on the heart of the one who has died, and *lacerate* – even more than *rend*
or *pierce* – makes clear that the pain he endured – while living – was not
just figurative but excruciatingly physical.

If Swift did not build his vivid phrase "Cor lacerare" ("lacerate the
heart") from a technical term in medical texts,[55] he might have been
remembering Bacon's "mentis laceratio et stimulatio perpetua et irrequi-
eta" – "laceration of the mind and vexation without end or rest" – (the
punishment of Prometheus), and might have thus signaled a link between
himself and another daring benefactor of mankind.[56] By shifting the site
of laceration from *mind* to *heart*, he emphasizes the emotional anguish.[57]
What lacerates the heart is not the conventional grief, or even sorrow for
sin,[58] but indignation. Most modern critics follow Bredvold in thinking that "Indignatio" is designed to link Swift to Juvenal, who famously
wrote in his first satire that "facit indignatio versum" (79).[59] But it is not

---

[54] Cf. Pope's "Elegy to the Memory of an Unfortunate Lady": "And the last pang shall tear thee
from his heart."

[55] Did Swift perhaps know, from his readings of medical experiments or his conversations with
Dr. John Arbuthnot, about a medical condition called cardiorrhexis (translated in medical dic-
tionaries as 'rupture of the heart' or 'laceration of the heart')? As Vienken ("'Nobody Has Ever
Written a Really Good Book about Jonathan Swift': Scoring the Recesses of the Swiftian Mind,"
in *Reading Swift: Papers from the Fourth Münster Symposium on Jonathan Swift*, ed. Hermann
Real and Helgand Störer-Leidig [2003], 147–57, 154) notes, Swift's library contained works by
thirty-one medical authors.

[56] From Bacon's decoding of the allegorical fable of Prometheus in *De Sapientia Veterum* (1609),
106. Swift owned a copy of Bacon's 1638 *Opera Omnia* (Passman and Vienken 2003: I, 126).

[57] Perhaps Swift remembered the linking of *laceration* and *heart* in a passage from Seneca the
Younger, as translated by L'Estrange: Sextius, who advised against the eating of meat, "would not
have Men inur'd to hardness of Heart, by the Laceration, and Tormenting of Living Creatures"
(*Seneca's Morals by way of Abstract*, 10th edn., [1711], 124). *Laceratio* appears in Seneca's Latin,
Epistulae Morales, 108. 18.

[58] Cf. Joel 2.13, "Rend your heart and not your garments." In *Grace Abounding*, Bunyan reported
that reading scripture "did also tear and rend my soul."

[59] Louis Bredvold, "A Note in Defence of Satire," *ELH* 7 (1940), 258. Swift cited Juvenal's phrase
in a May 1, 1733 letter to Pope (Woolley 1999–2007: III, 637) but stipulates that it "is only to be
applyed when the indignation is against general vilany, and never operates when a vilain writes

often observed that while Juvenal's indignation produces poetry, Swift's, lacerating the heart, produces nothing but pain. (Swift's epitaph in no way reminds us that he was a writer.) Johnson (1953: 821) noted that indignation is characteristic of the Old Testament God,[60] but not that while an indignant God punishes, it is the indignant Swift who is punished, or punishes himself.

If the middle section of the epitaph focuses on what Swift suffered, the final one focuses on his actions: he strenuously championed liberty. Johnson thought (1953: 284) that by *libertas* Swift meant both liberty of conscience and Irish liberty. But given Swift's support of the Test Act, his deep distrust of Roman Catholics, Protestant Dissenters, and such "freethinkers" as William Woolaston and Thomas Woolston, and his belief that, although the state could not control what a man thought, it could and should certainly control what he published, it is very unlikely that he would have called himself a "vindicator" of religious "liberty." But he was probably aware that some of his contemporaries readily claimed such a mantle. One such vindicator was Jonathan Jones, who in his *Liberty Vindicated* (1730?) came to the defense of *Discourse on the Miracles of our Saviour* (1727)[61] by Thomas Woolston – a writer whom Swift loathed. Another was the author of the anonymous *Vindication of Liberty of Conscience; of the Toleration of Protestant Dissenters; and of the Present Happy Establishment* (1734). The fact that "Liberty Vindicated" could be used as the title of a work of religious controversy by a defender of Woolston suggests that when Swift called himself *Libertas Vindicator* he was sardonically aware that he was using contaminated words.

Most scholars think that by *libertas* Swift meant primarily Irish liberty, and compare the famous lines from *Verses on the Death of Dr. Swift*:

> Fair LIBERTY was all his Cry,
> For her he stood prepar'd to die;
> For her he boldly stood alone;
> For her he oft expos'd his own. (347–50)

to defend himself" (as Hervey and Lady Mary had done, he implies, by placing Juvenal's phrase as an epigraph on the title page of the *Verses Address'd to the Imitator of Horace*).

[60] Nahum 1.6, Psalms 69.24, Micah 7.9.

[61] See Swift's note to *Verses on the Death of Dr. Swift* (281n): "Wolston was a Clergyman, but for want of Bread, hath in several Treatises, in the most blasphemous Manner, attempted to turn Our Saviour and his Miracles into Ridicule. He is much caressed by many great Courtiers, and by all the Infidels, and his Books read generally by the Court Ladies." Jones also published *Instructions to the Right Reverend Richard [Smalbroke] Ld. Bishop of St. Davids, in Defence of Religious Liberty* (1729), in reply to Smalbroke's *A Vindication of the Miracles of our Blessed Saviour, in answer to Mr. Woolston*, 2 vols. (1729–31).

Some critics have suspected, probably rightly, that these lines harbor some irony, if only because of the hyperbolic "Cry" and the repeated "For her ... for her ... for her" – Swift being on the whole congenitally suspicious of most kinds of emphatic utterance and overstatement. But it seems unlikely that Swift intended any subversive irony in the epitaph, just as there seems to be none in his letter bequeathing Pulteney an epitaph and complimenting him and one or two of his friends on their "spirit of liberty." (In darkly considering the extent of English *"Power"* – as in the Drapier's fourth letter – Swift may have felt that the only liberty he succeeded in preserving was the Irishman's "Liberty of *roaring*" as he was stretched upon the rack.) Although by May 1740, when Swift wrote his will, Pope was already having doubts about whether Pulteney would remain true to his principles, Swift seems to have continued to admire him, and might in his own epitaph have intended to suggest that he himself was among the "one or two friends." The letter to Pulteney also suggests that Swift's words "Libertatis Vindicatorem" were not intended to mean that as a result of his efforts liberty had indeed been preserved in the nation at large, but only that its spirit was alive in a few people: "it is altogether impossible," the letter to Pulteney had continued, "for any nation to preserve its liberty long under a tenth part of the present luxury, infidelity, and a million of corruptions" (Woolley 1999–2007: III, 66). The call to imitate Swift, *if you can*, is thus a grim and angry challenge, even a taunt, rather than a battle cry in anticipation of victory.

Vindicator is another term requiring some interpretation. Following Luce (1967: 78), Ross and Woolley observe (1984: 694) that *vindicator* is not classical Latin, but a late ecclesiastical coinage, the classical term being *vindex*. *Vindex* means "defender," "deliverer," "protector," "guarantor," but also "avenger" or "punisher" (as with *Jupiter Vindex*). *Vindicator* has the same range of meaning. Although Frank Boyle has recently suggested that Swift regarded himself as a kind of avenger,[62] it seems clear that in the epitaph he is a defender or champion (though not necessarily, as I have suggested, a successful one). Because Swift was a trained Latinist, he would have known the difference between the classical *vindex* and the late Latin *vindicator*: *vindex* probably had for him associations with Cicero, who uses it in combination with *libertas*,[63] and

---

[62] Frank Boyle, *Swift as Nemesis* (2000). Swift sometimes (e.g., "The Day of Judgement") indulged the fantasy that he was a kind of vengeful God, and his ambivalence toward the Irish included fantasized punishment (e.g., *Modest Proposal*) of their truckling.

[63] *De Legibus*, III, 39: "habeat sane populus tabellam quasi vindicem libertatis" ("a sound people might be allowed the ballot as a vindicator of liberty").

Livy, for whom *vindex libertatis* is a recurrent heroic epithet, used especially of the tribunes of the people. *Strenuus* is also used regularly by
Livy – "vir fortis ac strenuus" – especially of tribunes, as opposed to
patricians,[64] suggesting that to the trained Latin reader Swift's epitaph
would have had both a classic and a class resonance: though not of high
birth himself, he boldly defends liberty against the actions of a tyran-
nizing aristocracy, linking himself (in the terms of his own *Contests and
Dissensions … in Athens and Rome*) with the Roman "Commons" rather
than "Nobles." Although "vindication," in eighteenth-century English
usage, often referred to a defense or justification of God's ways, Swift's
use suggests that he is not linking himself to a tradition of theological
vindicators,[65] but summoning the reader to remember the word's political resonance.

It was probably William King's tribute, in the Latin footnote to *The
Toast*, where Swift is praised because "he defended liberty" ("Libertatem
Vindicavit") that he particularly remembered. Still, it may have given
him pause when he recalled that the Emperor Augustus – whom Swift
regarded as the destroyer of the liberty of the Roman Republic[66] – had
made the same claim: the opening sentence of the *Res Gestae Divi Augusti*
("Deeds of the Divine Augustus") declares that he had freed the people
from the domination of faction – "rem publicam dominatione factionis
oppressam in libertatem vindicavi."[67] This is a claim that Swift implicitly rejected: as Weinbrot remarks (1978: 83), Gulliver in Glubbdubdrib
does not find Augustus among the "Restorers of Liberty to oppressed and
injured Nations." History suggests that anyone – a Caesar or a Walpole –
might claim to be a champion of "liberty," whether Roman or British.
Roman coins proclaimed that the Emperor Caesar, son of the Divine
One, was "LIBERTATIS P[opuli] R[omani] VINDEX" – "Vindicator of the

[64] Francesca L'Hoir, "Heroic Epithets and Recurrent Themes in 'Ab Urbe Condita,'" *Transactions of the American Philological Association* 120 (1990), 224–27. Cf. also Horace, Epistle I, 7 (a poem Swift imitated): "strenuus et fortis" (I, 46). Swift perhaps knew too that a *vindicatio in liber-tatem* – Cicero uses the term – was in Roman law a legal action brought against someone for wrongfully holding a free man as a slave (Alan Watson, "Vespasian: Adsertor Libertatis Publicae," *Classical Review* n.s. 23, 2 [December 1973], 127–28).
[65] As suggested by Peter Davidhazi, "A Monumental Inscription: The Transcultural Heritage of Swift's Epitaph," in *Moment to Monument: The Making and Unmaking of Cultural Significance,* ed. Ladina Lambert and Andrea Ochsner (2009), 51–70.
[66] Octavian, so Swift wrote in 1701, "entailed the vilest Tyranny that Heaven in its Anger ever inflicted on a Corrupt and Poison'd People … Here ended all Shew or Shadow of Liberty in Rome" (*Contests and Dissensions … in Athens and Rome*, 39–40).
[67] Like Swift's instructions for the inscription on his monument, the *Res Gestae* is a set of instruc-tions in Augustus' will for the inscription he wanted recorded on monuments after his death.

Liberty of the Roman People."⁶⁸ Thus it was perhaps to avoid the classical phrase *Libertatis Vindex*, contaminated by its association with Augustus and already in his time a "shop-worn catch phrase,"⁶⁹ that Swift chose the late Latin *Vindicator*.

Vindicator might also have appealed to Swift because the English word "vindicator"⁷⁰ had been used in combination with "indignation" and "liberty" – the three key terms in the epitaph – in a well-known passage about Juvenal in Dryden's *Discourse on the Original and Progress of Satire*: "His Indignation against Vice is more vehement; ... he treats Tyranny, and all the Vices attending it, as they deserve, with the utmost rigour [compare "Strenuum pro virili"]: and consequently, a Noble Soul is better pleased with a Zealous Vindicator of *Roman* Liberty; than with a Temporizing Poet, a well Manner'd Court Slave."⁷¹ This not only solidified Swift's link to the angry and declamatory Juvenal, but it implicitly re-argued his long-held position, in the ongoing discussion with Pope (who sometimes preferred compliance and oblique resistance) about how to respond to a corrupt court, that the only "Noble" response was to speak out boldly. By bidding the compliant Horace to "blush" in the 1738 epitaph, Pope may have signaled that he had moved toward Swift's Juvenalian view.

If "indignatio," "vindicator," and "libertas" are the key terms in Swift's epitaph, it comes as a slight surprise to recall that Pope never uses the English equivalent of the first of them; uses the second, "vindicate," in a completely different sense (he "vindicates the ways of God to man" by mounting an informal philosophical defense of God's justice, or offers, in the *Epistle to Dr. Arbuthnot*, what he calls a "just vindication" against

---

⁶⁸ Abbreviated as "IMP CAESAR DIVI F COS VI P R VINDEX" on a famous silver coin minted at Ephesus in 28BC (Mattingley, *Coins of the Roman Empire in the British Museum*, vol. 1 [1923], nos. 691–93), cited in Watson, "Vespasian," 127n. Swift's friend Sir Andrew Fountaine was one of the country's great coin collectors. As Vienken, ("'Nobody Has Ever Written,'" 152–53) notes, Swift's library contained a large number of volumes on numismatics as well as Gronovius's *Theasaurus Graecarum Antiquitatem*, 13 vols. (1697–1701).

⁶⁹ C. Wirszubski, *Libertas as a Political Ideal at Rome during the Late Republic and Early Principate* (1950). For a more recent discussion of the claims made by and on behalf of Augustus as liberator – Cicero declared that he liberated ("liberavit") the *res publica* – and for controverted meanings of *libertas* in Roman political discourse, see Karl Galinsky, *Augustan Culture* (1996), 42–57.

⁷⁰ Swift does not use the word "vindicator" in his poetry but uses the verb "vindicate" in a 1731 letter in reference to his controversial epitaph on Schomberg: although he has been criticized by the court, "the publick prints, as well as the thing it self, will vindicate me" (Woolley 1999–2007: III, 416).

⁷¹ Quoted from Dryden, *Works* (California edition, 1974), IV, 65. It is sometimes overlooked that Dryden went on to say he "preferr'd the Manner of *Horace*... to that of *Juvenal*" (71). Swift's epitaph is implicitly an answer to Dryden. The similarity between the Dryden passage and Swift's epitaph was first suggested by Luce (1967: 79).

slanders and slanderers);[72] and although fond of the third, "liberty," rarely uses it in a political sense. When he does, it is with sharp irony, as when King George is praised as "Great Friend of LIBERTY" ("Epistle to Augustus," line 25), or old Cotta's son zealously devotes himself to "GEORGE and LIBERTY" (*Epistle to Bathurst*, line 207).[73] When used unironically, it means (as noted earlier) the personal freedom of private life, as Pope confirms by linking liberty and friendship in "Libertati & Amicitiae," the motto, he declared to Marchmont in 1741, that he would place over his door at Twickenham.[74] In the terms of the opening sentence of Cowley's essay "Of Liberty," Swift champions "The Liberty of a People ... in being governed by Laws which they have made themselves," and Pope the "Liberty of a private man" in "being Master of his own Time and Actions."[75]

"Vindicate" had other Popean associations, and Swift may have been implicitly marking off his difference from them. He probably knew Warburton's *Vindication of Mr. Pope's Essay on Man, From the Misrepresentations of Mr. De Crousaz*, published on November 15, 1739, just six months before he wrote his will (and probably also knew Warburton's own work of self-defense, the 1738 *Vindication of the Author of the Divine Legation of Moses*). In declaring himself a "vindicator," Swift hinted at the difference between the interested defense of accused persons and the disinterested championing of a cause. Viewed from this angle, Swift's epitaph reads as the last of his replies to Pope. He champions a different kind of liberty. And he offers a different kind of vindication. But the core of his claim – that he defended liberty – is in fact close to the praise that Pope had offered him just three years earlier in the "Epistle to Augustus": "The Rights a Court attacked, a Poet saved."

Shortly before Pope's relations with Swift effectively ended in March 1741, he composed a third epitaph for himself. It was first printed in one of his friend Dodsley's new ventures, the short-lived *Publick Register; or, Weekly Magazine*, no. 2 (January 10, 1741).

> Under this Marble, or under this Syll,
> Or, under this Turf, or e'en what you will;
> Whatever an Heir, or a Friend in his Stead,
> Or any good Christian lays over my Head;

[72] In a December 1734 letter to Caryll (Sherburn 1956: III, 447).
[73] One exception is *Windsor-Forest*, "Fair *Liberty*, Britannia's Goddess" (91).
[74] October 10, 1741 (Sherburn 1956: IV, 365). See above, p. 208. If there is a political resonance to "libertati," it is faint.
[75] From *Several Discourses by Way of Essays* (p. 79), in *Works* (1668).

> Lies one who ne'er car'd, and cares not a Pin,
> What they said, or may say of the Mortal within.
> But who Living and Dying, resign'd, still and free,
> Trusts in God, that *as well as he WAS, he shall BE.*[76]

Playfully alluding to the formulas of classical and Christian epitaphic writing, Pope in effect dismisses them: it really doesn't matter to him where he is laid – contrast Swift's "Hic depositum." But this is not for the conventional reasons that the body is a mere shell and the soul has flown to heaven, or even that, as Milton suggested, the true Christian is always in his great taskmaster's eye. It is "the Mortal" who speaks: here lies not "the body" but "one" who never cared and (as if alive) still cares not a pin. (As Johnson remarked disapprovingly, Pope "confounds the living man with the dead.")[77] Pope here recalls and extends the Roman idea of a life *sine cura* ("without care"), except that it now means not "carefree" but "indifferent." ("Cares not a pin" is blithely dismissive, even Swiftian.)[78] His condition has not altered much since his death: there is little sense that the way he "*shall BE*" will differ from the way he "*WAS.*" Thus Death is cause for neither distress nor joy, a sharp contrast with both Pope's "Heathen to his departing Soul" (his translation of Hadrian's famous "Animula vagula …") and "Dying Christian to his Soul" (Pope's Christian imitation),[79] and too with Swift's epitaph, where life meant a laceration of the heart and death a cessation of indignation. Pope's "as well as he *WAS*, he shall *BE*" finds comfort in the essential fixity of his state. Swift's "I am what I am, I am what I am" – reportedly uttered in a moment of dark lucidity at the end of his life – finds only imprisonment.[80]

Pope had in fact speculated in several letters to Swift about the nature of life after death. In an April 1733 letter, responding to Swift's critique of his epitaph on Gay, Pope (ignoring the critique) laments the separation from Gay, wishing that he and Swift "might walk into the grave together … contentedly and chearfully," and concludes with the thought that wherever they find themselves after death "it will be exactly what

---

[76] Pope may have remembered lines from Prior's recently reprinted "For my own Monument": "And if in passing thou giv'st him a smile, or a tear / He cares not" (*Miscellaneous Works* [1740], 131).

[77] Lonsdale (2006: IV, 92).

[78] Pope never uses the proverbial phrase elsewhere in his poems. But Swift was fond of redeploying proverbs: see "Sell the Nation for a Pin" (*The Legion Club*, line 48) and "It would not signify a Pin" ("The Dean's Reasons for not building at Drapier's Hill," line 25).

[79] Written in 1713, but not printed until 1730, and reprinted as late as 1737 and 1742 (Ault 1954: 91–95).

[80] Reported by Deane Swift to Orrery in a letter of April 4, 1744, and reprinted in Orrery's *Remarks* (1752: 142).

region or state our Maker appoints." Eighteen months later, as Arbuthnot is dying, Pope again writes to Swift of death that would at first separate him from Swift but then "re-unite us," though he goes on to wonder whether "the affections of this life should, or should not continue into the other," before resolving that "doubtless it is as it should be." The closing words of his own epitaph might be thought of as a continuation of that conversation.[81]

Just as Pope claims not to care where he is buried, so he does not care how he is remembered by those left behind. Although nominally an address to the living, it in effect ignores the *viator* or *lector*. The contrast with Swift is again a clear one: Swift's epitaph, like *Verses on the Death of Dr. Swift* before it, seems sharply focused on trying to control the way the dead will be remembered. But in turning away from the reader Pope is not (like Gray at the end of the "Elegy," for example) turning toward God: the epitaph voices an insouciant refusal to worry about the future, and simply (and without prayer or fervent hope) "Trusts" in what awaits him.

If we were to take Pope's poem literally – I don't care where I'm buried, and I don't care what anybody says about me – we would have to conclude that it is profoundly disingenuous. For it is very clear from Pope's instructions for the design of his family monument and the public utterance of his *Epistle to Dr. Arbuthnot*, to say nothing about his letters, that he cared very much about both matters. (Technically, as David Morris notes, Pope's epitaph says he wants to be remembered "as not caring how he is remembered." Perhaps it would be more accurate to say, with Pope himself, that he was "Divided between Carelessness and Care."[82]) Thus we cannot readily draw conclusions about the way that the poem reflects Pope's epitaphic definition of himself – except to note that writing disingenuously and facetiously about his death and burial marks him as capable of a kind of Swiftian playfulness on a grave occasion that Swift declined to adopt. Swift's epitaph is a grim summons: he presents himself as indignant and lacerated; Pope's is a light-hearted *bon mot* or *bagatelle*: he affects to be unruffled and untouched.

Although Pope never acknowledged the poem or included it in editions of his *Works* during his lifetime, he may well have taken the trouble

[81] Woolley (1999–2007: III, 630; IV, 29).
[82] Morris, *The Genius of Sense: A Reading of Alexander Pope* (1984, 30). *The Second Epistle of the Second Book of Horace Imitated* (1737), line 291. Spence reports that Pope quoted the line on his deathbed (Osborn 1966: I, 266).

to revise it.[83] When reprinted five months later by Curll, and three years later in a miscellany,[84] its text included several verbal variants suggesting Pope's continuing (and characteristic) attention to significant detail.[85] In line 2, should he say "what you will" (playing with the idiomatic expression, and pointedly addressing the reader) or "what they [i.e., the heir or friend] will"? In line 4 should he say the conventional "Christian" or the more pagan "Creature?" In line 7, should he say "resign'd" (suggesting religious acceptance) or "serene" (underlining the lack of any anxious worry)?

The poem should be regarded intertextually. As Johnson observed long ago, its beginning appears to be an imitation of Ariosto's epitaph for himself:

> Ludovici Areosti humantur ossa
> Sub hoc marmore, vel sub hac humo, seu
> Sub quicquid voluit benignus haeres
> Sive haerede benignior comes.

('The bones of Ludovico Ariosto are buried under this marble, or under this earth, or under whatever pleases his kind heir, or a kinder friend...')[86] But what Johnson does not observe is that while Ariosto carefully notes that the lines were written "while he was alive," and that he was then indifferent for the conventional reason that he had no care for the future of his "empty corpse," Pope makes no such distinction: by deliberately "confound[ing] the living man with the dead" he declines to adopt the sentiment that the grave holds nothing but mortal remains. Scodel (631) adds the point that Pope, unlike Ariosto, omits his own name – his is an epitaph for one who claims to care nothing for fame. Pope's poem can also be seen as an emulative (and corrective) response to Gay's facetious epitaph for himself – "Life is a jest, and all things show it; / I thought so once, and now I know it" – another poem in which the deceased seems to speak lightly from the grave, dismissing any care about mortal life and

---

[83] Warburton included it in his 1751 edition. It also survives in three contemporary mss.: Portland Papers, Longleat, xviii; BM Cowper Papers, MS Add. 28101; and Bodleian MS Ballard 50.

[84] As the final litem in *Dean Swift's Literary Correspondence* (June 1741), where it is entitled "Epitaph for *himself*, by Mr. Pope," and in *The Norfolk Poetical Miscellany*, vol. II, (1744) 85, as "Mr. P – 's Epitaph *on Himself.*"

[85] The variants could, of course, have been introduced by a printer, or the editor or scribe of the contemporary transcriptions.

[86] Printed in Ariosto's *Opere* (1730), II, 399, as quoted in Johnson's "Life of Pope" (Lonsdale 2006: IV, 92–93). Johnson could have found Ariosto's epitaph in Hackett's *Select and Remarkable Epitaphs*, I, 67.

any anxiety about what lies in prospect.[87] But Pope takes care to make his epitaph a "Christian" one and to convert Gay's "jest" into the serene confidence that he had long before suggested to Martha Blount should be the stance of one who faced death, possessed of a "Conscience of a life well spent."[88]

Perhaps too, as a kind of *bagatelle*, the poem is an implicit response to Swift, one final correction of the sort Pope in his "philosophical" mood had repeatedly sent to Swift, inviting him to shed his anger and his bitterness and adopt Pope's favorite pose of serene ease, a summons to Swift to remember his own favorite "rule" – "Vive la bagatelle"[89] – and an emulative tribute to a writer whose comic "bagatelles" he admired and preferred above the poems of savage indignation.

---

[87] Scodel (1988: 632) suggests that the anapestic tetrameter of Pope's final couplet recalls the "willful nonchalance" of Prior's well-known "For my own Monument."

[88] See Pope's "To Mrs. M. B. on her Birth-day" (1723), reprinted in Ault (1954: 244–45), where death is a Sabbath's "sleep" before she wakes "to Raptures in a Life to come," and his "Epistle to Miss Blount, with the Works of Voiture" (1710), with its epitaphic couplet summing up Voiture's life: "Thus wisely careless, innocently gay, / Chearful, he play'd the Trifle, Life, away."

[89] Woolley (1999–2007: III, 501), and Pope's *Imitation of the Sixth Epistle of the First Book of Horace*: "And Swift cry wisely, 'Vive la Bagatelle!'" (128).

LIBRARY, UNIVERSITY OF CHESTER

Selective bibliography of works cited

Ault, Norman, ed. (1935), *Pope's Own Miscellany*.
   ed. (1936), *The Prose Works of Alexander Pope, vol. I, The Earlier Works, 1711–1720*.
   (1949), *New Light on Pope*.
   ed. (1954), Alexander Pope, *Minor Poems*, completed by John Butt (vol. VI of Twickenham Edition).
Baines, Paul and Rogers, Pat (2007), *Edmund Curll, Bookseller*.
Barnett, Louise (2007), *Swift in the Company of Women*.
Bateson, F. W., ed. (1951), Alexander Pope, *Epistles to Several Persons* (vol. III–II of the Twickenham Edition).
Butt, John, ed. (1939), Alexander Pope, *Imitations of Horace* (vol. IV of Twickenham Edition).
   (1954), "Pope's Poetical Manuscripts," *Proceedings of the British Academy*, 40, 23–59.
Cowler, Rosemary, ed. (1986), *The Prose Works of Alexander Pope, vol. II: The Major Works, 1725–1744*.
Cruickshanks, Eveline and Erskine-Hill, Howard (2004), *The Atterbury Plot*.
Cummings, Robert (1987), "Windsor-Forest as a Silvan Poem," *ELH*, 54, 63–79.
Davis, Herbert (1931), "Verses on the Death of Dr. Swift," *Book-Collector's Quarterly*, 57–73.
Davis, Herbert, et al., eds. (1939–68), *The Prose Works of Jonathan Swift*, 14 vols.
Delany, Patrick (1754), *Observations upon the Remarks on the Life and Writings of Dr. Jonathan Swift*.
Ehrenpreis, Irwin (1962–83), *Swift: The Man, his Works, and the Age*, 3 vols.
Elias, Archibald, ed. (1997), *Memoirs of Letitia Pilkington*, 2 vols.
   (1998), "Swift's Don Quixote, Dunkin's Virgil Travesty, and Other New Intelligence: John Lyon's 'Materials for a Life of Dr. Swift,' 1765," *Swift Studies*, 13, 27–104.
   (2000), "Swift and the Middling Reader: Additions to the Faulkner Reprints of Pope's Satires, 1733–1735," *Swift Studies*, 15, 61–75.
Elwin, Whitwell, and Courthope, W. J., eds. (1871–89), *The Works of Pope*, 10 vols.
Erskine-Hill, Howard (1975), *The Social Milieu of Alexander Pope*.
   (1982), "Alexander Pope: The Political Poet in his Time," *Eighteenth-Century Studies*, 15, 123–48.

(1996), *Poetry of Opposition and Revolution: Dryden to Wordsworth.*

(1998), "Pope and Slavery," in *Alexander Pope: World and Word*, ed. Erskine-Hill, Proceedings of the British Academy 91, 27–54.

Ferraro, Julian (1998), "From Text to Work: The Presentation and Re-presentation of *Epistles to Several Persons*," in *Alexander Pope: World and Word*, ed. Howard Erskine-Hill, Proceedings of the British Academy 91, 111–34.

(2008), "Pope: Pen and Press," in *Literary Milieux*, ed. David Womersley and Richard McCabe, 116–39.

Fischer, John Irwin (2000), "Swift's Miscellanies, in Prose and Verse, Volume the Fifth: Some Facts and Problems," in *Swift Studies*, 15, 76–87.

(2003), "'Love and Books': Some Early Texts of Swift's *Cadenus and Vanessa*," in *Reading Swift: Papers from the Fourth Münster Symposium on Jonathan Swift*, ed. Hermann Real and Helgard Stöver-Leidig, 285–310.

Foxon, David (1975), *English Verse, 1701–1750*, 2 vols.

(1991), *Pope and the Early Eighteenth-Century Book Trade*, rev. and ed. James McLaverty.

Goldgar, Bertrand and Gadd, Ian, eds. (2008), Jonathan Swift, *English Political Writings, 1711–1714*.

Griffin, Dustin (1978), *Alexander Pope: The Poet in the Poems.*

(1987), "Augustan Collaboration," *Essays in Criticism*, 37, 1–10.

(1996), *Literary Patronage in England, 1650–1800.*

(2002), *Patriotism and Poetry in Eighteenth-Century Britain.*

Griffith, R. H., ed. (1922–27), *Alexander Pope: A Bibliography*, 2 vols.

Guthkelch, A. C. and Smith, D. N., eds. (1958), Swift, *A Tale of a Tub*, 2nd edn.

Halsband, Robert (1970), "'The Lady's Dressing Room' Explicated by a Contemporary," in *The Augustan Milieu*, ed. Henry K. Miller, Eric Rothstein, and George R. Rousseau, 225–31.

Hammond, Brean (1995), *Professional Imaginative Writing in England 1670–1740: "Hackney for Bread."*

(1998), "'Low and Ungentleman-like Reflections': Swift and Pope," in *Reading Swift: Papers from the Third Münster Symposium on Jonathan Swift*, ed. Hermann Real and Helgard Stöver-Leidig, 309–20.

(2003), "Swift's Reading," in *Reading Swift: Papers from the Fourth Münster Symposium on Jonathan Swift*, ed. Hermann Real and Helgard Stöver-Leidig, 133–46.

Harth, Philip (1985), "Swift's Self-Image as a Satirist," in *Proceedings of the First Münster Symposium on Jonathan Swift*, ed. Hermann Real and Heinz Vienken, 113–21.

(1998), "Friendship and Politics: Swift's Relations with Pope in the Early 1730s," in *Reading Swift: Papers from the Third Münster Symposium on Jonathan Swift*, ed. Hermann Real and Helgard Stöver-Leidig, 239–48.

Higgins, Ian (1994), *Swift's Politics: A Study in Disaffection.*

Hodgart, Matthew (1978), "The Subscription List for Pope's *Iliad*," in *The Dress of Words: Essays on Restoration and Eighteenth-Century Literature in Honor of Richmond P. Bond*, ed. R. B. White, Jr., 25–34.

Hooker, Edward N., ed. (1943), *The Critical Works of John Dennis*, 2 vols.

Johnson, Maurice (1953), "Swift and 'The Greatest Epitaph in History,'" *PMLA*, 68, 814–27.

Jones, Emrys (1968), "Pope and Dulness," *Proceedings of the British Academy*, 54, 231–63.

Karian, Stephen (2002), "The Authorial Strategies of Swift's *Verses on the Death*," in *Representations of Swift*, ed. Brian Connery, 77–98.

(2008), "Edmund Curll and the Circulation of Swift's Writings," in *Reading Swift: Papers from the Fifth Münster Symposium on Jonathan Swift*, ed. Hermann Real, 99–129.

Kelly, Ann Cline (1988), *Swift and the English Language*.

Kerby-Miller, Charles, ed. (1950), *Memoirs of Martinus Scriblerus*; rpt. 1988.

Kirkley, Harriet (2002), *A Biographer at Work: Samuel Johnson's Notes for the "Life of Pope."*

Leranbaum, Miriam (1977), *Alexander Pope's "Opus Magnum" 1729–1744.*

Lonsdale, Roger, ed. (2006), Samuel Johnson, *The Lives of the Most Eminent English Poets*, 4 vols.

Luce, J. V. (1967), "A Note on the Composition of Swift's Epitaph," *Hermathena*, 104, 78–81.

Mack, Maynard (1945), "Letters of Pope to Atterbury in the Tower," *Review of English Studies*, 21, 177–25.

ed. (1950), Alexander Pope, *An Essay on Man* (vol. III–I of the Twickenham Edition).

(1982), *Collected in Himself: Essays Critical, Biographical, and Bibliographical on Pope and Some of His Contemporaries.*

(1984), *The Last and Greatest Art: Some Unpublished Poetical Manuscripts of Alexander Pope.*

(1985), *Alexander Pope: A Life.*

McLaverty, James (1984), "The Mode of Existence of Literary Works of Art: The Case of the *Dunciad Variorum*," *Studies in Bibliography*, 37, 82–105.

(1985), "Pope and Giles Jacob's Lives of the Poets: the *Dunciad* as Alternative Literary History," *Modern Philology*, 83, 22–32.

(2001), *Pope, Print, and Meaning.*

(2008), "The Failure of the Swift–Pope *Miscellanies* (1727–32) and *The Life and Genuine Character of Doctor Swift*," in *Reading Swift: Papers from the Fifth Münster Symposium on Jonathan Swift*, ed. Hermann Real, 131–48.

Orrery, Roger Boyle, Earl of (1752), *Remarks on the Life and Writings of Dr. Jonathan Swift.*

Osborn, James, ed. (1966), Joseph Spence, *Observations, Anecdotes, and Characters of Books and Men*, 2 vols.

Passman, Dirk F. and Vienken, Heinz J. (2003), *The Library and Reading of Jonathan Swift: A Bio-Bibliographical Handbook*, 4 vols.

Pollak, Ellen (1985), *The Poetics of Sexual Myth: Gender and Ideology in the Verse of Swift and Pope.*

Potter, Dorothy Bundy Turner, ed. (2002), *The Journal of Mary Freman Caesar, 1724–1741*.

Probyn, Clive (1986), "Swift's *Verses on the Death of Dr. Swift*: the Notes," *Studies in Bibliography*, 39, 48–62.

Rawson, Claude (1973), *Gulliver and the Gentle Reader*.

(1994), *Satire and Sentiment 1660–1830*.

Rees, Christine (1973), "Gay, Swift, and the Nymphs of Drury Lane," *Essays in Criticism*, 23, 1–21.

Richardson, John (2001), "Alexander Pope's *Windsor Forest*: Its Context and Attitudes toward Slavery," *Eighteenth-Century Studies*, 35, 1–17.

Rogers, Pat, ed. (1983), Jonathan Swift, *The Complete Poems*.

(1994), "Literary and Biblical Allusions in Swift's Correspondence," *Notes and Queries*, 41 [June], 194–96.

(2004), *The Symbolic Design of Windsor-Forest: Iconography, Pageant, and Prophecy in Pope's Early Work*.

(2005a), *Pope and the Destiny of the Stuarts: History, Politics, and Mythology in the Age of Queen Anne*.

(2005b), "John Philips, Pope, and Political Georgic," *Modern Language Quarterly*, 66, 411–42.

Rosenheim, Edward (1970), "Swift and the Atterbury Case," in *The Augustan Milieu*, ed. Henry K. Miller, Eric Rothstein, and George R. Rousseau, 174–204.

Ross, Angus and Woolley, David, eds. (1984), *The Oxford Authors: Jonathan Swift*.

Rumbold, Valerie (1989), *Women's Place in Pope's World*.

ed. (1999), Alexander Pope, *The Dunciad in Four Books*.

ed. (2007), *The Poems of Alexander Pope, vol. III: The Dunciad (1728) & The Dunciad Variorum (1729)*.

Schakel, Peter (1993), "'Friends Side by Side': Theme, Structure, and Influence in the Swift–Pope *Miscellanies* of 1727," in *Reading Swift: Papers from the Second Münster Symposium on Jonathan Swift*, ed. Richard Rodino and Hermann Real, 103–12.

(1994), "What Success It Met: The Reception of *Cadenus and Vanessa*," in *Reading Swift: Papers from the Third Münster Symposium on Jonathan Swift*, ed. Hermann Real and Helgard Stöver-Leidig, 215–24.

Scodel, Joshua (1988), "'Your Distance Keep': Pope's Epitaphic Stance," *ELH*, 55, no. 3 (Autumn), 615–41.

Sherburn, George, ed. (1929), *The Best of Pope*.

ed. (1956), *The Correspondence of Alexander Pope*, 5 vols.

Stephanson, Raymond (2007), "Letters of Mr. Alexander Pope and the Curious Case of Modern Scholarship and the Vanishing Text," *Eighteenth Century Life*, 31, no. 1, 1–21.

Sutherland, James, ed. (1963), Alexander Pope, *The Dunciad* (vol. v of Twickenham Edition), 3rd edn.

Vander Meulen, David (1991), *Pope's Dunciad of 1728: A History and Facsimile*.

Vienken, Heinz (1995), "Jonathan Swift's Library, His Reading, and His Critics," in *Walking Naboth's Vineyard: New Studies of Swift*, ed. Christopher Fox and Brenda Tooley, 154–63.

Weinbrot, Howard (1978), *Augustus Caesar in "Augustan" England*.

(1993), *Britannia's Issue: The Rise of British Literature from Dryden to Ossian*.

Weis, Charles and Pottle, Frederick, eds. (1970), *Boswell in Extremes, 1776–1778*.

Williams, Harold ed. (1948), *Journal to Stella*, 2 vols.

ed. (1958), *The Poems of Jonathan Swift*, 2nd edn., 3 vols.

ed. (1963–72), *The Correspondence of Jonathan Swift*, rev. David Woolley, 5 vols.

Winn, James (1977), *A Window in the Bosom: The Letters of Alexander Pope*.

Woolley, David, ed. (1999–2007), *The Correspondence of Jonathan Swift, D. D.*, 4 vols.

Index

Throughout the index, "AP" stands for "Alexander Pope" and "JS" for "Jonathan Swift."

'Vertumnus and Pomona' (AP), 39
Vindication of Liberty of Conscience (anon.),
    239
'Vindication of Lord Carteret' (JS), 143
Virgil, 234–35
    Aeneid, 110, 234–35
    AP's imitations, 29, 31
    Dryden and, 35
    Dunciad and, 107, 118
    Georgics, 39, 44, 49
    influence on AP, 235
    JS and, 33, 39, 186

Wales, Caroline, Princess of, 131
Wales, Frederick, Prince of, 131, 207, 213, 218
Waller, Edmund, 28, 40
Walpole, Sir Robert, 1, 83, 131, 138, 151, 152, 210,
    213, 226, 241
Walsh, William, 19, 29, 35, 126
Walter, Peter, 135–36
Warburton, William, 79, 183, 222, 224–25,
    230, 243
Welsted, Leonard, 104, 153
Wesley, Samuel, 51
Whiteway, Mrs. Martha, 211, 218,
    223, 229
Wilford, John, 151
Wilkes, Thomas, 229

William III, King of England, 48
Williams, Harold, 45, 61, 221
Wilson, Revd. Francis, 228
Winchelsea, Anne Finch,
    Countess of, 16, 39, 224
Windsor-Forest (AP)
    and *Conduct of the Allies*, 9, 43–60
    JS's opinion of, 25, 30, 31
    slavery, 91
Withers, Henry, 232
Wood, William, 220
Woolaston, William, 239
Woolley, David, 70, 199, 202, 203,
    204, 217, 240
Woolston, Thomas, 239
Wordsworth, William, 12–14
Wotton, William, 26, 34
Wright, John, 175
Wycherley, William, 16, 28, 29, 37, 40,
    96, 126, 197

Yeats, William Butler, 231
Young, Edward
    AP on, 19, 124–25, 167
    JS on, 153, 156–55
    JS's poetical epistle to, 16, 152

Zinck, Christian Friedrich, 228

Lightning Source UK Ltd.
Milton Keynes UK
UKOW06f1200210815

257300UK00010B/214/P